Computer
Organization

PRENTICE-HALL INTERNATIONAL, INC., *London*
PRENTICE-HALL OF AUSTRALIA, PTY. LTD., *Sydney*
PRENTICE-HALL OF CANADA, LTD., *Toronto*
PRENTICE-HALL OF INDIA PRIVATE LTD., *New Delhi*
PRENTICE-HALL OF JAPAN, INC., *Tokyo*

Computer
Organization

IVAN FLORES

Computer Consultant

Professor of Statistics, Baruch School of Business
The City University of New York

PRENTICE-HALL INC., ENGLEWOOD CLIFFS, N.J.

Current printing (last digit):

10   9   8   7   6   5   4   3

13-165902-2

Library of Congress Catalog Card Number 77-76871

Printed in the United States of America

PREFACE

This book describes extant computer systems in terms of functional block organization and relates the organization to software components in their operating systems. The book is aimed at those with some knowledge of both software and hardware. This includes several classes of individuals who have a "need to know":

- The computer user who wants to know more about his computer.
- The user-programmer and the system programmer who could write better programs if they understood how their machine functioned.
- The hardware or software student who would like to contrast different organizations.
- The maintenance engineer who would like to have a clearer picture of the whys and wherefores of the machine he services.

Assemblers and compilers make computers seem more similar than they are. This text examines the organization of typical word-, field-, and byte-oriented machines, and it emphasizes their similarities and differences.

Knowledge of the organization and function of several computers is essential to the researcher and scholar in computer science. Its place in the graduate curriculum is acknowledged. The computer science "grandfather" should be as well informed as the second or third generation computer science graduate.

Both the system and problem programmer will learn something about the hardware of each of the machines for which they program; the computer designer will learn something about the software intended for the machine he designs; the serious user will learn enough about the software to get his problem running, and enough about the hardware to get the problem stated properly. All of these groups should be able to follow this text. The first chapter is a leaven to the readers and, so, is the starting point for my investigation.

In conducting my research for this book, I had to wade through vast quantities of manufacturer-supplied information. Incidentally, I am indebted to IBM, RCA, UNIVAC, and other manufacturers for making available much of their confidential hardware information. Just one manufacturer would have no part of my venture (guess who—I'm being politic!) and I had to divine his techniques.

Anyway, I saw the mounds of paper the field engineers had to endure. I expect this volume to supplement (supplant?) these mounds by providing a survey of machine properties and techniques at a hardware level, information which the FE-in-training should absorb at the earliest possible moment.

Of singular importance to the development of the computer field to its present point is the CHANNEL CONTROLLER concept. It has evolved to its present stature in more than ten years. Although this concept is taken for granted by many, Chapter 2 is the first presentation to treat it comprehensively and interrelate it to cycle stealing and interrupt.

Equally salient is the interrupt principle presented in Chapter 3. Its effectiveness depends on its cohesion with the software provided for it. Functional aspects of both are examined to apply to systems of both the second and third generation. The contrast between cycle stealing and interrupt cannot be overemphasized.

One third generation concept is level or mode control, where commands are available or unavailable, depending on the mode in which the program resides. The concept has been coalesced in the machine design with those of the CHANNEL CONTROLLER. After the mode control principle is presented in Chapter 4, it is welded to the previous work to form a massive truss, the superstructure of present systems. This truss is, of course, the program status word. Its functional details are fully expounded in Chapter 4. Later, this principle is incorporated into two machine designs, IBM System 360 and RCA Spectra 70; how the PSW is integrated into the total system is answered in Chapters 9 and 10.

The DEC PDP-8 is thoroughly explained in Chapter 5 as being the most typical and popular of its class. Then Chapter 6 discusses four more smaller computers in less depth.

Chapter 7 examines the IBM 1401 in detail for several reasons:

- It is the most popular second generation machine.
- It is the first totally field-oriented machine.
- It is the first and most successful totally business-oriented machine.
- It is the basis for the entire third generation Honeywell System 200 product line.

This leads us to Chapter 8 where the Honeywell 200 line is examined.

Chapter 9 covers System 360 in depth and, consequently, its length is considerable—but after all, it is the most *important* machine of our time (no, I didn't say best!). Since the RCA Spectra 70 and the Univac 9000 are designed to be machine language compatible, it is important to see in Chapters 10 and 11 in what respects they differ from System 360.

At this point I want to bring out the limitations imposed upon this book. I designed it to be most useful to the largest number of people. To do that, I restricted my exposition to the most popular computers. By *popular* I mean those which, by number, are most prevalent in the field. Hence, sheer number dictated those computers which I chose to describe in detail. Of course, I have been selfish in this. I am interested in selling the book to the most people. With a large number of people interested in the book, perhaps I will be encouraged to write further books on the organization of the more obscure, more exotic, and possibly even more interesting computers.

What happened is that the most popular computers turned out to be of the Princeton type. Hence this is not a general book on computer organization; it is alright that the emphasis is on the simpler type of construction.

Although programming and software are discussed, advanced aspects such as multiprogramming, real-time systems, and so forth, do not get much attention.

For the record, I suppose some of you would like to know what was omitted. In fact, maybe you would like to see if *I* know what was omitted. I am not going to give you an exhaustive list, but here are a few of my major omissions.

Stacks   The Burroughs machine, the B5500, is the most prominent machine that uses the stack principle in the hardware design. It is a fine machine which places hardware design much closer to the higher-level language in which the user usually programs. Its organization is different and complex. I think, if I ever get a chance, I could write a *whole book* just about this computer.

Multiperipherals   The CDC 6600 is a special beast with one large computer and many small ones; more important, it is run by one of the small computers. This is a fascinating concept, especially when we make the CENTRAL PROCESSOR multifunctional. That is, it can carry on several processes at once: floating point division, editing, etc.

Virtual memory   Two computers have been designed to have hardware facilitation of virtual memory and paging so as to make multi-access computing supposedly more feasible for these machines. We have the IBM System 360, Model 67, and the GE 645 with Multics. Both of these are very interesting, but we are not yet sure if they have solved the problem which they supposed to.

Look ahead   At least four computers are designed to have look ahead. Philco made the 2000, Model 212. IBM has constructed STRETCH, System 360, Model 91, and is in the process of releasing System 360, Model 85. All of these process more than one command at a time. Certainly this is an interesting concept which seems to have succeeded; but again, I could write half a book about this.

Multiplexor   I have described SELECTOR CHANNELS in detail and how input and output information is handled generally. I have not given much attention to the MULTIPLEXOR CHANNEL. The MULTIPLEXOR is a CHANNEL which deals with slower DEVICES and can have many such DEVICES operating simultaneously. The details of how this is done seemed less important to me than the other features included in this book. Perhaps, at a later date, I can add this information to a revised edition.

Controller   I think the DISK CONTROLLER is reaching major proportions as an important hardware item. I have discussed this topic, devoting a whole chapter to it, in my forthcoming book, *Data Structure and Management*. Possibly, it too should be included in this book. But at this point in time, I feel it is more important to get the book out to the public for their criticism than to include all available topics (which would make it a seven volume set instead of a single volume).

Programming   This is not a book on programming but new hardware certainly tries to satisfy many of the programmer's needs. The features which facilitate multiprogramming are present in third generation computers and are, namely, MEMORY PROTECT and the CHANNEL CONTROL-LER. A system of dynamic paging is helpful but this need not be done by hardware facilitation. Again, multitasking is a software feature. Multiaccess programming requires the use of consoles and TELECOMMUNICATION DEVICES as well as a MULTIPLEXOR CHANNEL. Again, a whole book might be devoted to describing the interrelations of a multiprogramming and hardware design.

Several of my friends, Andre Godefroy, Al Brooks, and Burt Walder, read the text and helped to improve its style and clarity. My secretaries Gladys and Helene shared their devotion in working long and patiently with me. Arlene and Chet Abend have created another beautiful cover and jacket design. My editors at Prentice-Hall, John Davis and Gregory Hubit, have shown me every consideration in this creation. Chris Nolan has done her usual fine job of editing the manuscript. Finally, thanks are due to Lt. Colonel Philip Enslow, Jr., Office of Telecommunications Policy, Woodbridge, Va., who is responsible for preparing the List of Abbreviations which appears on the endpapers.   I. F.

CONTENTS

1

INTRODUCTION

1.1 CONVENTIONS

In discussing computers in a system environment, we are concerned with many things:

- the hardware itself;
- problem-solving programs;
- the programming systems and parts of them;
- the language elements with which the programmer speaks to the computer;
- signals floating about in the hardware for internal communications.

The printed book is a way for the author to talk to the reader—for me to talk to you. This communication can be more effective if ambiguity is removed, and one way of doing this is to use different typefaces to distinguish different kinds of objects. That is the device I use in this book—different typefaces refer to different classes of things.

The conventions I employ follow; you should become familiar with them to facilitate your reading of this volume.

1. Whenever definitions are made, the object being defined appears in **bold-faced** type. Generally, these definitions are interspersed in the text. The use of boldface permits the reader to find the term more quickly when it's needed for reference.
2. The names of all kinds of hardware units appear in SMALL CAPITALS.

I

This applies to everything from subsystems through functional units to logical units.

3. When software is discussed by name, this name appears in script. Thus, the name for the system supervisor is 𝒮𝒴𝒮𝒯𝒮ℳ. All capitals are used for the largest systems, initial capital and lowercase are used for routines, and lowercase only is used for subroutines.

4. The programmer deals with several kinds of programming languages. These range from high level down to assembly language and, in some cases, machine language. I deal here mainly with assembly language and mnemonics. Whenever these are used, they appear in uppercase sans serif type. For example, when the programmer specifies addition, he uses the mnemonic ADD.

5. When parts of the hardware communicate with one another by control signals, the names of these signals appear in lowercase sans serif type. Thus, start is a signal to initiate some computer process.

1.2 THE COMPUTER SYSTEM

Since this is an advanced book about computers, it is assumed that the reader has background in digital computers. However, for the sake of uniformity, this chapter is a brief review of both hardware and software fundamentals. Let's begin by examining the modern computer.

The modern computer   When I speak of a **computer,** I refer to an automatic problem-solving device whose main purpose is handling information which is represented electrically. However, since many devices can be used for problem solving, it is important to limit our field of interest.

The computer is **digital** when it handles information represented in discrete levels. *Electrical* devices which have exactly two states have been found to be most economical and accurate. Hence most digital computers are **binary;** but this is not a necessity.

Electronic computers are distinguished from electric computers: the former use only solid state and vacuum tube devices for processing, whereas the latter use electromechanical devices.

The speed at which basic actions take place in the modern computer can be rated in nanoseconds or microseconds, terms for billionths and millionths of a second, respectively. That is why the modern computer is a **high speed device.**

The directions by which the computer operates are stored in its MEMORY. These directions are available to the computer not only for examination but also for alteration. In this sense, the modern computer can modify its own behavior; hence, it is an **internally programmed** or **stored program** computer.

Use In the past, computers were roughly contrasted by their use:
- The **scientific computer** solves problems involving a large amount of calculation but generally producing only one or a few results.
- The **commercial computer** is applied mainly to accounting problems where very little calculation is done but where voluble output is produced.

Third generation computers aim at solving both types of problems simultaneously. But, as a consequence of their versatility, they are less effective than a single-minded system in solving either type of problem.

Another way to classify computers is according to the variety of applications in which they can be used:
- The **special purpose computer** is designed for a specific class of problems. This is exemplified by the missile computer or the elevator traffic control computer.
- The **general purpose computer** is hardly limited in the number of applications of any given type for which it can be used.

This book is devoted solely to general purpose computers.

The classical system Figure 1.2.1 is a block program of first and second generation computers. The MEMORY is central. It receives information from INPUT DEVICES and furnishes information to OUTPUT DEVICES. The CONTROL SUBSYSTEM obtains the

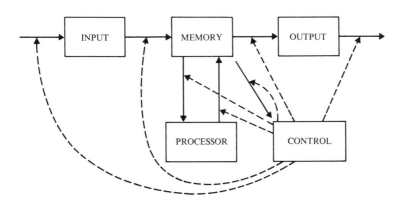

Fig. 1.2.1 The classical computer system.

program from MEMORY and assigns tasks, one at a time, to the other SUBSYSTEMS. The PROCESSOR receives data from the MEMORY under the direction of the CONTROL SUBSYSTEM; it returns processed data to the MEMORY.

The modern   The modern computer block diagram is
system   presented in Fig. 1.2.2. The difference that
we note immediately is that the devices, whether for input or output, do not report directly to the MEMORY but are reached through the CHANNEL

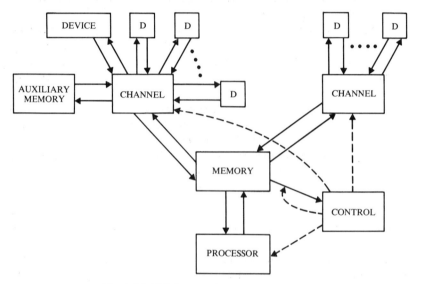

Fig. 1.2.2 Third generation computer system.

CONTROLLER. This is the main difference between the classical and modern computer systems. Chapter 2 is devoted to the operation and implementation of the CHANNEL CONTROLLER method for IO.

1.3   BUILDING BLOCKS

Language   The form of information, both internal and
external to the computer, is dictated by the nature of the available circuits and components. The simplest, most rapid, and most economical devices are bistable. There are two states in which a **bistable device** may be found; it will maintain a given state until a signal demands that it enter its other

state. Relays were used in the first computers; modern computers use FLIPFLOPS. The first FLIPFLOPS consisted of a pair of tubes; now, they consist of a pair of transistors or integrated circuits with dual active elements. These elements work reciprocally. When one of them passes current, the other refuses to pass current; when one of the pair is on, the other is off. Other names for the FLIPFLOP circuit are BIT STORAGE, MULTI, TOGGLE, etc.

The two states of a bistable device are arbitrarily labeled 0 and 1. Since there are only two possibilities, they are called **binary digits,** contracted to **bits.**

To represent humanly recognizable information, numeric or alphabetic, in binary form requires translation. Each character used by a human is represented by a set of bits. A computer dealing only with numeric information might use a set of four bits to represent each decimal number. Table 1.3.1 lists the decimal digits and the corresponding bit set called

Table 1.3.1 THE NATURAL BINARY
CODED DECIMAL CODE

Digit	Code
0	0000
1	0001
2	0010
3	0011
4	0100
5	0101
6	0110
7	0111
8	1000
9	1001
	1010 ⎫
	1011 ⎪
	1100 ⎬ forbidden
	1101 ⎪
	1110 ⎪
	1111 ⎭

NBCD by which the computer could store the decimal information. **BCD** or **binary coded decimal** codes use a different four-bit combination for each decimal digit. When the combinations all correspond to the binary counting representation, the code is called **NBCD** or **natural BCD.** For all BCD codes, there are sixteen different combinations of four bits each, and six of these combinations are unassigned. Thus, when decimal information is handled in this fashion, there is a loss in efficiency.

If six bits were used for each symbol, they could be combined in sixty-four different ways, enough to translate both letters and numbers. **Alphanumeric,** defined as combined alphabetic and numeric information, can therefore be represented with a minimum of six bits per character.

It is often more suitable to handle larger chunks of information of a fixed size. A specified number of combinations, each representing a **character,** are assembled together into a **word.** This word can be rated by the number of characters, letters, or numerals it contains, or by the number of bits in it. Thus the Honeywell 800 has a forty-eight bit word. Information can be stored in this word in eight alphabetic characters of six bits each, or in twelve numeric characters of four bits each.

We use one definition for **word size:** the number of bits *recalled* or *memorized* on a single, main memory cycle; the memory cell size (see p. 12). By this definition, *all* computers have a *fixed* word size, the size of a datum in MAIN MEMORY. For some computers, since words are so small, i.e., single characters, the command can specify multiple characters (words) for processing. Such machines as the RCA 501, 301, and Spectra 70, the IBM 1401, 1410, and Series 360, and the Univac 1050 are **character-oriented machines.** They handle single or multiple characters as specified in the command or data punctuation. There is a relation of word size to the character which is clarified in later chapters for specific machines.

It is possible to translate from a decimal number into a totally binary number. When this is done, no digit in the original decimal number need be represented in any group of bits in the binary number. The bits in the computer word are used as they are used for counting in a binary system. Thus, 37 is represented in binary by 00100101, but no combination of bits corresponds to 3 or to 7 here.

Even though information is stored in the computer word in binary, and although there is no *direct* translation between bit sets and characters, our concept of data processing is not affected. Two words may be added together, regardless of their representation in the machine, as long as they are numerical. On retranslation into human terms, the result must be the same no matter what the representation of numbers in the machine.

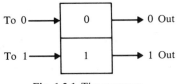

Fig. **1.3.1** The FLIPFLOP.

Hardware atoms   Engineering considerations have led to the conclusion that the most reliable, smallest, economical, and all-around best hardware atom is the BISTABLE DEVICE or FLIPFLOP. The symbol for the FLIPFLOP appears in Fig. 1.3.1. Two lines enter the block. A signal on the line labeled **to 0** sets the device to its 0 state regardless of its present setting; a signal, **to 1**, sets the device to the 1 state regardless of its present reading. The output line records the present setting of the device.

The FLIPFLOP holds one bit of information. It can be set in a nanosecond or so, and it can be read instantaneously—as fast as a signal can scan the output. However, the FLIPFLOP costs more per bit than other storage devices. When speed is not of the essence, the preference is for less expensive devices or even core MEMORIES. Usually, we rely on FLIPFLOPS to act as temporary, fast-access storage devices within the PROCESSOR where speed *is* important.

The REGISTER   The REGISTER is a set of BIT STORAGE DEVICES or FLIPFLOPS holding a fixed number of bits. This number of bits, the chunk of information dealt with by the PROCESSOR and CONTROLLER, is often, but not necessarily, a *word*.

The word   "Word" as it is used here refers *only* to the size of the MEMORY CELL. The twenty-five bit word could represent a twenty-five bit natural binary number. One of the bits could be reserved for a sign, and the twenty-five bits might then be viewed as a twenty-four bit binary integer.

Coding schemes enable us to store decimal information where a set of four bits can represent any one of the decimal digits. Since there are six sets of four bits available in our twenty-five bit word, such a word can represent a signed, six-digit decimal number.

In business applications we manipulate alphabetic as well as numeric information. Six bits are required to represent an alphabet of characters, numerals, and special symbols; sometimes seven or eight bits are used for a more complete alphabet. Our twenty-five bit word can store four six-bit alphanumeric symbols plus a sign or tag when necessary.

Some computers permit us, under control of the program, to alternate between two or more of the character-handling capabilities just specified. Thus, some pieces of information can be treated as alphanumeric, while others can be treated as straight numeric.

REGISTER layout   REGISTERS are set most quickly in parallel: the bits are set at once. Figure 1.3.2 depicts the parallel REGISTER. The double line indicates that several signal lines set information into the REGISTER.

The serial REGISTER can receive and transmit only a single bit of information at a time. The symbol for the serial REGISTER is in Fig. 1.3.3.

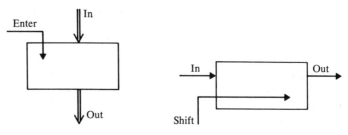

Fig. 1.3.2 The parallel entry REGISTER.   **Fig. 1.3.3** The serial entry REGISTER.

A compromise between these is achieved with the serial-parallel REGISTER, where a character of information can be entered into or withdrawn from the REGISTER during a single time interval. Since a character consists of several bits, we say that the REGISTER is serial by character and parallel by bit. The symbol for this appears in Fig. 1.3.4.

SWITCHES   A SWITCH permits or prohibits the passage of a signal through a line or set of lines. By this definition, the SWITCH might be operated remotely or automatically, incorporating a mechanical or electromechanical device. It is then called a RELAY. The first computers were constructed mostly of relays. Although the RELAY is inexpensive and bistable, it does not operate fast enough to serve in a high speed computer.

In the electronic SWITCH, one electronic signal permits or prohibits the passage of another electronic signal along a signal path. Both the actuator and the signal are electronic in nature, and it is difficult to differentiate between them. The symbol for an AND GATE, or simply AND, is shown in Fig. 1.3.5. A signal appears at the output of this DEVICE only when signals are present on *both* input leads. This function is identical with the logical connective *and*, from which it derives its name.

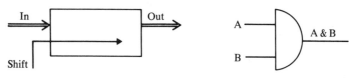

Fig. 1.3.4 The serial-parallel REGISTER.   **Fig. 1.3.5** The AND gate.

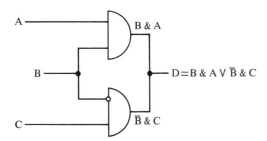

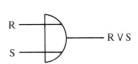

Fig. 1.3.6 The double throw, single pole switch.   **Fig. 1.3.7** The OR gate.

Connecting two ANDs together as in Fig. 1.3.6, we form a TWO THROW SWITCH. Notice that an output signal appears when both *A* and *B* are present *or* when both *C* and *B* are present. There is a little circle on AND2 in the figure. This indicates that the signal *B* entering that GATE is inverted; a signal appears at the output of AND2 when the signal *C* is present and the signal *B* is absent. In other words, the circuit of Fig. 1.3.6 produces an output on line *D* identical with the input *A* or the input *C*, according to whether signal *B* is present or absent. It thus acts as a TWO THROW SWITCH, where the signal *B* throws the switch in the up direction, and the absence of signal *B* throws it in the down direction.

In Fig. 1.3.6, if the outputs of two ANDs are shorted together as shown, trouble may arise. It can be avoided with the OR GATE or OR, shown in Fig. 1.3.7, which

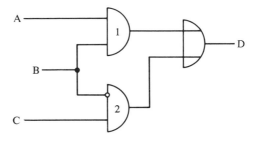

Fig. 1.3.8 An improved double throw, single pole switch.

produces an output if either or both inputs are present. OR produces the *effect* of the shorting wire as far as the output is concerned, but the input signals do not interact.

The OR in Fig. 1.3.8 provides the function of the OR in Fig. 1.3.6 without the interaction of the latter.

THE TWO THROW SWITCH

MULTIPOLE SWITCHES

Combinations of ANDs and ORs form both MULTIPOLE SWITCHES and MULTITHROW SWITCHES. MULTIPOLE SWITCHES affect several information paths; MULTITHROW SWITCHES route signals to several places. SWITCHES are among the most important components of the computer because they automatically route information. They permit one COMPUTER SUBSYSTEM to control what happens in another SUBSYSTEM.

A large multipole SWITCH is often indicated in diagrams by an oval. The ANDs and ORs which comprise the SWITCH may be omitted entirely and must be assumed.

Functional units   A FUNCTIONAL UNIT is a larger component of a computer SUBSYSTEM. The function performed by a unit can be stated in words. The logical designer takes this verbal statement and converts it into symbols using logic. This results in a set of equations which is symbolic but not mathematical and says the same thing as the original verbal statement. The designer uses certain rules of simplification in restating the equations so that they assume a more compact form.

Since each *and* or *or* connective in a statement corresponds with a logical atom, AND or OR, simplification of the equation results in simplification of the hardware. When the symbolic equations are reduced to their simplest forms, they then yield the most economical hardware. The designer then converts the equations to a pictorial form which represents the modular structure of the hardware. It is then simple to convert this modular representation to the physical structure of the computer.

Presented below are the verbal descriptions of some FUNCTIONAL UNITS used in the computer.

ADDER

The heart of the ARITHMETIC UNIT is the ADDER. As shown in Fig. 1.3.9, it adds a pair of quantities (*A* and *B*) together, producing a third. The ADDER is indicated by a rectangle with "ADDER" inside it.

ENCODER

The ENCODER is a translator. When presented with a character, the ENCODER produces the bit set of the user's code corresponding to the character. There is a separate input line for each character for which a code is desired. The output is in the code, a bit set corresponding to the input character, as shown in Fig. 1.3.10. For one and only one character input signal, none, one, several, or all of the output lines may contain signals corresponding to the proper code. If several input signals are applied, nonsense results.

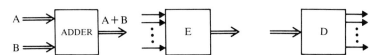

Fig. 1.3.9 The ADDER.   **Fig. 1.3.10** The ENCODER.   **Fig. 1.3.11** The DECODER.

The DECODER provides the inverse function of the ENCODER. It takes a code, a bit set, and translates it into the corresponding character, as shown in Fig. 1.3.11. None, one, several, or all of the coded input lines may contain signals; only one output line produces a corresponding signal. If some bit sets are **invalid,** they correspond to no valid character; a single, output signal line may convey this.

The COUNTER counts the number of discrete signals which appear on the line. Incoming signals appear as pulses on the **count line.** The COUNTER has a limit which, when exceeded, resets the COUNTER to 0. Thus, if the maximum count for a COUNTER is 15 and we enter a 16th pulse, it sets the COUNTER to 0; the next pulse sets it to 1; and so on. As shown in Fig. 1.3.12, another input line, the **reset line,** may reset the COUNTER to 0 regardless of its present state. The **output lines** of the COUNTER convey a set of signals which record a binary count. To represent a count of $2^n - 1$ (for instance, 31) only n (5 in this example) lines are needed.

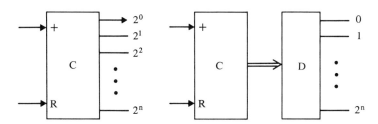

Fig. 1.3.12 The COUNTER.   **Fig. 1.3.13** A COUNTER-DECODER combination.

Frequently the COUNTER is used in conjunction with the DECODER, as shown in Fig. 1.3.13, so that the count is automatically available as a signal on only one of a number of output lines from the DECODER. A scale-of-31 COUNTER having five output lines connected to a NBC DECODER with thirty-two outputs will produce signals on these lines in sequence as pulses are supplied to the counter line.

1.4 THE MEMORY

Use   MEMORY stores large amounts of information. It makes a little of this information rapidly available to the other subsystems when the proper command is received. Under direction, MEMORY receives information from any other SUBSYSTEM and blindly stores it in the specified location.

The MEMORY consists of a MEMORY CONTROL UNIT, REGISTERS, and a storage area. The storage area contains a large number of CELLS, each specified by an address.

CELL

The CELL stores exactly one *word*, a fixed number of bits. As noted earlier, *our* definition of *word* relies on this quantity, the CELL size. By this definition the IBM 360/30 has a different word size from the 360/65, for example.

ADDRESS

The **address** is a unique label for the CELL; the address of a CELL is distinct from the contents.

RECALL

The MEMORY functions to **recall** information when it is supplied with the address of the CELL containing the desired information. After being instructed to *recall*, it goes to the proper CELL, brings forth the contents, and passes them to the requesting unit. It is important to note that *recalling* is nondestructive, just as it is for humans. If you bring forth a piece of information, it is not removed from your memory. Thus, when you tell the Motor Vehicle Bureau your birthday, you still retain the knowledge in your memory—it is **nondestructive recall.**

The properties of the components used in the MEMORY are easily confused with their actual functions. Thus magnetic cores which have a destructive read property are used in MEMORIES that function in a nondestructive manner. Functionally, all MEMORIES in modern computers maintain information in a CELL, even after a datum has been *recalled* and transferred elsewhere.

MEMORIZING

For the MEMORY to **memorize** information, two things must be supplied: the *address* of the CELL into which the item is to be inserted, and the *item* to be memorized. Upon receiving these and a request for *memorization*, memorize, the MEMORY will perform its task and report when it is done. Naturally, *memorizing* is destructive since it is impossible to both maintain an old word in a specific CELL and also insert a new word in the same CELL.

A MEMORY is said to be a **random access** MEMORY when it requires a fixed time, called the **cycle time,** regardless of whether it is *memorizing* or *recalling* and regardless of the address of the datum in question. However, for some MEMORIES, when a datum is *recalled*, it may be made available *before* the end of the cycle.

MEMORY
subsystem
structure

The MEMORY subsystem contains:
- the CELLS
- the MEMORY ADDRESS REGISTER
- the MEMORY DATA REGISTER
- the CONTROL UNIT

This is shown in the block diagram, Fig. 1.4.1, which is referred to in the rest of this section.

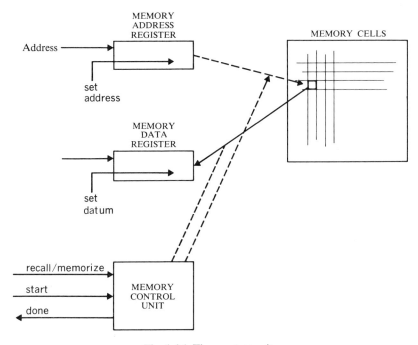

Fig. 1.4.1 The MEMORY unit.

To summarize, each CELL:

1. contains a single word;
2. does not have its contents destroyed by *recall;*
3. may have new information written into it (but at the expense of destroying existing information);
4. has a unique address (label) for reference.

MAR

The MEMORY ADDRESS REGISTER (MAR) holds the *address* of the CELL with which the MEMORY is currently concerned. It receives this address from some other unit. The MEMORY ADDRESS REGISTER in Fig. 1.4.1 has parallel lines entering from outside, indicating an address furnished by another subsystem. Notice a line labeled set address entering the MAR from the source subsystem. Via this line, the source subsystem notifies the MAR when it should accept the address supplied by that source subsystem.

MDR

The MEMORY DATA REGISTER (MDR) holds a datum. During *recall*, the information from the CELL pointed to by the MAR is placed temporarily in the MEMORY DATA REGISTER by the MEMORY CONTROL UNIT. It is available to the requesting subsystem when done appears.

During *memorizing*, the datum to be stored is placed by the originating subsystem into the MDR by set datum. It is emptied into the CELL by the MEMORY CONTROL UNIT when the location pointed to by the address in the MAR has been found.

MCU

The MEMORY CONTROL UNIT (MCU) controls the memory cycle. It is instructed by the requesting unit either to *recall* or *memorize*. This request is not final, for the source subsystem may change its mind without messing up the MEMORY's operation. The request *is* final when start is supplied to the MEMORY. After start is received, the MCU keeps the two registers, MAR and MDR, locked out from interference by other subsystems until the MEMORY's job is done. The MCU finds the CELL and times the flow of information between the MDR and the chosen CELL. When the job is completed, the MCU issues a completion signal indicated in the figure as done.

RECALL

Operation An address is supplied to the MAR. It is *entered* there when set address arrives. Next the MCU is told to recall. Finally, start is supplied to the MCU. The MCU finds the location specified in the MAR and places its contents in the MDR. Done is issued by the MCU signalling that the datum in the MDR is available to the rest of the computer. The computer transfers the MEMORY DATA REGISTER to its destination. A lockout is provided so that another request does not interfere during *recall*. A further lockout may be added to permit subsystem access to the MDR while preventing activation of the MEMORY till the cycle is over.

1.5 THE PROCESSOR

Constituents A typical PROCESSOR is illustrated in Fig. 1.5.1. It has three REGISTERs providing temporary storage of one word

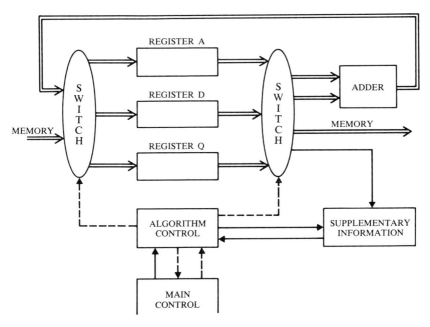

Fig. 1.5.1 PROCESSOR.

each. REGISTERS hold operands, intermediate results, and final results. An **operand** is a datum to be operated on. The PROCESSOR contains an ADDER which does addition and other processes of arithmetic. It also has a COMPLEMENTER which implements subtraction by complementation and addition.

SWITCHES control the flow of information by guiding information from one REGISTER to another, either through the ADDER or bypassing it.

The PROCESSER CONTROL UNIT (PCU) is usually autonomous. It supervises the activity of the PROCESSOR. When informed of the instruction to be done, the PCU times and monitors the process.

AUXILIARY DEVICES are also required. COUNTERS indicate how many cycles of a process have been performed so far or how many bits of a word have been examined. Other INDICATORS summarize the present state of affairs and the properties of the information being handled. For instance, when two negative numbers are multiplied, a FLIPFLOP stores the information that the product is positive.

The arithmetic The labels applied to the REGISTERS vary from
function computer to computer. A typical set includes
the AR, or ACCUMULATOR, for holding the results of arithmetic. Two other

REGISTERS are labeled DR and QR in deference to their function of holding the *divisor* and *quotient* during division. They serve supplementary purposes during other processes. Information from MEMORY can be sent to any one of these REGISTERS by an appropriate command. Such commands will be referred to later using mnemonics. X is the symbol for a transfer (information copying); M is the symbol for the MEMORY location used as a source or destination; the name of the source or destination REGISTER in the ARITHMETIC UNIT is incorporated in a mnemonic. Thus the command XMA brings information from a location in MEMORY to the A REGISTER. Transfer from a REGISTER to MEMORY is indicated similarly. Thus XQM indicates that the contents of the Q REGISTER are stored in MEMORY.

Each arithmetic command specifies a location in MEMORY and/or a REGISTER from which an operand is to be brought. This operand goes to one of the three REGISTERS and arithmetic is performed on it. It ends up in one of the three REGISTERS as specified by the designer. A new command may be required, depending upon the computer, to return the result to MEMORY.

During the time in which the operand appears in the PROCESSOR and the result is produced, many steps take place. These are supervised by the PROCESSOR CONTROL UNIT. Further subcontrol units known as ALGORITHM CONTROL UNITS may also be present. These take over control and supervise the operation of individual arithmetic or editing commands.

Editing   **Editing** consists of entering new information into words or deleting information from words. For example, the result of a business transaction might appear in MEMORY as 0001598000. Editing is required to get this into final form for output. Actually, the amount of the transaction is $159.80. Thus the editing to be done requires that the three initial zeros and two of the three terminal zeros be removed. Then the dollar sign must be inserted to the left of the 1, and a decimal point must be placed between the 8 and the 9.

One of the editing tasks used in this example is **extracting**—in which the meaningful part of a word is skimmed off the word like cream from milk. Using this process, we discarded the unwanted zeros. Another editing function required shifting. This properly orients the information within the REGISTER and moves characters with respect to the word so that decimal points, for instance, can be inserted. Insertion of new information requires **masking**—in which new characters are written over parts of a word according to a mask, similar to the way a stencil allows us to print characters on top of a package. Thus the dollar sign and decimal point can be inserted without affecting the other characters in the word. Other editing facilities to serve special purposes are provided by some computers.

1.6 THE CONTROL SUBSYSTEM

Function The CONTROL SUBSYSTEM (or CONTROL) is the master control for the computer. It supervises all operations including those of the MEMORY, PROCESSOR, INPUT/OUTPUT, as well as itself. Depending upon the design of the computer, the CONTROL SUBSYSTEM may or may not be able to relinquish its autonomy to one of the other subsystems. Even when it does so, the subsystem in question returns authority to the CONTROL SUBSYSTEM when the subservient subsystem has completed its operation.

Complete directions are supplied to the CONTROL by the program, the sequence of instructions or commands. The instruction repertoire differs from one machine to another, but there are certain basic similarities. I will later note some of the differences and similarities of the commands which are the basic atoms that make up the machine language program. CONTROL recognizes and interprets these atoms as it encounters them.

The instruction list The list of instructions to the computer is stored in locations in the MEMORY. Although each instruction is comprehensible to the computer but may not be directly readable by the human, this sequence is called the **machine language program.**

Each of these instructions generally requests the processing of one or more data. The data are all stored in the computer MEMORY, but not necessarily in order of reference. There are three reasons for this:
- Some items are referred to several times.
- It may be convenient to store data in order of human generation.
- Intermediate results may also be on the data list.

A datum to be operated upon by the computer is called an **operand.** Some computers can refer to more than one operand in a single machine language command. For the moment, we confine our attention to single-address (one operand) commands.

CONTROL operation CONTROL operates in two cycles, *fetch* and *execute*. A **fetch** cycle brings the next instruction from MEMORY to a location in CONTROL where it is examined and interpreted. With certain exceptions, CONTROL gets its next command from the location right after the one where it got its last command.

Next CONTROL interprets and performs the instruction it has fetched, the **execute** cycle. Usually, a command requires an operand, the procurement of which is delegated to the MEMORY. CONTROL sets up the destination for receipt of the new operand. When this operand is passed over to the destination subsystem, it instructs that subsystem what to do and may delegate full authority for the performance of the remainder of the command.

When the destination subsystem has completed its task, it signals CONTROL which goes over to a **fetch** cycle and gets its next command.

Control subsystem structure   In Fig. 1.6.1, the INSTRUCTION COUNTER (or IC) is a REGISTER which can be counted and which stores the address of the instruction being executed or to be executed next, depending on the computer. The bit storage device F indicates which cycle

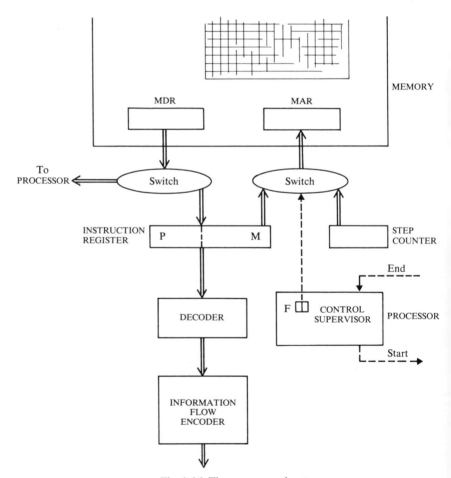

Fig. 1.6.1 The CONTROL subsystem.

of operation is in progress, *fetch* or *execute*. The INSTRUCTION REGISTER (or IR) receives the command. This command consists of:

- the opcode—the process to be performed;
- location—generally the address of the operand address;
- tags or supplementary information.

The INSTRUCTION DECODER examines the opcode of the command in the IR. A number of lines emanate from it, one corresponding to each instruction in the computer's repertoire. For an admissible instruction under examination, one and only one of these lines carries a signal. The INSTRUCTION ENCODER interprets the signals produced by the DECODER, chooses the destination subsystem, and sets up the flow of information to, from, and within it. To provide timing and supervision for CONTROL, there is a CONTROL UNIT contained therein. To avoid confusion, we refer to *this* CONTROL UNIT as the MASTER CONTROL.

1.7 THE MACHINE REPERTOIRE

The machine repertoire is the set of commands comprehensible to the computer. The set of FLAP commands which constitute the repertoire of the FLAPJAC computer discussed completely elsewhere† is presented in Table 1.7.1 as an example to the reader and to illustrate an expressive notation for conveying the commands.

The command   Consecutive MEMORY locations contain consecutive tasks to be performed by the computer. In one or more CELLS of the program sequence, a computer command is stored in machine language. It is impossible to tell whether a word in MEMORY is a datum or an instruction word. As far as the computer is concerned, any word can be treated as a datum. At times it is requested to process an instruction. If, by mistake, it is requested to perform a datum, trouble may arise. If the datum does not have a proper combination of bits to be interpreted as a command, then the computer is unable to proceed further. It may stop dead and signal the operator of its confusion. Or else it may turn control to the other software (the executive system) by means of an interrupt.

Command content   The command *must* contain one thing: an indication of the process to be performed. The opcode field conveys this. The least demanding of any command is NOOP. This is an abbreviation

OPCODE

---

† Ivan Flores, *Computer Programming* (Englewood Cliffs, N.J.: Prentice-Hall, Inc., 1966).

Table 1.7.1 Flores Assembly Program (FLAP) Mnemonics

Line						Indexable
	Transfers					
1	To	XMR	$(M) \to R$			Yes
2	From	XRM	$(R) \to M$			Yes
3	Between	XRR'	$(R) \to R'$			No
4	Special	X0M	$0 \to M,$	X0R	$0 \to R$	Yes
	Logic					
5		ANDTA	$(A) \,\&\, (M) \to A$	ANDTM	$(A) \,\&\, (M) \to M$	Yes
6		ORTA	$(A) \lor (M) \to A$	ORTM	$(A) \lor (M) \to M$	Yes
	Shifts					
7	Out	SRR	$0 \xrightarrow{M} R$	SLR	$R \xleftarrow{M} 0$	No
8	Around	ERR	$(R) \xrightarrow{M} R$	ELR	$R \xleftarrow{M} (R)$	No
9	Long	LSR	$(A) \xrightarrow{M} Q;\ (Q) \xrightarrow{M} A$			No
	Arithmetic					
10		ADD	$(A) + (M) \to A$	ADA	$(A) + |(M)| \to A$	Yes
11		SUB	$(A) - (M) \to A$	SBA	$(A) - |(M)| \to A$	Yes
12		MLR	$(M) \times (D) \to A$	MUL	$(M) \times (D) \to A, Q$	Yes
13		DIV	$(A) / (M) \to Q$			Yes
	Decision and action					
14	Unconditional	NOOP	$\Rightarrow I + 1$	STOP	⟂	No
15		UCJ	$\Rightarrow M$			Yes
16	Decision	CMP	$(A) > (M)\ 1 \to G$ $\quad (A) = (M)\ 1 \to E \quad$ $(A) < (M)\ 1 \to L$		$0 \to E, L$ $\quad 0 \to G, L \quad$ $0 \to G, E$	Yes
	Conditional					
17		JOG	$G = 1 \Rightarrow M;\ G = 0 \Rightarrow I + 1$			Yes
18		JOE	$E = 1 \Rightarrow M;\ E = 0 \Rightarrow I + 1$			Yes

No.	Mnemonic	Operation			
19	JOL	L = 1 ⇒ M; L = 0 ⇒ I + 1			Yes
20	CAS	(A) > (M) ⇒ I + 1	(A) = (M) ⇒ I + 2	(A) < (M) ⇒ I + 3	No
	Index manipulations				
	Fill				
21	XMN,n	$(M_M) \to n$	XNM	$(n) \to M_M$	No
22	XAN,n	$(A_M) \to n$	XNA	$(n) \to A_M$	No
23	XPN,n	M → n			No
	Increment				
24	NPP,n	(n) + M → n	NMP,n	(n) − M → n	No
	Compare				
25	CMPN,n	(n) > M 1 → G 0 → E, L	(n) = M 1 → E 0 → G, L	(n) < M 1 → L 0 → E, G	No
	Compare and jump				
26	JNP,n	(n) ⩾ 0 ⇑ M	(n) < 0 ⇑ I + 1		No
27	JNNZ,n	(n) ≠ 0 ⇑ M	(n) = 0 ⇑ I + 1		No
28	JNN,n	(n) < 0 ⇑ M	(n) ⩾ 0 ⇑ I + 1		No
	Increment, test, and jump				
29	TUN,n	(n) + 1 → n	(n) < 0 ⇑ M	(n) ⩾ 0 ⇑ I + 1	No
30	TDN,n	(n) − 1 → n	(n) > 0 ⇑ M	(n) ⩽ 0 ⇑ I + 1	No
	IO				
31	READ	(Input) → M			Yes
32	WRITE	(M) → Output			Yes
33	REWIND	rewind device			No
34	JOIE	indication ⇒ M	no indication ⇒ I + 1		Yes
	Subroutine linkage				
35	JAS	I + 1 → M − 1 ⇑ M			Yes
36	JSR	I → RJR; ⇑ M			Yes
37	JRA	⇒ (RJR) + M			No
38	JSN,n	I → n; ⇑ M			No

for no operation; it simply specifies that the computer do nothing but go on to the next command. The opcode is a specification of the task to be performed (or, as in the NOOP instance, not performed).

The next field, called **location,** usually found in the command contains one or more operand addresses. Most commands require operands, and *location* will generally contain the *address* of the one or more operands.

Scientific computers generally have space in their command for only one location. The IBM 7090/94 and the Philco 2000 contain room for one location field in a single operand specification. These machines are referred to as **single address machines.**

When the computer word is large enough, several operand locations can be inserted into a single command. Thus the Honeywell 800 provides a command with locations for three operand addresses; and it is consequently called a **three address machine.**

Supplementary information frequently incorporated in the commands of some computers indicates the kind of addressing required by the command, or other details.

Command structure Since the command is always decoded by CONTROL, it is entered in a fixed position in the INSTRUCTION REGISTER. Therefore, the location in the command of each function field is fixed.

By the laws of combinations and permutations, n bits allow us to specify 2^n different items. If our command repertoire must contain forty-seven different commands, five bits provide thirty-two combinations, and six bits provide sixty-four combinations. For the forty-seven commands, six bits are the minimum that we can reserve for the opcode.

Sometimes more bits than the minimum are provided for convenience in coding or simpler hardware implementation. Thus, one of the bits in the opcode may be reserved to indicate whether the result of the command is to be returned to MEMORY; another bit may indicate whether arithmetic is to take place; and so forth. With this procedure, ten bits may become reserved for the opcode when irredundant coding would require only six, for instance. It is common for the designer to allot anywhere from four to twenty bits for the opcode.

The number of bits required to specify the operand address depends, of course, on the number of available MEMORY CELLS. Certainly, the minimum number of such locations depends upon the minimum machine configuration; the maximum depends upon the maximum MEMORY size option available to the customer. Usually the maximum size is provided for.

Operands   Scientific computers, such as the IBM 7090 and the PDP 8, are called **fixed word length computers.** This phrase is meaningless, per se, for we know by definition that all computers have a fixed word size. This jargon conveys that commands can specify the transfer or processing (with the exception of IO) of only one word at a time. Other computers, such as the Honeywell 200 and RCA Spectra 70, operate on chunks which may vary in size. I call these **variable field length** computers because they handle sets of words whose size is specified in the command. They are sometimes misnamed **variable word length** computers.

The definition of *word* size is always the size of each main MEMORY CELL. It may be as small as seven bits for the IBM 1401 or sixty bits for the CDC 6600, but it is *fixed.*

For the PDP 8, each command is word size, or twelve bits. No variation is possible. Variable field length machines, such as the RCA 301, may also have **fixed length commands.**

Valuable memory space is conserved if the command can expand or contract to suit the amount of information required for its specification. We see later how this is done for the IBM 1401 and System 360 which have **variable length commands.**

1.8   ADDRESSING

Using the FLAP command repertoire, Table 1.7.1, we discuss the following kinds of addressing:
- implied
- immediate
- direct
- indirect
- relative
- indexed

We assume that the addressing method is distinguished in the command by a *tag*.

Implied addressing   Every transfer of information has a source and destination. Commands which process information usually refer to two operands—data which are operated upon. Each of these is stored somewhere. If the command has room for only a single address, how then can we refer to two operands or to both source and destination? The REGISTERS provide the solution. One or both locations can be REGISTERS; their use is *implied* in the command. Thus, the command XAM addresses the AR as the source of information by implied addressing. In fact, both source and destination may be implied; witness XQD.

Another way to imply the source or destination is through the index specification digit. Thus the command XAM addresses by implication an INDEX REGISTER. The particular INDEX REGISTER is specified by the digit which follows the command code.

Immediate addressing   The computer may deal with operands of a full word length, and such operands cannot be transmitted with the command. However, an operand of address length may be presented in the *location* field of a command when **immediate addressing** is used. Thus, index-associated commands often use immediate addressing to fill or increment an index with a quantity in the *location* field.

Direct addressing   The normal way to specify an operand is by **direct addressing** using the *location* field in the command.

Indirect addressing   Suppose we know the address of a CELL which contains the address of a desired operand, and we want the operand. We go to the CELL, get the address which is there, and use it to procure the operand. With **indirect addressing,** the location field in the command contains the address at which the operand address is stored.

For direct addressing the operand is (M). For indirect addressing the operand is ((M)), where M is specified in the address portion of the command and ($\Box$) means "the contents of."

To indicate indirect addressing, the tag, 1, follows the command mnemonic. Thus, if ADD indirectly addresses CELL 237, and 237 contains the address 111, then ADD actually addresses 111. Thus we have:

$$\text{ADD,I}\quad 237 \equiv \text{ADD}\quad 111 \quad \text{for}\quad (237) = 111 \qquad (1.8.1)$$

where $\equiv$ means "is equivalent to."

MULTIPLE INDIRECTION

The operand address in a command word may take us to a CELL which contains an address of a CELL which contains an address and so forth and so on. Finding the operand is like a treasure hunt: we move from one CELL to the next looking for clues with the hope that a treasure will be found.

The treasure hunter can distinguish between a clue and the treasure itself by its specific nature. A datum, however, does not have a specific nature to distinguish it from a clue (address). How, then, do we know that we are at the end of the trail? When a CELL is known to contain an address, it is only the address itself that is of use; other bits of the word are free to be used as *tags*. Just as a command word has a tag to indicate indirect addressing, so too the address word can contain a tag showing further indirect addressing. The command word tag, I, used in indirect addressing takes us to the first address. We examine the tag at this address. If it indicates direct addressing, we know the next CELL we reach contains the operand. If it is tagged as indirect, we examine the next CELL as an address. We continue this as long as indirect tags are present. The first direct tag indicates that the very next CELL to be examined contains an operand.

Relative   For relative addressing, we determine the
addressing   effective address by adding the location field
to the contents of a BASE ADDRESS REGISTER (BAR). Thus,

$$\text{effective address} = (\text{BAR}) + \text{M} \qquad (1.8.2)$$

One purpose of relative addressing is to increase the address range of a command in a small, low cost computer where the command size is small. If the location field of a command is necessarily small because the command is small, then the number of CELLS that this set of bits addresses is small compared with the full MEMORY. Relative addressing ameliorates this difficulty. It is seldom used in larger machines, except for the byte-oriented third generation computers.

The address in the command could be interpreted relative to any REGISTER in the machine or even to any CELL. The INSTRUCTION COUNTER is especially useful for relativizing. For jump commands it comes in handy to be able to indicate the jump location relative to the current step, (IC). For **self-relative** commands, the effective address is given by

$$\text{effective address} = \text{M} + (\text{IC}) \qquad (1.8.3)$$

The tag in the command word which indicates self-relative addressing is *. We have

$$0\text{I}7 \quad \text{UCJ,*} \quad 4: \Rightarrow 2\text{I} \qquad (1.8.4)$$

The unconditional jump on step 17 is self-relative by an amount of 4. This is equivalent to a jump to step 21. Similarly,

$$07\text{I} \quad \text{JOL,*} \quad -3 \quad \text{L} = 1: \Rightarrow 68$$
$$\text{L} = 0: \Rightarrow 72 \qquad (1.8.5)$$

The above *jump on less* is self-relative by -3; for *less*, the jump takes us three steps backward from 71, landing us on 68.

Indexable commands An indexable command is one which may specify an INDEX to modify the operand address. An indexed command takes the form in FLAP:

$$\text{mnemonic, digit, tag   address} \tag{1.8.6}$$

Here *digit* is a decimal digit. Thus a nonzero digit specifies the INDEX REGISTER corresponding to the digit; if it is zero or blank, no indexing is done. Indexable FLAP commands are so indicated in Table 1.7.1.

EFFECTIVE ADDRESS

The effective address of the operand for an indexed command is given by:

$$\text{effective address} = \text{address} + \text{(index digit)} \tag{1.8.7}$$

The contents of the INDEX REGISTER specified by digit is added to address.

EXAMPLE

ADD is indexable. ADD, specifying INDEX 3 and operand address 245 actually adds the contents of CELL 272 if INDEX 3 contains 27:

$$\text{ADD,3   245} = \text{ADD   272   for   (N3)} = 027 \tag{1.8.8}$$

Index manipulations The power of the INDEX REGISTER can only be exploited if we do other things with it besides using it to modify commands. The tasks that we examine are:

- transfers
- increments
- tests
- combinations

TRANSFERS

A transfer into an INDEX REGISTER sets it up for future use. Transfers out of an INDEX REGISTER save index quantities for future use in other segments of the program.

INCREMENTS

The ability to add or subtract from an INDEX quantity permits us to move up and down within a list being processed.

TESTS

Tests upon INDEX REGISTER contents can determine when a list has been processed.

When one command can replace two or more, the program can be written with less space and can be executed in a shorter time. Combination index commands fulfill several purposes.

Transfers   Transfers between MEMORY and an INDEX REGISTER use commands on line 21 of Table 1.7.1. *Digit* specifies the source or destination INDEX REGISTER. It does not indicate that the command is being indexed. On the contrary, this command is not indexable.

The INDEX REGISTER stores only the number of digits required to specify an address. Hence a transfer to or from a MEMORY CELL involves only the location field of the word. For FLAP, these are the three right-hand digits. For a transfer into MEMORY, zeros are placed in nonaddress positions. Thus, to store the contents of INDEX 5 in CELL 345 we use

$$\text{XMN,5} \quad 345 \quad \text{for} \quad (N5) = 123, \quad 000000123 \rightarrow 345 \qquad (1.8.9)$$

To fill an INDEX from the AR or to transfer the contents of an INDEX into the AR, the nonaddress portion of the AR is preserved. This allows us to change only the address portion of a word (desirable for address alteration).

Since the INDEX REGISTER and the location field of a command are the same size, it is possible to fill an INDEX REGISTER directly from a command word. The location field of the command is entered into the INDEX. To put 15 into INDEX 3 we use

$$\text{XPN,3} \quad 015 \quad 15 \rightarrow N3 \qquad (1.8.10)$$

There is no command to transfer the quantity from an INDEX into the program!

Incrementation   The two commands on line 24 of Table 1.7.1 permit us to add or subtract quantities from INDEX REGISTERS. The index to be augmented is specified by *digit*. The increment is in the *location* field. To increase index 7 by 3, we give the command iNdex Plus Program,

$$\text{NPP,7} \quad 003 \quad (N7) + 3 \rightarrow N7 \qquad (1.8.11)$$

Reflexive   Reflexive commands relating to INDEX REGISTERS can be single or multiple in nature:
- test
- test and act
- increment, test, and act.

With more complexity, more is implied by the command.

   The index comparison command CMPN tests the contents of *digit* against the quantity in the *location* field. The result of the command sets one of the three FLIPFLOPS in control, L, E, or G, and resets the other two (as with CMP). To compare the contents of INDEX 3 with 75, we give the command

$$\text{CMPN,3} \quad 075 \quad \text{(N3): 75} \qquad (1.8.12)$$

   If the comparand for a test quantity is implied, action may also be specified in the command. The most likely quantity for testing is zero. The three commands on lines 26 through 28 of Table 1.7.1 permit us to test an index and *jump* if the accompanying condition is not met. The *jump index nonzero* command in CELL 41 requires us to return to step 37 if INDEX 3 does not contain 0; we continue to step 42 if the INDEX REGISTER contains exactly 0:

$$041 \quad \text{JNNZ,3} \quad 037 \qquad (\text{N3}) \neq 0 \Rightarrow 37$$
$$(\text{N3}) = 0 \Rightarrow 42 \qquad (1.8.13)$$

   For incrementing by 1, a triple combination command may be used. This is useful when we process a list contained in contiguous CELLS. The Tally-Down iNdex command (TDN) permits us to reduce a positive index toward 0, testing it to see if it is 0, jumping if it is not 0, and continuing to the next command when it is 0. The Tally-Up iNdex command (TUN) permits us to increase by 1 a negative index quantity in a similar fashion. These commands are on lines 29 and 30 of Table 1.7.1.

   Summary   The kind of addressing for the command is conveyed to CONTROL by tags in the command. It is possible to combine two or more modes of addressing. Thus we can have indexed indirect addressing, where the effective address of the next address is obtained by adding the contents of the tagged INDEX REGISTER to the operand location. Any address participating in multiple indirect addressing can be indexed.

   The tag conventions and the permissible combination of tags are presented in Table 1.7.1.

1.9   SOFTWARE

   I define **software** as those programs which do not solve the user's problem directly. They are generally designed not by the user, but by the system programmer. The remainder of this chapter discusses specific software tasks and their relation to hardware.

1.10   TRANSLATORS

Introduction   Most programming today is not done in
machine language. We say that the program is in **machine language** when
it can be fed directly into the computer where, after being placed in
MEMORY, it is ready to run. A **source language** program requires one or
more stages of translation to produce the machine language program.

Source languages   We distinguish several kinds of source
languages according to their use.

Languages which convey information with a syntax and word structure
similar to that used by the programmer in expressing himself in writing out
his algebraic or business problem are **procedure oriented languages,**
abbreviated POLs. They include FORTRAN, ALGOL, PL1, and
COBOL. These are also called **compiler languages** after the programming
system which translates them, the compiler.

Problem oriented languages state a problem for which a general
solution has already been programmed. For instance, Report Generator
Language enables us to state the design of a given report; the Sort Generator
Language allows us to communicate the nature and format of records to
be sorted.

Special languages are structured for the statement of special kinds of
problems. A System Simulator Language is designed to state the properties of a system which is being simulated on the computer. IPL-V (Information Processing Language Number Five) is designed to express
problems which simulate human thinking.

Assembly languages   **Assembly language** provides commands which
are very close to machine language commands, and it falls into the three
categories which will be discussed. The mnemonic language introduced in
Section 1.8, FLAP, is an assembly language. Other extant assembly
languages for IBM machines include BAL, FAP, and AUTOCODER;
Univac assembly languages include UTMOST and ALMOST.
   The three kinds of assembly languages we distinguish are:
   • absolute assembly language   AAL
   • symbolic assembly language   SAL
   • macro assembly language   MAL

An absolute assembly language differs in two ways from actual machine language:
- A mnemonic—a set of letters—is substituted for the binary command code.
- A letter or number code is used for the address of a MEMORY CELL instead of the binary representation of this code.

AAL is a shorthand notation for machine language commands. These are translated to machine language by a clerk or by a very simple assembler. No storage allocation is done.

For a symbolic assembly language, the location of data is denoted symbolically and need not be allocated by the programmer. The assembler does the full allocation of storage and keeps track of all MEMORY CELLS. To talk to the assembler about the nature and format of data, pseudo-commands are used. The SAL can also deal with arrays and provide address modification by addition and subtraction.

Most notably, the macro assembly language permits the programmer to define and name an open subroutine and then to call for a copy of it to be inserted any place in the program that he desires. This feature, programmer defined macros, along with conditional assembly, built-in macros, and other extensions, make up the modern MAL.

AL—POL **contrast**   Absolute assembly language has the characteristic that each source language command is represented by exactly one machine language command. Symbolic assembly language translations present a one-to-one structure—one machine language command for one source language command. For MAL, a sequence of machine language commands is substituted for a macro call right there in the program.

For the procedure oriented language, one source language statement is usually translated into many machine language statements. More important, the sequence of statements produced is a function of the POL compiler and the object machine; it is not at all evident in the source language statements.

The most important differences between the AL and POL are:
- The sequence of machine language steps is nowhere implied in the POL.

- The one-to-many characteristic is customary in the compiler, whereas in the assembler it is an exception.

Mixed　　　　　　　There is no incentive to incorporate AL **characteristics**　　　characteristics in the POL. When POL characteristics are incorporated into assembly language, categorization becomes difficult.

Lists—sets of data—are handled in assembly language by:
- indexing
- operand address modification

Both of these features are built into the assembler. Index specification uses the command tag. Index manipulation is done just as in machine language. Pseudoinstructions allow a set of contiguous locations to be set aside and attach to the first of these locations a label by which the set can be referenced. For instance, if we call such a set DATA, elements of the array are referenced relative to DATA; the fourth element in the array is, hence, DATA + 3. This feature may also be used to reference backward from a given landmark; information can be addressed by a description such as DATA − 6.

Some assemblers permit arithmetic expressions to be used as operand addresses where such expressions include multiplication (∗) and division (/). They tolerate an expression such as,

$$3 * A + (B - 3)/2 \qquad (1.10.1)$$

A and B in (1.10.1) are values supplied to the assembler or with the data. In the first case, the assembler must evaluate the arithmetic expression, but in the second case, a string of machine language commands must be substituted in the object program to evaluate the expression. In any case, the procedure is not one which falls under our definition of an assembler; this is definitely a POL facility.

Translator names　　　Occasionally a company issues a translator which does not follow our definitions. A company may produce a simple assembler which it calls an assembler and a symbolic or macro assembler which it calls a compiler. This may be misleading.

On the other hand, some "assemblers" provide compiler features such as the use of arithmetic expression for operand address.

1.11   LOADERS

Need   There is a constant need to enter new programs into the computer and properly position them in the MEMORY.

Programs may be of several kinds: **object language programs** which perform operation on problem data; **translator programs** to produce an object program (results from the translator) from a source language program (data for the translator); **service routines** which perform tasks on other routines or libraries of routines (data for the service routine); or the program to be brought in may be the loader itself.

A simple sketch of the activity of the loader (henceforth called ℒ𝒪𝒜𝒟) is found in Fig. 1.11.1. When ℒ𝒪𝒜𝒟 is entered, it brings a set of information from the outside into a desired position in the MEMORY.

The bootstrap   A **bootstrap** is a loader that loads itself.

When the computer MEMORY is empty, as it would be when first installed, then there is also no loader in the computer to start things off. Some intermediate medium which holds a copy of the loader program is mounted at one of the input subsystems. The operator starts the ball rolling by entering the first load instruction into the computer at the computer console. This causes the computer to bring in a portion of the loader which then brings in the remainder of the loader. The loader can then bring in other programs.

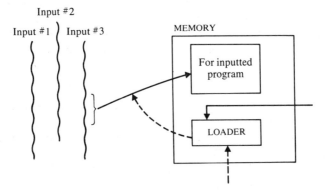

Fig. 1.11.1 The ℒ𝒪𝒜𝒟, acting on instructions, enters the proper program into its assigned area and then relinquishes control to it.

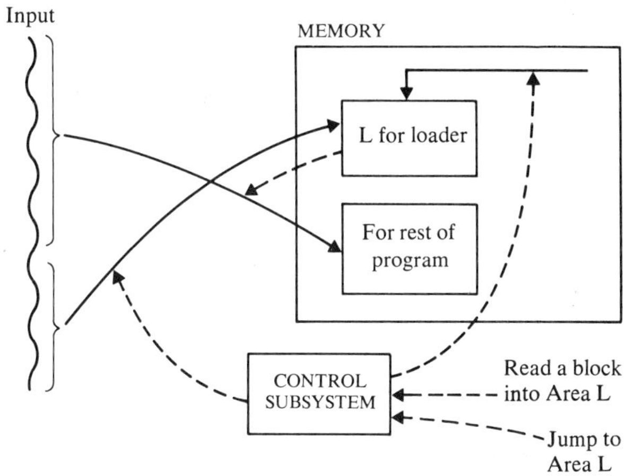

Fig. 1.11.2 The bootstrap brings in a program segment and then transfers to it so that the rest of the program is brought in.

Bootstraps may be more or less elaborate and may be more or less facilitated by commands peculiar to a given computer. The bootstrap loader for the LGP30 requires only a single command to be entered at the console. The loader is prepunched onto paper tape, which is then read in through the paper tape reader. The console command initiates this. Characters from the paper tape are loaded consecutively into MEMORY until a special character is encountered. This causes the computer to terminate loading and to start taking its next instructions from the program just loaded. The bootstrap activity is diagrammed in Fig. 1.11.2.

Relocation As above, any program is placed into MEMORY starting at the same location every time or at a location indicated by the programmer. But it is difficult for the programmer to foresee what else is in MEMORY while his program is running. Hence, the practice now is to forget about trying to properly place the object program, which is then written for a standard starting location and relocated during loading as shown in Fig. 1.11.3.

Another alternative is to write references within the program relative to the starting position, which need not be known at the time the source program is prepared. This requires special hardware, such as the BASE REGISTER for System/360 discussed in Chapter 9.

Since most programs must be relocated, and this relocation is the function of LOAD, LOAD must be aware of the present allocation of MEMORY. LOAD is part of a larger system which includes a monitor or executive routine (called SYSTEM). It is usually the task of SYSTEM to

Input

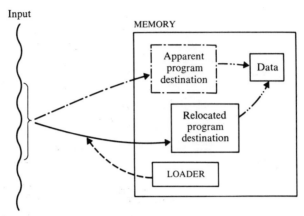

Fig. 1.11.3 The 𝓛𝓞𝓐𝓓 is responsible for relocating programs and assuring that data reference is proper.

know the placement of everything in the MEMORY and to convey this information to 𝓛𝓞𝓐𝓓. 𝓛𝓞𝓐𝓓 then uses this information to place incoming information properly. The responsibility for assigning locations for incoming information may be in 𝓛𝓞𝓐𝓓 or in 𝓢𝓨𝓢𝓣𝓔𝓜. However, this has little effect on the operation of 𝓛𝓞𝓐𝓓.

Information usually preceding the program tells 𝓛𝓞𝓐𝓓 which subroutines are used by the program so that they can be brought from the library. 𝓛𝓞𝓐𝓓 allocates space for each subroutine and copies the subroutine from the library tape into memory. In addition, it creates or

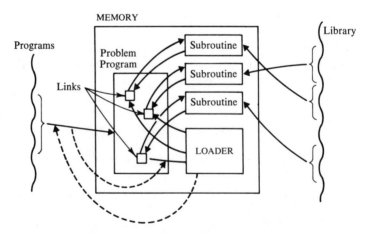

Fig. 1.11.4 The 𝓛𝓞𝓐𝓓, besides entering the program into memory, brings in subroutines from the library and may even create links within the program to get to them.

validates links from the program to the subroutine and from the subroutine to the program. The activity of $\mathcal{LOAD}$ with respect to library programs is diagrammed in Fig. 1.11.4.

Conversion   Some loaders transform incoming data. In binary machines, information often enters in decimal, and conversion is made to binary to store it. $\mathcal{LOAD}$ may take charge of this conversion routine. Besides conversion, scientific numbers must be interpreted and sometimes put into floating point format. This may also be supervised by the loader.

Other space   To supervise the distribution of space in the **allotment needs**   computer MEMORY, $\mathcal{LOAD}$ is concerned with a number of topics which are discussed next.

$\mathcal{LOAD}$ constantly monitors the MEMORY to verify that new information being brought in does not overwrite important information which is to be saved. Whenever incoming information has used up all available space, this condition is signaled and trouble indicated to $\mathcal{SYSTEM}$, or even to the human operator.

The incoming program usually contains a header with the storage requirements for the program proper. This tells $\mathcal{LOAD}$ how to distinguish data and the amount of space required for typical data sets. This prediction is produced by the assembler or compiler or sometimes by the programmer. Sometimes space predictions can be completely accurate, but they may have a range of variability. For instance, a subroutine used by the program may be generated. That is, at the time of use, a special routine creates the desired subroutine. The length of the generated subroutine varies according to the parameters appearing in it; therefore, its length may not be predictable. Further, library routines may not be tagged for length, so that $\mathcal{LOAD}$ cannot foresee the space required.

For scientific problems, a given program may be repeated on a number of sets of data entered via the program INPUT DEVICE. The program communicates to $\mathcal{SYSTEM}$ when it has finished with one set of data. $\mathcal{SYSTEM}$ may delegate $\mathcal{LOAD}$ to enter the data, relocate it in the MEMORY and, occasionally, allocate additional storage if the new data set is larger than that previously handled.

MEMORY BOUNDS

ANTICIPATED REQUIREMENTS

NEW DATA

A program frequently needs working storage to hold intermediate results. ℒ𝒪𝒜𝒟 must provide such storage and protect from interference if desired.

Occasionally, a program is written which is too large to fit into MEMORY together with the data and the software. In that case it is **segmented**— divided into two or more sections which are run one after the other or among which we alternate. ℒ𝒪𝒜𝒟 supervises the running of a segmented program. It learns when one segment is completed, brings in the next segment, and then turns over the operation of the computer to that segment. This is called **overlay.** Sometimes a later segment of the program turns over control to an earlier segment. In that case, ℒ𝒪𝒜𝒟 must have the capability to return to this earlier portion of the program. For a tape installation, this would require the ability to rewind tapes and restart them at the proper position.

1.12 LINKAGE EDITOR

For the larger computers and larger programming systems, ℒ𝒪𝒜𝒟 has a very large job:

- It is responsible for loading and relocating the machine language program.
- It communicates with the segments of the main program.
- It gets the names of, brings in, locates, and links to the sub-routines from the subroutine library.
- It brings in overlays when they are required.
- It monitors the contents of MEMORY to be sure that MEMORY bounds are not exceeded.

It is difficult to make a loader having all these responsibilities yet occupying a sufficiently small portion of memory. This latter quality permits more free space at load time.

To make the loader more effective, third generation systems remove many of these functions, performing them on a different pass. This pass is done by the linkage editor, ℒ𝒥𝒩𝒦. Before discussing what it does and how it operates, I will examine the operation systems containing the linkage editor.

The modern operating system of Fig. 1.12.1 shows all the passes which can exist in a modern operating system. On the top horizontal line we find hexagons containing the name of software routines. These routines are in control when the dashed line from that hexagon enters the box labeled COMP.

Arrows enter or leave the *computer* box connecting it to other symbols representing peripheral devices. The box for the computer appears as many times as there are routines in control. All these routines need not, and probably do not, apply to any single job. Indications in the figure are for a tape-oriented system, but a disk-oriented system operates similarly.

The supervisor, $\mathcal{SYSTEM}$, is always in charge in going from one job to another. It reads in cards or card images from the CONTROL DEVICE. These cards contain directions to $\mathcal{SYSTEM}$ telling it what to do next. In the example, FORTRAN compilation is to be done first. $\mathcal{SYSTEM}$, via the system loader, brings in the compiler program, $\mathcal{FORTRAN}$, which will then take over and perform translation. $\mathcal{SYSTEM}$

The translator takes over and reads control cards, thereafter performing the translation as required. It produces a printout for the programmer and an assembly program for assembly. In third generation computers, compilation often goes directly from source language into machine language. However, in some cases, an assembly language printout is produced. At the end of compilation, control may go to one of these three:

- $\mathcal{BAL}$, the assembler language (AL) used in the system shown;
- $\mathcal{LIBR}$, the librarian for the relocatable library;
- $\mathcal{LINK}$, the linkage editor.

I shall take the longest path.

The assembler reads the AL program and performs a translation to relocatable machine language. During this pass it may incorporate AL routines from the AL subroutine library. $\mathcal{BAL}$

If this program is to be inserted on the relocatable machine language library. $\mathcal{LIBR}$ intervenes, places its title in the table of contents, and stores the program so it can be retrieved easily. $\mathcal{LIBR}$

The linkage editor takes a program from the library, from $\mathcal{BAL}$, or from some other input and converts it into absolute machine language. At this time all subroutines which are in the relocatable library or elsewhere are appended to the program and properly linked thereto. At this stage, if a program exceeds the core limits, it is rejected. $\mathcal{LINK}$

After editing, the absolute program is given to one of two routines:

- $\mathcal{LIBA}$, librarian for the absolute ML library;
- $\mathcal{LOADA}$, loader for absolute ML programs.

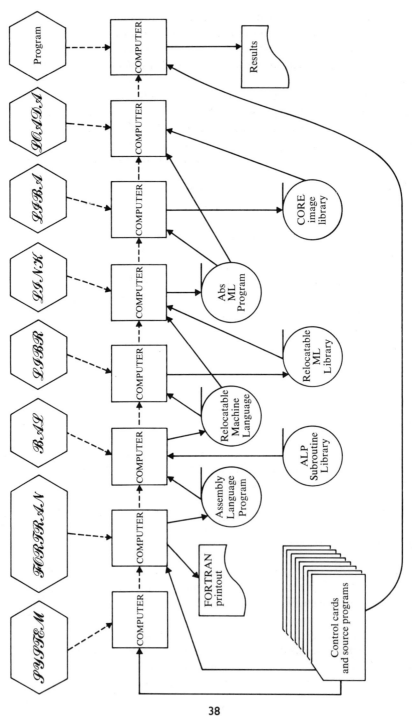

Fig. 1.12.1 A modern operating system in operation with emphasis on the linkage editor £$\mathcal{LINK}$.

38

The directions for loading are obtained from the CONTROL DEVICE by 𝓛𝓞𝓐𝓓𝓐. A program may be loaded from the CONTROL DEVICE, another INPUT DEVICE, or from the absolute library. The functions of 𝓛𝓞𝓐𝓓𝓐 are now very simple: It places the ML program directly in MEMORY, one location after another, until the program is loaded. It then turns control over to the program.

Once the program is in control, it brings in its own data, acts upon it, and produces results. The translator has replaced the command STOP by UCJ, the object of which is a point in 𝓢𝓨𝓢𝓣𝓔𝓜. This permits 𝓢𝓨𝓢𝓣𝓔𝓜 to take over and determine the next job from the control cards.

𝓛𝓘𝓝𝓚   It is clear that all linkage, relocation, and allocation functions previously in 𝓛𝓞𝓐𝓓 are now incorporated in 𝓛𝓘𝓝𝓚. This certainly reduces the complexity of 𝓛𝓞𝓐𝓓𝓐 but may increase the total machine time since two passes are necessary. But only one pass is required for often used programs which reside in the absolute library often referred to as the **core image library.**

1.13   THE INPUT/OUTPUT CONTROL SYSTEM, IOCS

What and how   The 𝓘𝓝𝓟𝓤𝓣/𝓞𝓤𝓣𝓟𝓤𝓣 𝓒𝓞𝓝𝓣𝓡𝓞𝓛 𝓢𝓨𝓢𝓣𝓔𝓜 is software which does many jobs concerned with the input and output of information.

For efficient operation, the program must have information ready when it is needed and must get rid of results as quickly as they are produced. IOCS helps by properly relating buffers to DEVICES, and by seeing that buffers get filled as soon as they become free, and emptied as soon as the computer is done using them.

BLOCKING, DEBLOCKING

Information is stored in the intermediate medium in blocks of size characteristic to that medium: in the punchcard, a block of eighty characters is customary. On the other hand, the record handled by the computer program may be larger or smaller than this block size. Deblocking is, hence, obtaining the next record from a multirecord block. Or it might consist of assembling several small blocks into a single multiblock record. Blocking is the function of assembling a block of information from multiple records or fracturing a single internal record suitably for output medium.

ERRORS AND EXCEPTIONS

A reel of magnetic tape may contain all the records pertinent to a particular facet of a concern's activities. The importance of protecting such a file cannot be underestimated. Even though duplicates of such files are customarily in fireproof vaults, all safeguards are taken to protect the originals. JOCS makes sure that all files of information are correctly titled and properly labeled after use. Similarly, when new sets of records are first examined, the label on the medium containing them is verified to be sure the proper set of records is referenced. (Label handling is usually an optional feature.)

ROLLBACK

When trouble arises that the program cannot eliminate, one alternative is to return to an earlier point in time when the program was known to be functioning correctly. This is called **rollback.** To provide rollback, the input and output media, the MAIN MEMORY, and machine REGISTERS are all recorded on some intermediate medium. When difficulty arises, the whole computer can be returned to the condition which prevailed at the most recent rollback point.

DEVICE ASSIGNMENT

Depending on the manufacturer, DEVICE assignment may be relegated either to JOCS or to SYSTEM. Sometimes, each does a portion of the job. The task is to assign physical device numbers to the symbolic device names used in the program. The assignment procedure takes account of previous assignments and other requirements.

Methodology   JOCS consists of subroutines and tables properly connected together. Its use consists of two phases. In the first phase the tables are set up. Information is supplied to JOCS regarding the activity it is to perform. For blocking and deblocking, for instance, it must know block size, record size, format, and so forth. During this setup period, internal reference tables are produced. Requests (calls) for the use of JOCS are found within the source program.

The second phase is the application of IOCS to the object program. Depending upon the original design, the software may now have become part of the object program. In other instances, it is called into play by the object program as it is needed, and exists as a separate entity in the computer MEMORY.

At least three choices exist for the design of IOCS:

- It can be transmitted to the object program as sets of open subroutines.
- Links can be transmitted to the object program to closed subroutines referred to at run time.
- It can be linked through the system monitor which calls in IOCS at run time.

DEVICE and buffer management   A given program may use many inputs and outputs. These are usually addressed symbolically instead of physically. IOCS, in cooperation with the FOREMAN, relates the symbolic and physical assignments. IOCS alone is responsible for obtaining a buffer, assigning it to an IO DEVICE, and knowing when to do this. Frequently multiple buffer areas are designated. IOCS monitors both the DEVICES and the buffer areas and properly alternates the computer activity between buffer areas. Similarly, it alternates DEVICE activity between the buffer areas as soon as it is determined that an area is free for DEVICE activity. When readdressing is necessary so that the same set of commands can be used to reference a new buffer area, IOCS is in charge of monitoring the alteration.

Blocking and deblocking   As it performs the function just discussed, IOCS must also ascertain that proper block and record sizes are observed. If a record for computer consumption consists of a number of blocks, IOCS makes sure that enough small buffers are kept full so that when the computer is ready to process the record, all the blocks which compose it are available. For multirecord blocks, IOCS makes available the next selected record for computer use. Similarly, it sees that a number of small records are assembled into a large block before that block is released for output.

Blocking is especially prominent in magnetic tape processing, where small records are concerned. Here the larger the block recorded on tape, the more efficient the input activity. This is because spaces of considerable size must be interspersed between blocks on the tape. The more records that are packed into a block, the fewer the spaces that appear on tape; consequently, less time and less tape are consumed for each record read. It is up to IOCS to disassemble the blocks into records as they are inputted and to assemble the records into blocks as they are outputted.

Errors and exceptions   The INPUT DEVICE can check the parity bit against the rest of the word or frame to detect errors. Similarly, an OUTPUT UNIT can check information when read-after-write facility is provided, in which case the read information is compared with what was intended to be written. When an error is detected, there are three ways to notify the computer:

1. The DEVICE can interrupt the computer, which means that the computer will be notified as soon as it completes the command now in process.
2. The DEVICE may store the error indication which it transmits to the computer upon *inquiry*.
3. The DEVICE stores the error information and becomes *disabled* until otherwise notified by the computer.

The *inquiry* method requires that the computer monitor the DEVICE and check with it after the DEVICE has completed each IO operation. The *disable* feature is applicable when all IO activity is delegated to the same IO CONTROL UNIT. In this case, the computer will be notified when it requests the next IO function.

In some few cases, such as the Honeywell 800, correction activity uses a built-in, error-correcting feature. A computer routine is called in, which, in most cases, can correct the block and proceed with the processing.

Few manufacturers have incorporated error-correcting schemes, and it is more common to request a reread or rewrite operation. To reread tape, we must back up a block and then read a block forward.

There is no guarantee that the reread operation will produce a correct block. So the system must provide for a number of such operations and then an alternative procedure if good information cannot be obtained. One such alternative is to reject the job entirely; another is to print a message that this record cannot be processed, and to continue to the next record.

Exception routines may be classified by whether human intervention is required or not. For the latter, an example is the *end of tape* signal which requires that JOCS report to the operator that he must put on a new tape. Usually JOCS will call in and reassign another INPUT DEVICE so that no lag in computation will result.

Disabling events, such as card jams, require the temporary halt of the computer.

FOREMAN   Hardware does not talk directly to JOCS. It can only speak to the FOREMAN, as I call it. Some manufacturers distinguish JOCS from the FOREMAN by calling them *logical* and *physical* JOCS, respectively; but I find this confusing.

1.14   SUPERVISORS

The job   The **supervisor,** $\mathcal{SYSTEM}$, otherwise called the **monitor,** the **system monitor,** and the **executive routine,** supervises the other software as well as problem program sequences entered into the computer; hence, it is indirectly responsible for data management too.

Paramount is its function of coordination. It delegates jobs to one of the software programs; where this program has finished its task, it reports to $\mathcal{SYSTEM}$, which determines what is to be done next. In the same way, $\mathcal{LOAD}$ is called to ready an object program to be run. $\mathcal{SYSTEM}$ terminates jobs when difficulty arises; no program has STOP in it, but ends with a jump to $\mathcal{SYSTEM}$. The supervisor has the usual management function of hiring, firing, and coordination.

$\mathcal{SYSTEM}$ may have several further functions. It does all the accounting required so that the proper people, contract, or division in the company will be charged for the use of the computer for the period when their job is being run. It does the followup when errors cannot be corrected, and it may dump a job. It talks with humans! When $\mathcal{SYSTEM}$ is present, it provides the main link among other software and the human. After all, top management (the human) would do better to talk with the section chief than with one of the crew (the other software).

The system   Let's face it, the larger our agglomeration of software, the more inevitable is auxiliary storage—the TAPE, DRUM, or DISK DEVICE. Here, large amounts of information are available at a moderate transfer rate. A large portion of $\mathcal{SYSTEM}$ is also on this external medium.

The collection of software for the installation is put together on something called a system record, system file, or system tape. This includes a portion of $\mathcal{SYSTEM}$, for we want to restrict the running program as little as possible. The less the software clutters MEMORY, the larger the production program it can accommodate.

In MEMORY at all times there is a portion of $\mathcal{SYSTEM}$ which we call the **system nucleus.** It maintains crucial information about what is going on and makes preliminary decisions; then it may call in from the system tape or disk such help as required to finalize the decision and carry it out. The system nucleus thus contains preliminary decision-making capability plus, possibly, selection and loading capability.

The system tape or disk contains the rest of $\mathcal{SYSTEM}$. It also contains translators, probably at least one assembler and one compiler. It contains the loader and a copy of JOCS. The subroutine library may be on this tape or on a separate tape, depending upon its length.

Typical control sequence

SYSTEM is most importantly employed in proceeding from one program to another. We now review a typical operation (Fig. 1.12.1) as seen from the "eyes" of SYSTEM. A group of jobs for the computer to do today is set up as the day's operations begin. When the program being run is finished, it indicates this to SYSTEM which now gets to work. SYSTEM may now do the accounting for the last run; it then clears the MEMORY and resets the system. It produces a printout so that the operator knows that this program is finished, how it was disposed of, and how long it took.

SYSTEM next makes a new initial assignment of IO DEVICES. It brings in the next program or a portion of it. The program may require translation. Whether or not it does, SYSTEM has found out enough information about the program to make further IO assignments.

For translation, SYSTEM has the loader bring in the translator and locate it properly in MEMORY. The program is read and translated, and output is produced. SYSTEM then determines if the program should be run and, also, if the program is in a condition to be run. If so, it resets MEMORY and calls in the loader.

LOAD or LOADA brings in the translated program for running and the data associated with it. The program is then activated and running begins. SYSTEM is relegated to the background, but it takes over should a catastrophic error occur, when the job is completed, or when its time has expired. It calls in the loader when segmentation is required.

The accounting function

For the accounting function, SYSTEM obtains information about program status, program running time, and the account to be charged. If different charges are made for problem and software time, the accounting procedure keeps track of activities separately. SYSTEM may also keep track of computer time spent on each job.

A program submitted may have associated with it one or more of several activities. It may be translated. It may be performed. The number of times it is performed may depend upon the number of data sets submitted with it. It may be debugged. It may be interrupted. Errors may occur which may or may not be corrected. If it is segmented, some of these segments may be done several times, while others are not performed at all. The program may be normally terminated or may be rejected before completion. Status change information is obtained by SYSTEM and printed out as soon as available.

A CLOCK incorporated in the computer reflects the real passage of time and, hence, is called a REALTIME CLOCK. It may use the same units of time as we do and, in this case, no conversion is required. However, this is not a necessity of the REALTIME CLOCK. The CLOCK reading is accessible to and sometimes is resettable by 𝒮𝒴𝒮𝒯ℰ𝓜 to time intervals rather than running continuously.

Some installations consider all computer time chargeable to overhead, and its cost is not accounted for. Most companies make a direct charge to a department or project in a department for computer time. The rate charged for computer time and how the time is calculated varies by installations. Cost may include
  • program run time
  • loading
  • translation
  • monitoring, and so forth.
It may even include a percentage maintenance charge. Also, the rate may differ from one job to another. This is especially true when jobs can be submitted not only from within the company, but also from outside customers who pay hard cash.

Often a time estimate submitted with a program prevents excessive looping or other program malfunctions. Such errors could produce a nonterminating activity which is very hard on the budget. The 𝒟uration 𝓜onitor can prevent them and can also protect against catastrophic computer errors.

Error routines   Detected errors are handled in several ways. The program may provide its own error subroutines. Uncorrectable errors in input and output are usually delegated to 𝒥𝒪𝒞𝒮.

Some errors have uniform recovery procedures. Intrasystem data transmission errors, arithmetic overflow errors, and other entirely computer-associated errors fall into this category. They are handled by the 𝒻𝒪ℛℰ𝓜𝒜𝒩.

Data transmission errors are eradicated by retransmission when the source and destination are known and intervening events have not affected the information. Otherwise, rollback may be incorporated into the program. When error cannot be removed, the program is dumped— removed—and the next one started. Arithmetic conditions, such as overflow and underflow, can be coped with if a means for recalculating the data is provided. 𝒮𝒴𝒮𝒯ℰ𝓜 usually requires some help from the programmer for this. He provides rollback points and indications of which quantities are to be rescaled and by how much.

DEVICE assignment   Either SYSTEM or JOCS or both may be responsible for allocating DEVICES. The symbolic designation furnished with the program should correspond to an available working DEVICE. When the monitor makes assignments, it communicates them to JOCS by establishing tables.

The basis for assignment is mainly *present availability status*. Some DEVICES have specific system assignments, such as the system tape and the library tape. Other DEVICES have less sacred reservations, intermediate storage for translation and output. Other DEVICES have concurrent job designations: output information from the last job ties up units which the operator is unloading. From those DEVICES which are free and working, SYSTEM assigns units for tasks in the program for which the programmer has not already made specific assignments taking into consideration buffer needs. It may do anywhere from none to all of this task. On occasion, it finds that there are not enough DEVICES free to perform the job, which must then be postponed.

Conversation with humans   Some information flows between the human and the computer in all systems.

TO THE HUMAN

Computers communicate by lighting one or more indicator lamps to convey prevailing conditions to the human. Greater versatility is provided through a written message on a CONSOLE DISPLAY. For the maximum in speed, there is the CATHODE RAY TUBE; however, the CONSOLE PRINTER is almost as effective.

When a program is completed, OUTPUT DEVICES require attention. Messages to this effect are produced by SYSTEM on the CONSOLE. They demand immediate service, for the DEVICES remain unused until the operator has freed them. Less routine difficulties are communicated to the operator by the CONSOLE PRINTER: SYSTEM can tell the operator when it encounters an unsolvable error or when no more programs are available.

Such catastrophies as DEVICE or computer hangup require immediate attention.

TO THE COMPUTER

Information is sent directly to the computer by CONSOLE BUTTONS or the CONSOLE TYPEWRITER, which can be utilized by SYSTEM without interrupting the program in progress. The information entered may be in response to a request of the SYSTEM which is ready to receive and interpret it.

Sometimes the operator talks directly to SYSTEM to request a new program sequence when a different program priority situation arises. In this vein, a new important program may appear. The operator tells

$SYSTEM$ about this, using the CONSOLE KEYBOARD. $SYSTEM$ can now have this program run out of turn. The operator can even interrupt the present activity to have the computer generate Christmas carols for visiting dignitaries!

$SYSTEM$ usually recognizes a CONSOLE activity with an interrupt routine in $FOREMAN$. It has on hand a series of canned messages. It selects a message appropriate to the situation and transmits this to the CONSOLE DEVICE.

Information entered into the CONSOLE KEYBOARD is obtained by $SYSTEM$ via an interrupt. The message is scanned by $SYSTEM$ and its format compared with a number of prepared samples. A comprehension subroutine corresponding to one of these samples is called in to "make sense" of the entry.

Multiprogramming,   When an operating system has to handle
multiaccess   multiple programs, regardless of why, its overhead in both time of operation and core residency, needless to say, must increase. Further, hardware features should be furnished in the form of:

- *memory protect* so one program won't clobber another;
- *interrupts* to inform $SYSTEM$ when a violation has been found;
- *dynamic relocation* is a luxury which facilitates, supposedly, quick interchange between users.

PROBLEMS

1.1 Give four pairs of adjectives that describe and distinguish computers, and explain them.

1.2 Write the sequence that occurs during (a) *recall;* (b) *fetch.*

1.3 Distinguish among a REGISTER, MEMORY CELL, and AUXILIARY MEMORY block.

1.4 What is the difference between arithmetic and editing?

1.5 How could the hardware do multiple indirect addressing?

1.6 Why aren't all commands indexable?

1.7 Why are separate commands needed to manipulate the contents of indexes?

1.8 What makes translators different from most other software?

1.9 Why is relocation necessary in today's computers?

1.10 Why is there a separate *LINK*?

1.11 What's the difference between *JOCS* and the *FOREMAN*?

1.12 What's a supervisor?

2

THE

CHANNEL

CONTROLLER

2.1 THE CONCEPT

Need The problem which the CHANNEL CONTROLLER is designed to alleviate is indicated schematically in Fig. 2.1.1. Information exists on some DEVICE **medium** which is so called because its use and availability is restricted to a single kind of (IO) DEVICE. Thus punchcards can be read only by a PUNCHCARD READER and not by a MAGNETIC TAPE UNIT.

A DEVICE communicates with its DEVICE medium and either accepts information from the medium or places information upon it. Present computer systems require that information from a DEVICE be passed over to the MAIN MEMORY, (MM), or that information destined for the device medium be passed from the MAIN MEMORY through the DEVICE onto the medium.

Transfers from We are *not* concerned with the various means
DEVICE to for transcribing information from the medium
MEMORY through the DEVICE or from the DEVICE onto
the medium, as this is a specialized study dependent upon the nature of the PERIPHERAL DEVICE. We *are* concerned with how a DEVICE communicates with MM, (MAIN MEMORY). In the simplest and least expensive machines which have few IO DEVICES, it is expedient to connect each DEVICE directly to MAIN MEMORY. However, in the medium and large scale computer field, DEVICES proliferate.

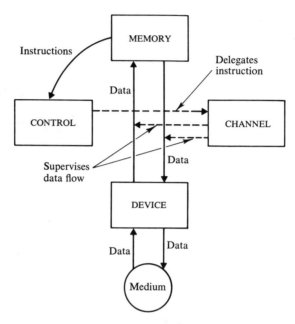

Fig. 2.1.1 The supervision of data flow between the
DEVICE and MEMORY.

We cannot permit direct communication between a DEVICE and MM for at least five reasons:

1. The difference in information flow rate between MM (one *word* per 1–2 microseconds) and that of the DEVICE (a few to a few hundred thousand *characters* per second).
2. The quantum of information handled by a DEVICE is different from the MM word.
3. Instructions must be given to each DEVICE, telling it the task it is to perform. If DEVICES were autonomous, CONTROL would have to communicate with each and every DEVICE.
4. Undoubtedly, occasions arise where several DEVICES want to talk to MEMORY at once. It is complex, if not impossible, to settle these conflicts at the DEVICE level.
5. Synchronization problems arise between the DEVICE and MM. The arrival of information rarely corresponds to the MM or the DEVICE is free.

**CHANNEL
CONTROLLER
functions**   The CHANNEL CONTROLLER (or CHANNEL, or simply CC) is a subsystem which acts autonomously by referring to a list of sub-commands stored in MAIN MEMORY. In this respect, the CHANNEL is like a

small computer:
- it has its own program in MEMORY;
- it has a CONTROL UNIT (CC CONTROL) and is attached to DEVICES which it supervises.

In some systems, separate computers were used to control IO functions; these computers were called **satellites** for, although they were autonomous, they were under the regulation of the central computer.

The CHANNEL has in its dominion a number of PERIPHERAL DEVICES. This number can have an upper limit in the hundreds or even thousands in the case of data lines. One task of CC is to select and talk with one or more of these DEVICES under the direction of CONTROL.

In performing an input function, the CHANNEL collects information from the DEVICE which the DEVICE has previously collected from the device medium. CC formats this information and assembles it into a quantum (word) convenient to the MM. It then causes this word to be placed in a preassigned location in MM.

The output function of the CHANNEL is to obtain a word from a known location in MAIN MEMORY which it then disassembles and sends to the DEVICE. The latter records the information on its own medium.

Autonomy   The CHANNEL performs a sequence of operations. The sequence is stored in coded form in a section of MM designated by the software or sometimes by the programmer. The program tells the CC where it is to get this sequence of instructions. Each instruction to the CHANNEL will be designated hereafter as a **subcommand.** Each subcommand describes a *set* of operations occurring for a given DEVICE, using a designated area of MAIN MEMORY.

Selection   The CC supervises many DEVICES as shown in Fig. 2.1.2. How these are connected is discussed in Section 2.2. A command in the main program tells the CHANNEL which DEVICE it will work with in the near future. No other DEVICE can be active under the jurisdiction of *this* CC. All subcommands which the CHANNEL receives pertain to the selected DEVICE until further notice from CONTROL.

Collection and   The CHANNEL is responsible for assembling
assembly   information into words for storage in MAIN MEMORY or for disassembling words from MM into pieces of convenient size for the DEVICE to handle.

Scattering and   One beauty of the CC concept is the ability to
gathering   scatter information from a DEVICE into different areas of MM. This is illustrated in Fig. 2.1.3, where six segments of

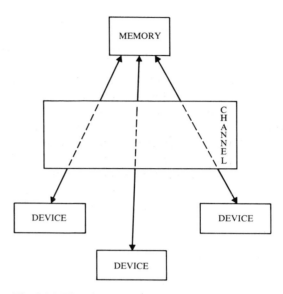

Fig. 2.1.2 The channel may supervise data flow between several DEVICES and MEMORY.

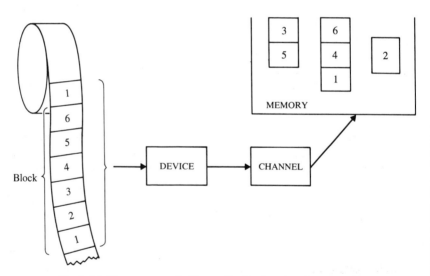

Fig. 2.1.3 The CHANNEL facilitates distributing data from a DEVICE medium to different parts of MEMORY-scatter read.

information are to be scattered into different areas of MM. With a single command, the main program delegates this task to the CC which performs this by using six separate subcommands stored elsewhere in MM.

Need   Some functions described above are necessary for the proper operation of all DEVICES. If a set of DEVICES can share hardware which can perform these functions for any one of the DEVICES, then this hardware is a less expensive solution than separate hardware for each DEVICE. Assembly and disassembly, for instance, are incorporated into the CHANNEL and hence need not be duplicated for each DEVICE. If autonomy existed on the DEVICE level, each DEVICE would have to incorporate means for assembly and disassembly.

The CHANNEL resolves conflicts among DEVICES.

An interrupt facility is a necessity to modern computing. If provided at the CC level, its need is removed from the DEVICE level.

The *gather* and *scatter* facility takes the burden of simple clerical matters away from the main program, placing it at the CHANNEL level.

2.2 DEVICE CONNECTION AND SELECTION

Crossbar   The crossbar connection is indicated sche-
connection   matically in Fig. 2.2.1. CONTROL addresses a number of CHANNEL CONTROLLERS, each of which is connected to all the DEVICES available in the system. This is somewhat analogous to a telephone center where any subscriber can talk to any other subscriber.

CONTROL delegates the DEVICE request to any free CC, since each can talk with every DEVICE. It chooses a CC by using a discipline incorporated into the hardware. Generally, this is done on a rotation basis: the next free CHANNEL picks up the request. If none is free, the request holds up processing until a CHANNEL becomes free.

CONTROL makes a request for a DEVICE by naming that DEVICE. Of course, the INSTRUCTION REGISTER originally gets this request from the program. Hence the program should name a specific DEVICE for an IO function.

Once a CHANNEL receives a request, it simply connects to the desired DEVICE and initiates its operation. If the DEVICE is already occupied because it is reporting to another CHANNEL, then the new request must wait until the DEVICE is free. Hence the controller becomes tied up in waiting for a busy DEVICE.

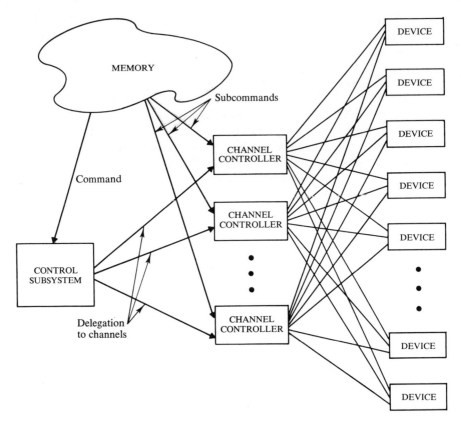

Fig. 2.2.1 The crossbar arrangement for the CHANNEL.

Crossbar   The crossbar method of connecting the
considerations   CHANNEL is particularly appealing to the user
because it permits any subset of DEVICEs to be active simultaneously (of
course, the number of active DEVICEs cannot exceed the number of
CHANNELs!). This is a costly solution because connections must exist from
all CHANNELs to every DEVICE. Further, each CHANNEL must know the
status of every DEVICE; otherwise, a CC would be unable to reject a request
for a busy DEVICE. Interlocks must be supplied so that two requests for
the same DEVICE will not be started simultaneously.

Finally, to incorporate an interrupt technique requires that certain
DEVICE statuses inhibit reinitiation for that DEVICE so that servicing of an
interrupt for that DEVICE can proceed with immunity. Thus, if a parity
error is detected on TAPE DRIVE 28 and an interrupt routine is servicing it,
the program or other software must not be able to start DRIVE 28 from *any*
channel until the DRIVE has been released or reassigned by the interrupt
routine.

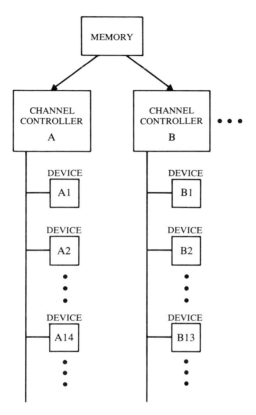

Fig. 2.2.2 Permanent DEVICE assignments to the
CHANNEL CONTROLLER.

Permanent Figure 2.2.2 shows a more popular arrange-
CHANNEL-DEVICE ment whereby each CHANNEL CONTROLLER has
assignment a number of DEVICES permanently assigned
to it. Any single DEVICE on a given channel can be activated. While this
DEVICE is active, no other DEVICE on that channel can be activated: the
CHANNEL CONTROLLER's facilities are dedicated to the DEVICE it serves;
these facilities are limited (by cost) and cannot be shared by another
DEVICE. This limits DEVICES which may be active simultaneously to a set
chosen, each from a different channel. This is not a severe limitation
because the programmer at assembly time or software at run time may
be able to ascertain which DEVICES will be active at the same time and, if
there are duplicate DEVICE types on different channels, try to assign
them properly. With this method, physical limitations may be over-
riding.

DEVICE names   We should clarify, at this point, three different references to DEVICES: symbolic, machine, and physical. The programmer refers to a DEVICE or a device function by a **symbolic name,** generally of mnemonic design: PAYROLL might be the name given to a master payroll file; it also designates an output (or input) DEVICE which already (hopefully) holds that file. The **machine designation** of a DEVICE in this assignment discipline consists of a CHANNEL designation and a DEVICE designation within the channel. Thus, B3 designates the third DEVICE on channel *B*.

Generally, DEVICES of one type can occupy only certain positions on a given channel. For instance, we may have the restriction that device B3 is a MAGNETIC TAPE UNIT (MTU). This does not restrict us to a specific machine. The **physical designation** of an IO UNIT is often by its serial number. For instance, TAPE UNIT 3D7928 may occupy position 3 on channel B. If this DEVICE should suddenly malfunction, nothing prevents us from disconnecting its cable, removing the physical DEVICE, and replacing it by the UNIT with serial number 4X39, say. Better still, since 4X39 is not in use, we might simply relabel it as B3.

Put in other terms, the programmer uses a *symbolic* name in referring to a DEVICE; the supervisor, monitor, or assembly language programmer refers to a DEVICE by its *machine* name; the service engineer refers to DEVICES by their *physical* names (or other epithets).

DEVICE CONTROL   In some computer systems it is necessary to
UNIT   insert an additional CONTROL UNIT between
the DEVICE and MAIN MEMORY, as shown in Fig. 2.2.3. The CHANNEL CONTROLLER performs functions for the DEVICES on the channel which are common to all DEVICES regardless of their type. There are additional functions which need be performed for DEVICES of one type but not of another. If these also can be incorporated into a single CONTROL UNIT, this reduces hardware cost. In the figure, we see a MAGNETIC TAPE CONTROL UNIT which supervises the operation of several MTUS. Some of the control hardware required for these MTUs has been removed and placed in a single DEVICE CONTROL UNIT.

The control hierarchy is then as follows:
- CONTROL in the computer delegates an IO operation to the CHANNEL CONTROLLER.
- This operation, for a given DEVICE, requires connection of the DEVICE CONTROLLER associated with that DEVICE.
- The CHANNEL CONTROLLER delegates an operation to the DEVICE CONTROLLER.

Although several CCs may be active separately, only one DEVICE CONTROLLER and one DEVICE can be active on any given channel: the CHANNEL

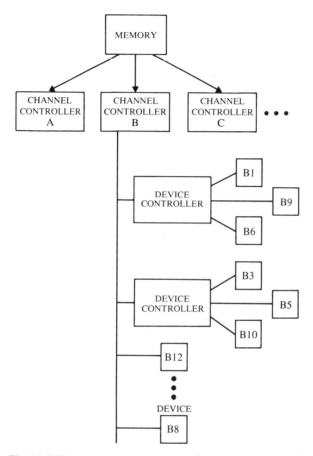

Fig. 2.2.3 The DEVICE CONTROLLER handles several DEVICES of
the same type.

CONTROLLER has only one set of registers, etc., which must be dedicated
for the use of the DEVICE CONTROLLER; similarly, the latter has but one set
of hardware, etc., for communication with the designated DEVICE.

MULTIPLEXOR   Most manufacturers are furnishing a CHANNEL
CONTROLLER which can handle not only the fast DEVICES we have described,
but also slow DEVICES such as TELETYPE and TELEPHONE LINES. Information
is exchanged with these DEVICES at such a slow rate that it is possible to
service tens or even hundreds with a single CHANNEL. Such a CHANNEL
CONTROLLER is termed a MULTIPLEXOR CHANNEL or simply a MULTIPLEXOR.

The principles of organization of the MULTIPLEXOR and its relation to the rest of the computer are very similar to those of the CHANNEL CONTROLLER. However, it is necessarily much more complex. Since the MULTIPLEXOR is gathering and disseminating data for more DEVICES "simultaneously," it must have a means for keeping track of each. To install hard REGISTERS for each DEVICE would indeed be expensive—price the manufacturer right out of the field.

The MULTIPLEXOR instead uses MM to control information and data for each *active* DEVICE. It must then have a means for associating MM CELLS with DEVICES.

It would sidetrack us to give inordinate attention to the MULTIPLEXOR. Instead, we plug away at the CHANNEL.

2.3 CHANNEL INITIATION

Program delegation Somewhere in the program sequence IO commands arise. In many systems, these are mediated by software of one form or another. Some systems depend on JOCS for IO commands. Whether JOCS is used or not, all IO commands are turned over to the SYSTEM automatically by an interrupt in third generation machines such as the IBM 360. This is discussed in more detail later.

Eventually, an IO command from the program sequence (which may be in the software) is placed into the INSTRUCTION REGISTER of CONTROL. The command has different symbolic forms. For our purpose, we assume the following form:

$$P \quad STARTIO \quad channel, device, M \qquad (2.3.1)$$

Here, *channel* is a machine language identifier of the channel addressed; *device* refers to the DEVICE number on the addressed channel; M is the location in MEMORY of a sequence of subcommands to which the CHANNEL refers.

If the CHANNEL addressed happens to be busy, this command cannot be accepted by that CHANNEL. The alternative action taken depends upon the hardware design. In some cases, the next main program command is skipped; in other cases, a jump to an error recovery routine is made—the specific location of this routine is a permanent location provided for the CHANNEL CONTROLLER; a further alternative is for the entire computer to be held up until the channel addressed becomes free. In any case, since the CHANNEL cannot accept one command while it is busy executing another, something must be done about the new command.

CHANNEL   The location M is the start of a sequence of
subprogram   commands to be referenced by the CHANNEL
addressed in the command. Each entity in this sequence is referred to
hereafter as a **subcommand.** The subcommand is interpreted by the
CHANNEL in reference to the DEVICE distinguished in the original IO
command. Each subcommand has a form something like this:

$$\text{function, \quad number, \quad location, \quad tags} \qquad (2.3.2)$$

Here, *function* may be specific to the DEVICE called upon; *number* specifies
the number of words, bytes, or other quanta of information to be transferred between the DEVICE and MAIN MEMORY; *location* is the starting point
in MM where information is to go (or come from) as it emanates from (or
goes to) the DEVICE; *tags* convey auxiliary information such as: data
transmission is not inhibited; this is not the last in the chain of subcommands; indexing; etc.

Function conveys the operation the DEVICE is to carry out. This may be
read or *write*: information is transferred toward or away from MAIN
MEMORY, respectively. It may also convey a nondata function: a request to
a MAGNETIC TAPE UNIT to REWIND tapes; a PUNCHCARD UNIT request to
select a specified hopper; etc. Finally, there are reflexive functions: halts
or jumps. For the latter, the CHANNEL CONTROLLER finds a new sequence
of subcommands at another location in MEMORY. Subcommand jumps
may be conditional or unconditional.

Simultaneity   From (2.3.1) the CHANNEL has been delegated
a subcommand sequence starting at M. *Both* these activities occur at the
same time:
- The CONTROLLER performs subcommands at M, M + 1, etc.
- The computer executes commands at P, P + 1, etc.

Of course, other CHANNEL CONTROLLERS may have assignments—subcommand sequences—which they are pursuing at the same time.

DEVICE   Let us examine communication with the
communication   INPUT DEVICE. A DEVICE provides information
in bytes or characters. Generally, this quantum differs in size from that
generally used for entering information into MAIN MEMORY (word size).
The CHANNEL is the liaison between the DEVICE and the MEMORY having as
one of its main functions the reformatting of information to suit the
MEMORY or the DEVICE, whichever it is addressing. Thus, on input, it
receives *characters* of information from a DEVICE and assembles them into
words. When a word is assembled, it is passed over to MAIN MEMORY.

For output, words are passed from MAIN MEMORY to the CHANNEL where they are disassembled into characters suitable for the DEVICE.

CHANNEL   How does the CHANNEL CONTROLLER operate
operation   when requested in the program? It receives
a command from CONTROL. If and when it accepts this command, it is ready to select and activate the DEVICE specified in the command. (Sometimes, as in the IBM 7094, two or more commands are required to get the CHANNEL going.) When it accepts the command, the CHANNEL goes to MAIN MEMORY and gets the first subcommand in the sequence.

The subcommand indicates the task which the DEVICE is to perform. The CHANNEL delegates this task to the DEVICE. Generally, this will involve the exchange of data. Let us examine *input*. Data begins to flow from the DEVICE to the CHANNEL. It is accepted and aggregated by the CHANNEL. When a word is assembled, it is passed over to MEMORY, and the subcommand is checked to see if the number of words to be transmitted has been reached. If not, we count down this number and alter the destination location so that the next data word will go into the next sequential word in MEMORY. We continue thus until the required number of words have been replaced in MEMORY.

The CHANNEL has completed a subcommand. It now goes to MEMORY, to the location right after the one where it obtained the last subcommand, and looks for its new subcommand there. It gets this subcommand, interprets it, and starts its execution.

Eventually, the CHANNEL obtains the last subcommand in the sequence. This is indicated by a tag in the subcommand; or the sequence may contain a HALT subcommand. After executing a tagged command or arriving at a HALT, the CHANNEL CONTROLLER enters either an idle or an interrupt condition. For computers where interrupt is not provided, it is up to the program to determine when a DEVICE has completed its task and what the effect of that completion is.

In modern computers, an interrupt is provided whereby the worker program is interrupted and a software monitor takes over to make sure that activity on the channel is properly recorded and that new activity is initiated if this is at all possible.

Interrupt schemes are discussed in the next chapter.

2.4   CYCLE STEALING

Communication between MEMORY and a CHANNEL is done by **cycle stealing.** This phrase contrasts with earlier or simpler techniques for IO communication. Early computer control subsystems maintained control of IO operations: when information was transmitted between an IO DEVICE and MEMORY, the rest of the computer was immobilized; no other references to MEMORY were possible as long as an IO DEVICE was activated.

The CHANNEL CONTROLLER principle permits information to accumulate while "useful" work is being done by the PROCESSOR and CONTROL. Information is transferred between the CHANNEL and MEMORY, without the awareness of CONTROL. As it were, the CHANNEL "sneaks" into MEMORY and steals a MEMORY cycle. This may postpone, by a MEMORY cycle time or so, the activities of CONTROL or some other subsystem. Sometimes the computer is not held up at all while an IO MEMORY transfer takes place.

How are conflicts   Requests for the use of MEMORY can arise from
resolved?   several subsystems of the computer. Actually, the PROCESSOR can use the MEMORY only under the jurisdiction of CONTROL. This leaves the CHANNEL CONTROLLERS as the other main users of MEMORY.

If there are several requests to use MEMORY, these could be settled by one of two schemes:
  • one which assigns MEMORY to requesting subsystems in a fixed order according to subsystem name, not request arrival order;
  • a queue scheme which orders requests according to their arrival, generally on a first-come, first-served basis.

A queue scheme requires extra hardware to keep track of the arrival sequence of requests. Such hardware is not justified.

A priority scheme could use either priorities fixed within the hardware, or these priorities could be assignable by the programmers. The programmable scheme would mean that priority for a subsystem would change from one program to the next. Such flexibility is not required for the operating system. It is available on computers where it may improve the effectiveness of the computer complex. We examine here only one fixed-priority scheme.

Protection   Suppose several programs are in MEMORY and each makes use of one or more IO DEVICES via CHANNEL CONTROLLERS; what's to prevent the CHANNEL/DEVICE combo from going wild and clobbering somebody else's MEMORY area? System/360 solves this by requiring the CHANNEL to access MEMORY with its own *key* supplied as the channel address word (see p. 103). Each sector of MEMORY has a *lock*; only those for which this key fits can be opened by the CHANNEL.

Single port   Consider a single-port MEMORY SUBSYSTEM as diagrammed in Fig. 2.4.1. Other subsystems access the port in a left-to-right priority sequence. If there is a request pending for CHANNEL #1, this

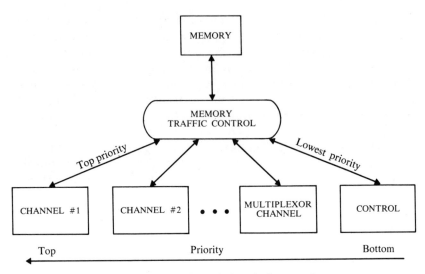

Fig. 2.4.1 Cycle stealing priority, single-port scheme.

request is served next, regardless of any others which may be waiting. If there are requests on *several* CHANNEL CONTROLLERS, the lower numbered CHANNEL always receives service first. Hence, we assign DEVICES of more importance as far as servicing is concerned to the lower number channels. For DEVICES which have the highest rate of information flow (such as DISKS) it is essential to pick up information before it is lost, being replaced by new information. This restriction should be tempered by the need to place DEVICES which would be working simultaneously for a given program on different CHANNELS.

DEVICE activity always receives MEMORY response before CONTROL. One wonders if there would be time left for CONTROL activity. *Fetch* and *execute* cycles require much less time than does a DEVICE for its activity; so generally, there will be time free for the program. But even in the worst case, CONTROL activity will not be held up indefinitely. IO activity will eventually expire and require that processing activity intervene before more IO activity can be dispatched.

Rate comparison   Let us examine information transmission speeds for IO DEVICES. They fall into three categories: slow, medium, and fast.

SLOW

PUNCHED PAPER TAPE DEVICES and communication lines are rated in operations per *minute*. Data words arrive in *seconds* or fractions thereof.

The best example of medium speed DEVICES is the PUNCHCARD READER, which operates at 600–1000 cards per minute (although some DEVICES read up to 2500 cards per minute). Consider a rate of 15 cards per second. The maximum number of filled columns in a card is 80, so that the maximum transmission rate required is 1200 characters per second. This is 300 words per second in a typical fixed-word machine, or 5 milliseconds per word.

High speed DEVICES include MAGNETIC TAPE TRANSPORTS and DISKS and DRUMS. These transmit information at the rate of 15,000–500,000 characters per second, or up to 125,000 words per second, from 8 microseconds to 250 microseconds per word.

Stealing   The CHANNEL CONTROLLER steals a cycle to transmit a word from the data medium into the MEMORY (or from MEMORY into the data medium). It must take care of a word of data before the DEVICE produces (or requires) the next word. In the fastest DEVICE examined above, we have 8 microseconds before another MEMORY access is required. Third generation computers have MEMORIES with cycle times of 1 microsecond or even one-half of a microsecond. This means that MEMORY would be completely loaded down only if eight high speed DEVICES were active simultaneously. Such a situation does not generally arise.

CHANNELS also steal a cycle once in a while to acquire another subcommand. The urgency of this is not as high as for servicing DEVICE needs.

A high speed DEVICE continues to produce (or consume) information at its high rate regardless of what is happening to the CHANNEL. Hence the CHANNEL should be prepared to accept another character as soon as the DEVICE issues it. For characters arriving at half a million per second, the CHANNEL must respond within 2 microseconds, as must MEMORY. However, the MEMORY will not be called upon to react that fast for another 8 microseconds. It turns out that, for current computers with a limited number of high speed DEVICES attached and intermittent DEVICE operation, MEMORY is seldom called upon to react up to its speed capacity. If it should happen that a character of any transmission is missed, interlocks are generally provided so that a retransmission can be requested under program control. Even this eventually can be eliminated by a DATA BUFFER REGISTER (discussed later).

The main program   Whenever a number of CHANNELS require servicing, the running program is inevitably held up. This is only a matter of a delay in execution of the steps of the program. CONTROL always remains aware of what command is to be performed next. If the cycle theft occurs between a *fetch* and the acquisition of an operand, then CONTROL suspends its animation until MEMORY becomes free for it to procure the desired operand.

It is emphasized that no other program or software is brought into play as a result of cycle stealing. This is in contrast to *interrupt* discussed in the next chapter.

2.5 COMMAND ACQUISITION FOR CHANNELS

Figure 2.5.1 shows a functional diagram of the composition of a typical CHANNEL CONTROLLER.

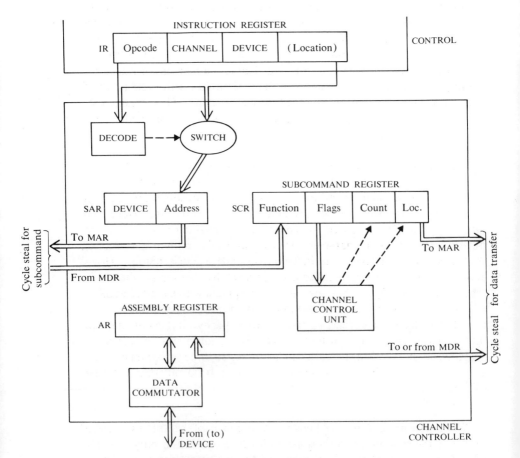

Fig. 2.5.1 REGISTER in the CHANNEL CONTROLLER.

REGISTERS   Several REGISTERS are provided in the CHANNEL in the figure, the COMMAND REGISTER, CR, holds a command provided by CONTROL. The SUBCOMMAND REGISTER, SCR, holds the subcommand that the CHANNEL has acquired on its own from MEMORY. The DATA REGISTER, DR, stores a word as it is assembled or disassembled. The CONTROL UNIT coordinates and times the functions of the CHANNEL CONTROLLER.

The command   An IO command is entered into the INSTRUC-TION REGISTER of CONTROL. It may come along as one of the commands in a running program. Generally, though, it will appear in a sequence of the software, probably IOCS.

After the command arrives, it is decoded and detected as an IO command by CONTROL which broadcasts *most* of the command to *all* the CHANNEL CONTROLLERS. That the opcode distinguishes *this* command as IO need not be broadcast. The remaining information, *channel*, *unit*, and *M*, is broadcast.

Each CHANNEL CONTROLLER has a CHANNEL DECODE UNIT which reacts only to the designation of *this* CHANNEL; no other CHANNEL reacts. It stores the UNIT and MEMORY *location* into the COMMAND REGISTER.

A portion of the operation code is broadcast in some computer systems when such portion contains information relevant to the command to be delegated to the CHANNEL.

In some systems (e.g., IBM 7040/90 series) two commands are needed to activate a CHANNEL. There are so many DEVICE/CHANNEL choices that a full command is needed to make this selection and function unambiguous. The second command tells the CHANNEL where it is to obtain its string of subcommands.

Subcommand   At the time the command (s) is received by the CHANNEL, no subcommand is presently available; *M* is dispatched to the MEMORY ADDRESS REGISTER and a *recall* requested. In the meantime, the DEVICE specified in the command is started either directly or under the auspices of the DEVICE CONTROLLER.

The datum procured by MEMORY is routed to the SUBCOMMAND REGISTER of this particular CHANNEL. Upon the arrival of the subcommand the CONTROL UNIT is advised, and a data acquisition sequence is initiated.

Data acquisition   We now describe the acquisition of data during *input*. The reader may revise the description to fit the *output* process if he desires.

The DEVICE called upon is activated on receipt of the command. The functions to be performed by the DEVICE are specified in the subcommand.

Here we examine data-directed commands. These require activation of the DATA COMMUTATORS.

Once the input DEVICE has been activated, it sends information to its CONTROLLER on a character or byte basis. Information is continually dispatched and continuously arrives at the DEVICE. It is intercepted there by the DATA COMMUTATOR, whose responsibility it is to insert the character in the proper section of the DATA REGISTER.

Once a word is assembled in the DATA REGISTER, the CONTROL UNIT is activated by the COMMUTATOR. The address where the word is to be stored, m, is dispatched to the MAR once a cycle can be stolen. Thereafter, the contents of the DATA REGISTER are passed over to the MDR and the information stored in MEMORY.

This action completed, the CONTROL UNIT is notified. It advances the address, m, so that the next data word will be stored in the next position in MEMORY. The count, n, is decremented.

Upon checking if the *count* has reached zero, the subcommand has been completed. Otherwise, we continue another data acquisition cycle.

NEW SUBCOMMAND

If the subcommand being executed has been completed, the CONTROL UNIT detects this and initiates the acquisition of another subcommand. The contents, M, of the CR are incremented to distinguish the position of the next subcommand. This address is sent over to the MEMORY and another cycle is stolen for *recall*. The datum acquired is passed in the SUBCOMMAND REGISTER and data acquisition continues.

Termination   Eventually, one of the subcommands placed in the SR will either be tagged to indicate that it is the last of a sequence, or else there will be a *halt* subcommand. This indicates to the CONTROL UNIT that, after data acquisition associated with the subcommand, the subcommand sequence is terminated, and the command is considered complete.

The action the CHANNEL takes depends upon the complete system into which it is incorporated. In the old computers, the CHANNEL would become idle, waiting to be interrogated. New systems have an interrupt facility, whereby the CHANNEL interrupts the main program as described in the next chapter.

ABORTION

Some systems require that, when an overwhelming obstacle arises, DEVICE operation terminates generally via the interrupt mechanism. Examples of such obstacles are parity errors and the reading of *end of tape* or even *end of file marks*.

2.6 DEVICE OPERATION

Selection   Figure 2.6.1 is a block diagram showing
DEVICES connected to the CHANNEL CONTROLLER through the DEVICE
CONTROLLER. A set of four busses communicates between the two
CHANNELS. One of these is the data bus which carries information between
the CHANNEL CONTROLLER and the chosen DEVICE. The second is a control
bus which indicates to the chosen DEVICE CONTROLLER what activity is
required of the DEVICE. The subchannel selector bus chooses the DEVICE
CONTROLLER from information decoded at the DEVICE CONTROLLER. The
DEVICE SELECTOR switches in the DEVICE indicated. Only two sets of busses
connect the DEVICE CONTROLLER to the DEVICE: one is for information
exchange; the second carries control information to direct the DEVICE
about activity it is to perform—over this, the DEVICE also transmits its
present status to the DEVICE CONTROLLER.

When a command is received by the CHANNEL, the selection lines which
emerge from it select the DEVICE CONTROLLER which, in turn, selects the
DEVICE. A through path is then made between the DEVICE and the CHANNEL
CONTROLLER. Control signals interpreted by the DEVICE CONTROLLER
activate the DEVICE and cause it to begin the desired activity. On input,

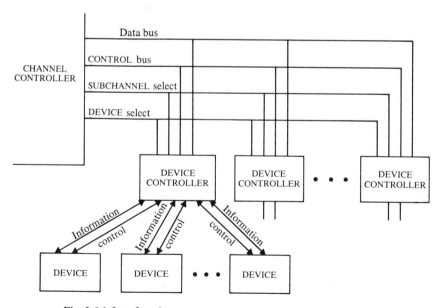

Fig. 2.6.1 Interface between CHANNEL CONTROLLER, DEVICE CON-
TROLLER, and DEVICE.

information emanates from the device medium as soon as that medium is up to speed and properly located. When this information arrives, it is sent to the CHANNEL CONTROLLER, where it is assembled. In some cases, the time between startup of a DEVICE and the arrival of the first information is quite lengthy—a matter of milliseconds for DISKS and PUNCHCARD DEVICES. The DEVICE, DEVICE CONTROLLER, and CHANNEL CONTROLLER are all waiting but unavailable for other activity, and hence, their status during this period is **busy**; but PROCESSOR activity continues unabated.

Data transmission   As shown in Fig. 2.6.2, information from the DEVICE flows through the DEVICE SELECTOR and into a SWITCH at the CHANNEL CONTROLLER. This SWITCH determines whether the information is coming in or going out, and it sets up a path between the DEVICE and the DATA COMMUTATOR.

For input, the SWITCH passes data *from* the DEVICE *through* the INPUT LOGIC *to* the COMMUTATOR. A character at a time is sent over to the DATA REGISTER. The COMMUTATOR determines which position the data is sent to in the word being assembled. It moves the characters along, one at a time, from left to right. When the COMMUTATOR reaches the end of the word, it sends a signal to the CONTROL UNIT of the CHANNEL CONTROLLER. A MEMORY cycle is stolen to place the word in MEMORY. This happens before the next character comes along from the DEVICE; it will be placed at the

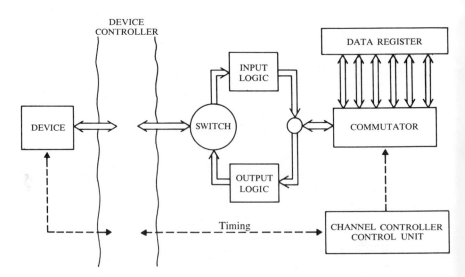

Fig. 2.6.2 Data transmission between DEVICE and CHANNEL CON-TROLLER.

left end of the word in the DATA REGISTER. If the DATA REGISTER has not been cleared, the old word will be written over and improperly stored in MEMORY. Hence, the reaction time of the MEMORY to the CHANNEL CONTROLLER must be less than the intercharacter period. This time can be lengthened by placing a BUFFER REGISTER between the DATA REGISTER and MEMORY, making a full word assembly time available during which cycle stealing may come about.

Result   The operation of a DEVICE terminates in one of several conditions. Hopefully, the DEVICE delivers the data properly to the MEMORY if that is the desired goal of its operation. There are other alternatives though: an *error* within the data may be detected by the DEVICE. Most IO DEVICES are provided with parity circuits which check the information by applying a checking algorithm. If the data do not pass this check, a parity error is communicated to the CHANNEL CONTROLLER. It causes the CHANNEL CONTROLLER to abort its operation.

There are choices of when it will abort, depending upon the machine design. Most often it continues recording data, indicating at the completion of its cycle that a parity error has occurred; the software will take appropriate measures. It could stop data transmission and turn control over to the software through an interrupt, accomplishing the same purpose; but further data have not been recorded since there is really no saving in ignoring the data after the error is noted. It is general practice to record them.

Occasionally, the DEVICE cannot satisfactorily complete its assignment. For instance, the PRINTER cannot print if there is no paper available for it; punchcards will not be fed if there are none in the hopper to feed; a MAGNETIC TAPE DRIVE will not read if the end of tape mark has been reached; the DISK arm will not *seek* if an illegal address has been provided to it. Hence, these situations cause an interrupt.

When the CHANNEL CONTROLLER is informed of the end of DEVICE activity, it goes into an interrupt operation as discussed in the next chapter. It records the DEVICE status or provides control line outputs which are available to CONTROL for appropriate posting during the interrupt operation.

PROBLEMS

2.1 Why do modern computers have CHANNELS?

2.2 What is assembly and disassembly? How are they done?

2.3 What is the CHANNEL program? Why isn't it wired in?

2.4 Why is a crossbar system used? What is the alternative? What is *its* advantage?

2.5 What are and why do we have three kinds of names for DEVICES?

2.6 How does the program talk to the CHANNEL? How does the CHANNEL talk to the DEVICE?

2.7 What is cycle stealing? How is it done? Why?

2.8 How does the CHANNEL get a subcommand?

2.9 How is data exchanged between MEMORY and a DEVICE?

3

INTERRUPT

3.1 AIM OF THE INTERRUPT

The new   The computer is working on some program
program, P′   called P. What choices are there for P? It may be

- a simple worker program;
- in the case of multiprogramming, it is one of a number of worker programs;
- in some cases, it may be doing one of the tasks required to keep the computer running efficiently. In any case, when an interrupt arrives from one of the possible sources (CHANNEL, program, etc.), a new program, designated as P′, is invoked.

P′ has complete access to all of the hardware of the computer. There is a risk that information being processed by the old program, P, and left in the REGISTERs of the computer will be destroyed. After operation with program P′, the interrupt program, we should return to program P at the point where we left off. Therefore, all information contained in the computer hardware *must* be preserved so that the program can be started properly later.

An interrupt scheme is designed to facilitate overall system operation. Define the overall system as the combination of software and hardware which operates a number of different programs for different users. An interrupt scheme calls for cooperation between software and hardware. Hardware is provided to facilitate the software and is designed with the software in mind. A good interrupt scheme depends upon interaction of the user's program with both the hardware and software systems to accomplish the overall system tasks.

How much of the interrupt operation is done by hardware and how much by software depends upon the overall system design provided by the manufacturer.

Need   An interrupt is necessary when the program in process, P, becomes less important to overall system efficiency (getting the most user's work done per unit time) than some other program, P', for one of several reasons:

1. A DEVICE needs attention. If it does not get this attention, overall system efficiency will drop.
2. A program is in trouble and cannot continue unless it is given special attention by the software.
3. The program now running expires.
4. The user has something to say immediately which affects the overall outlook of the system to user's programs by changing some function such as the priorities of activities.

Further, the new activity, P', cannot be handled entirely by the hardware. If this were the case, the operation might be handled by some expedient such as cycle stealing, rather than interrupt. Hence, the program P' must take over the computer completely to properly fulfill its needs, thus requiring all the provisions available in the interrupt scheme.

To put it another way, the interrupt facility permits the problem program to maintain control of the computer until an infrequent event (such as IO completion) requires its attention. Otherwise, the program would have to periodically check for the event, a time-consuming activity.

3.2   ACTIVITY

Phases of interrupt   We distinguish several distinct phases in interrupt activity. Depending upon system design, there are many different **sources** of interrupts. These can be divided into five (or more) **source classes,** enumerated as follows.

INITIATION

- CHANNEL CONTROLLER—IO completion or exception.
- EXTERNAL DEVICE—from DEVICES to which no task was delegated by the program; interrupts arising from the operator's console, communication lines, realtime clock, or the user's console.

- program—errors found by CONTROL, such as incorrect command codes or addresses; sometimes the program itself can request an interrupt to the system.
- PROCESSOR—overflow, underflow, and other errors arising from calculations or operations.
- MEMORY protect—when a worker or software program addresses an area in MEMORY not available to it.

From this list it is evident that each subsystem can be the source of one or more classes of interrupt.

Signals from *sources*, regardless of *class*, initiate interrupt activity.

■ PROGRAM CESSATION. Some time after initiation of an interrupt, the program being interrupted is brought to a halt.

■ STORAGE OF OLD PROGRAM INFORMATION. Before a new program can be placed in control, all pertinent information about the old program is collected and stored.

■ INTERRUPT PROGRAM INITIATION. The purpose of this whole thing is to get an interrupt servicing routine started. This includes selection of the proper subroutines for servicing the interrupt.

■ TERMINATION. When the interrupt activity is complete, we determine what further activity is required and transfer control to it. Eventually, control passes to the interrupted program.

■ RESTORATION. To reinitiate the interrupted program, it is necessary to retrieve REGISTER information and so forth, restoring the status of the computer to that which was in force at the time of the interrupt.

Hardware, software, and program interrelation
An interrupt facility is possible only if provisions have been made in the hardware. Such provisions must be made for performance of all the phases of the interrupt activity. The initiating signal from the various subsystems is detected by the hardware. The information is stored in a HARDWARE DEVICE, namely, a FLIPFLOP. The setting of this FLIPFLOP is used to halt the program at just the right spot. Hardware is necessary to supervise the storage of sufficient information to get the software started. The means for transferring control to the interrupt program is also implemented in hardware. Finally, the means for restoring the old program may also be of hardware design.

Most of the REGISTER and status information is put away in storage by interrupt *software*. All interrupt servicing, including determination of the device number, device type and kind of error is the responsibility of the software. Choice and method of return to the old program often reside in the software.

USER'S PROGRAM

One beauty of this interrupt scheme is that the problem-solving program of the user need make no provision for interrupts. The problem programmer may be unaware of the interrupt system as he writes his program. However, the installation system programmer may be required to supply routines for servicing interrupts which are peculiar to that installation or which perform tasks for which the software manufacturer has not made provisions.

Software Let's take a more intensive look at interrupt software. It's generally aimed at handling DEVICE halts, especially those produced by CHANNEL CONTROLLERS.

- Its first task is to get information remaining in the REGISTERS from the interrupted program out of the way in a safe place and prevent *itself* from being interrupted.
- The second phase is diagnostic: What was the reason that the program was interrupted?
- The third phase is selective: What is to be applied to this difficulty?

One consideration in designing interrupt software is the diversity of DEVICES to be handled and the multiplicity of difficulties which can arise for *each* DEVICE. Such a large number of permutations results in an impossibly extensive software system. One way to trim this system is to supply service routines only for those DEVICES included in the installation. A further way is to provide only for those exceptions which might reasonably arise in the installation activity. Finally, we might expect that a large user with many system programmers might wish to tailor routines to his own needs.

The logical result of the preceding software description is a requirement for modularity. Early interrupt schemes did not provide such modularity, with consequent cumbersomeness—the user would often alter the system to suit his needs with unpredictable results.

With regard to alterability, modularity provides the alternative of removing one subroutine and replacing it according to the user's wishes.

3.3 MULTIPLE INTERRUPTS

Problem For simplicity let us examine what to do when exactly two interrupts arrive sequentially at two CHANNEL CONTROLLERS in a system consisting of several CCs alphabetically labeled. Imagine a **trap** (another name for interrupt, briefer and more appealing) occurring on channel *B*. This causes us to enter the *trap* routine to service the channel

B trap. Suppose further that, while doing this, a trap occurs on channel *E*. What implementation is invoked as the first step in servicing any given interrupt?

There are several answers:

1. Completely ignore further traps.
2. Record further traps, but do not let them "happen."
3. Permit traps and make facility for traps within traps.

The first solution, ignore traps, is, of course, mostly unacceptable. Here when channel *E* traps during the processing of the channel *B* trap, it is ignored—nobody knows that channel *E* is done. The only way thereafter to find out that channel *E* is done is to inquire of it. Then after every trap, to be sure that nothing pending is left unserviced, a series of channel inquiries must be initiated—rather unappealing.

IGNORE

The solution which permits traps within traps requires a system of priorities and a means for going back and forth among the trap routines. Although seemingly complicated, this scheme has actually been implemented on the Sigma 7 and the GE 4020 computers. We eschew an explanation of this approach in favor of the more popular one below.

PERMIT

We next describe techniques for implementing the second scheme of recording traps but inhibiting them from interrupting.

RECORD

Suspend   A routine is working on the trap for channel *B*. The first steps of this routine place "Do Not Disturb" signs on all doors. A single command, SUS, when given by the software, suspends or causes all (or selected) source lines to remain energized, but none can interrupt the currently working trap subroutine. Hence the trap subroutine can go to completion without interruption from *other* traps. After completion, it remains to reinstate (*restore*) the original (unsuspended) status. It is then possible to accept one of the waiting interrupts which has occurred during the trap processing.

Restore   When trap software has completed its task, there should be a way to restore the status of the computer before the trap occurred. A final set of operations places all the REGISTERS and INDICA-TORS in the condition in which they existed before the trap occurred then the *restore* operation takes "Do Not Disturb" signs off the doors—traps are restored. But a delay should be inserted. This delay permits us to jump back to the original program without interference. We want the new interrupt to occur in the original program and not in the trap servicing routine. Hence, *restore* has a built-in delay to give us this assurance.

After return to the interrupted program is made, whatever trap is waiting takes over and initiates *another* interrupt. Immediately this trap is given service; no step of the old program is actually performed. The new trap routine stores the location of the interrupted program as the new trap routine is initiated.

Several traps   While we were servicing the trap on channel *B*, a trap on channel *E* arrived but was *suspended.* Suppose another trap arrives, this one from, say, channel *A*. What happens now when the interrupted program is restored?

One alternative is *first come, first served.* Then we would have to take the trap on channel *E* before channel *A*. But this would require much accounting, which would be messy to implement in hardware.

The simplest and even the most effective solution is to service the waiting traps in a fixed order, from lowest to highest priority, regardless of the arrival order of these traps. Examine the case where greatest priority goes to a channel with the letter which ranks first, alphabetically. Here, although *A* trapped after *E*, both were *suspended.* When traps are *restored*, channel *A* is serviced first because "*A*" comes before "*E*."

Some systems are designed to handle this problem more efficiently by permitting traps within traps. A priority scheme again handles the most important traps first, but recognizes the traps of lower priority. We examine the *program status word* technique for implementing this in the next chapter.

3.4   OVERVIEW OF ONE IMPLEMENTATION

Second generation hardware   The function of the trap hardware in a typical second generation system, the IBM 7090, is illustrated in Fig. 3.4.1. Two CELLS in MEMORY are reserved for each CHANNEL CONTROLLER or other class of interrupt source. This pair of CELLS participates in every trap occurring on the channel with which they are associated. In this sense, they are reserved; they should not be used by the programmer. Actually, he could refer to them if he programs at the machine language level. Naturally, this would mess things up for the trap software. If he tries to reference them in absolute assembly language, protection is often provided by the assembler. Protection is not necessary during symbolic assembly since programs are safely relocated by the loader.

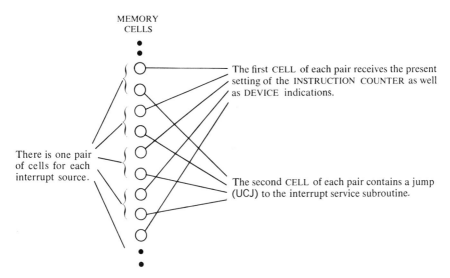

MEMORY
CELLS

The first CELL of each pair receives the present setting of the INSTRUCTION COUNTER as well as DEVICE indications.

There is one pair of cells for each interrupt source.

The second CELL of each pair contains a jump (UCJ) to the interrupt service subroutine.

Fig. 3.4.1 CELLS in MEMORY participate in hardware function of the interrupt.

The first CELL of each pair will hold the contents of the INSTRUCTION COUNTER after a trap has occurred. There is room in the CELL for other information. The number of the DEVICE causing the interrupt is also stored there.

The second CELL of the pair holds the starting location of the trap routine dedicated to this channel.

When a trap occurs, these actions take place:

1. The contents of the INSTRUCTION COUNTER are placed in half of the first CELL—this is the return point to the old program.
2. The number of the DEVICE causing the interrupt is stored in the other half of the CELL.
3. CONTROL uses the contents of the second CELL as the location for the next command which it then *fetches*.

Software   A block diagram of interrupt software functions is presented in Fig. 3.4.2.

Before anything else, a SUS command *suspends* all other traps. Recall that this means that other traps remain active; they are recorded when they occur but are not permitted to interfere. In some cases, it might not be desirable to *suspend all* traps. For instance, we might not *suspend* the CONSOLE entry trap—this permits the operator to enter information at the

SUSPEND

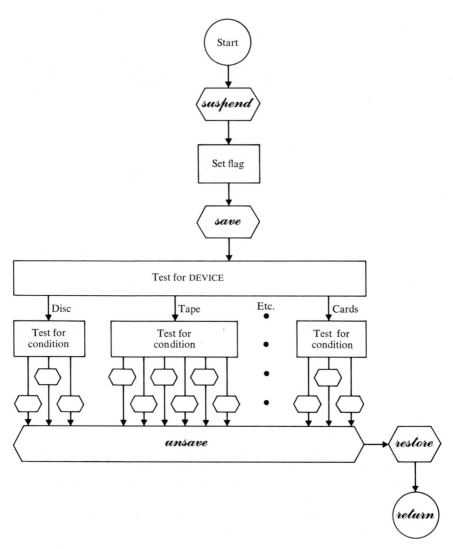

Fig. 3.4.2 Block diagram of interrupt software functions.

CONSOLE for the computer during trap servicing. In this way, a trap could ask questions of the operator. After answers are received, trap servicing continues followed by eventual return to the problem program.

Second generation systems often provide many entry points for servicing many channels. Part of this servicing is common for all channels.

FLAG

To enable routines to keep track of the original channel causing the trap, a flag is set.

The machine still has information being processed by the old program in some of its REGISTERS. The *save* routine puts this information away in known locations of storage. This is one of the common routines mentioned earlier.

SAVE

Now that the whole machine is available to service the trap, it is ready to investigate the cause of the trap. We process the *flag*, checking this against tables to determine the type of DEVICE. This, in turn, takes us to one of a set of DEVICE testing routines. Such routines inquire of the DEVICE how that DEVICE has terminated its operation and its present condition. This singles out the service routine unique to the DEVICE type and condition.

TESTS

The service required is dependent upon the conditions tested above. These are discussed in detail in my *Computer Software*.

SERVICE

This routine serves the opposite purpose from the *save* routine: it returns the computer to its original condition.

UNSAVE

We now re-enable the traps, recognizing that there is a short delay before new traps may intervene.

RESTORE

We have enough time to get back to the original program before the traps react.

RETURN

3.5 THE FOREMAN

Who is he? The 𝓕𝓞𝓡𝓔𝓜𝓐𝓝 is my name for the software routine which carries out the clerical tasks associated with input and output. This routine is known by other names for systems provided by other manufacturers: Input-Output Executor (𝒥𝒪𝓔𝒳); physical 𝒥𝒪𝒞𝒮; trap supervisor. I think that none of these appellations describes the tasks done by this routine as well as 𝓕𝓞𝓡𝓔𝓜𝓐𝓝.

The reader might have some acquaintance with the input/output control system (𝒥𝒪𝒞𝒮). It generally facilitates IO commands to such an extent that a simple call is sufficient to initiate a 500 or 1000 step routine.

JOCS would be nearly impossible without a 𝓕𝓞𝓡𝓔𝓜𝓐𝓝 as a mediator between the DEVICES and the larger overall system. In some systems, JOCS is viewed as consisting of two parts: *logical* JOCS and *physical* JOCS. The latter is what I refer to as the 𝓕𝓞𝓡𝓔𝓜𝓐𝓝, and the former is my true JOCS.

TASKS

Below are listed many of the tasks which the 𝓕𝓞𝓡𝓔𝓜𝓐𝓝 carries out:

- He gives all the *actual* IO commands to the CONTROLLERS. A macrocommand (or, more properly, a call) to JOCS is interpreted by it and converted into a series of commands which are delegated to the 𝓕𝓞𝓡𝓔𝓜𝓐𝓝. He, in turn, converts them into machine language as they arrive, and they are provided to the CHANNEL.
- He receives all the traps. Each hardware-initiated trap is routed to its own initial subroutine. Eventually, however, control is passed to the 𝓕𝓞𝓡𝓔𝓜𝓐𝓝.
- He posts results of IO operations in areas available to the other software.
- He may have to convert DEVICE information into a form readable by the other software such as JOCS or SYSTEM.
- He keeps track of DEVICE activity.
- He provides error-recovery machinery. When a parity error, for instance, is detected by hardware, it is reported to the 𝓕𝓞𝓡𝓔𝓜𝓐𝓝, who, in the case of magnetic tape, supervises multiple reads of the faulty block, hopefully being able to reread it eventually. The user is entirely unaware of the error. It is, however, recorded for the use of the installation supervisor for maintenance purposes.
- Hence, another task is recording and diagnosis of error activity.
- Conversion from medium language to computer language may be done in the 𝓕𝓞𝓡𝓔𝓜𝓐𝓝.
- Error and exception messages originate in the 𝓕𝓞𝓡𝓔𝓜𝓐𝓝.

WHO USES THE 𝓕𝓞𝓡𝓔𝓜𝓐𝓝?

In a complete system, the 𝓕𝓞𝓡𝓔𝓜𝓐𝓝 is indispensable. In a partial system, the 𝓕𝓞𝓡𝓔𝓜𝓐𝓝 is still essential; we have to have some method of handling traps and printouts. The user might eliminate JOCS because of the space it occupies, but rarely would a programmer wish to eliminate the 𝓕𝓞𝓡𝓔𝓜𝓐𝓝.

Interrelation with   The sketch in Fig. 3.5.1 shows the relation of
other software   the 𝓕𝓞𝓡𝓔𝓜𝓐𝓝 to other software. Here,
CAB represents the channel activity block. There is one such area in
MEMORY for posting the activity of each channel. It is available for
inspection by the other portions of the system software for which it is a
communications "channel."

The 𝓕𝓞𝓡𝓔𝓜𝓐𝓝 is responsible for initiating a DEVICE by communicating with the CHANNEL CONTROLLER to which the DEVICE is connected.
He must give machine language commands when he is in control of the
computer. When DEVICE operation is complete, the CHANNEL CONTROLLER
interrupts the computer. When the 𝓕𝓞𝓡𝓔𝓜𝓐𝓝 gets control again, he
handles the trap.

The 𝓕𝓞𝓡𝓔𝓜𝓐𝓝 handles command delegation to the DEVICES by
talking to the CHANNEL CONTROLLER; he handles DEVICE requests by talking
to the initiating software: 𝓙𝓞𝓒𝓢 or 𝓢𝓨𝓢𝓣𝓔𝓜.

𝓢𝓨𝓢𝓣𝓔𝓜 manages the rest of the software under the directions that it

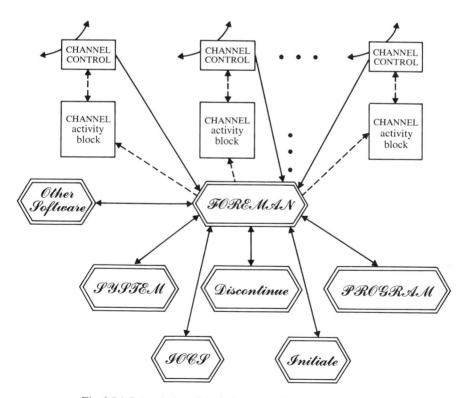

Fig. 3.5.1 Interrelation of 𝓕𝓞𝓡𝓔𝓜𝓐𝓝 with other software.

receives from the user in the form of control cards or control messages. We may speak to $SYSTEM$ directly through the CONSOLE, but it is best to speak with it through a CONTROL DEVICE.

Discontinue and initiate　　Two routines which have frequent conversation with the $FOREMAN$ are called $Discontinue$ and $Initiate$, which are now examined.

$Discontinue$ receives the trap analysis furnished by $Trap$, a part of $FOREMAN$. $Trap$ does the preliminary processing required to absorb descriptive information about the completion of the task delegated to the IO DEVICE, performing any translation required before posting the information. $Discontinue$ examines the results of $Trap$ to determine what should be done next. If necessary, $Discontinue$ posts information; otherwise, it delegates another task to IO. In other words, $Discontinue$ determines what is going to happen next and provides communication between the $FOREMAN$ and other software.

$Initiate$ takes over when the $FOREMAN$ receives an IO request; it analyzes the request and determines that an IO command should be given. $Initiate$ creates the machine language command for that DEVICE and furnishes it to the $FOREMAN$ who actually issues the command to the CHANNEL CONTROLLER.

$Discontinue$ and $Initiate$ are known by other names in some manufacturer's software. For instance, the IBM 7090 package designates these as $Select$ $-$ and $Select$ $+$. The two routines should be available in $IOCS$; however, $IOCS$ is not a compulsory item. When it is not provided, the $FOREMAN$ must have available $Discontinue$ and $Initiate$ in one of these forms:

- as part of the object program;
- in another portion of the software—possibly provided by the user;
- in the $FOREMAN$.

Normal trap events　　The most important use of the $FOREMAN$ is for servicing traps; this activity is presented in Fig. 3.5.2 and is discussed below.

After the small source routine has been performed, control passes to the routines contained in the $FOREMAN$. The first routine, $Trap$, analyzes the cause of the interrupts. Errors may have occurred which require further handling by $Trap$. Normally, however, it completes its analysis and

Discontinue
Initiate
WHO ARE THEY?

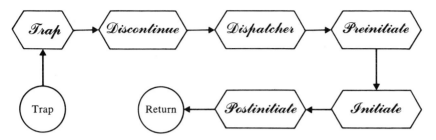

Fig. 3.5.2 Normal chain of routines used in 𝓕𝓞𝓡𝓔𝓜𝓐𝓝 in a trap activity. 𝓘nitiate and 𝓓iscontinue may be in 𝓙𝓞𝓒𝓢.

posting activities and turns over control to 𝓓iscontinue. 𝓓iscontinue makes a further analysis of the interrupt with respect to the program in progress. Some activities may require special handling, such as the occurrence of end of file while reading. This is not an error; it is a major exception, and 𝓙𝓞𝓒𝓢 is immediately informed to take further action.

When there are no exceptions, the 𝓓ispatcher is called upon to investigate what new tasks are waiting for service on this channel. The 𝓓ispatcher assigns a new task to the trapped channel. Before returning to the program, we want to activate either the trapped DEVICE or some other DEVICE on the trapped channel so that useful IO work can be done while the main program functions.

The 𝓓ispatcher turns over control to 𝓟reinitiate in the 𝓕𝓞𝓡𝓔𝓜𝓐𝓝 which checks the request and, if it is valid, calls 𝓘nitiate to construct the command.

𝓘nitiate fabricates the next command for the trapped channel, presenting it to the 𝓕𝓞𝓡𝓔𝓜𝓐𝓝. 𝓟ostinitiate in the 𝓕𝓞𝓡𝓔𝓜𝓐𝓝 *gives* the command to the IO DEVICE via the CHANNEL CONTROLLER. If the 𝓕𝓞𝓡𝓔𝓜𝓐𝓝 has no other chores to do, it returns control to the program.

3.6   HARDWARE FOR INTERRUPT

Problems   We discuss here some of the problems encountered in implementing an interrupt system and how they were solved in second generation systems. The next chapter discussed third generation approaches using the *program status word*.

First, when do we interrupt? The interrupt should be recorded immediately; however, it cannot become effective until a convenient breakoff point is reached. If operand acquisition is necessary, the MEMORY is used and the command finished before the trap takes effect. In newer systems, commands can be interrupted *during* execution. But we do not discuss this technique here.

What if a *fetch* cycle is in progress and CONTROL is getting its next command? In some systems, we can interrupt now without fouling things up.

As for other problems, these are itemized directly below and then discussed.

1. How is the trap recorded?
2. How is the place in MEMORY for storing information obtained?
3. How is the new subroutine initiated?
4. How is *suspend* applied?
5. How is *restore* done?

Recording   A single FLIPFLOP is sufficient to record the presence of an interrupt regardless of the channel on which it occurs. As shown in Fig. 3.6.1, all sources of interrupt signals can be entered into one large OR. This prevails regardless of whether the source is a CHANNEL CONTROLLER, PROCESSOR, CONTROL, or MEMORY, or something external. Then any source signal sets FLIPFLOP FI which is examined only by CONTROL and only after a command has completed execution. Right after the INSTRUCTION COUNTER is tallied, we would like to jump to the interrupt subroutine.

Cutting out   Before we leave the main program, the contents of the INSTRUCTION COUNTER should go to the interrupt location. The next command is obtained from the CELL just *after* the interrupt location. Let's see one way that this might be done.

The interrupt logic takes over just after INSTRUCTION COUNTER tally. The contents of the INSTRUCTION COUNTER are sent to the MEMORY DATA REGISTER. Also, interrupt information from the CHANNEL CONTROLLER or other source is entered into the MDR. The interrupt location obtained as described below is placed in both the MAR and the IC.

Memorize is furnished to the MEMORY. From here on, this is handled as though it were a *memorize* command. At the end of the *memorize* cycle, the IC is advanced to point to the CELL after the interrupt location. We *fetch* the next command from *that* CELL which should contain an unconditional jump to the trap subroutine.

Interrupt source   There is one line for each source, the same line used to record the interrupt. It gates the source identification. The signal is applied to an ENCODER. There is one ENCODER for each possible

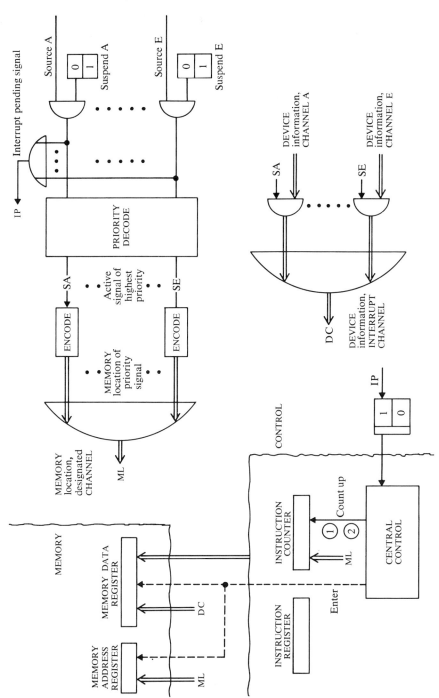

Fig. 3.6.1 Interrupt hardware.

85

source. It is activated only when there is a signal on that source line. When activated, it produces the code for the interrupt location corresponding to that source. Only one source signal appears, the one with highest priority.

The ENCODER outputs are passed to a multiple input OR. Since only one ENCODER is active, the output of this OR *is* the identification of the interrupt location; it is passed to the MAR and the IC.

Cause identification Each source, besides having interrupt lines, has other lines which tell the reason for the interrupt. These pass through gating arrangements similar to the identification ENCODERS just described. The information will eventually be fed to the MDR as shown in Fig. 3.6.1.

Sequencing FLIPFLOP FI indicates that an interrupt procedure is ready to start or is in progress. It turns off normal sequencing in CONTROL and causes CONTROL to enter interrupt sequencing.

The interrupt sequence consists of the following steps:

1. Load the MAR, MDR, IC as above.
2. *Memorize.*
3. Tally the IC.
4. Continue to the next cycle.
5. Initiate a one cycle delay after which FLIPFLOP FI resets.

Suspend/restore One *suspend* FLIPFLOP is provided for *each* source. It inhibits the transmission of information on the source trap lines. Thus, if a SUSPEND FF is set, a trap from that source cannot cause an interrupt sequence to take place. The source in most cases will maintain the signal interrupt even though SUSPEND FF is set.

A command which we call SUS sets the SUSPEND FFs which it designates. In the operand address position of *this* command is a series of zeros and ones which is a **suspend mask.** Where there are ones in the mask, the corresponding sources are *inhibited;* when there are zeros in the mask, the corresponding sources are *enabled.*

SUS appears early in the trap servicing sequence—almost immediately. This way other traps are prevented from intervening.

SUS serves also as a *restore* command. If the mask contains nothing but zeros, all traps on all channels are *restored.*

It is important that SUS is delayed for one execution cycle. The need for this when suspending is apparent. When using SUS for restoring, it is necessary to have a chance to return to the problem program before the suspended traps call in.

Once back to the problem program, we might find several traps pending. The order of acceptance of these traps is generally on a fixed priority basis: regardless of arrival order, the highest priority trap is accepted first. The others are *suspended* by the software when it takes over.

3.7 SOFTWARE-HARDWARE INTEGRATION
FOR TRAP PROCESSING

Immediate role   Trap takes us immediately to the second CELL
of software   of the interrupt location pair which contains
a jump to a distinctive subroutine for processing this source. If this
UCJ were lacking, we might take commands from interrupt locations,
probably clobbering the whole system.

The first command in the service subroutine is SUS. This masks out
other sources from interrupting, but it may not mask out all of them.
Further, the subroutine sets a FLAG CELL to store information from the
interrupt location about the trap source. The FLAG CELL serves two
functions: it provides the common subroutine with a means for returning
to the problem program; it is referenced when making DEVICE tests
appropriate to the source. Some *saving* of information may be required
within the "source" subroutine to clear a REGISTER used in preparing the
flag, for instance.

Common   The first task of the command subroutine is
subroutine   to *save* REGISTERS and INDICATORS. Next,
through a *source-specific* subroutine, it makes tests to determine the
DEVICE causing the trap. Then, through *device-specific* subroutines, tests
determine the *cause* of the interrupt. Finally, a service routine is chosen
and entered according to the DEVICE and *cause* of the trap. Other parts of
the 𝓕𝓞𝓡𝓔𝓜𝓐𝓝 are called in as required.

Interrupt   After interrupt service, we wish to return to
completion   the problem program; we use the flag set up
in an earlier step with the INSTRUCTION COUNTER information stored
in the interrupt location. We return to the original program with a jump,
indirectly through the interrupt location or to another jump found at the
interrupt location.

But we should not do this immediately. First we reinstall the computer
to its former condition; we *unsave*. The 𝓕𝓞𝓡𝓔𝓜𝓐𝓝 knows where
REGISTERS and INDICATORS were stored. He takes the contents of these

locations and returns them to the REGISTERS and INDICATORS. Now we are ready to *restore* the status of the computer by issuing SUS. Since this command *sets* the interrupt mask it can also be used to *restore* the mask. Again this gives us just one cycle respite in which we make the indirect jump to the problem program for SUS.

PROBLEMS

3.1 Why is interrupt necessary? How does it differ from cycle stealing?

3.2 What are interrupt causes?

3.3 When and how is an interrupt initiated?

3.4 What is the relation of interrupt to software?

3.5 How are several interrupts handled?

3.6 List the functions FOREMAN and JOCS to clearly distinguish between them.

3.7 What are *suspend* and *restore* and why are they needed?

4

SYSTEM

360

INTERRUPTS

4.1 THE PROGRAM STATUS WORD

What is it? The program status word is so very important because it is an integral part of IBM System 360. Further, this concept has been adopted by both RCA and UNIVAC for their series of computers which are almost identical in command structure to their IBM counterpart.

Purpose The **program status word** (or simply **PSW**) holds all information pertinent to the program presently in control. It is automatically stored when control is changed to another program. The program status word for the program in control is stored in the PSW REGISTER (PSWR). To change control to another program, we merely swap PSW's. This is under hardware supervision; it is a result of an interrupt.

The interrupt causes an interchange of PSW's—but when is this done? As with all interrupts, the command being executed is permitted to continue to completion. After *execution*, the next *fetch* cycle is inhibited. We withdraw a new PSW from a location automatically determined, and we place the old PSW in another (predetermined) location to save it.

The new PSW, placed in the PSWR, governs the interrupt service routine which is immediately on its own. Generally, this routine *saves* the contents of REGISTERS which it will be using before it begins its job; it will *unsave* these REGISTERS when it completes the job.

When the interrupt service is finished, control returns to the problem program by placing ths problem PSW in the PSW REGISTER. At this point, the problem program does not know that it was interrupted and continues as though nothing had happened.

PSW contents   We mention here some of the items contained in the PSW without going into detail.

The INSTRUCTION COUNTER, which indicates the location of the next command to be executed, is in the PSW. After an interrupt is noted, the command continues to completion but does not use the INSTRUCTION COUNTER in the PSW now in the PSWR.

Inhibit masks are contained in the PSW. There are several masks for different kinds of interrupts. But we could look at them as a single mask which allows or disallows given conditions to cause interruption. The problem program generally permits a wide range of interrupts; the software restricts interrupts which may occur while it is in control; different pieces of software allow many or few kinds of interrupts, depending on the nature of the piece of software.

Later, we describe how the protect key incorporated in the PSW can protect some areas of MEMORY from use or abuse by a problem program.

Mode describes the extensiveness of the command repertoire available to the program in control.

The source of the interrupt is also stored in a portion of the PSW as it's being put away. This area can also be used to hold information regarding the condition of the program in progress.

Two bits in the PSW are devoted to the **condition code (CC),** information about what has happened during the command just executed. For instance, in *comparison* operations it indicates the outcome as *less, greater,* or *equal;* for arithmetic, it may indicate a *positive, negative,* or *zero* result. The program manual describes condition code settings after command completion for those commands which alter the CC (not all do).

Mode   Several alternative modes are available according to the settings of the PSW mode bits. The mode determines the scope of commands available to the program. All commands are generally available to SYSTEM. Problem programs have a limited range. For instance, they are not permitted to play around with the PSW's. They are not even permitted to give IO commands; for IO it must resort to a program-initiated interrupt such as the SUC described later.

Keeping harmful commands away from problem programs assures the safety of both software and other problem programs. In uniprogramming, software could be clobbered by a problem program if the command repertoire were not restricted. In multiprogramming, problem programs are protected from each other by the same feature. The feature can be extended if several levels are provided so that subroutines have more or less autonomy.

Sources of   There are five alternatives for classes of
interrupts   interrupt sources for IBM System 360:

1. **External**—from the console or communication lines—undelegated.
2. **Supervisor call**—the program itself requests the interrupt.
3. **Program**—error arises in the command or incorrect specification of data.
4. **Machine**—errors arising from parity checks or other detected machine failures.
5. **IO**—CHANNEL CONTROL interruptions.

For each class of interrupts, there are two reserved locations in MEMORY. The first is the old PSW location, where the PSW from the current program is stored. The second, the new PSW location, follows directly in MEMORY and contains the PSW to be placed into the PSW REGISTER to initiate the interrupt servicing program.

The source of the interrupt signals the class to which it belongs. This determines the two locations to be used for the next steps which are:

- The cause of the interrupt is placed in the PSWR.
- The PSW now in the PSW REGISTER is stored in the *old PSW location.*
- The PSW is withdrawn from the *new PSW location* and stored in the PSW REGISTER.

This method for implementing interrupts *may* reduce the amount of hardware required.

Miscellaneous   Other information provided in the PSW includes an indication of the character code by which the IO DEVICES are addressed. It also includes wait/run status. Another piece of information in the PSW is the instruction length of the last executed instruction.

Source of PSW's   We have been tossing PSW's around as though they came from out of the blue. Actually, the source of all PSW's is in the software.

First note that PSW's for all interrupts are stored at the *new PSW location.* They are loaded into those locations when the software is initiated at an installation. They can be changed when the software itself is altered. Notice also that the only convenient way to get to the software is through interrupts, generally.

Then how do programs get their PSW's? When the program is terminated, control passes to SYSTEM through a supervisor call placed by the COMPILER in the problem program. At this point, $\mathcal{SYSTEM}$ determines the next job to be done and then turns control over to the loader ($\mathcal{LOAD}$). MEMORY areas to be used by the program are assigned by $\mathcal{SYSTEM}$, which also assigns a protect key and sets up the key in these areas for the use of the problem program. It then sets up a program status word which it relays to $\mathcal{LOAD}$.

When $\mathcal{LOAD}$ takes over, it brings in the new program and turns control over to that new program by placing the assigned program status word in the PSW REGISTER.

4.2   INTERRUPT AGAIN

Interrupt a la mode   The discussion of interrupt is oriented towards the IBM System 360. There are two modes of operation: problem and supervisor. For supervisor mode, there is no restriction on the commands which may be executed. In problem mode, certain commands are disallowed. When an interrupt occurs, the software which takes over is obviously in a supervisory mode.

Technique   Figure 4.2.1 illustrates the IBM System 360 hardware technique for handling interrupts. Hardware causes one of five software packages to take over to service the interrupt. Each of the software packages consists of at least four kinds of routines:

1. Setup *saves* information from REGISTERs which may be used in later routines.
2. Test determines the DEVICE and cause involved and assigns further operations to Service.
3. Service is tailored to the cause and DEVICE interrupting, and it performs activities geared to posting, servicing, and removing the interrupt cause.
4. Return contains tests to see if further servicing is to be done by the software. If so, the proper routine is called upon, and service continues. Should service be complete, Return checks if another piece of software must be called in (such as $\mathcal{SYSTEM}$). If not, it is also responsible for *unsaving* and for making a return to the problem program.

Hardware a la mode   As usual, a trap does not initiate action until the command in progress has been executed. In Fig. 4.2.2, the steps taken thereafter are according to the circled numbers in that figure.

Problem Mode   Supervisor Mode

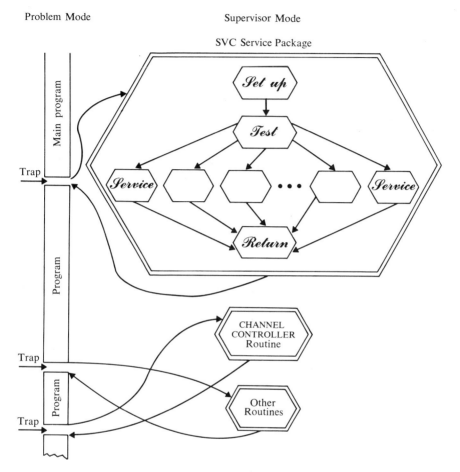

Fig. 4.2.1 A cause-specific routine is initiated by a cause-specific trap.

After the trap arrives and the command in progress is completed, the interrupt source determines where the word in the PSW REGISTER will be stored:

1. The contents of the PSW REGISTER are placed in the source-specific old PSW CELL.
2. The contents of the new PSW CELL are placed in the PSW REGISTER.
3. CONTROL goes to Trap for the source class. The PSWR now permits activity to proceed in the supervisory mode. The next command placed in the INSTRUCTION REGISTER, therefore, is from Setup.
4. The interrupt routines proceed.

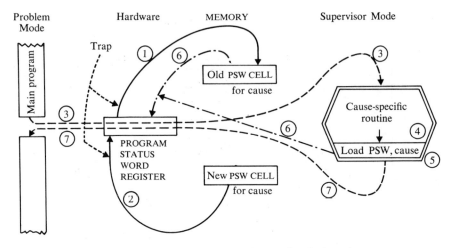

Fig. 4.2.2 Hardware-software interaction during a trap.

5. The last command executed in supervisory mode is the last command in Return,

$$\text{LOAD PSW,} \quad \text{cause} \qquad\qquad (4.2.1)$$

6. This command (performed only in supervisor mode) places the contents of the old PSW CELL associated with the trap source in the PSWR.

7. The next command to be executed is the one in the problem program just following the occurrence of the trap. Since the problem PSW was restored from the old PSW CELL for the source, the problem mode pertains to commands which occur thereafter.

The foregoing discussion applies when no other interrupts are pending. An interrupt pending on return to the problem will not take effect until the problem PSW is returned. At that moment, *fetch* will be inhibited; no problem command ever gets into the INSTRUCTION REGISTER. Instead, another trap is initiated by the exchange of PSW's, etc.

IO   For IO interrupts, the source is one of four CHANNEL CONTROLLERS (four is the maximum present in System 360). Regardless of which CHANNEL is responsible, all interrupts of this class go to the same service routine. The identity of the CHANNEL and the DEVICE causing the trap is stored in the interrupt code of the old PSW. Generally, the new PSW masks *all* interrupts. Since alteration of PSW's is under the control of the software, a service routine may unmask interrupts if it desires.

CONTROL
subsystem

Traps arising in CONTROL are called program interrupts. Here are examples:

1. *Instruction*—an opcode is not recognized by the machine because
   (a) it is an illegal combination of bits, or
   (b) this command is absent from the repertoire for *this* model of the system.
2. *Mode*—a command permissible only in supervisory mode is given in the problem mode.
3. *Command sequence*—the only example of this for System 360 is that an *execute* command cannot address another *execute* command.
4. *Address*—an area of MEMORY is addressed which lies outside the bounds of the MEMORY for this configuration.
5. *Specification*—many kinds of errors arise in this category such as
   (a) byte boundary errors,
   (b) improper REGISTER specification,
   (c) improperly specified data, and so forth.
6. *Data*—the data to be manipulated by the command are not in the proper form.
7. *Arithmetic*—errors include underflow, overflow, etc.
8. MEMORY *protect*—see below.

The interrupt code in the old PSW ascribes the cause of a control interrupt to one of the factors above.

MEMORY
protection

MEMORY is divided into many recognizable segments (4096 bytes for System 360). The number of segments depends upon the size of the MEMORY provided in the installation. Each segment has a **protect key** (or, more unequivocally, I call it a **protect lock**) associated with it consisting of exactly four bits. There is a SEGMENT REGISTER for each segment which holds its *protect lock*. The segment is protected according to the setting of this *lock*. A SEGMENT REGISTER can be set only by SYSTEM; it cannot be affected by the program.

In the PSW for each program, there is also a four bit (properly named) protect key. Whenever MEMORY is accessed by a program, the *lock* in the MEMORY SEGMENT REGISTER is checked against the *key* in the PSWR. If the two are identical, the program may "open" this segment—may use words in this segment; otherwise, a protection interrupt is invoked.

Several segments may be identified with the same *lock* to hold large programs which need a lot of MEMORY space. Thus only one *key* is needed by any program, even a large one.

SYSTEM must be able to access all of MEMORY. If SYSTEM became locked out by an incorrect MEMORY *lock*, we would be in trouble! A program containing zeros in the *key* of its PSW has permission to access *any* MEMORY area. Thus, 𝒮𝒴𝒮𝒯𝒠𝒨 has a **pass key:** all MEMORY is accessible to it.

Similarly, there may be unprotected or *unlocked* work areas in MEMORY unassigned to any program. A program is free to use this area, noting, of course, the risk of having this area altered by *other* programs.

External   External interrupts are, by their nature, spontaneous. That is, DEVICES are not *assigned* a task; they interrupt whenever the need arises.

Examples clarify this:

1. The TIMER addresses a fixed CELL in MEMORY. This TIMER is synchronized to the line frequency. Every sixteen milliseconds or so, the TIMER updates its assigned CELL in MEMORY by cycle stealing. This CELL is monitored by the interrupt hardware. When the TIMER CELL is decremented to zero, an interrupt occurs. Control is turned over to 𝓔𝓍ternal after the source is posted in the old PSW as being due to the TIMER interrupt.
2. The operator may interrupt the computer via the INTERRUPT CONSOLE BUTTON. In so doing, he initiates 𝓔𝓍ternal. The old PSW records the cause of interrupt as the operator.
3. Six other external interrupt lines are provided.

4.3   THE SUPERVISOR CALL

What is it?   The supervisor call has the mnemonic SVC in assembly language. It is a programmable interrupt. The programmer uses the supervisor call to request software intervention. The program asks that it be interrupted! SVC is treated like any other trap.

One would expect that there would be few occasions where the programmer *wants* to talk to the software. Ostensibly, this is true. However, when he writes IO requests (e.g., IO macros), which seem to him like ordinary commands, they are reinterpreted by the assembler as communication with the software. To elucidate this, consider the IO request, OPEN. The programmer is given a number of mnemonics like this which elicit IO operations. However, none of them is translated directly into single machine language commands. Instead, each is converted into either a BAL (*branch and link*) or an SVC. A code which indicates the function to be performed is inserted by the assembler in the address portion of the SVC command. SVC makes the computer trap and the code is transmitted to SYSTEM. It turns over control to the proper software routine (OPEN here) by interpreting the code associated with the SVC.

FIELDS

In Basic Assembly Language, BAL, there are three fields in an assembler-defined macro. The first indicates the call; the second indicates the type of call; the third gives the details of where information pertaining to this call type is found.

Other examples No IO command can be requested *directly* by the programmer—all are re-interpreted by the assembler as SVC or BAL.

There are other reasons for which the programmer writes SVC to the assembler. Some of these are discussed below.

MSG

When the programmer wants a message printed out, such as in an exception routine, he writes a macro for this. The macro name and its fields indicate a message request and the nature of the message. For instance, PPROUT might be the name of the message which, when printed out, says "Printer out of paper."

The macro is translated by the assembler which inserts in the program stream the SVC command code. When encountered, this causes a trap. SYSTEM picks it up and determines that it should be handled by FOREMAN. The latter interprets the code and goes to the selected service routine. In the example, this routine goes to an area which contains the message and prints it out. The computer then enters a wait condition since this program requires operator intervention. Control is returned to the computer when the operator indicates he has performed the function requested of him. When SYSTEM sees that the job is done, return is made to the problem program.

EOJ

The *end of job* call EOJ is used to communicate to SYSTEM that the program has solved its problem. SYSTEM then selects the next job for performance and passes control to LOAD. Control proceeds as in normal software after STOP has been detected.

EXIT

The use of EXIT for user-supplied software is explained in the next section.

FETCH

This call, FETCH, is used to get a subroutine from the library. After trapping, SYSTEM recognizes the need for a subroutine, the name of which is found in the third field. It turns over control to the library loader. It loads up the SR name in the library directory and then gets the SR from the library after space in core has been allocated by SYSTEM for the SR. When the subroutine is available, return is made to the user program.

Action It should be clear that the action for SVC is similar to that for any other trap. An exchange of PSW's is performed. This places SYSTEM in control. It analyzes the cause of the call and delegates the task to whatever software is required. Control passes to this piece of software. After this job is done, the supervisor itself gives the command, LOAD PSW, and then returns control to the problem program.

4.4 TRAPS WITH INSTALLATION-SUPPLIED SOFTWARE

In this section we discuss software supplied by the sophisticated user. "User" is the term which requires clarification.

There is a whole range of "users" from the job-shop user with a simple program to the maker of very large program application like insurance or bank accounting. The former has no truck with software; the latter must include his own within his program. In between, there is the installation system programmer who writes special software which is hidden from the casual user.

In this section, "user" refers to anyone who has recourse to *some* software design.

Need Third generation hardware and software are provided with some software modularity: some pieces of the software may be removed and replaced if you dare. Certainly the user should take advantage of this. If new software is to reside within the main software package, it must be placed there by the Library Editor. The latter has access to SYSTEM and may insert the package so that it operates in supervisor mode. Such a package must be completely debugged before it is entered into the system.

Installation-supplied software can provide for differences in:

- number and type of devices
- device configuration
- installation procedures
- special services

In the last category, we find Time and many other accounting routines unique to a given installation. The installation needs these services to account for computer usage. Initiation of such routines is trap-dependent. The routines themselves may, however, reside in the software or in the user's program.

Privileged software   An example of a user software-resident routine is Initiate. Although generally incorporated in JOCS, the installation may create its own. Initiate fabricates a command for the device used on the file presently addressed. Figure 4.4.1 shows how Initiate comes into use. The steps are numbered below to correspond to the numbers in circles in the figure.

As an example of its use, Initiate may be called in when an interrupt occurs on a DEVICE specific to *this* Initiate. There are several Initiates provided, one for each DEVICE type. However, the trapped DEVICE may not necessarily be dispatched this time. We examine the case of an input file when it is initially opened. Here, generally, Initiate is employed provided the DEVICE and CHANNEL are free. Now look at the sequence.

1. The problem program is interrupted by SVC which requests opening a file. This causes a trap to SYSTEM.
2, 3. SYSTEM recognizes that this trap should be serviced by JOCS and turns control over to it. After performing file management procedures which are necessary to open the file, JOCS delegates command initiation to FOREMAN.
4. FOREMAN checks the various activity blocks associated with the CHANNEL, DEVICE, and file to see whether it is possible to give a command to the associated DEVICE. It may either
   (a) place the request in a queue and quit, or
   (b) ask Initiate to fabricate a command to be given to the DEVICE. Initiate fabricates the required subcommands and returns the control to FOREMAN.
5. For step 4(b) Initiate fabricates the subcommands and returns control to FOREMAN.
6. FOREMAN gives the SIO command which uses the newly fabricated subcommands and returns the control to JOCS.
7. JOCS posts information about the command just given on the activity blocks; then it returns control to SYSTEM.
8. SYSTEM returns control to the problem program.

Program-incorporated routines   Sometimes it is beneficial to incorporate a service routine into the user's program. Yet it is desirable to have this routine triggered off by a trap of some sort. Some mechanism should then permit return to the problem program after the routine has been employed.

An example of this in the case of a TIMER routine is presented in Fig. 4.4.1. The lines are numbered within squares to correspond to the steps below which we use to explain the diagram.

Problem Mode   Supervisor Mode

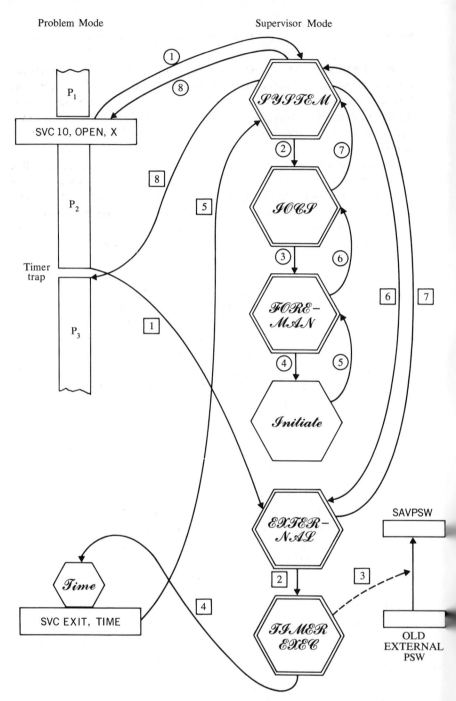

Fig. 4.4.1 Privileged installation-supplied software (numbered circles) and unprivileged user software (numbered squares).

Let us first examine the purpose of the user's routine, 𝒯ime. It is to be brought into play specifically when an external trap is caused by a TIMER interrupt. The user has previously asked 𝒮𝒴𝒮𝒯ℰℳ to set up the TIMER which runs for a fixed length of time and then traps. At this point, the user wants to perform the functions incorporated into his routine, 𝒯ime. Then he wishes to return to his own program at the point where he was interrupted. The procedure outlined below permits him to do this.

1. In the figure, we see that a TIMER trap occurs in the user's program between segments P_2 and P_3. This takes us to the external trap routine, ℰ𝒳𝒯ℰℛ𝒩𝒜ℒ.
2. ℰ𝒳𝒯ℰℛ𝒩𝒜ℒ notes that the interrupt was due the TIMER and turns control over to the 𝒯imer ℰxec.
3. One job of the 𝒯imer ℰxec is to put away the old PSW into a MEMORY position which we call SAVPSW. Control of this is indicated by the dashed line in the figure; the transfer is indicated by the solid line.
4. The 𝒯imer ℰxec now turns control over to 𝒯ime somewhere in the user's program. This is done with the command:

$$\text{LPSW   TIME} \qquad (4.4.1)$$

to *load* the PSWR. This sets up the PSW in problem mode, which includes a setting of the INSTRUCTION COUNTER referring to the start of 𝒯ime.
5. At the end of the subroutine 𝒯ime, we wish to return to the beginning of the main program segment P_3. To do this, we return to 𝒮𝒴𝒮𝒯ℰℳ by giving the supervisor call:

$$\text{SVC   EXIT   TIME} \qquad (4.4.2)$$

6, 7. 𝒮𝒴𝒮𝒯ℰℳ recognizes from EXIT that an exit to the user's program is required. The PSW for doing this was placed in SAVPSW. 𝒮𝒴𝒮𝒯ℰℳ may be aware of this; if not, it may ask ℰ𝒳𝒯ℰℛ𝒩𝒜ℒ to find the address, or it may get the address from a communication table.
8. 𝒮𝒴𝒮𝒯ℰℳ makes a return to the segment P_3 using:

$$\text{LPSW   SAVPSW} \qquad (4.4.3)$$

(Actually, the absolute address of SAVPSW may be installed in a BASE REGISTER referenced by 𝒮𝒴𝒮𝒯ℰℳ for this return.)

Installation of
user's routine   A control message is needed to notify 𝒮𝒴𝒮𝒯ℰℳ where 𝒯ime resides in the program. One way is to have the loader talk to 𝒮𝒴𝒮𝒯ℰℳ. It can do this only

through the linkage editor. Hence control information for the $\mathcal{SYSTEM}$ should be entered by control cards to $\mathcal{LINK}$ at linkage edit time.

$\mathcal{LINK}$ passes the information to $\mathcal{LOADA}$ who gives it to $\mathcal{SYSTEM}$. Finally, $\mathcal{SYSTEM}$ passes the location of $\mathcal{Time}$ over to $\mathcal{EXTERNAL}$, also furnishing a table position such as SAVPSW for $\mathcal{EXTERNAL}$ to use.

As far as the programmer is concerned, he contends only with $\mathcal{LINK}$ and simply supplies a couple of control cards which are the communication link.

4.5 MACHINE LEVEL IO

IO commands There are only four IO commands, SIO, HIO, TIO, and TCH, which mean, respectively, Start IO, Halt IO, Test IO, and Test CHannel. None of these commands can be given by the problem program; all are given in the supervisor mode. The way the user gets to an IO DEVICE is through the $\mathcal{JOCS}$. The IO macro is translated into a BAL to the $\mathcal{JOCS}$ with operands designating the file to be accessed and processing required for it. If the CHANNEL needed is busy, and it probably is, the request is turned over to $\mathcal{FOREMAN}$. He queues it up. An IO command is not generally given, and a *trap* occurs. Then $\mathcal{FOREMAN}$ receives the trap and gives an SIO referencing the proper subcommand list. More about this in the next section.

COMMAND An IO command consists of three fields: an opcode for one of the four commands designated above; the CHANNEL and DEVICE fields indicate the CHANNEL and DEVICE to be used.

STATUS In dealing with IO, we recognize three levels:

1. The CHANNEL CONTROLLER reports directly to the CONTROL SUB-SYSTEM.
2. The SUBCHANNEL reports to the CHANNEL CONTROLLER.
3. The DEVICE reports to the SUBCHANNEL.

Four statuses may prevail at any of these levels.

1. The level may be **available.**
2. The level may have an **interrupt pending.**
3. The level may be **working.**
4. The level may be **nonoperative.**

Thus a DEVICE, SUBCHANNEL, or CHANNEL each has one of these statuses. An IO task may be assigned only if the DEVICE, SUBCHANNEL, and CHANNEL are *all available.*

The purpose of SIO is to start the DEVICE on the CHANNEL specified in the command. This is done only if the DEVICE, CHANNEL, and SUBCHANNEL are *available*. The overall prevailing status is recorded in the condition code of the PSW whether the command is accepted or rejected. If the DEVICE cannot be started, there is a hierarchy of rules for disposing of the command. These rules are complicated and would add little to this presentation—the reader is referred to the IBM publication "Principles of Operation."

Other commands have been tailored to serve the software, especially JOCS. The details are also quite complicated and so only the general purpose of these commands is examined:

1. TIO—test IO—restores the status of some interrupt conditions and, in general, helps process traps.
2. HIO—halt IO—halts the activity when certain conditions prevail.
3. TCH—test CHANNEL—reports the status of a CHANNEL and generally does nothing else.

Channel address word   The **channel address word,** hereafter abbreviated **CAW,** is always found in the same location; in System 360, this is location 72.

The CAW has two fields:

1. A protect key provides access to prescribed blocks of MEMORY.
2. An address points to the start of a subcommand list. This is a list of channel control words discussed below.

All the subcommands being given to the addressed DEVICE are in a list. The address of the *start* of this list is in the CAW. If the wrong CAW is at the CAW location, then the DEVICE will do the wrong activities if the CHANNEL can interpret the subcommands in the list at all. Therefore, it is very important that the proper CAW be installed before SIO is given. That is one reason why the user is kept away from SIO commands. JOCS and FOREMAN make many preparations and tests before SIO is given.

The CAW is only a pointer to the subcommand list. The list of subcommands relative to a given IO operation reflects the needs of JOCS in reference to this latest macro.

Before SIO is given, JOCS and/or FOREMAN do these things:

1. Determine what tasks are required of the DEVICE after it is started.
2. Fabricate or have fabricated subcommands for each of these tasks.
3. Set up the subcommands in a list.
4. Insert the start of this subcommand list in the CAW.
5. Determine and insert the protect key in the CAW.

SIO

OTHER COMMANDS

Channel control word The **channel control word** (hereafter **CCW**) *is* actually the subcommand. The CAW points to a list of CCW's.

After SIO is *accepted* by a CHANNEL CONTROLLER, it places the CAW in the COMMAND REGISTER. Thereafter, the COMMAND REGISTER always points to the next CCW.

Now the CHANNEL CONTROLLER goes to the address in the COMMAND REGISTER to get the first CCW. This is placed in the SUBCOMMAND REGISTER. We find in that REGISTER the four items described in Chapter 2:

1. A subcommand code specifying the subcommand to be executed.
2. A data address.
3. Flags.
4. A count.

DATA CHAINING

Data chaining is described in Chapter 2. For instance, during *read*, we may *scatter* portions of a block from a MAGNETIC TAPE DRIVE into several different MEMORY areas. Similarly, during writing we can *gather* data from several MEMORY areas, forming them into a single block on the OUTPUT DEVICE.

COMMAND CHAINING

A feature, new with System 360, is the ability to chain unrelated subcommands. For instance, a *scatter read* might be followed by a *block skip* operation which, in turn, is followed by another *scatter read.* These subcommands will be performed in sequence provided that an exception condition does not arise on any one of them. When an exception arises in the middle of a subcommand sequence, that sequence is terminated and a trap initiated. The status of the CHANNEL is posted in the channel status word as the trap takes effect, as described next.

Channel status word A location in MEMORY is reserved and assigned to store the **channel status word** (hereafter **CSW**). Information about a task is posted here. This happens *whenever* a SIO, TIO, or HIO is issued whether accepted or not. It is also done whenever a trap occurs.

The information in the CSW is not altered until the next IO command is given or an interrupt occurs. The CSW contains the following:

1. The protect key. (The same one as in the CAW.)
2. The subcommand address. In general, this is the address of the *next* CCW to be executed. When a CCW string has been fully executed, it is the location of the last CCW which appears here.

3. A status field specifies subcommand terminated. As an example, the CCW might terminate because of a unit check, a unit exception, a proper end, etc.
4. The present count. Thus, if the subcommand has requested that twenty-two words be read from a block, but the *end of file* was encountered on the eighth word, the *count* would read fourteen $(8 + 14 = 22)$.

4.6 IO SOFTWARE

Translator   We look first at the translator because the programmer produces all IO commands in source language. The programmer writes in a higher language such as FORTRAN, COBOL or PL/1, or assembly language. Today, most higher language translators go immediately into machine language. Nevertheless our discussion is directed to assembly language for three reasons.

1. Although the original IO statements may be in high level language, they generally take an intermediate form equivalent to AL IO macros.
2. It is easier to explain what happens to IO at the assembly language level.
3. The macro translates into AL equivalents.

System 360 IO macros are assembly-incorporated macros. The assembly language programmer gives a macrocommand which the assembler interprets. When a macro is encountered, a sequence of machine language commands is substituted for it. Some of these commands are tailored to fit the parameters contained in the macro call.

For the 360 IOCS, there are two kinds of macros:

1. The file definition macro, DTF (for "define the file") for DOS and DCB (for "data control block") for OS360, is a description of a file which is supplied to IOCS at assembly time. The IOCS described in *Computer Software* was able to accept file definitions at run time. OS360 also provides this facility with the DD statement. But both OS360 and DOS require file descriptions from the programmer at assembly time using DTFs or DCBs. Many kinds of DTFs permit different kinds of file processing as well as different DEVICE sources.
2. Imperative macros such as OPEN and GET permit the programmer to "demand" that actions he requires take place when he wants them to.

Most imperative commands given at a high level require a complete software system and are directed to 𝔍𝒪𝒞𝒮. Imperatives can be directed to the ℱ𝒪ℛℰℳ𝒜𝒩 in a truncated software system specified by the user, usually only at the assembly language level. In 𝒪𝒮360 this is done with the macro EXCP.

To examine IO properly, we should understand not only what IO macros do but also what happens to them from the time they are written to the time they are executed. We examine, therefore, what happens in the software system.

Assembly program   The reader should review the relation of the assembler to other software, especially as presented in Fig. 4.6.1.

IO macros   What happens to a program written in an assembly language using 𝒟𝒪𝒮 with IO macros is shown in Fig. 4.6.1. At the beginning of this program, DTF commands present a complete file definition to the assembler. These are translated by the assembler into one or more SVCs. These specify that an IO operation is required, namely, an initialization of the system. 𝒮𝒴𝒮𝒯ℰℳ or 𝔍𝒪𝒞𝒮 later places this information into a communication area contained within 𝒮𝒴𝒮𝒯ℰℳ.

IO imperatives written by the programmer are preserved by the assembler, which converts them into a call sequence. It also places a subroutine of some size at the end of the program which is linked to the calling sequence.

ℒℐ𝒩𝒦 edits the program and ℒ𝒪𝒜𝒟𝒜 loads the program together with subroutines produced by the assembler into MEMORY. On the right of Fig. 4.6.1, we see how the SVC causes parameters associated with the file to be placed within the communication area. We also see how calls to 𝔍𝒪𝒞𝒮 are handled similar to subroutine calls.

IO calls at run time   Figure 4.6.2 shows what happens at run time to a call such as OPEN whose machine language equivalent appears in the program. When the call appears, control turns over to the 𝔍𝒪𝒞𝒮 routine 𝒪𝒫ℰ𝒩 which was brought in with the program. 𝒪𝒫ℰ𝒩 refers to the file, CHANNEL, and DEVICE blocks associated with the file name. From the file block it determines what data are to be posted and where. It transmits this information to ℱ𝒪ℛℰℳ𝒜𝒩 by performing an SVC call. Of course, 𝒮𝒴𝒮𝒯ℰℳ mediates this call, but it's actually performed by the ℱ𝒪ℛℰℳ𝒜𝒩.

The ℱ𝒪ℛℰℳ𝒜𝒩 examines the CHANNEL and DEVICE blocks to determine if the command can be executed. If not, it may have to be posted on queues for the CHANNEL and/or for the DEVICE. If an SIO is to be

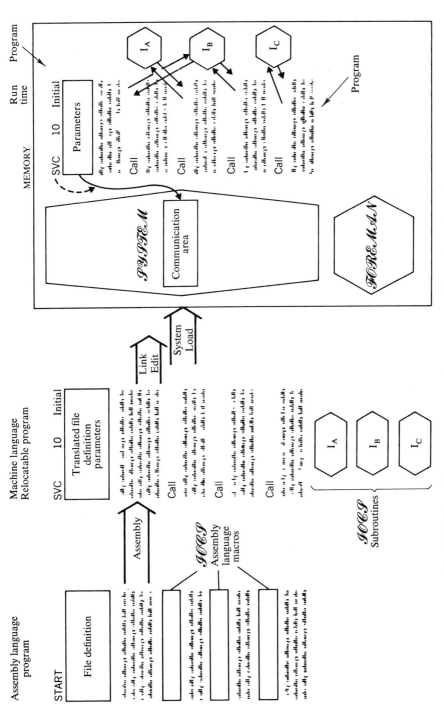

Fig. 4.6.1 Effect of IO macros on routine MEMORY and ML relocatable program.

107

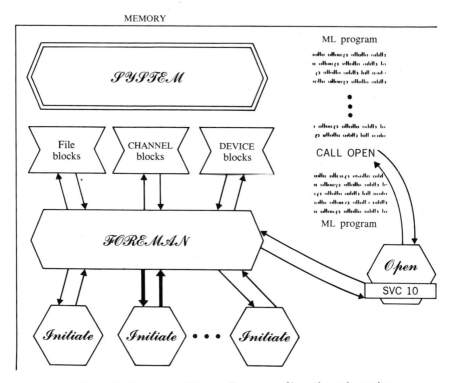

MEMORY

Fig. 4.6.2 Operation of the IO call to open a file as shown in routine MEMORY.

executed, 𝓕𝓞𝓡𝓔𝓜𝓐𝓝 turns control over to 𝓘nitiate. Here a CAW is fabricated and a sequence of CCW's selected, and control returns to the 𝓕𝓞𝓡𝓔𝓜𝓐𝓝. The 𝓕𝓞𝓡𝓔𝓜𝓐𝓝 gives the SIO which causes the CHANNEL to bring in data and place them in the proper area in MEMORY. After the SIO, control returns to 𝓞𝓟𝓔𝓝 from the 𝓕𝓞𝓡𝓔𝓜𝓐𝓝 via 𝓢𝓨𝓢𝓣𝓔𝓜 using a *load* PSWR command, LPSW. 𝓞𝓟𝓔𝓝 may have further processing to do, after which it returns control to the main program by a simple *return jump*.

4.7   INTERRUPT HIERARCHY

Multiple interrupts   During the execution of a single instruction, several interrupts may arise—any of the following five classes:

1. Machine
2. IO

3. External
4. Program
5. Supervisor call

In what order are the interrupts treated? We have several choices:
- arrival order
- by priority
- nested according to one or the other schemes
- a combination

If we assign a processing order, what should it be? The order in which the interrupts are listed above is our preference. Let us see why.

A machine interrupt occurs when a machine malfunction is detected. We don't want to do anything else until this trouble is corrected.

Neglected IO operations decrease the efficiency of the computer:
- ignored data may be lost
- unassigned CHANNELS lie idle

It is important to get DEVICES serviced and CHANNELS reassigned as soon as possible. External interrupts are similar in their urgency to IO operations, except that the information exchange rate for these DEVICES is slower. Hence they have a lower priority.

A program interrupt and supervisor call cannot both occur at the same time. If a command is recognized as a supervisor call, then it cannot cause a program interrupt, and vice versa. Either operation requires the immediate attention of the computer: it is more important than the program; it is less important than any other interrupt.

The combined   We now describe the reasoning in the hierarchy
hierarchy scheme   scheme provided for System 360.

Machine interrupts are given top priority. When one arises, all other interrupts are left hanging. If other interrupts are pending, nothing is done with them. This gets the machine out of difficulty if possible or else terminates service before irreparable damage is done.

Excluding machine traps, should other interrupts occur belonging to one of four other classes, they are treated in order of *reverse* priority. But when an interrupt PSW gains control, the remaining interrupts are allowed to take effect: traps are permitted and the higher priority one then takes place. This is best explained with reference to Fig. 4.7.1.

In the figure, it is assumed that all possible classes of interrupts except machine become pending during the execution of the present command. This means that three classes may be pending at the termination of the

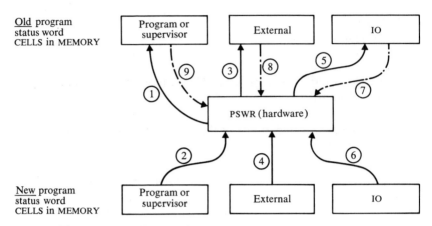

Fig. 4.7.1 How the hardware implements the interrupt hierarchy.

command. The activities proceed as indicated in solid lines and then in dash-dotted lines. The sequence of operations is indicated in the figure with circled numbers corresponding to the following steps:

1. First the present program status word is removed from the PSWR and placed in the location provided for the *old program* PSW (or supervisor call) trap (depending on the cause of this trap)— remember, only one or the other is permitted, not both.

2. The new program status word for the program (or supervisor call) interrupt handling routine is installed in the PSWR. However, it permits either external or IO interrupts.

3. Hence the pending external interrupt causes the contents of PSWR to be stored away in the CELL provided for the *old external* PSW.

4. The *new external* PSW is placed in the PSWR. It permits IO interrupts.

5. Hence a pending IO *trap* causes the present contents of the PSWR (the external interrupt PSW) to be stored in the *old* IO PSW CELL.

6. The *new* IO PSW is installed in the PSWR. It masks off all interrupts except machine failures. Hence, without further interruption, it may now begin servicing the IO trap.

7. Upon completion of IO trap service, the *old* IO PSW is installed in the PSWR. It contains the location of 𝓔𝓧𝓣𝓔𝓡𝓝𝓐𝓛. The external interrupt service routine takes over.

8. When service is completed, the *old external* PSW is installed in the PSWR. This is the location of the program (or SVC) trap service routine. It keeps control until trap service is done.

9. Thereupon, the PSW from the *old program* (or SVC) PSW is installed in the PSWR. This is the problem program PSW, and hence we are back in business.

If an 10 trap occurs during the servicing of an external interrupt, it may or may not stop external trap service and initiates 10 service immediately, depending upon how 𝓔𝓧𝓣𝓔𝓡𝓝𝓐𝓛 is masked at that time. If so, when 10 service is done, we return to 𝓔𝓧𝓣𝓔𝓡𝓝𝓐𝓛 at the place where service was left off.

Similarly, during a supervisor call (or program) trap, both external and 10 traps may be permitted at certain times during the routines. The service of the SVC (or program) interrupt is kept in abeyance while the other trap is serviced. The SVC (or program) trap is then reinstated and continued.

This combined priority scheme provides better trap service. There is very little likelihood that service of an important trap will be postponed until it is *too* late and human intervention becomes necessary. The slight price is that service for some of the less important traps *is* postponed.

PROBLEMS

4.1 What is the program status word? Distinguish among
(a) PSWR   (b) Old PSW   (c) New PSW
(d) Old PSW location   (e) New PSW location

4.2 (a) What is the condition code?
(b) What are all the places where it is found?
(c) What does it have to do with interrupt?

4.3 What is mode? Why is there more than one mode for third generation computers?

4.4 (a) Name the five classes of interrupts.
(b) Why are there five?
(c) List them in order of importance.

4.5 (a) How do we leave an interrupted program?
(b) How do we return to an interrupted program?

4.6 Can software be interrupted? Can we interrupt in the Supervisor? Why (or why not)?

4.7 Why would the program be able to interrupt itself? Give details.

4.8 How can the user supply his own pieces of software? How does he get back and forth? How does he provide for this?

4.9 How is *status* applied to 10? Name the four statuses. What is their meaning at the channel, subchannel, and device level?

4.10 Define, describe, give the need for and tell where we find:
(a) CCW   (b) CAW   (c) CCW

4.11 What is a macro? What is the difference between OPEN and 𝓞𝓟𝓔𝓝?

4.12 What happens when several interrupts arrive at the same time? In what order are they serviced? May the service of an interrupt be interrupted? How?

5

THE

PDP-8

5.1 THE SMALL-WORD PROBLEM

The market With the formalities out of the way, we are now ready to give an intensive look at modern computers. It is our aim to examine typical computers in each general category to see the problems faced by the designer, especially with regard to hardware but without neglecting its relation to software.

The small computer is a particular design challenge for:
- keeping cost low
- making ability high
- selling the product by demonstrating its overall usefulness
- providing satisfactory software

Smaller word size in the MEMORY offers the best potential for cost cutting. But it brings along many auxiliary problems discussed below.

Small memory The PDP-8 uses a twelve-bit MEMORY word.
word This is sufficient for many applications of the computer where the precision of calculations can be kept low. It is particularly appropriate for measurement and control applications.

The data word is defined as a simple twelve-bit datum. Operations upon it are performed either by bit picking (editing and masking) or by considering it as a natural binary number (counting number) and performing arithmetic operations on it.

As a binary number, the quantity is manipulated as an unsigned integer. The programmer must then use subroutines which provide signed representations of his numbers. One way is to convert signed numbers into two's complement notation. The computer, of course, is unaware of the sign and manipulates such representations like binary integers. Two's complement notation assures a properly signed result. The OVERFLOW FLIPFLOP, the LINK, is provided for checking overflow.

The command problem Since MEMORY words contain exactly twelve bits, one problem is to fit command information into such a small word. The MAIN MEMORY supplied with the computer is generally 4K or 4096 words, the twelfth power of two. Hence, to address even this small MEMORY with the most common addressing base number, 2, it is necessary to use twelve bits. All small-word machines have this problem. It may be alleviated for all by a paging system similar to that described in Section 5.3.

Even paging requires some compromise between address size and the number of command bits available to specify the command.

Command structure In Fig. 5.1.1, the command word is examined. Three bits are provided for opcode; hence, eight *basic* commands are available. The command repertoire is expanded by providing an *operate* code. **Operate** is really the opcode of an entire class of additional commands—those which do not require operand addresses. Thus the entire address field is free to distinguish a number of nonoperand commands. A second of the eight opcode combinations distinguishes the class of IO operations using an expanded format discussed later. This leaves six actual combinations for use as command codes. These are discussed in Section 5.5.

Seven bits allocated for address can address 128 words of MEMORY using the paging scheme described later. The two remaining bits convey **addressing mode:** The first may request single indirect addressing; the second conveys whether the current or a base page is being accessed.

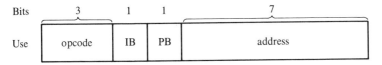

Fig. **5.1.1** The PDP-8 command.

5.2   ORGANIZATION

Aim   The aim of the PDP-8 design is to implement
a small, effective, inexpensive, high speed, scientific computer with as
little hardware as possible. The computer should interface with conventional IO DEVICES. It should also be able to talk to analog equipment
and measuring devices which function on-line for measurement and
control application. And when it's free, it can act as a normal, small,
general purpose calculator.

The plan   The plan of the computer is presented in
                           Fig. 5.2.1.

MAR

The MEMORY of the basic unit contains 4096 locations. To address them
all uniquely, the MEMORY ADDRESS REGISTER must contain twelve bits.

MDR

All words brought from MEMORY are placed in the MDR and are twelve
bits long. The MDR is a versatile REGISTER since it is also used as part of
the CONTROL SUBSYSTEM. Further, it holds one of the operands used in
addition or subtraction. Finally, it is incrementable for use with the
autoindexing feature described later.

IC

The INSTRUCTION COUNTER is called the PROGRAM ADDRESS REGISTER
by the manufacturer. It holds twelve bits and hence addresses all of
MEMORY. The IC is incrementable.

IR

A three-bit INSTRUCTION REGISTER holds the command opcode during
execution. Three bits can convey all commands except *operate* and IO,
which get special treatment.

AR

The A REGISTER, AR, or ACCUMULATOR, accumulates numbers during
addition and subtraction. It has an OVERFLOW REGISTER called the LINK
associated with it.

ADDER

A parallel binary ADDER provides fast two's complement addition of
binary numbers. The AR and MDR are added together and the result
placed in the AR.

CONTROL

CONTROL monitors all the activity which is taking place.

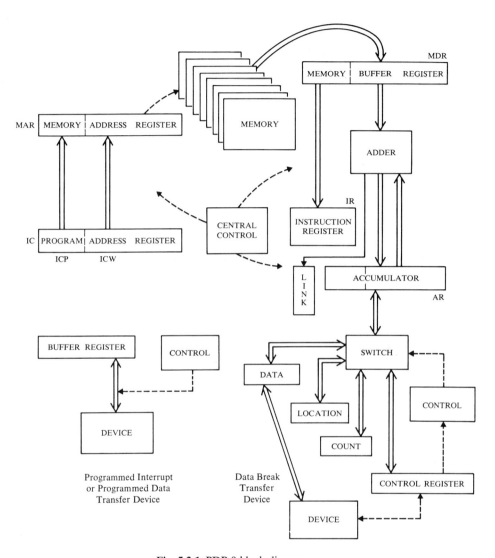

Fig. 5.2.1 PDP-8 block diagram.

IO   Two kinds of IO interfacing are provided.
For slow DEVICES, an interrupt causes the problem program to go to
a service routine whenever the DEVICE needs servicing. This is less
sophisticated than the CHANNEL CONTROLLER principle, but it is especially
useful in this small machine.

For fast DEVICES, cycle stealing is provided and called data break; it is
described later.

5.3 PAGING

Current page   The INSTRUCTION COUNTER consists of two parts: the leftmost part (the most significant five bits) contains a page number; this SUBREGISTER is indicated here as ICP. The seven right-hand bits comprise a word number on the page in ICP; this SUBREGISTER is referred to as ICW. Hence, the total IC points to one word in MEMORY using its absolute address.

At the end of a command, the INSTRUCTION COUNTER is incremented by adding one to its contents. Generally, ICW is increased by one, and ICP is unaffected: we advance from one word to the next on the same page. Eventually we get to the last word on the page; this word is numbered 177_8. Now when we add one to the IC, (ICW) becomes 000_8, and the page number is increased by one. Thus, program sequencing flows from page to page without interruption.

The contents of ICP distinguish the **current page,** one of thirty-two possible pages.

Data address   Data can be accessed in one of four possible ways using the indirect bit, IB, and the page bit, PB, both in the command word.

PRESENT PAGE

To get data from the present page the *indirect* bit, IB, is set to 0, and PB is set to 1 to indicate that we are accessing the present page directly.

PAGE ZERO

To obtain information from the base page, page 0, PB is set to 0 and IB is set to 0, indicating direct access to page 0.

INDIRECTLY, EITHER PAGE

Data may be accessed indirectly from either the present page or the base page according to the setting of PB. IB is set to 1. Only single indirect addressing is allowed. The address of the datum in twelve-bit absolute form is obtained from the present or base page, as determined by PB. This address, which can refer to any page in the computer MEMORY, is then accessed for the actual datum.

5.4 FETCH AND OPERAND
ACQUISITION

Fetch   Operations for *fetch* are presented in Fig.
5.4.1 and are discussed below according to the numbers in that figure:

0. Before *fetch* occurs, the signal end provided to CONTROL causes the
   INSTRUCTION COUNTER to be incremented.
1. (INSTRUCTION COUNTER) is passed over to the MAR and a MEMORY
   recall is initiated.
2. The MEMORY produces a datum in the MDR.
3. The opcode extracted from the MDR is inserted in the IR.
4. (IR) determines if this is an instruction operand. If so, the operand
   is acquired; see below. Otherwise, execution begins immediately;
   see Section 5.6.

Direct access,   The acquisition of a directly accessed operand
present page   in Fig. 5.4.2 is discussed below according to
the numbers which appear in that figure:

1. The present page indicator, ICP, is transferred to the page portion
   of the MAR, MARP.
2. The word portion of the MDR, MDRW, is transferred to the word
   portion of the MAR, MARW.

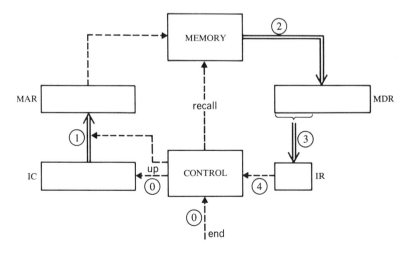

Fig. 5.4.1 PDP-8 *fetch.*

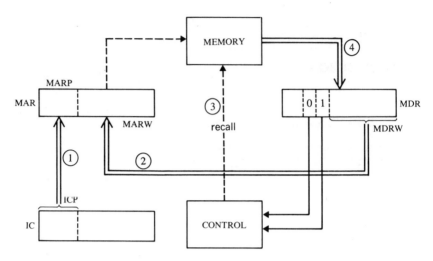

Fig. 5.4.2 Direct access, present page.

3. *Recall* is requested.
4. The contents of the address presently in the MAR are placed in the MDR, replacing this instruction which was just there. Whatever was needed is now in IR.

Direct access of page 0   This is shown in Fig. 5.4.3.

1. MARP is set to 0 because the page bit is 0.
2. The contents of the MDRW are placed in MARW.
3. *Recall* is requested; the datum is placed in the MDR.

Indirection   This is illustrated in Fig. 5.4.4.

1. Depending on the setting of the page bit, either MARP is set to 0 or the contents of ICP are placed there.
2. *Recall* is requested.
3. The pointer addressed by the MAR is placed in the MDR.
4. The entire contents of the MDR, the pointer, are placed in the MAR. This is our indirection cycle.
5. *Recall* is initiated.
6. The datum pointed to is placed in the MDR.

Autoindexing   The PDP-8 computer has no indexing or other form of automatic address modification. This is generally a severe

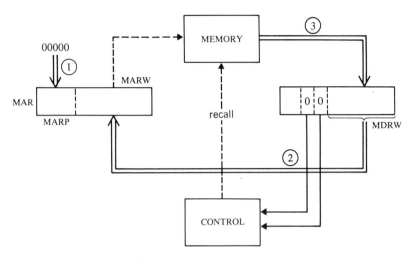

Fig. 5.4.3 Direct access, page 0.

limitation of all small computers in doing loops. One way around this is the autoindexing feature. It permits certain CELLS of MEMORY to be incremented automatically when they are used indirectly.

The autoindexing feature is invoked only under the following conditions:

1. CELLS 10_8 through 17_8 are referenced.
2. They are referenced indirectly.

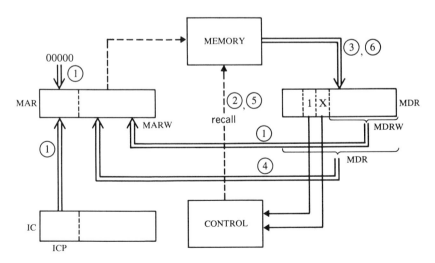

Fig. 5.4.4 Indirect addressing.

When these CELLs are referenced directly, they are not autoindexed; when these CELLs are addressed indirectly, we cannot avoid autoindexing; no other CELLs can be autoindexed.

The autoindexing feature causes the incrementation of the contents of the directly addressed CELL *before* it is used as an address. The new quantity is returned to MEMORY at its former position. It is also a pointer to the data.

EXAMPLE

Consider the command

$$\text{ADD} \quad \text{IO} \quad 012 \tag{5.4.1}$$

It references MEMORY indirectly through CELL 12, page 0, requesting autoindexing. Suppose that CELL 12 contains octal 5432; thus

$$(12) = 5432_8 \tag{5.4.2}$$

The contents of CELL 12 are incremented before being used as a pointer to the desired data. Hence the octal command executed is

$$\text{ADD} \quad 5433 \tag{5.4.3}$$

At the end of the execution of this command, CELL 12 contains the new address quantity 5433.

EXECUTION

A command using autoindexing is performed as illustrated in Fig. 5.4.5.

1. The instruction is placed in the MDR.
2. The mnemonic is ADD. The three-bit command code is placed in the IR.
3. The INDIRECT FLIPFLOP is set to 1, indicating that indirection is required.
4. 0's are placed in the MAR.
5. 12_8 is placed in the MAR.
6. The autoindexing detector determines that this is an autoindexing instruction. (Address is 10_8 through 17_8, indirect, page 0.)
7. The MEMORY CELL on page 0 is accessed and its contents brought to the MDR.
8. These contents are incremented by 1.
9. The incremented quantity is returned to MEMORY.
10. The contents of the MDR are placed in the MAR.
11. The datum is placed in the MDR.
12. The rest of the command proceeds in the *execute* phase in the normal fashion.

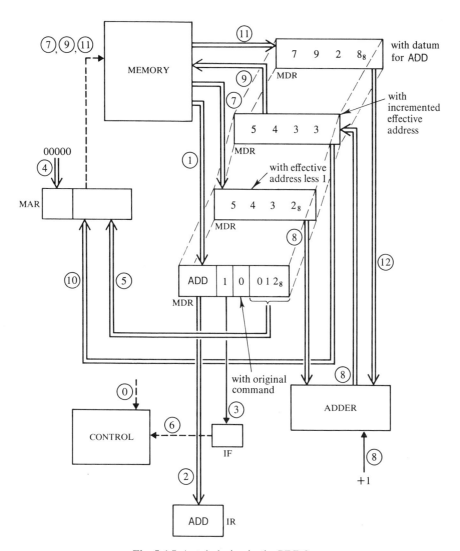

Fig. 5.4.5 Autoindexing in the PDP-8.

5.5   COMMANDS

Main commands   The main commands, with one exception, fall into the pattern established for FLAPJAC. The mnemonics the Digital Equipment Corporation uses for these commands are different and are presented in Table 5.5.1. The operation codes are designated by the

Table 5.5.1 PDP-8 COMMANDS

Octal	Mnemonic Flap	Mnemonic PDP-8	Arrow Notation
0	ANDTA	AND	(A) & (M) → A
1	ADD	TAD	(M) + (A) → M
2		ISZ	(M) + 1 → M; M ≠ 0 ⇒ I + 1
			M = 0 ⇒ I + 2
3	XMA	DCA	(M) → A
4	UCJ	JMP	⇒ M
5	JAS	JMS	I + 1 → M; ⇒ M + 1
6		IO	
7		Operate	

first octal digit in the command word and range from 0 to 6 for operand address.

ISZ   The one different command is called *Increment and Skip if Zero*. It brings the contents of the selected MEMORY location into the MEMORY DATA REGISTER. There this quantity is incremented by 1 and stored in the CELL indicated by (MAR). Next we test to see if the MDR contains 0. If not, we continue the program by getting the next instruction from the next CELL in sequence. If the MDR contains 0, a skip is requested. To do this, we doubly increment the INSTRUCTION COUNTER before the next *fetch*.

IO   IO operations are requested with the command with code 6_8 and the mnemonic IOT for INPUT *and* OUTPUT *transfer:*

$$IOT: \quad 6_8, \text{ device, event} \qquad (5.5.1)$$

Here *device* is a six-bit designator for one of the possible peripheral DEVICES which might be attached to the computer. *Event* permits or inhibits pulses at different times to be transmitted to the selected DEVICE. These pulses inform the DEVICE of its task or test the DEVICE to see how it has completed its operation. More detail is provided about this later.

Operate   Since we have only a small command repertoire so far, we need a way to enlarge it. We do this with a special set of *operate* commands—they do not require explicit reference to an operand.

All *operate* commands have the same first digit, 7_8. The meaning of the rest of the bits in the command word is somewhat specific. To increase the number of such meanings, we divide *operate* commands into two groups according to the fourth bit in the command word.

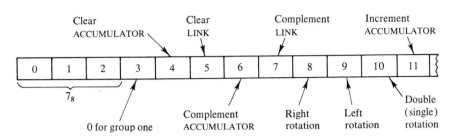

Fig. 5.5.1 Group one *operate* instructions.

Group one *operate* instructions are diagrammed in Fig. 5.5.1. Bit 3, the fourth bit in the command word, is 0 for group one *operate* commands. The meanings of the other bits are presented in the figure. Several of the bits require clearing or complementing either the ACCUMULATOR or the LINKS (overflow bits). Bits 8, 9, and 10 are used for single or double left or right rotation. The last bit, bit 11, designates incrementation of the ACCUMULATOR.

Several of these bits may be 1 at once. For instance, to get 000000000001 ACCUMULATOR, we can clear and increment the ACCUMULATOR.

A most useful command requests that the ACCUMULATOR be complemented and incremented. Since negative numbers are represented with two's complement notation, this command is used for making a positive number negative. Complementation means the one's complement. This makes subtraction possible where no explicit subtract command exists in our repertoire, and it is illustrated in Table 5.5.2. The subtrahend is

Table **5.5.2** PDP-8 SUBTRACTION

XMA	Y	$Y \rightarrow$ AR
CIA		$-Y \rightarrow$ AR
ADD	X	$X - Y \rightarrow$ AR

placed in the ACCUMULATOR with the command XMA. The two's complement of the subtrahend is found using CIA. Now the minuend is added into the ACCUMULATOR with the command ADD. The difference is hence found in the ACCUMULATOR.

The group two commands illustrated in Fig. 5.5.2 request skips of various sorts. The conditions for skipping are found in bits 5, 6, and 7. If all these conditions are present (logical *and*), a skip is requested. Otherwise we do the next command in sequence.

GROUP ONE

GROUP TWO

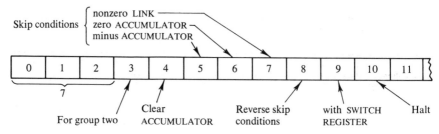

Fig. 5.5.2 Group two *operate* instructions.

To request that the conditions be reversed, 1 is placed in bit 8. Now if the condition called for is absent, a skip is required. This is best demonstrated in Table 5.5.3, where some *operate* commands are presented.

Table 5.5.3 *Operate* COMMANDS

Mnemonic	Octal Code	Arrow Notation	Meaning
NOOP	7000	$\Rightarrow I + 1$	No operation
RTL	7006	$A \xleftarrow{2} (A)$	Rotate two left
CMA	7040	$C(A) \to A$	Complement AR
CIA	7040	$C(A) + 1 \to A$ or $-(A) \to A$	Complement and increment AR
STOP	7402	$\not\Rightarrow$	Halt
SKIP	7410	$\Rightarrow I + 2$	Unconditional skip
SZA	7440	$(A) = 0: \Rightarrow I + 2$	Skip on zero AR
SNA	7450	$(A) \neq 0: \Rightarrow I + 2$	Skip nonzero AR

Consider these examples. To skip on zero ACCUMULATOR, we use the mnemonic SZA having a 1 in bit 6, but 0 in bit 8. To request a skip on nonzero ACCUMULATOR, we again place 1 in bit 6 and also 1 in bit 8.

5.6 IO

Types　　　　　　　　　　There are three kinds of IO operations possible:

1. Dedicated, called a **program data transfer.**
2. Interrupt, called the **program interrupt.**
3. Cycle steal, called **data break transfer.**

A dedicated IO operation is one where no processing or control operation takes place. There is no simultaneity. All processing operations are held up until the IO operation is completed.

For an *interrupt* IO operation in the PDP-8, a single word transfer between IO and MEMORY is delegated to an IO DEVICE; when this single operation is complete, an interrupt of the problem program occurs. This is most suitable for very slow DEVICES where processing may then proceed as we wait for a delegated IO operation to take place.

Only certain IO DEVICES and CONTROLLERs operate with cycle stealing, similar to the CHANNEL described in Chapter 2 except that no *subcommands* are involved. A single command delegates an IO interchange of several words to a DEVICE CONTROLLER. As each new access is required, a MEMORY cycle is *stolen* for the transfer of information between MEMORY and the DEVICE.

The remainder of this section is devoted to dedicated IO; interrupt and cycle stealing are discussed in Section 5.7.

Dedicated IO   Control for a DEVICE is unidirectional; but some DEVICES are bidirectional! Then separate control is required for each data transfer direction for the DEVICE. For instance, when the TELETYPE-WRITER enters information into computer MEMORY, it's addressed differently from when the computer prints out information from MEMORY on the TELETYPEWRITER.

The first digit of all IO commands is 6_8 to indicate IO. The next two digits provide a choice of 64 CONTROL UNITS. The fourth octal digit designates one or more pulses supplied to the DEVICE.

Figure 5.6.1 indicates control information going to the CONTROLLER. The last three octal digits are broadcast to all CONTROLLERs over the IO CONTROL bus when the command code 6_8 is decoded. The two middle digits appear on the DEVICE selection bus. Each DEVICE CONTROLLER has a unique DECODE which responds only to the code for this DEVICE. When that code is received, the output of DECODE permits the iot pulses to activate the DEVICE. They direct the DEVICE to perform one of several tasks. We continue the explanation by providing an example.

TELETYPEWRITER   The TELETYPEWRITER is bidirectional and contains an eight-bit DEVICE BUFFER. We now examine commands which apply to the TELETYPEWRITER when used as a TELEPRINTER.

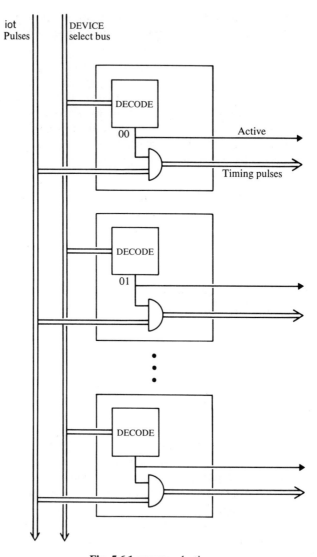

Fig. 5.6.1 DEVICE selection.

The IO command begins with 6_8. 04_8 is the address of the TELEPRINTER—the TELETYPEWRITER when it is being used for printing. 1_8 is a query to determine if the DEVICE FLAG is set. We skip if it is set; otherwise, we do the next sequenced command.

Figure 5.6.2 shows how the select pulses are supplied to the DECODE. Since we address unit 04, that DECODE produces an enabling signal to the

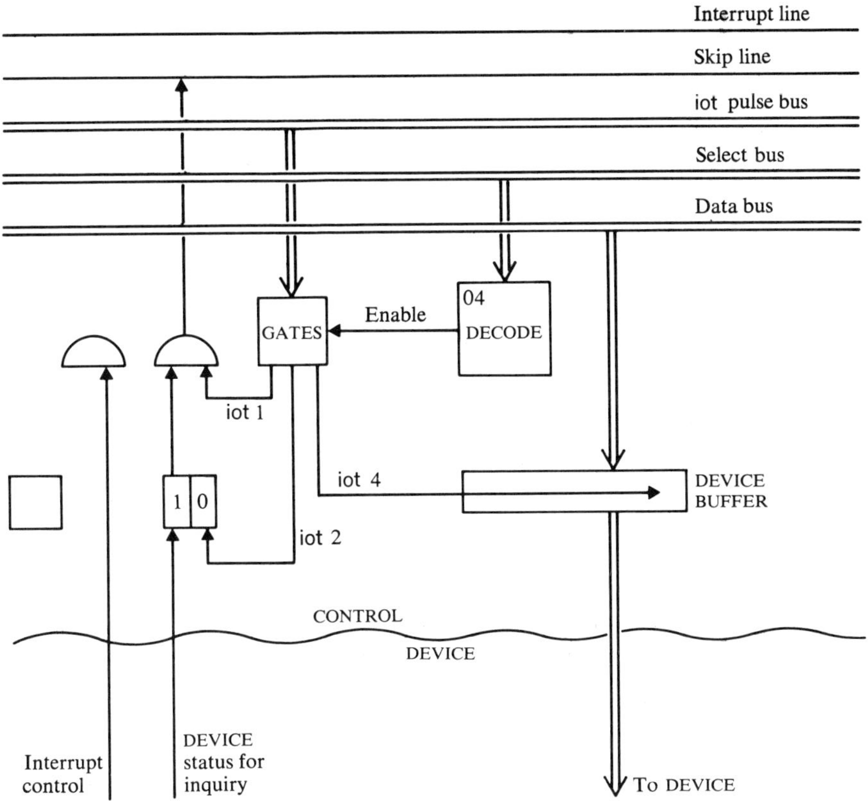

Fig. 5.6.2 Output interface as found in the TELETYPEWRITER.

GATES. Next the iot pulses arrive. Only iot1 is sent out; it tests the FLAG FLIPFLOP: if set to 1, a signal appears on the skip bus; none appears if it is reset to 0. That bus returns a skip signal to the computer. A skip is done only when there is a signal on the bus.

This request to clear the TELEPRINTER FLAG is portrayed in Fig. 5.6.2 where the reader can follow its execution.   6042

This request loads the DEVICE BUFFER, the TELEPRINTER CHARACTER BUFFER. The information source is the ACCUMULATOR. A character must have been placed in the AR by an earlier command. The command 6044 permits iot4 to transfer the character from the AR into the DEVICE BUFFER. After the character code is received in the DEVICE BUFFER, the DEVICE types this character on the TELEPRINTER.   6044

Fig. 5.6.3 Sequence to print character only after TELE-
PRINTER is found free.

6046

This performs both 6042 and 6044 by permitting iot2 and iot4 to activate the TELEPRINTER. Hence, this command does a data transfer and then clears the FLAG.

PROGRAM

Figure 5.6.3 is a three-step program which permits us to dispatch a character for printing, making sure that the printer has accepted the character before continuing the program.

Read   Let us see the commands applicable to the PAPER TAPE READER, an INPUT DEVICE. It too contains an eight-character BUFFER.

6011

This is a *skip-on-flag* command. Since the FLAG is set after a character is put in the BUFFER, this is a "don't skip if bus" command. When the BUFFER is full, it permits us to continue the program.

6012

This transfers the character in the DEVICE BUFFER into the ACCUMULATOR.

6014

This requests that the DEVICE CHARACTER BUFFER be filled from the PAPER TAPE READER. It activates the READER to get a new character.

PROGRAM

Figure 5.6.4 is a dedicated program to read from the PAPER TAPE READER. First we request that the BUFFER be filled. Then we see if a character is available. If none is available, we do not skip; instead, we return to the command which does the checking. When the CHARACTER

FIRST	RFC	(6014)	Fill BUFFER from tape
	RSF	(6011)	Skip if BUFFER filled
	UCJ	* — 2	
	CLA		Clear AR
	RRB	(6012)	BUFFER to AR

Fig. 5.6.4 Sequence to get next character from HIGH SPEED
PAPER TAPE READER, waiting for completion.

BUFFER *is* loaded, we clear the ACCUMULATOR and place the character from the BUFFER therein.

Processing during   Dedication is not mandatory! It would be
IO   folly to waste time in an IO unless:
- IO data are required before more processing can be done.
- There is nothing else to do.

With an inquiry scheme, it is up to the programmer to make the best use of his time. From the manufacturer's timing charts he can determine the length of IO and of intervening commands. He can place enough commands between *delegation* and *inquiry* so as to keep the DEVICE going at *almost* its maximum rate and yet make use of processing time.

5.7   INTERRUPT; CYCLE STEALING

Interrupt procedure   There is an INTERRUPT FLIPFLOP, IFF, in each DEVICE CONTROLLER for which an interrupt can take place. This is illustrated in Fig. 5.7.1. IFF can be set by the DEVICE CONTROLLER when the

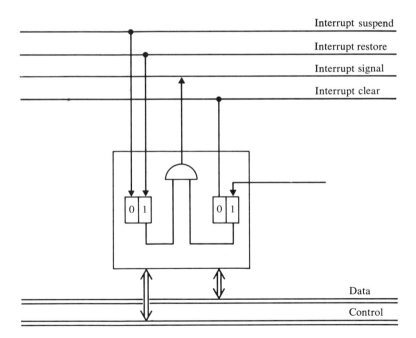

Fig. 5.7.1 Interrupt control.

interrupt-causing condition arises in the DEVICE; IFF can be reset by programmed computer signal.

The SUSPEND FLIPFLOP, designated SFF, in the PROCESSOR is used to inhibit the interrupt signal. A single signal from the computer is used to *suspend* interrupts for *all* the DEVICE CONTROLLERS; a similar signal is used to *restore* interrupts for *all* DEVICES.

When a condition calling for an interrupt occurs for a DEVICE and no other interrupt has prevailed, this condition sets the IFF on. If the SFF is also set, this enables the interrupt signal from IFF to appear on the interrupt line. An interrupt is initiated when the PROCESSOR next becomes free to accept it.

The interrupt   An interrupt for the PDP-8 operates exactly as though the following command were given

$$\text{JAS} \quad 000 \qquad\qquad (5.7.1)$$

As with any other command in the instruction sequence, it can take place only after the current command has completed *execution*. Whenever a signal appears on the interrupt line, it sets a FLIPFLOP, IPFF, indicating that an interrupt is pending. At *execution* completion IPFF forces (5.7.1) into the INSTRUCTION REGISTER. This causes the INSTRUCTION COUNTER to be stored at CELL 0, page 0, and the address for the next command comes from CELL 1, page 0.

Software   There is only one kind of interrupt— interrupts from all DEVICES are handled in the same fashion. It is up to the software to distinguish the interrupt source and cause.

An interrupt forces a jump to CELL 1, page 0, which contains an unconditional jump to the first step in the service routine. PDP-8 interrupt service is similar in concept to the earlier description:

1. *Suspend* all interrupts.
2. *Save* REGISTERS as required.
3. Make tests. The order in which the tests are made establishes priority in servicing DEVICES.
4. Each test looks for a CONDITION FLAG. When the FLAG is present, it causes a skip to the service routine.
5. The service routine places a DEVICE in operation again where possible and provides IO services to the program.
6. *Unsave* REGISTERS.
7. *Restore* interrupts. A delay is provided here to let us get back to the main program.

8. Return to the problem program.

$$\text{UCJ} \quad \text{I} \quad 000 \qquad\qquad (5.7.2)$$

Priority interrupt   With the system just outlined, can we permit an interrupt while servicing a previous interrupt?

The system *does* permit multiple interrupts. However, the software must be designed to cope with this. Suppose that we have a low speed DEVICE for which service is less important. Its priority, then, is low. The interrupt routine, when initially entered, shuts off all interrupts. It then checks to find the interrupting DEVICE. It checks the highest priority DEVICES first. Upon reaching a certain priority level, it can permit interrupts in testing and servicing.

This must be preceded by an operation which saves the contents of CELL 0 in some safe location and also sets a FLAG to indicate that this is the case. Now we can proceed to check and service the low priority interrupt which has occurred.

In the meantime, another interrupt may occur, presumably one of higher priority. When it does, we make tests regarding it. Eventually, we find the source and cause of the second interrupt and service it. During this process, other interrupts have been suspended.

At the end of servicing the second interrupt, we check to see if a FLAG has been set (indicating the presence of a former interrupt). If not, we return to the main program by an indirect jump through CELL 0.

If we were servicing a low priority interrupt at the time of the high priority interrupt, then the FLAG was set before interrupts were restored. Before continuing to service the first interrupt, we return its former contents to CELL 0. This was stored safely somewhere before second interrupt servicing began. Now we have required the return mechanism for problem program after servicing the low priority interrupt.

Data break   The DATA BREAK FACILITY (DBF) is a stripped down CHANNEL CONTROLLER. Unlike the CHANNEL CONTROLLER, there is no subcommand string which indicates a sequence of operations to be performed.

The DBF can perform as single command the transfer of a number of words of information between an IO DEVICE and MAIN MEMORY. This command is delegated from the program by the computer to the DBF which is available for high speed DEVICES.

The command issued to the DBF is generally in two or three parts.

1. An address indicates the place in CORE where the transfer is to begin.
2. A location for the intermediate medium indicates the other source

or destination of the information for the IO DEVICE. This location may be implied. For instance, in the case of magnetic tape, it is assumed that the *next* block is to be read or written.

3. The quantity of information to be transferred is supplied. Again, where information is dealt with in chunks of fixed quantity, this information may be omitted.

To convey the command to the DBF, we store control words at known locations in MEMORY. The program delivers these portions of the command to the ACCUMULATOR using XMA; the information is then imparted to the DEVICE using a command whose mnemonic might be XAI. After the control information is delivered to the DEVICE, it is started by one more command.

MEMORY is a single port subsystem. We should have a TRAFFIC CONTROLLER to determine which facility next has access to the MEMORY. We may consider entry to the TRAFFIC CONTROLLER as consisting of a number of channels with a priority associated

The DBF is identical to a channel stealing operation.

1. A break takes place after the execution of the present command.
2. The MDR and the MAR are now free.
3. A location is supplied the MAR by the DATA BREAK FACILITY.
4. Data is sent to or received from the MDR by the DATA BREAK FACILITY BUFFER.
5. The DATA BREAK FACILITY increments the core location number and decrements the count.

PROBLEMS

5.1 What is the small word problem? What are some solutions to it?

5.2 What components belong to or are shared by the five subsystems of the PDP-8?

5.3 Why is *paging* so-called? How is it done?

5.4 Why are the MAR and MDR divided into two parts?

5.5 How is autoindexing done? Why is it needed?

5.6 Assuming a symbolic assembler which includes lateral facility, write a PDP-8 program to 12 numbers at LIST, placing the result after the list and using the autoindexing feature. Assume the list is on a different page from the program.

5.7 Explain how the command repertoire of the PDP-8 is expanded with *operate* commands. Why are there two groups? How are *operate* commands combined within a group?

5.8 How is simultaneity achieved?

5.9 How is interrupt done? How can multiple interrupt requests be handled?

5.10 What is *data break*?

6

OTHER

SMALL

COMPUTERS

6.1 DEPARTURES

The market for very small computers is extremely large. A stripped down model in this category ranges in price from $8,000 to $25,000 or so. Hence the user can afford to purchase a computer and have it dedicated to a single application. It can be part of a control system for a manufacturing process or simply be a stand-alone general purpose computer for a design group. The small computer provides tough competition to the multiaccess computer concept where a large main computer services many consoles, making each console look to its user as though he has a small computer.

Since the field is wide open, there is competition among the manufacturers to provide an inexpensive computer which is easy to use and program. To do this, they have conceived changes in the concept presented in the last chapter as embodied in the PDP-8. Let us look at some of the features.

Longer word   Every bit that we add to the word size of a computer increases the cost of the computer. The cost per bit must be multiplied by the number of words of MEMORY that the basic model comes with. The more demanding user may buy extra modules of MEMORY. These, too, cost more because he must pay for each little bit more of word size.

When increasing word length, we should consider the convenience of the word size with respect to arithmetic and editing operations. Twelve is a very convenient size because it is divisible by 2, 3, 4, and 6. Thirteen, of course, is a prime number and does not contain any factors. Thirteen bits would be usable, but the additional bit might not hold extra data—it could be used for parity. In this case, the programmer sees the useful word as being only 12 bits long anyway.

In the *small* size range, we find computers with word length of 16 and 18. A 24-bit word is already twice as large as the 12-bit word of the PDP-8. I consider this word size to be in the medium computer class; this study is postponed to another volume. The 18-bit word size is not common. Therefore, the only other size that we consider is the 16-bit word.

INDEX REGISTER   To me, an INDEX REGISTER is indispensable for adequate programming. However, it is costly in two respects:

1. The cost of the REGISTER itself.
2. A bit in the command word to indicate that indexing is required.

It is interesting to see how some manufacturers have gotten around the second difficulty, anyway.

Another   It is nice to have another REGISTER when doing
ARITHMETIC   arithmetic. It is almost indispensable in
REGISTER   doing multiplication and division. However, the small computers generally do these latter processes with a subroutine package. Still, the computer can *also* use this extra REGISTER for indexing.

Double length   We have seen the difficulty facing the PDP-8
instruction word   in addressing all of its MEMORY from the command word and, at the same time, conveying sufficient information about the command and the addressing method. A single 12-bit word is really inadequate to do all this. Some manufacturers have, therefore, gone to double word command. This double word naturally requires two accesses of MAIN MEMORY. Also, when obtained, command information requires space.

Variable command   Variable size commands such as provided in
length   the IBM 1401 would really complicate the design for a small computer. However, if we are providing double word commands, it is a simple matter to permit *some* commands to be double

word size while others are single word size. For instance, *operate* commands might be single length, whereas *operand* commands might be double length.

Double precision   It is easy to see that a 12-bit word provides accuracy of only 1 part in 4096. Often, this would not be satisfactory, and we have to go to double precision processing to achieve the accuracy required in some scientific calculations. It is simple to do this by programming, but this is always time consuming during writing and running, and the routine uses up valuable MEMORY. When the programmer and designer are on speaking terms, the designer can provide some few extra commands which will greatly facilitate programming double precision arithmetic. In fact, why not have some double word commands as in the IBM 1130?

Separate data   We have seen how a program is written in
pages   page size sections. Reference to information within the page is simple using the paging system provided by the manufacturer. It is also simple to refer to information on page 0. But page 0 has a limited amount of space. To refer to information on other pages requires indirection which consumes both time and space. With small page size, a working program travels over several pages. This means that to reference data in a fixed location will generally require indirection. A remedy for this is to provide a PAGE REGISTER for data referencing separate from the PAGE REGISTER for commands. Then, regardless of which page the program is operating on, reference to the data can be made directly via the DATA PAGE REFERENCE REGISTER.

Priority interrupt   It is valuable to have a hierarchy of interrupts whereby some servicing will get done for an important DEVICE even though other DEVICE servicing is going on. This is not expensive to implement, and it is quite useful for on-line processing systems.

Commands   If there is space in the command word for additional command codes (hah!), why not create new commands which might help the programmer. These should always be evaluated for trade-off between usefulness and cost.

The main   As we look at the different machines in this
difficulty   chapter, the emphasis seems to be on the command word and what it conveys. This is actually the case because the

main difference among these machines is how the command word is set up and how it is interpreted by the hardware.

The programmer's view of a new machine is through the command repertoire available with the hardware.

The different types of addressing which the manufacturer makes available and the tags in the command word he uses for requesting these addressing types are most apparent to the programmer. It's surprising what variations we find from one machine to the next. Ingenuity in handling addressing is so important for the small machine because this is its main problem: although its MEMORY is small, the number of locations it contains may require most or all the command word for specification.

With the small computer, the user can often afford to have processing stop while IO takes place. But as the user wants to do more and more advanced programming, he looks for simultaneity. This can be done most efficiently only by incorporating the CHANNEL CONTROLLER principle or a variation thereof as described in Chapter 2. This involves cycle stealing and/or interrupt.

6.2 SDS 92

Scientific Data Systems makes a number of computers. But the only one which concerns us is their Model 92, a small, general purpose computer.

Instruction form   The interesting thing about the SDS 92 is its use of a double word command. Furthermore, according to the command code, either a single or a double command may be called for.

The command format is shown in Fig. 6.2.1. The first word is divided into five fields:

- The first (leftmost) six bits designate the operation to be performed.
- The seventh bit, call it S, is a page 0 bit. The manufacturer calls page 0 the scratch pad because it is directly addressable from a single command word.
- The eight bit, call it I, is used for indirection.
- The ninth bit, call it N, designates indexing.
- The remaining three bits, call them M1, constitute the higher-order portion of an address when a full address is used.

The second word of the two word command constitutes twelve bits, all of which we call M2 and which make up the low-order portion of the

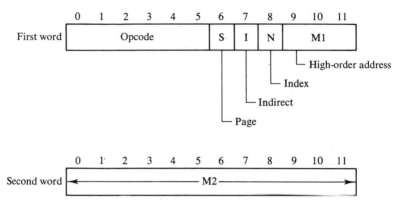

Fig. 6.2.1 SDS 92 command format.

operand address. Then the operand address M consists of the concatenation of M1 with M2.

Addressing   Several forms of addressing are available for this double word command.

For direct addressing, SIN=000. The operand addressed is at location M.

For indexing, SIN=001; it is done by *subtracting* the contents of the A REGISTER from M. We should note that M is a fifteen-bit quantity, whereas (AR) is a twelve-bit quantity. This is taken care of by the ADDER.

To address page 0, SIN=1XX. Here *XX* comprises two higher-order bits which are concatenated with M1 to form a five-bit address which designates some location in MAIN MEMORY ranging from 1_8 to 37_8. Notice that 0_8 is not an admissible address on page 0. Further, addressing the scratch pad uses *single* word commands.

When SINM1=100000, immediate addressing is called for. It requests that we use the contents of the *next* location following *this* command as the operand. For example, a command located at CELL 123 with opcode for ADD containing indicia for immediate addressing finds its operand at 124; that is, (124) will be added to the ACCUMULATOR.

SIN=010 requests indirect addressing using M (described for direct addressing) as the pointer address.

Fetch and operand acquisition   It is interesting to see what hardware is required to implement a double word command. REGISTER configuration for the SDS 92 is shown in Fig. 6.2.2; only the names of the REGISTERs have been changed (but not to keep their identities secret).

To *fetch* the first word of a command, the contents of the INSTRUCTION COUNTER are passed over to the MAR, and the IC is incremented. The

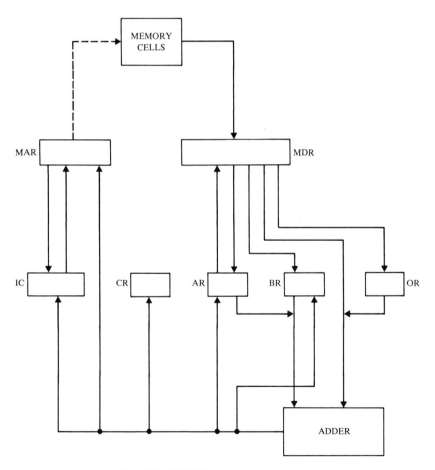

Fig. 6.2.2 SDS 92 hardware arrangement.

MEMORY brings forth the word and places it in the MDR. From there, the full word is sent to the CONTROL REGISTER, designated as CR. The upper half of the word is duplicated in the operation register, OR. What happens hereafter is determined by the contents of the CR—whether another cycle of *fetch* is required.

For double word commands, another *fetch* cycle is initiated when the need for it is determined by the CR. The only reservation is that, when the word gets to the MDR, it is not copied into either the CR or the OR as this would clobber the first half of the instruction.

When an operand is to be acquired directly as indicated by SIN=000, the contents of the MDR are passed over to the right-hand portion of the MAR. At the same time, M, which is in CR, is passed over to the higher portion of the MAR. A word is procured by the MEMORY and placed in the MDR.

Now it is the contents of OR which determine where the contents of the MDR are routed.

Indirect addressing for a double word command is done similarly to the direct addressing as described above, except for a few things:

1. We are getting an address which necessarily consists of fifteen bits.
2. Two REGISTERS are required to hold the address: part of the CR; the MDR.
3. The first word that is brought from MEMORY is broken up, and the lower half is placed in the CR.
4. The MAR is incremented before we use MEMORY again.
5. The incremented address in the MAR points to the next portion of the address that we desire.
6. That word is placed in the MDR.
8. Further indexing or indirection may be required as indicated by SIN now in the CR.

For indexing, from M we *subtract* (A) to get the effective address. Note that *subtraction* is used for indexing. For the hardware man, it makes little difference whether indexing is adding or subtracting. The programmer does different things for each—but not that different!

M is spread out over the MDR and a portion of the CR. To index, this information is gated into one input of the ADDER; the contents of the AR are gated into the other input, and *subtraction* is called for. The result, the effective address, is routed to the MAR. The MEMORY procures the word and places it in the MDR from whence it is routed to a DESTINATION REGISTER.

Other features   As is evident from Fig. 6.2.2, the SDS 92 has two ARITHMETIC REGISTERS. Both of these are available to the programmer. The first bit of the command code indicates whether AR or BR participates where arithmetic or editing is specified. As noted earlier, when indexing is called for, it is the AR which participates. Hence, for looping which involves adding or subtraction, it is desirable to maintain a sum or difference in the BR.

The manufacturer speaks about the IO CONTROLLER as though it were a CHANNEL CONTROLLER. But all communication between MEMORY and the PERIPHERAL DEVICES takes place using the ACCUMULATOR. No other processing can take place during IO since no cycle stealing is provided. A single word of information is brought into the ACCUMULATOR by a word input command, WIN; a word of information is provided to an OUTPUT DEVICE from the ACCUMULATOR by WOT.

It is possible to request a sequence of words to be brought in or written out with the "record" commands, RIN and ROT. The "CONTROLLER" keeps track of the number of words which comprise the record and determines when transfer is complete. However, the PROCESSOR is immobilized during this period, since IO transfers takes place through the AR.

Interrupt is provided which permits a DEVICE to cause a jump to a specific location in MEMORY when it's completed a task. Though cycle stealing is absent, interrupt is desirable. On output, for instance, WOT delivers a datum to a DEVICE after which the computer is free while the DEVICE is *busy*. If the computer does not know when the DEVICE is done, it has to keep asking the DEVICE (the programmer must space requests). This is where the interrupt helps.

Further, there is a hierarchy of priorities so that, when one DEVICE is being serviced, another may interrupt that service routine to call servicing of the second (interrupting) DEVICE.

6.3   SCC 650

Scientific Control Corporation makes several computers, the smallest of which is the model 650 having a twelve-bit word.

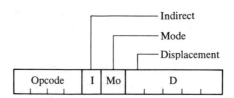

Fig. 6.3.1 The SCC 650 command format.

Command The command format for the SCC 650 is shown in Fig. 6.3.1. We immediately notice two differences between it and the PDP-8.

1. The opcode uses four bits (instead of three).
2. The operand address, D, uses six bits (instead of seven).

There are two more bits included:
- The indirection bit, I, is set to 1 when indirection is called for, and it is 0 otherwise.
- The mode bit, P, serves a double purpose:
  * When it is 0, it indicates addressing on page 0.
  * When it is 1, it indicates reference to current page.

Current page reference, P=1, is either indexed or self-relative, according to the setting of the INDEX STATE FLIPFLOP, ISF, discussed later. With a six-bit operand address, we reference 64 words. This, then, is the page size. Hence page 0 contains 64 words. The operand address quantity, D, is an offset for relativizing or is a displacement during indexing when P=1.

There is no simple direct addressing for the current page; it must be either indexed or self-relative.

Hardware Figure 6.3.2 shows the hardware configuration of the SCC 650. Notice that there is a separate INSTRUCTION REGISTER, IR, an ACCUMULATOR, AR, and the normal two REGISTERS associated with the MEMORY, the MAR, and the MDR.

There are three additional registers:

1. XR serves as a second ACCUMULATOR or an INDEX REGISTER, depending on the command in progress.
2. ZR is an AUXILIARY REGISTER which holds the second operand taking part in arithmetic as it's being entered into the ADDER.
3. SR is a STATUS REGISTER consisting of several SUBREGISTERS used for control operations. It contains the following:
  * ISF is the INDEX STATE FLIPFLOP.
  * CYR is a set of FLIPFLOPS storing carry information.

* PBR is the PROGRAM BANK REGISTER used when indirection is not indicated.
* IBR is the BANK SETTING REGISTER when indirection is called for.
* Other FLIPFLOPS.

In Fig. 6.3.2, the MAR has fifteen bits; the first three bits are bank bits. This part of the MEMORY address is set either from the PBR or the IBR according to information conveyed by the command and the setting of ISF. A different bank (set of 64 pages) of MEMORY is used as determined by the setting in PBR or IBR according to the type of addressing called for.

Addressing The several different forms of addressing are now discussed.

When both the indirect bit (I) and the mode bit (P) are 0 (IP=00), reference is to page 0 regardless of the INDEX STATE FLIPFLOP (ISF). In this case, operand address on page 0 (0) *is* the effective address of the operand. (PBR and IBR are disregarded.) If we call the setting of ISF S, then we have for IPS=00X, EA=D.

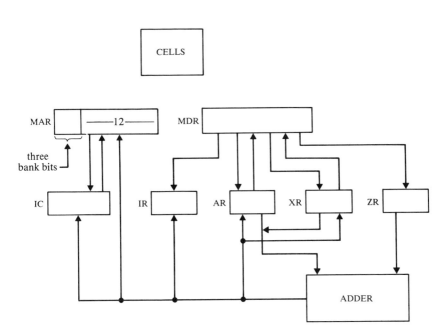

Fig. 6.3.2 SCC 650 hardware.

For IPS=010 self-relative addressing is called for. D is added to (IC) to obtain the effective page address; (PBR) is the bank address.

A novel feature with respect to this kind of addressing is brought into play when P=1. Here the datum is in the CELL following this command. Normally, this would mess up the command sequence. However, the 650 automatically increments the IC so that for the command

$$207 \quad ADD,* \qquad 1 \tag{6.3.1}$$

The next command automatically is drawn from 209.

When IPS=11X, indirection is called for. A pointer address is determined as described before for the effective address in the case of self-relative or indexed addressing. The contents are obtained from the MDR. This is a twelve-bit word. It is placed in the MAR on the right side. The contents of the IBR are placed in the left side of the MAR. We are now ready to obtain a datum (from a bank different from the program bank).

Fetch A *fetch* procures the next instruction as indicated by the INSTRUCTION COUNTER and from the program bank. This is indicated in arrow notation:

$$(\text{PBR}) \smile (\text{IC}) \rightarrow \text{MAR} \rightarrow (\text{MDR}) \rightarrow \text{IR} \tag{6.3.2}$$

Addressing The reader may work out how addressing is done using Fig. 6.3.2 and the equations given in arrow notations below:

$$0 \smile M \rightarrow \text{MAR} \tag{6.3.3}$$

Self-relative This mode of addressing uses a program bank and is relevant to the INSTRUCTION COUNTER:

$$(\text{PBR}) \smile (\text{IC}) + M \rightarrow \text{MAR} \tag{6.3.4}$$

For the case where M=1, we have

$$M=1: \quad (\text{IC}) + 2 \rightarrow \text{IC} \tag{6.3.5}$$

otherwise,

$$M=0: \quad (\text{IC}) + 1 \rightarrow \text{IC} \tag{6.3.6}$$

$$(\text{PBR}) \smile (\text{XR}) + M \rightarrow \text{MAR} \tag{6.3.7}$$

The pointer address is obtained by one of the foregoing methods. Call it PA. Indirection uses the INDIRECT BANK REGISTER, IBR, and hence is given by these two equations:

$$(\text{PA}) \to \text{MAR} \tag{6.3.8}$$

$$(\text{IBR}) \smile (\text{MDR}) \to \text{MAR} \tag{6.3.9}$$

6.4 IBM 1130

Characteristics   The IBM 1130 is a small machine like the others we have discussed, except that it has a larger word size, namely sixteen bits. The extra four bits almost put it into another category. There are a number of other machines of sixteen rather than twelve bits. They have attractive characteristics but their cost is necessarily high.

The IBM 1130 MEMORY has a basic size of 4K and can be expanded to a size of 8K, but no more.

The machine is said to have *indexing*. I prefer to restrict this term to machines which have hard REGISTERs immediately accessible for holding index quantities. However, the IBM 1130 does have access to three index quantities which are held in reserved positions in CORE. The three indexes numbered 1, 2, and 3, respectively, occupy MEMORY locations 1, 2, and 3.

The IO method does not have the sophistication of some of the smaller machines: it is not CHANNEL CONTROLLER oriented. Each DEVICE is controlled and activated separately. However, an interrupt system is supplied which permits a DEVICE to cause the CP to jump to fixed locations in CORE, one for each DEVICE (or sometimes a set of DEVICES). A novel feature of the IBM 1130 is its ability to use both data and commands which are either in single or double word format. A single word datum contains a left-hand sign bit and is sixteen bits long. The double word is thirty-two bits, again with the sign in the left-hand position. In both cases, words are in two's complements integer binary format where double or single data words are addressed as determined by the command code. Whether a command is single or double word is determined by the command configuration itself, that is, a command field signified as F distinguishes single from double word commands.

Command   The two kinds of commands are presented in Fig. 6.4.1. The fields which comprise the command are discussed in detail below.

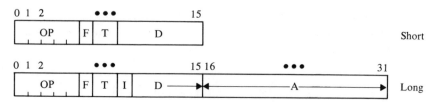

Fig. 6.4.1 Long and short command formats.

The first five bits in both short and long commands are reserved for the opcode, and the field is called OP. This allows for thirty-two separate commands.

The F field, which consists of a single bit, distinguishes short from long commands. Most commands can take either long or short form as distinguished by this bit.

The two-bit tag field, T, determines the kind of addressing to be done. 00 indicates generally direct addressing. When the tag is 01, 10, or 11, this designates, respectively, the use of INDEX REGISTERS 1, 2, and 3 from MEMORY locations 1, 2, or 3. The content of the designated INDEX REGISTER is added to the displacement. Note that the INDEX REGISTER is neither a REGISTER (it is in MM) nor is its use reserved for indexing (it is often used for relocation like a BASE REGISTER).

There are eight bits left in the command word. This field is called the **displacement** by IBM and is designated D. For short commands only, either it is added to an INDEX REGISTER, or the INSTRUCTION COUNTER (when T=00) to form the operand address. It is not large enough when used alone to address all of MEMORY.

For the long command, all of the second word is the address field designated A. The D field is ignored. The address, A, is manipulated as described later to form an effective address. Although sixteen bits are available, only up to fourteen are useful because of the limitation in CORE MEMORY size.

For the long command, the bit after the tag field, N, is designated I; instead of being part of displacement, it indicates if indirection is required. Then, for the long commands, the displacement field, D, consists of only seven bits.

Addressing   There are a variety of ways in which the effective address, which we call M, can be fabricated according to the contents of the various fields described before.

For short commands where F = 0, the tag field N indicates the index quantity to which the displacement is added. Then we have

$$N \neq 0: \quad M = (N) + D \tag{6.4.1}$$

Here N also indicates the INDEX REGISTER indicated by the tag. When the tag is 0, we have

$$N = 0: \quad M = * + D \tag{6.4.2}$$

The asterisk indicates the present contents of the INSTRUCTION COUNTER.

For F = 1 and I = 0, we request direct addressing of a long command. For this we have

$$N \neq 0: \quad M = (N) + A \tag{6.4.3}$$

$$N = 0: \quad M = A \tag{6.4.4}$$

where N is the index number. Here A is the address field, the entire second word; the displacement, D, is completely ignored.

For long commands with indirect addressing, we have F = 1, I = 1. The address is prepared as before, but it is only a pointer. We go to that address to get the address for the operand desired. In this mode we have

$$N \neq 0: \quad M = ((N) + A) \tag{6.4.5}$$

$$N = 0: \quad M = (A) \tag{6.4.6}$$

(margin labels: SHORT · LONG DIRECT · LONG INDIRECT)

Hardware   Figure 6.4.2 is a block diagram of the IBM 1130 hardware. Let us examine the REGISTERS and their functions in the equipment.

■ *memory address.* The location in CORE which is being addressed is in a STORAGE ADDRESS REGISTER, SAR, equivalent to our MAR.

The datum from MEMORY or to be stored is temporarily held after retrieval or before storage in the STORAGE BUFFER REGISTER, SBR, equivalent to our MDR.

■ *opcode.* The opcode for the command to be *executed* is placed in the OPERATION REGISTER, OPR.

■ *tags.* The F bit, the two tag bits, N, and the indirection bit, I, are all stored in the TAG REGISTER, TAG.

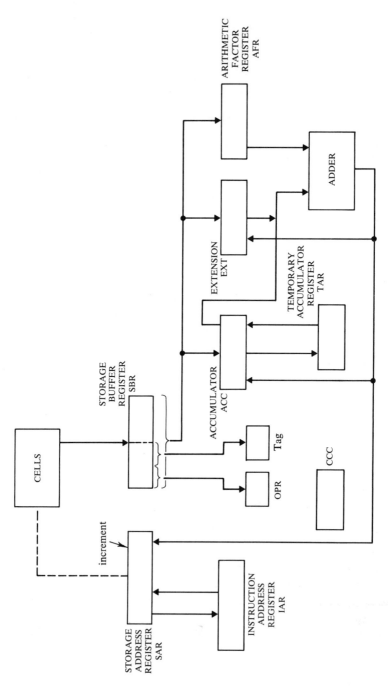

Fig. 6.4.2 Block diagram of the IBM 1130.

148

■ INSTRUCTION COUNTER. The address of the *next* instruction is held in the next ADDRESS REGISTER, IAR, for all but branch instructions.

■ ACCUMULATOR. The ACCUMULATOR, ACC, receives the results of all arithmetic operations. It can be loaded from or stored in CORE storage. Shifts and logical instructions are directed to the ACC.

■ *extension*. The ACCUMULATOR extension, EXT, holds the less significant word in double precision arithmetic. It also takes part in multiplication, division, and double word shifts.

■ *operand*. In arithmetic or editing, the address of the second operand is generally contained in the second command word. When the operand is obtained, it is placed in the ARITHMETIC FACTOR REGISTER, AFR.

■ TEMPORARY ACCUMULATOR. During the calculation of the effective address, the ACCUMULATOR is required. Its contents are moved from ACC temporarily. TAR is the REGISTER which holds the contents of ACC during address calculation.

■ *cycle contents*. For multiplication and division, it is necessary to count the number of cycles of arithmetic. CCC does this; it also counts up and down for shifting.

Fetch; address   *Fetch* can be followed in Fig. 6.4.2. It is
accumulation   initiated at the end of an *execute* cycle. The
IAR contains the address of the next instruction. (IAR) is passed over to the SAR. The datum arrives at the SBR; the first part of this word is sent over to the OPR, and the TAG is to control the next set of activities. What happens next depends on the F bit which tells us whether we have a short or long command. With only a few exceptions where an address need not be calculated, the contents of the ACC are temporarily stored in the TAR, so that the ACC will be free for the calculation.

For short commands, the displacement D is sent over from the SBR to the ACC which is filled with 0's as needed. Now the two bits, T, determine how the calculations proceed. Immediately, if T = 00 the IAR contents are sent over to the AFR.

When T is not 00, T determines the INDEX REGISTER to be used. The INDEX REGISTER contents must be procured from MEMORY. To do this, the T bits are jammed into the least significant bits of the SAR, and 0's fill it up. When the INDEX contents arrive at the SBR, they are routed to the AFR.

Whatever the tag bits were, we are now ready to do addition. The contents of ACC and AFR are sent to the ADDER. The results of addition are entered in the SAR, for this is the address to be used next. The contents of the ACC are restored from their temporary location, the TAR. Generally, MEMORY will be called upon next to *recall*, but there are some cases, such as *store* commands, where a *memorize* is done next.

SHORT

LONG

When a long command is observed because $F = 1$, address calculation cannot proceed until we obtain the next word from MEMORY. One or two of the reflexive commands may be an exception to this, as the reader may determine. To obtain the next word, the IAR contents are sent over to the SAR. Whenever (IAR) goes to the SAR, it is automatically incremented there and then returned to the IAR. In this way we are sure that the IAR always points to the next command word.

The A field is sent to the SBR and from there, directly to the ACCUMULATOR. If $T = 0$, the ACCUMULATOR now has the operand address. If T is not 0, we obtain the INDEX REGISTER contents and place them in the AFR as described before. Addition of the contents of the ACC and the AFR produce the effective address which is then sent to the SAR.

INDIRECT

When indirect addressing is called for because $I = 11$, the long command address calculation operation proceeds as described directly above. However, when the datum indicated by the SAR arrives at the SBR, it is routed to the SAR, and another *recall* cycle is initiated. At this point, the I bit in the IAR is reset to 0 so that only one cycle of indirection may occur.

Load and store commands   Table 6.4.1 displays the entire command repertoire for the IBM 1130. The first column designates a class of commands. The second column describes the commands in each class verbally. The third column gives the assembly language mnemonic. The last column gives the opcode in octal.

The first set of commands is described as *load and store*. Generally, it is the ACCUMULATOR which is *loaded* or *stored*. Load means entering information *from* MEMORY; store means entering information *into* MEMORY.

The double word commands load (or store) information at M and $M + 1$ into (from) ACC and EXT. Thus we have, in arrow notation,

$$\text{LDD:} \quad (M) \rightarrow \text{ACC}; \quad (M + 1) \rightarrow \text{EXT} \qquad (6.4.7)$$

$$\text{STD:} \quad (\text{ACC}) \rightarrow M; \quad (\text{EXT}) \rightarrow M + 1 \qquad (6.4.8)$$

The command LDX loads the index, N, with D for $F = 0$; for $F = 1$, it loads N with A, for $I = 0$ or with (A) for $I = 1$. STX stores (N) in the effective address calculated as described earlier, leaving (N) unchanged. Carry status is stored in a pair of FLIPFLOPS—one for carry and one for overflow.

Arithmetic   The action of the add command is given in arrow notation as

$$\text{A:} \quad (M) \rightarrow \text{AER} \qquad (6.4.9)$$

$$(\text{ACC}) + (\text{AFR}) \rightarrow \text{ACC} \qquad (6.4.10)$$

Table 6.4.1 IBM 1130 INSTRUCTION SET

Class	Command	Mnemonic	Octal Opcode
Load and store	Load accumulator	LD	30
	Load double	LDD	31
	Store accumulator	STO	32
	Store double	STD	33
	Load index	LDX	14
	Store index	STX	15
	Load status†	LDS	04
	Store status	STS	05
Arithmetic	Add	A	20
	Add double	AD	21
	Subtract	S	22
	Subtract double	SD	23
	Multiply	M	24
	Divide	D	25
	And	AND	34
	Or	OR	35
	Exclusive or	EOR	36
Shift‡ (left)	Shift left accumulator†	SLA	02
	Shift left accumulator and EXT†	SLT	02
	Shift left and count accumulator and EXT†	SLC	02
	Shift left and count accumulator†	SLCA	02
(right)	Shift right accumulator†	SRA	03
	Shift right accumulator and EXT†	SRT	03
	Rotate right†	RTE	03
Branch	Branch and store IAR	BSI	10
	Branch and skip on condition	BSC	11
	Modify index and skip	MDX	16
	Wait†	WAIT	00
IO	Execute IO	XIO	01

† Valid in short format only.
‡ Modified by bits 8 and 9.

Double add performs the same task on the high-order word; additionally, it acts on the low-order word as follows:

$$AD: \quad (M+1) \to AFR \tag{6.4.11}$$

$$(AFR) + (EXT) \to EXT \tag{6.4.12}$$

The other arithmetic and editing commands are single word commands; they are fairly clear cut so that we need not dwell upon them.

Reflexive commands   The set of reflexive commands is interesting because it produces some techniques not seen in other machines we have examined.

WAIT

The WAIT command is simply a NOOP.

BSC

BSC, *branch and skip on condition*, has interesting ramifications. In this command, the field, D, contains a mask for conditions which may prevail in the ACCUMULATOR. For short commands this mask is checked against prevailing conditions, and if *all* the conditions in the mask are true, a skip occurs to * + 2. If *one or more* of the conditions is false, we take the next command, the one at * + 1.

For the long BSC, again we check the mask against prevailing conditions. If *any* one of them is true (not *all* this time), we take the *next* command in sequence * + 1. If *none* of them is true, we jump to the address, A. By proper management of the mask and the F bit, we can produce a NOOP or a UCJ from BSC.

BSI

A *branch and store* IAR, BSI, is just like the *branch and link* instruction for many other computers and JAS for FLAP. Its action is given as:

$$\text{BSI:}\qquad (\text{IAR}) + 1 \rightarrow \text{M};\qquad \Rightarrow \text{M} + 1 \qquad\qquad (6.4.13)$$

The double arrow indicates a jump. BSI becomes much more complicated in the long instruction format; we will skip this option.

Figure 6.4.3 shows how BSI and BSC are used for subroutine linkage. The first step in the diagram is the jump to the subroutine entitled SR. However, the location of SR is empty. Into it we place (IAR) + 1 using BSI. We actually jump to the step *after* SR. At the end of the subroutine we find BSC which is tagged as indirect (I = 1). It addresses the location SR. The mask in this command is set to give us an unconditional jump, (UCJ). Since this jump is indirect through the location SR which contains (IAR) + 1, we return to the next step in the problem program.

MDX

The *modify index and skip* command, MDX, is powerful because of the many variations which are possible in its specification. In the cases described here, whatever is modified is also always checked. If there is a sign change or if a REGISTER quantity becomes zero, a skip occurs, * + 2; otherwise, the next command is taken in sequence, * + 1.

For the short command, the tag determines which REGISTER is incremented. When the tag is zero, it is the INSTRUCTION ADDRESS REGISTER to which the displacement is added

$$T = 0: \qquad (\text{IAR}) + \text{D} \rightarrow \text{IAR} \qquad\qquad (6.4.14)$$

For a nonzero tag, the INDEX REG-
ISTER indicated is incremented

$$T \neq 0: \quad (N) + D \to N \quad (6.4.15)$$

In the long format, the action
performed depends on both the
tag and the indirection bits.
When the tag is zero, the displacement is added to the contents of the address pointed to
by A.

$$T = 0: \quad (A) + D \to A \quad (6.4.16)$$

When the tag is nonzero, an
INDEX REGISTER is indicated. For a zero indirection bit, the A quantity
itself is added to this INDEX.

$$T \neq 0, \quad I = 0: \quad (N) + (A) \to N \quad (6.4.17)$$

To see how the MDX command is used in facilitating loop action,
examine Fig. 6.4.4. At the end of the loop at the position entitled TEST,
MDX adds the quantity Q to INDEX REGISTER 3. As long as N3 remains
nonzero, we go to the next command at ACT. Here we find BSC which
acts like UCJ to the location, LOOP. However, when processing is
finished, we jump out of the loop by finding the index zero or changing
sign. This causes a skip to MORE.

IO   All IO operations are initiated with command
mnemonic XIO. It contains an address which is a pointer to an IO control
command (IOCC). This IOCC occupies two words in a location in
MEMORY assigned by the program. The format of the IOCC is displayed
in Fig. 6.4.5. Here *address* is a location in MEMORY with which information
is transferred. *Device* identifies a DEVICE to be activated and follows the
assignment shown in Table
6.4.2. *Function* conveys to the
DEVICE a task which the latter
is to perform. *Function* codes
are presented in Table 6.4.3.
Finally, *modifier* communicates
additional operations or operation modifications unique to
DEVICE.

Most IO DEVICES operate on
a word basis. A single word is

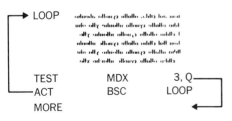

Fig. 6.4.4 Using MDX for testing and BSC
for looping.

Fig. 6.4.5 The IOCC.

interchanged between MEMORY and the DEVICE. Into this word may be packed one or more characters according to the DEVICE specification.

Only the DISK and the LINE PRINTER operate in a multiple-word mode. While information is interchanged with the DISK, computation cannot proceed. However, the PRINTER operates by cycle stealing.

The IBM 1130 provides an interrupt facility whereby, upon completion of an assignment, the DEVICE causes the computer to jump to a MEMORY location reserved for interrupt servicing. This jump is indirect. By forcing

Table 6.4.2 DEVICE DESIGNATIONS

Device Code (Octal)	Device
02	Card reader-punch
05	Printer or plotter
04	Disk
03	PT Reader, punch
01	Console keyboard, printer
07	Console entry switches

the BSI command, using the address of the interrupt location, we go through the interrupt location to the service routine. Because indirect addressing is available, we have a powerful tool for performing interrupts which occur *during* interrupts. These are set up on a priority basis. When a low priority interrupt is handled, a high priority interrupt takes precedence and causes initiation of a service routine for the high priority device. Upon completion, we return to continue service on the low priority device, and when done, we return to the problem program.

Table 6.4.3 FUNCTION DESIGNATIONS

Function Code (Octal)	Function
1	Write from *address* to DEVICE
2	Read from DEVICE to *address*
3	Load interrupt status word into ACC
4	Control DEVICE from *modifier*
5	Write by cycle steal
6	Read by cycle steal
7	Load DEVICE status word into ACC

PROBLEMS

6.1 Make a list of small computer features which one might encounter.

6.2 What is scratch pad addressing?

6.3 How are the arithmetic registers in the SDS 92 handled by (a) program; (b) hardware?

6.4 Comment on hardware self-relative addressing. Contrast it with paging. Describe the problems of each.

6.5 For the SCC 650, how are the PBR and IBB used? How might this affect the design of an assembler?

6.6 Describe all the ways MEMORY can be addressed in the IBM 1130 and when one might use each.

6.7 What is the effect of two command lengths on
(a) assembler design;
(b) AL programming;
(c) the paging problem?

6.8 Describe a *fetch* for both *short* and *long* commands.

6.9 State how double length arithmetic commands might be used.

6.10 How might the variations of the MDX command be used?

6.11 What provisions are there for simultaneity and interrupt for the IBM 1130? Explain and contrast with other alternatives.

7

THE
IBM
1401

7.1 FORMAT

The word Earlier we defined *word* as the unit of information obtained from MEMORY during one access. For the IBM 1401, *exactly one character* is obtained on each MEMORY access. Further, data manipulation in the PROCESSOR is one character at a time. Therefore, this machine has a word length of one character.

Character content is presented in Table 7.1.1. Each character (or word) in MEMORY contains exactly eight bits. The eighth or higher-order bit is called a **word mark (WM)** bit by IBM. I prefer to call it a **field mark**. It marks the beginning or end of fields of several characters, as described later. The parity bit is next (bit 7): it is made 0 or 1 so that the number of 1's in the succeeding bits which comprise the word is always odd. It is also called a check bit and designated as "C" by IBM.

Bits 6 and 5 are zone bits. They are 00 for numerals and have one of three remaining combinations to designate letters or special characters. The bits are labeled B and A, respectively.

The remaining four bits are used to convey numeric information, using a BCD code. In collaboration with the zone bits, letters are represented. They are labeled, in order, 8, 4, 2, 1 to reflect their weights.

Character representation The IBM 1401 was designed to replace electronic accounting machines (EAM) of the totally punchcard variety—"tab equipment." The character code was

Table 7.1.1 USE OF EACH POSITIONAL BIT IN EACH
WORD—A CHARACTER—IN MEMORY OR
DURING PROCESSING

Position	Function	Designation
8	Field	W (or underscore)
7	Parity	C
6	Zone	B
5	Zone	A
4	Numeric	8
3	Numeric	4
2	Numeric	2
1	Numeric	1

designed to appear at least somewhat familiar to the EAM user. This similarity is emphasized in Table 7.1.2. The twelve hole sites and their values are portrayed in the center column of the table. The two zone bits encode the three top card hole sites, which convey zone information. The four numeric bits represent the numeric hole sites according to the weights assigned to these bits. For instance, in the table a hole in row five is represented by numeric code 0101 to get weights 4 and 1 as in NBCD code. Notice that, generally, only one zone and one numeric hole may occur, determining the zone and numeric bits. Multiple holes get special handling.

Table 7.1.2 THE ZONE BITS RESEMBLE
THE ZONE HOLES AND THE
NUMERIC CODE RESEMBLES
THE NUMERIC HOLES ON
THE PUNCHCARD

Zone Code	Hole	Numeric Code
BA		8 4 2 1
1 1	12	XXXX
1 0	11	XXXX
0 1	0	1 0 1 0
XX	1	0 0 0 1
XX	2	0 0 1 0
XX	3	0 0 1 1
XX	4	0 1 0 0
XX	5	0 1 0 1
XX	6	0 1 1 0
XX	7	0 1 1 1
XX	8	1 0 0 0
XX	9	1 0 0 1

ZERO HOLE SITE

Two complications arise with the zero hole site. When a hole is present at this site, its coding is determined by its use in the card: If it is the only punch in that column, it should be coded as numeric; if there are other punches, it should be coded as a zone. The input and output circuitry takes care of this problem.

The second problem involves the numeric code for the single zero punch. In the NBCD code, the representation of zero is 0000. However, this code is reserved for a blank. The IBM code for zero is hence 001010, the hexadecimal "A" worth ten.

Since all other numerics are represented as NBCD characters, we might call this the modified NBCD code or simply MNBCD.

Use of the field   Both data and instructions are accessed in
mark   MEMORY using a three character address. This
determines the character which starts the field; termination of a field is determined by the word mark. A complication arises because the machine accesses data in one direction and instructions in another direction. This is illustrated in Fig. 7.1.1.

DATA

Data are referenced by giving the address of the *right-hand* terminal character of the field (the character with highest address). Data are used or examined until a character accessed contains a word mark. Figure

Location	340	341	342	343	344	345	
Code	11000000	00111000	0011001	00101001	00101001	01011000	10—
Character	b̲	H	A	R	R	Y	—

(a) The address of bHARRY is 345

Location	95	96	97	98	
Code	11100100	0011001	00101001	01011000	
Character	M̲	A	R	Y	—

(b) The address of MARY is 98

Location	701	702	703	704	705	706	707	708	709	710	711	712
Character	K̲	2	1̲	A̲	0	7	2	4	2	3	2̲	A̲

(c) location of instruction "K̲2" is 701
location of instruction "1̲" is 703
location of instruction "A̲072423" is 704
location of instruction "2̲" is 711

Note: WM is leftmost bit in character.
Parity is the next character bit.
Two *zone* bits come next.
The four right bits in the character are the *numeric*.

Fig. 7.1.1 Format of data and instructions.

7.1.1a shows how the field bHARRY is stored in MEMORY and accessed. The character Y, coded 01011000, is at location 345; it is the right-hand character of the field. To obtain this field, characters are accessed from right to left until we arrive at the character b̲† (a blank). Notice that the six data bits of this character are all 0, since this is a representation for a blank. The parity bit is 1, so that the character contains an odd number of 1's. Finally, there is a word mark present which halts the accessing process.

Figure 7.1.1b shows how the field MARY is stored at the address 98. Data fields are stored from right to left for a most practical reason. Often, arithmetic is done on data fields. Addition generates carries from a less significant digit to the digit of next higher significance. Subtraction generates borrows in the same fashion. Since higher significance digits are accessed after lower significance digits and after addition has been performed on them, then a carry can be taken into account in manipulating these digits. Carry handling would be very difficult if data were referenced in the other direction.

Instructions are stored in MEMORY from left to right. The lowest address contains the most significant character of an instruction field. The instruction consists of an opcode character and a number of address digits and/or designator characters. One character is sufficient to convey the entire command code of the IBM 1401. This opcode character is always obtained first. Other characters which follow are modifier or address characters.

The order of storage, left to right, is dictated by the ease of handling program information by the *programmer* this time. He is accustomed to writing commands from left to right, opcodes first, then address. Of course, he could write them that way and have the *Assembler*, Autocoder, produce them in reverse order. This would permit a consistent word mark position. However, in debugging a program, code appears backwards and patching would be very difficult. Hence this compromise is handled effectively by hardware:

- Data are read right to left.
- Commands are read left to right.

Figure 7.1.1c shows several instructions in MEMORY. Each instruction begins with a word mark character, and access continues until the next word mark character is encountered—it is discarded. Foregoing information is kept and recognized as the instruction to be executed.

In Figure 7.1.1c we note four instructions stored as described in the legend.

---

† An underlined character represents one for which a *word mark* is present.

Addresses   MEMORY size for the IBM 1401 varies from
1200 characters to 16,000 characters (*not* 16K). It is impossible to address
this much MEMORY with three digits alone. However, we have three
characters available, not three decimal *digits*. The zone bits in these three
characters distinguish the thousands decade in which the characters lie.
The numeric bits give the location in terms of hundreds, tens, and units.
Table 7.1.3 shows the numeric addressing value of each bit in the three
characters.

Table 7.1.3 THE USE OF NUMERIC AND ZONE BITS IN
FORMING ADDRESSES

Character	Hundreds	Tens	Units
Value B	2000	X	8000
A	1000	X	4000
8	800	80	8
4	400	40	4
2	200	20	2
1	100	10	1

By combining the numeric values of the numeric position of the three
addressing characters in hundreds, tens, and units with the zone bit values
in thousands, the exact operand address in MEMORY is fixed. Figure 7.1.2
shows several examples of how addresses are represented in the IBM 1401.

Code			Address
01000011	00000100	01000101	345
00010011	00000100	01000101	1,345
01110011	00000100	01000101	3,345
01000011	00000100	00100101	8,345
01110011	00000100	01110101	15,345

Fig. 7.1.2 Several addresses and their codes.

7.2   REGISTERS AND SUBSYSTEMS

Functional units   The REGISTERS and FUNCTIONAL UNITS of the
IBM 1401 computer are presented in Fig. 7.2.1. The dash-dot line
separates the UNITS into the SUBSYSTEMS, but it should be clear that

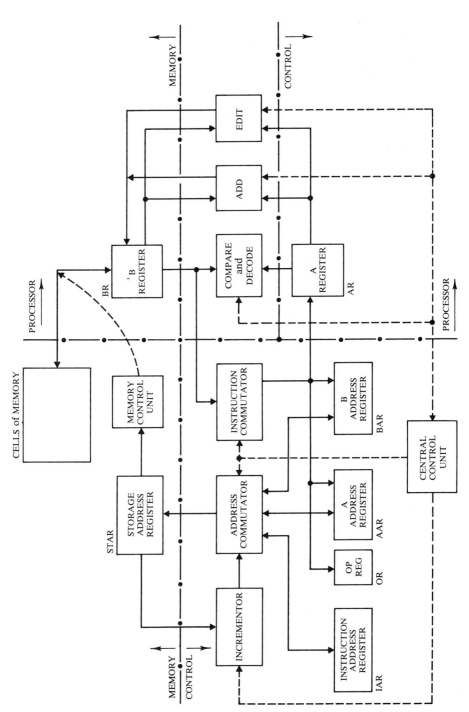

Fig. 7.2.1 Functional units of the IBM 1401 (except IO).

161

REGISTERS and other equipment are *shared* among the SUBSYSTEMS. Sharing makes for improved efficiency of REGISTER use and hence lowers the total cost of the computer. This does slow down the computer, since simultaneous activities do not occur.

Memory The MEMORY SUBSYSTEM contains two important REGISTERS: the STORAGE ADDRESS REGISTER, STAR, and the B REGISTER, BR. The former holds the address of an operand being accessed and corresponds to our MEMORY ADDRESS REGISTER. The B REGISTER holds the datum during *recall* and *memorization* and corresponds to our MEMORY DATA REGISTER. Notice that, contrary to classical design, the DATA REGISTER is much smaller than the ADDRESS REGISTER. This fits in with the previous description: Each data word is exactly one character; three characters are required to specify each MEMORY address.

Processor The PROCESSOR consists of two registers, BR and AR, which store the operands being manipulated. All operations are performed on a character at a time; hence, the AR and BR store one character each.

The PROCESSOR consists of a single digit ADDER, a COMPARISON UNIT, and EDIT LOGIC.

CONTROL Three addresses are of importance to the activity of this computer:
- the instruction address
- the addresses of each of the two operands

These three REGISTERS are called, respectively, the INSTRUCTION ADDRESS REGISTER, IAR, the A ADDRESS REGISTER, AAR, and the B ADDRESS REGISTER, BAR.

The OPERATION REGISTER, OR, holds the code for the operation to be performed. A definition character, when required for some commands, is placed in the A REGISTER, AR. MEMORY can be addressed from any of the three ADDRESS REGISTERS, IAR, AAR, or BAR. To create a path between one of these REGISTERS and the STAR, an ADDRESS COMMUTATOR is used. After use, the address is generally incremented or decremented. This operation could be done at the respective ADDRESS REGISTER or at the STAR. Hardware is saved by passing the address from the STAR through an INCREMENTOR under the direction of CONTROL on its way to the ADDRESS COMMUTATOR.

An INSTRUCTION COMMUTATOR during *fetch* distributes characters which comprise the instruction. The DECODE takes part in this operation in detecting the word mark.

Input and output   The logic for controlling input and output operations is not displayed in Fig. 7.2.1; its description is postponed to Section 7.8.

7.3 FETCH

Variable length   A command is placed in MEMORY starting at a
commands   lower numbered CELL and proceeding to a higher numbered CELL. It lies between two word marks: it includes the lower WM character but not the upper WM character. The number of characters in a command varies from one to eight as described below. *Fetch* obtains characters from MEMORY starting at the command address in IAR and continuing until a character with the word mark is found. This is discarded. (It remains in MM.) The desired command is then found in the IR.

A command can consist of 1, 2, 4, 7, or 8 characters. An example of each is given below. First the Autocoder mnemonic is given, followed by the machine language character underlined in parentheses. The underline is the written representation of character with 1 in its word mark.

$$W \quad (\underline{2}) \qquad\qquad\qquad (7.3.1)$$

This is a request to print from the output area, a fixed MEMORY region, onto the HIGH SPEED PRINTER. Only one command character is required since addressing is implicit; the area in MEMORY addressed and the DEVICE desired are both implied.

$$SS \quad (\underline{K}) \quad d \qquad\qquad\qquad (7.3.2)$$

This request selects one hopper of CARD READER. $\underline{K}$ conveys the command; the second character, $\underline{d}$, designates the hopper.

$$B \quad (\underline{B}) \quad AAA \qquad\qquad\qquad (7.3.3)$$

This unconditional jump includes an address of three characters specifying the destination.

$$A \quad (\underline{A}) \quad AAA \quad BBB \qquad\qquad\qquad (7.3.4)$$

This command adds the operand specified by AAA to the operand specified by the BBB and places the result at BBB. One set of three characters is required for each of the two address fields.

$$BCE \quad (\underline{B}) \quad AAA \quad BBB \quad d \qquad\qquad (7.3.5)$$

The *branch character equal* is a jump to the address AAA if the character at BBB is the same as that specified by d.

PRINT

SELECT

BRANCH

ADD

BCE

The INSTRUCTION REGISTER, IR, in Fig. 7.3.1 can contain the maximum of eight characters required for the largest command. It consists of four SUBREGISTERS:

OR, the OPERATION REGISTER, contains one character for the command.

AAR, the A ADDRESS REGISTER, holds three characters.

BAR, the B ADDRESS REGISTER, holds three characters.

AR stores the d-character.

Fetch cycle *Fetch* in Fig. 7.3.1 shows only those parts of the computer which participate. It can consist of one to eight phases, all identical. A typical phase is described. The circled numbers in the figure indicate the ordinal number of a step of this typical phase.

1. The contents of the INSTRUCTION ADDRESS REGISTER, (IAR), are passed over to the STAR through the ADDRESS COMMUTATOR.

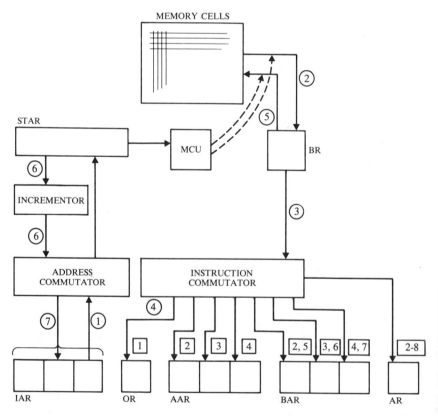

Fig. 7.3.1 *Fetch* cycle for the IBM 1401.

2. MEMORY obtains the character (stored at the address in the STAR) and places it in the BR.
3. It is passed over to the INSTRUCTION COMMUTATOR.
4. The INSTRUCTION COMMUTATOR routes it to the proper position in the IR.
5. The character in the BR is restored to MEMORY.
6. The address in the STAR is passed to the INCREMENTOR where 1 is added to it.
7. This address is returned to the IAR.

The numbers contained in the squares in Fig. 7.3.1 indicate where a character is routed during a phase corresponding to that number in the *fetch* cycle.

It is emphasized that one more phase takes place than there are characters in an instruction. Therefore, a *fetch* cycle can consist of 2, 3, 5, 8, or 9 phases. When the DETECT examining the BR notes a word mark, this is the last cycle. The *word mark* is in the first character of the command which *follows* the one scheduled for execution. That character is discarded. This initiates *execution* of *this* command.

Example   Figure 7.3.2 gives an example of *fetch* for an eight-character instruction. Shorter instructions are terminated earlier, as should be evident after examination of this cycle.

The example is a *fetch* of the instruction B567123Q, residing at 345. This is a request to jump to location 567 *if* the character at location 123 is "Q."

The first column of the figure indicates the ordinal number of the phase being performed. Succeeding columns indicate the contents of REGISTERS

Memory

Location	345	346	347	348	349	350	351	352	353
Contents	B	5	6	7	1	2	3	Q	S

Phase	STAR	IAR	OR	BR	AR	AAR	BAR
Previous	XXX	3 4 5	X	X	X	XXX	XXX
First	3 4 5	3 4 6	B	B	X	XXX	XXX
Second	3 4 6	3 4 7	B	5	5	5 b b	5 b b
Third	3 4 7	3 4 8	B	6	6	5 6 b	5 6 b
Fourth	3 4 8	3 4 9	B	7	7	5 6 7	5 6 7
Fifth	3 4 9	3 5 0	B	1	1	5 6 7	1 b b
Sixth	3 5 0	3 5 1	B	2	2	5 6 7	1 2 b
Seventh	3 5 1	3 5 2	B	3	3	5 6 7	1 2 3
Eighth	3 5 2	3 5 3	B	Q	Q	5 6 7	1 2 3
Ninth	3 5 3	3 5 3	B	S	Q	5 6 7	1 2 3

Fig. 7.3.2 *Fetch* of the command B567123Q stored at 345.

which participate in the *fetch*. These are listed *after* the phase specified in the first column has terminated.

The previous instruction *fetch* was terminated because B̲ was brought into the B REGISTER and a word mark detected. The IAR contains 345 after the last *execution* cycle of the previous command. The contents of other REGISTERS are unknown.

On the first *fetch* cycle we get the opcode, B̲, from 345 in MEMORY and install it in the OR. The address 345 is returned from the STAR through the INCREMENTOR to place 346 in the IAR.

On the second cycle, 5, which is the next character in the command, is distributed to four different places: BR, AR, the first character of AAR, and the first character of BAR. The other positions in AAR and BAR are cleared by setting in blanks (b).

At the end of the fourth cycle, AAR and BAR both contain the A address, 567. We next get characters for the BAR, which occupies us for phases 5, 6, and 7. On the eighth cycle, the character, Q, is brought and deposited in the AR. Finally, the ninth cycle brings S̲ to the BR. The word mark is detected and *fetch* terminated.

Large addresses   The IBM 1401 can have MEMORIES which range in size from 1,200 words to 16,000. The addressing scheme for the machine was discussed earlier. These addresses are stored as three characters. Hence, the AAR and BAR are both three characters long, each character consisting of seven bits. Since the display for the operator converts this information into straight decimal form, some manuals portray these REGISTERS as four or five position REGISTERS. The extra addressing information is transmitted between the IAR, AAR and BAR, and STAR. The "thousands" information is decoded in the STAR.

7.4   REFLEXIVE COMMANDS

We examine reflexive commands first, because they are the simplest and they illustrate the use of the ADDRESS COMMUTATOR. These commands include *jumps*, *halts*, and *noop*.

Unconditional   This is a four character command, BAAA.
jump   From Fig. 7.4.1 we see that as the *fetch* cycle ends, the command is contained in the OPERATION REGISTER and the address in the AAR. All that is necessary to execute this command is to request that the ADDRESS COMMUTATOR access the AAR instead of the IAR for the next

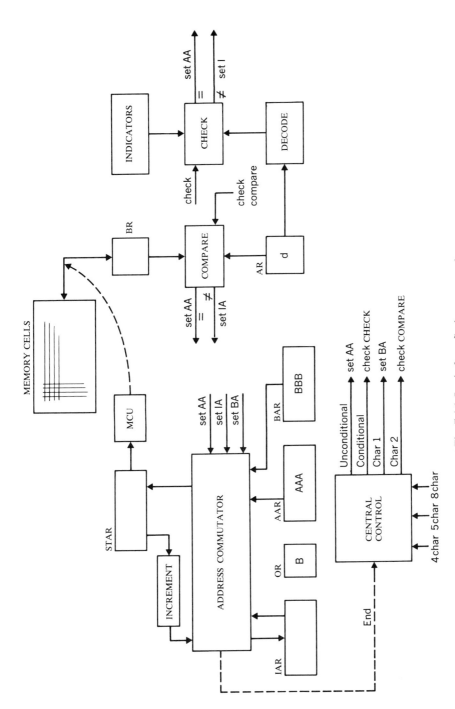

Fig. 7.4.1 Logic for reflexive commands.

167

fetch. This is done by CONTROL by activating the set line. CONTROL recognized the *jump*; it has kept count of the number of characters obtained during the *fetch.* This *jump* is distinguished from others by containing exactly four characters.

Conditional jumps   This five character command is B̄AAAd. It requests a *jump* if the condition conveyed by d has been set previously. If the condition is not met, the next sequential instruction is fetched.

The setting of d determines the INDICATOR examined. A list of d character interpretations is in Table 7.4.1. Each condition is stored as a FLIPFLOP setting, switch setting, or other bistable DEVICE setting.

Table 7.4.1 MEANING OF d̲ CHARACTER FOR B̲ COMMANDS

Autocoder Mnemonic	d̲ Character	Branch On
B		Unconditional
BC9	9	Carriage channel #9
BCV	@	Carriage channel #12
BLC	A	"Last card" switch (sense switch A)
BSS‡	B	Sense switch B*
BSS‡	C	Sense switch C*
BSS‡	D	Sense switch D*
BSS‡	E	Sense switch E*
BSS‡	F	Sense switch F*
BSS‡	G	Sense switch G*
BEF	K	End of reel*†
BER	L	Tape transmission error*
BIN‡	N	Access inoperable*
BIN‡	?	Reader error if IO check stop switch is off†
BIN‡	!	Punch error if IO check stop switch is off†
BPB	P	Printer busy (print storage feature)*
BIN‡	≠	Printer error if IO check stop switch is off†
BU	/	Unequal compare (B ≠ A)
BIN‡	*	Inquiry clear*
BIN‡	Q	Inquiry request*
BPCB	R	Printer carriage busy (print storage feature)*
BE	S	Equal compare (B = A)*
BL	T	Low compare (B < A)*
BH	U	High compare (B > A)*
BIN‡	V	Read-write parity check or read-back check error*
BIN‡	W	Wrong-length record*
BIN‡	X	Unequal-address compare*
BIN‡	Y	Any disk-unit error condition*
BAV	Z	Overflow†
BIN‡	%	Processing check with process check switch off†

* Special feature.
† d-modifier character must be coded in the operand portion of the instruction.
‡ Conditions tested are reset by a *branch if indicator on* instruction.

At the beginning of *execution* $\underline{B}$ is in OR; the jump address AAA is in AAR, and the d character is in the AR. CONTROL recognizes a five character command. The d character is interpreted by DECODE. CHECK is a unit which takes information from DECODE and from the INDICATOR and determines whether the condition described has been met. If so, CHECK issues set aa signal; otherwise, CHECK transmits set ia. This causes the next command address to be drawn from the AAR or IAR, respectively.

Character jump   This eight character command requests a *jump* to address AAA if the character stored at BBB is the same as the d character. CONTROL is aware that this is an eight character jump from the *fetch* count. The first task, to get the addressed character from MEMORY, is directed by sending set ba to the ADDRESS COMMUTATOR. This causes the contents of the BAR to be sent to the STAR. The character is brought to BR from MEMORY.

The COMPARE is now attached to examine the AR and the BR. The result of this comparison sets the ADDRESS COMMUTATOR for the next *fetch:* equal produces set aa; unequal produces set ia.

Word mark jump   This command, similar to the character jump, is an eight character command, ∨AAABBBd. It checks the character at address BBB for word mark and zone and jumps to AAA only if the combination of conditions specified is met. These combinations are listed in Table 7.4.2. The command is executed similarly to the $\underline{B}$ command.

Table 7.4.2 MEANING OF $\underline{d}$ CHARACTER FOR $\underline{V}$ COMMANDS

$\underline{d}$ Character	Condition
1	Word mark
2	No zone (No-A, No-B-bit)
B	12-zone (AB-bits)
K	11-zone (B, No-A-bit)
S	Zero-zone (A, No-B-bit)
3	Either a word mark, or no zone
C	Either a word mark, or 12-zone
L	Either a word mark, or 11-zone
T	Either a word mark, or zero-zone

CONTROL knows that a *word mark jump* (not a *character jump*) is performed. Hence, the contents of BR only are checked to form set aa or set ia; (AR) is disregarded.

Others   NOOP, <u>N</u>, does nothing. It starts another
                               fetch.

HALT, <u>.</u>, causes the machine to stop. If an address follows the
command character so that we have .AAA, then the next command to be
executed after the restart button is pressed is obtained from AAA.

7.5   COMPARE, MOVE

Compare   This is the simplest double data movement
                               command:

$$C \ (\underline{C}) \quad AAA \quad BBB \qquad\qquad (7.5.1)$$

The field stored at AAA is compared with the field at BBB. The result
of comparison is stored in INDICATORS. Thus, the INDICATORS will store
whether the first quantity is *greater than, equal to, less than,* or *unequal to*
the second quantity. The INDICATORS can be interrogated with the *jump
command*, <u>B</u>.

CONTROL places an A character in the AR and then a B character in the
BR. The two are compared and, if equal, we continue without setting any
INDICATORS (the *equal* INDICATOR was set initially). When the two characters
are unequal, we set the INDICATORS according to the direction of the
inequality.

The circled numbers in Fig. 7.5.1 show the steps that take place in a
cycle of the *compare* operation. These are described in similarly numbered
steps below.

1. The A address is sent from AAR to the ADDRESS COMMUTATOR.
2. It is passed over to the STAR.
3. The A character goes to BR.
4. It is passed over to the INSTRUCTION COMMUTATOR.
5. It is placed in AR.
6. It is also returned to MEMORY at the address now held by the STAR.
7. This address is passed over to the INCREMENTOR, where 1 is subtracted from it.
8. It leaves there through the ADDRESS COMMUTATOR.
9. The address returns to AAR.
10. The B address is passed to the ADDRESS COMMUTATOR.
11. Then it is passed to the STAR.
12. The B character goes to BR.
13. The COMPARE sets COMPARE INDICATOR if this is required.
14. The B character is returned to MEMORY.

EACH CYCLE

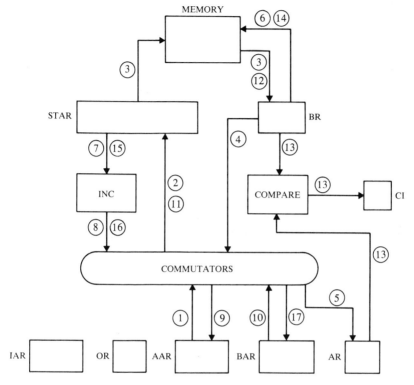

Fig. 7.5.1 Action of the IBM 1401 for COMPARE.

15. Its address is passed to the INCREMENTOR, where 1 is subtracted from it.
16. It goes to the ADDRESS COMMUTATOR.
17. The B address is returned to the BAR.

COMPARE is terminated where a word mark is detected in either the A or B character. This is signaled to CONTROL (13), and no more characters are brought thereafter.

Move   The move command is:

$$MLC \ (\underline{M}) \ \ AAA \ \ BBB \qquad (7.5.2)$$

It reproduces information from A field into the B field. The operation is halted by the first word mark encountered in either field. One cycle is performed for each character to be transferred. The details of a single cycle are presented in Fig. 7.5.1 by numbers enclosed in squares alongside the arrows indicating the flow of information. The steps of a typical cycle are presented below with numbers corresponding to those enclosed in squares.

1–9. The A character is brought from MEMORY and placed into AR. The address of the next character address is made in STAR by subtracting 1—this is placed in the AAR.

10–12. The B address from the BAR is placed in the STAR. The B character is placed in BR.

13. The seven lowest bits of the A character are taken from the AR and placed in BR. We now check to see if either AR or BR contains a word mark. If so, a signal is returned to CONTROL to end *execution*.

14–17. The new character for the B field is now in the BR. It is returned to MEMORY at the B address now in the STAR. B address is altered when it is passed through the INCREMENTOR. It is returned to the BAR through the ADDRESS COMMUTATOR.

Other moves   A number of other move commands are provided for the user. These include the following.

MCS (Z)	move and zero suppress	(7.5.3)
MLNS (D)	move numerics	(7.5.4)
MLZS (Y)	move zeros	(7.5.5)
MLCWA (L)	load characters to WM in A	(7.5.6)
SW (,); CW (□)	set or clear WM	(7.5.7)

Only (7.5.3) requires special activity, called a *rescan*, to do zero suppression. A similar operation is described in connection with EDIT in Section 7.7.

7.6   ARITHMETIC

Two commands do addition and subtraction:

$$A \quad (A) \quad AAA \quad BBB \qquad (7.6.1)$$

$$S \quad (S) \quad AAA \quad BBB \qquad (7.6.2)$$

They add (or subtract) the contents of the A field to (from) those of the B field, placing the result at BBB. The operation is terminated when a

word mark is encountered in the B field. This suggests that the B field is
equal to or longer than the A field. If the two fields are unequal in length
and the B field should be longer, then the process continues, using zeros
instead of referring to the A field after a word mark is encountered in the
A field. If there is no A field word mark, or if that field is larger than the B
field, the B field word mark ends the operation.

Operand   The sign of an operand is in the zone of the
least significant digit. Numbers are positive except when AB=01 for the
LSD. The zone in the intermediate characters is stripped during addition
and subtraction. The zone bits of the *most* significant digit are set when
overflows occur. For a single overflow, AB=01; for a double overflow,
AB=10; for a triple overflow, AB=11. If a fourth overflow should occur,
the zone bits are restored to 00. Therefore, it is encumbent upon the
programmer to check these bits in case overflows occur.

Arithmetic   The very first thing to be done is to determine
what arithmetic is *done*. Signed addition or subtraction was requested.
Whether addition or subtraction is actually done is determined from a
hardware-contained table such as Table 7.6.1. At the same time, we find
the sign of the result, assuming that no recomplementation is required.

Table 7.6.1 TYPES OF ADD CYCLES AND SIGN OF RESULT FOR ADD AND SUBTRACT
OPERATIONS

Type of Operation	A Field Sign	B Field Sign	Type of Add Cycle	Sign of Result
A D D +	+	+	True	+
		−	Complement	Sign of field with larger magnitude
	−	+	Complement	
		−	True	−
S U B T R A C T −	+	−	True	−
		+	Complement	Sign of field with larger magnitude
	−	−	Complement	
		+	True	+

Next we set about to do the process. Finally, when subtraction is done, it may be necessary to recomplement the result and change its sign.

A discussion using flow charts suffices to explain the general principles of the operation.

Sign cycle   The cycle required to determine the sign of the result is shown in the flow chart in Fig. 7.6.1. This is a nonmove cycle: an A and a B character are obtained from MEMORY, but neither the A nor B address is altered as it is returned from the STAR to the AAR or BAR, respectively. The least significant character of both augend and the addend contains the sign of the number in that field. This cycle uses *only* the sign to determine which process is performed as in Table 7.6.1.

Should *complement add* be performed, the sign returned to the B field is in standard form: $+ = 01$, $- = 11$. Since B$=1$ in both cases, it is a FLAG during recomplementation.

Add cycle   To add, an A character is placed in the AR, the B character in the BR, and the two added together using the ADDER. The A character is obtained using the simple A cycle presented in Fig. 7.6.2. The A character address is obtained from the AAR for the STAR. The contents of the STAR are decremented before being returned to the AAR. At the end of a simple A cycle, AAR points to the next digit (to the left) for addition.

B cycle   A B cycle for both *true* and *complement add* is presented in Fig. 7.6.3. The A character is in AR. We now bring the B character to the BR. If this is the first cycle of addition (i.e., the rightmost pair of digits are being added), check to see if this is *true* or *complement* addition. *Complement* addition requires not only the complementation of the A character but an extra precarry.

For other cycles we enter an additional 1 for previously recorded carry whether *true* and *complement* addition is performed. Where a carry was previously recorded, it is cleared after addition. Then the sum digit is returned to the BR from the ADDER, and thence to MEMORY.

The ADDER remains energized, producing a carry for *this* digit if one is called for until the carry can be recorded on a CARRY-IN FLIPFLOP after it has been cleared of the previous carry in.

Now the new B address is obtained by decrementing the contents of the STAR as they are returned to the BAR.

We look for a word mark in the B character which is still in the B REGISTER. Should there be one, we determine the overflow condition. For *true add*, we record this in the B zone bits. Where no carry has occurred

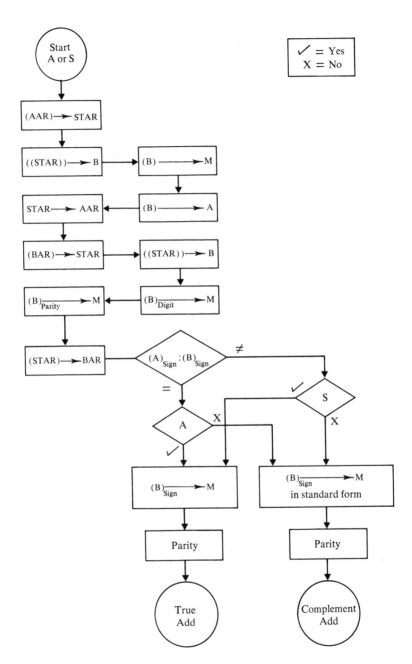

Fig. 7.6.1 Initial nonmove cycle.

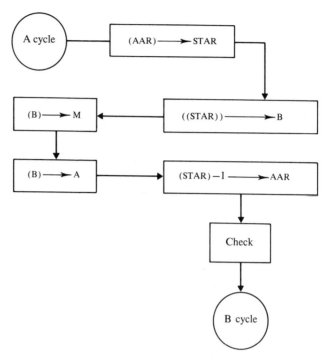

Fig. 7.6.2 A simple A cycle.

for the word mark character during complement addition, a *recomplement* cycle is requested.

When a B character does not have a word mark, do further addition cycles. It is possible that the A character may have contained a word mark. If a word mark was encountered presently or previously in the A character, A cycles are suppressed. Zero is placed in the AR immediately and before each new B cycle thereafter.

Recomplement   The *recomplement* cycle is sketchily presented in Fig. 7.6.4. To recomplement the result, we reset the BAR to the address of the least significant digit by bringing successive B characters from left to right to the B REGISTER for examination. We look for a 1 in the B bit of the zone of the character. Recall that the sign of the character was placed in *standard form*. If there is a zero in the B bit, we continue the search. Since we examine characters from left to right, we *add* 1 to the B address as it goes from STAR to BAR.

When we find the least significant digit, we change to a forward scan, complementing characters as we do: We pass the character from BR to AR; we clear the BR; we perform a complement addition. The resulting

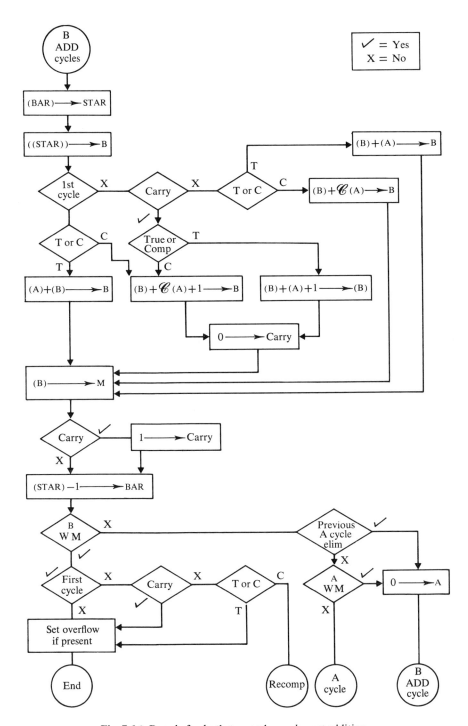

Fig. 7.6.3 B cycle for both *true* and *complement* addition.

177

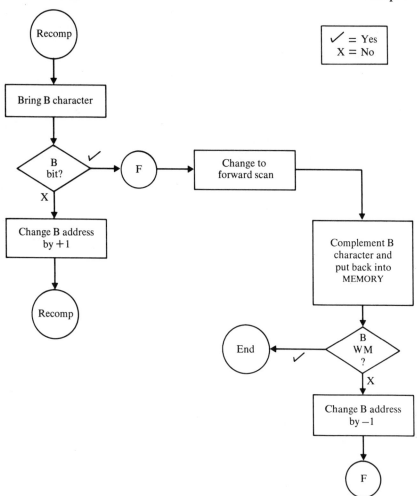

Fig. 7.6.4 *Recomplement* cycles.

character in BR is returned to MEMORY. We continue thus with forward complementing scans: We get characters from right to left, recomplement them, and return them to storage. When the character obtained contains a word mark, the *recomplement* cycle is over and so is addition.

7.7 EDIT

Command   The *edit* command is

$$\text{MCE} \quad (\underline{\text{E}}) \quad \text{AAA} \quad \text{BBB} \qquad (7.7.1)$$

It moves information from AAA to BBB, carrying out editing as requested in the mask contained at BBB. The data to be edited are at AAA. Instructions on how to edit them are at BBB.

The B field contains characters which describe what is to happen as information is moved there. Some characters in the B field give directions to CONTROL. Others replace characters in the first field. Still others direct alteration of characters as they pass from the A to the B field.

Example   First examine the example presented in Fig. 7.7.1. It contains representations of MEMORY before and after *edit*. The least significant digit in the destination field is at 300; the most significant character in the destination field is at 284 and is $. The source field begins with character 789 and continues to 782 which contains a word mark. E is at location 901. The command extends to location 907. It requests that information from 789 be edited and placed at location 300.

Edit tasks are determined by characters in the destination field.

This example demonstrates the use of mask symbols. The two right-hand asterisks are copied as is. The ampersand is replaced by a blank. The credit symbol is kept only if the source datum is negative; otherwise, it is to be replaced by a blank. The ampersand at 295 is replaced by a blank.

The blanks (indicated as "b") are replaced by data characters. Thus the blanks at 293 and 294 are replaced respectively by 2 and 6. Proceeding to the left, the period and dollar sign are kept. Zeros and blanks in the destination field are replaced by corresponding digits in the source field.

The zero in the destination field at 291 requests suppression of zeros to the left of the most significant digit should it appear at or to the left of the mask zero. This requires a rescan of the field. The result of the editing, you notice, has replaced the two left-hand zeros by blanks as requested by the zero suppression symbol.

Mask symbols   Table 7.7.1 shows which characters are used in the mask to control the editing. The decimal point, asterisk, and dollar sign are retained in the destination field regardless of the contents of the source field. The credit and minus sign are retained if the source field is negative; they are replaced by blanks otherwise. The blank is always replaced by a source character unless preceded on the right by 0 for zero suppression. Zero is replaced by the source character or a blank, according to the zero suppression function described later. The comma is kept except when the zero on its left has been suppressed.

Operation   *Edit*, although complicated in function, is simple to implement. Processing for our example is explained in tabular form in Fig. 7.7.2.

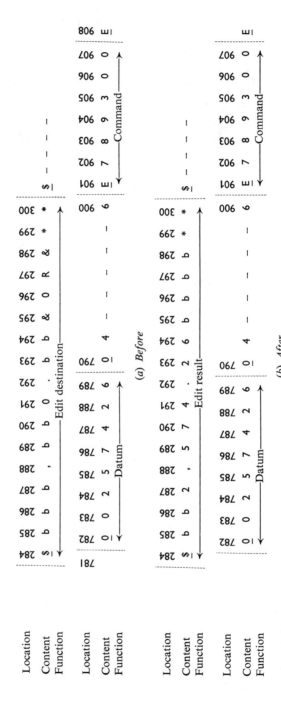

Fig. 7.7.1 The contents of MEMORY (a) before and (b) after the execution of an edit command, E at 901.

Table 7.7.1 CONTROL CHARACTERS FOR EDITING

Character	Name	Purpose
b	blank	A field character replaces B field blank.
0	zero	Indicates the rightmost beginning of zero suppression. All nonsignificant zeros at or to the left of this position are suppressed.
.	decimal point	Retained in B field.
,	comma	Retained in B field. Removed during zero suppression if it is at left of most significant nonzero digit.
CR	credit	Retained for negative datum; removed for positive datum.
—	minus	As for CR
&	ampersand	Replaced by blank, b.
*	asterisk	Retained.
$	dollar	Retained.

Edit starts by placing the first A character in the AR. Then the first B character is placed in the BR; it controls what is returned to storage next:

1. If the character in the BR is a comma, period, dollar sign, or asterisk, it is returned to the B address.
2. If the BR contains a credit symbol or minus sign, the contents of the A REGISTER are checked for sign. If negative, the symbol in the BR is returned to MEMORY; otherwise a blank is returned.
3. If the BR contains a blank, the contents of the AR are placed in the BR which is then *memorized*. A word mark in AR is removed.
4. If the BR contains zero, the contents of the AR are placed in the BR and memorized; a *word mark* is added to facilitate *rescan*. This is then *memorized*.

These four rules suffice to provide the complete editing facility. Notice that some cycles obtain and store a B character and do not refer to the AR. Other cycles store the A character and hence require a pair of character acquisitions to fill both the AR and BR for the next character to be placed in the destination field.

Zero suppression requires *rescan*, as illustrated in Fig. 7.7.2; it is not done otherwise. Characters from the B field are placed in the BR and examined. When zeros are encountered, they are replaced by blanks *until* a nonzero character is encountered. Thereafter, characters are transcribed as encountered. *Rescan* continues until the word mark character is encountered. The word mark is *removed* and the character returned. We rescan *up to* the word mark and remove it, stopping editing at this point. A word mark present in the destination field might interfere with printout.

RESCAN

Line	Cycle	AAR	BAR	B	A	Store	B Field
0	*Start*	789	300	X	0	X	$bbb,bb0.bb&CR&**$
1	A	788	300	6	6	6	$bbb,bb0.bb&CR&**$
2	B	788	299	*	6	*	$bbb,bb0.bb&CR&**$
3	B	788	298	*	6	*	$bbb,bb0.bb&CR&**$
4	B	788	297	&	6	b	$bbb,bb0.bb&CR b**$
5	B	788	296	R	6	b	$bbb,bb0.bb&Cb b**$
6	B	788	295	C	6	b	$bbb,bb0.bb&b b b**$
7	B	788	294	&	6	b	$bbb,bb0.bb b b b b**$
8	B	788	293	b	6	6	$bbb,bb0.b6 b b b b**$
9	A	787	293	2	2	2	$bbb,bb0.b6 b b b b**$
10	B	787	292	b	2	2	$bbb,bb0.26 b b b b**$
11	A	786	292	4	4	4	$bbb,bb0.26 b b b b**$
12	B	786	291	.	4	.	$bbb,bb0.26 b b b b**$
13	B	785	290	0	4	4	$bbb,bb4.26 b b b b**$
14	A	784	290	7	7	7	$bbb,bb4.26 b b b b**$
15	B	785	289	b	7	7	$bbb,b74.26 b b b b**$
16	A	784	289	5	5	5	$bbb,b74.26 b b b b**$
17	B	784	288	b	5	5	$bbb,574.26 b b b b**$
18	A	783	288	2	2	2	$bbb,574.26 b b b b**$
19	B	783	287	,	2	,	$bbb,574.26 b b b b**$
20	B	783	286	b	2	2	$bb2,574.26 b b b b**$
21	A	782	286	0	0	0	$bb2,574.26 b b b b**$
22	B	782	285	b	0	0	$b02,574.26 b b b b**$
23	A	781	285	0	0	0	$b02,574.26 b b b b**$
24	B	781	284	b	0	0	$002,574.26 b b b b**$
25	B	781	284	$	0	$	$002,574.26 b b b b**$
26	B	781	285	$	0	$	$002,574.26 b b b b**$
27	B	781	286	0	0	b	$b02,574.26 b b b b**$
28	B	781	287	0	0	b	$bb2,574.26 b b b b**$
29	B	781	288	2	0	2	$bb2,574.26 b b b b**$
30	B	781	289	,	0	,	$bb2,574.26 b b b b**$
31	B	781	290	5	0	5	$bb2,574.26 b b b b**$
32	B	781	291	7	0	7	$bb2,574.26 b b b b**$
33	B	781	292	4	0	4	$bb2,574.26 b b b b**$

Fig. 7.7.2 Edit example.

7.8 IO

Concept   The IBM 1401 is priced low; there is no attempt to provide simultaneity between IO and processing. PROCESSOR and CONTROL are dedicated to IO when it occurs. IO operations have access to the computer REGISTERS and MEMORY. There is a small portion of the IO cycle which leaves the PROCESSOR and MEMORY free so that some processing can proceed even during a dense sequence of IO commands.

All (nonoptional) IO requires **corner turning**: operations upon a set of characters are performed on a portion of each character, and the effect is recorded. This is repeated many times for the entire set. The details become clear later as corner turning is discussed with respect to the three important IO processes.

Fixed areas in MEMORY are assigned to each IO DEVICE: CARD READER, CARD PUNCH and PRINTER. Each character in each of these areas must be reviewed a number of times before successful IO transfer is achieved. These multiple accesses of MEMORY require much time and the complete dedication of the computer.

We now explore in some detail IO for the three important DEVICES.

Card reader   A card is read a row at a time as in Fig. 7.8.1. The ninth row enters the READ STATION first. The task of the computer is to enter into MEMORY a proper image of information stored on the card. Assume for the moment that only one hole exists in any given column.

The MEMORY area assigned to the CARD READER includes CELLS 0 through 80. The card image occupies CELLS 1 through 80. CELL 0 contains a code (the BCD value) corresponding to the row presently being scanned.

The first task of the LOGIC, when it detects that a row has been positioned, is to create the code for that row and place it in CELL 0. In Fig. 7.8.1, the code for row 9 which is being examined has been placed in CELL 0.

Next the HARDWARE scans each column at the READING STATION. The example shows a hole present in columns 9, 28, and 63.

A flow chart of the activity appears as in Fig. 7.8.2. Each of the eighty CELLS in MEMORY is accessed and brought out to the B REGISTER. As this is done, the number of the column is available in the STAR, and the input from the READ STATION is checked. If a hole is present, the code in CELL 0 (and also in the AR) is placed into the BR and stored in MEMORY. If no hole is

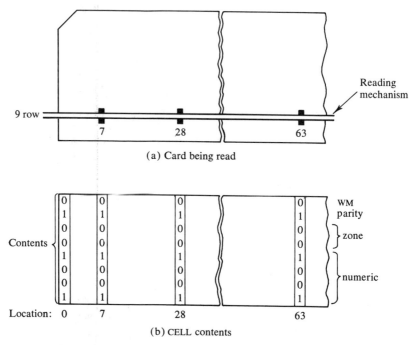

(a) Card being read

(b) CELL contents

Fig. 7.8.1 How a code is entered into corresponding CELLS of
MEMORY for each column of a card being read which
contains a 9 punch.

detected in a column, the B character is returned unaffected. The first time
this is done (row nine), either all 0's or a 9 code (10001001) is placed in a
CELL.

After the entire row is scanned, there is plenty of time for the card to
move so that the next row comes into position. The new code corresponding to that row is prepared and made available in the AR and CELL 0
for entry as each column is scanned.

During later row scans, it is possible to encounter a double punch. A
double punch is permissible only if *one* of the punches is in row 8. If this is
encountered, the two codes are combined by addition to record the double
punch. Should an illegal double punch occur, an error is recorded, and the
card image may be rejected.

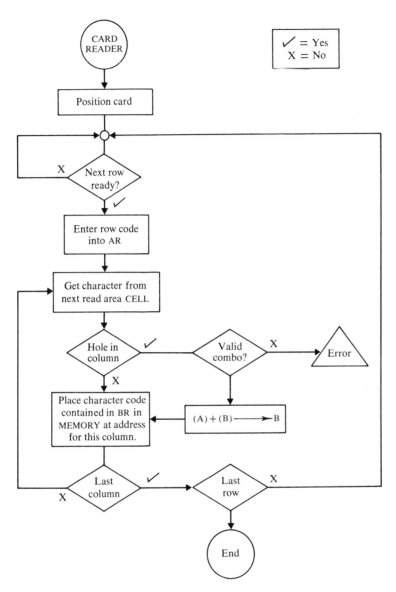

Fig. 7.8.2 Flowchart; CARD READER.

ZONE PUNCH

A punch in row 0 is converted to a 1 in the A bit; a punch in row 11 is a 1 in the B bit; a punch in row 12 produces a 1 for both the A and B bits. Only one zone punch is permitted; this is checked as the information is entered.

ZERO PUNCH

If no numerical punch has been recorded for a character, a 0 punch is converted into its numerical equivalent, 1010, with no zone code supplied. Conversely, if a numerical punch *has* been recorded, 1 is entered in the A bit.

TIMING

When the CARD READER is started, 21 milliseconds elapse during which no work is done *and* the PROCESSOR is locked out from computation. Reading and recording are performed in the next 44 milliseconds. If another card is to be read, a new command must be given within the next 10 milliseconds. These 10 milliseconds are free for computation.

PUNCH   PUNCH operation is the reverse of *read*. As before, the code of the row being scanned is set up in the CELL just preceding the punch MEMORY area. As a row comes beneath the punch magnets, the characters in the MEMORY area are scanned and compared to the code in the A REGISTER. If the two are equal, the PUNCH MAGNET is energized; if unequal, the PUNCH MAGNET is not energized. Equality is checked on numerics and zones separately. Again 0 is a special case. After the scan, *this* row POSITION MAGNETS are set up. The PUNCH MECHANISM is energized, and holes are punched in that row. This continues until all rows in the card are punched.

PRINTER   The IBM 1401 system uses a CHAIN PRINTER which is similar to the DRUM PRINTER, the operating details of which are described elsewhere.† In Fig. 7.8.3, we see a CHAIN containing a string of dissimilar characters which is presently positioned beneath the paper so that the "A" occupies the first print position. At that moment, we scan the CHAIN and the message to see if there are letters on the chain in the same position in which they belong in the message. When this is the case, a HAMMER in that position is struck so as to cause an imprint of the character to appear on the paper.

In the example, we are printing out a part number which has an "A" as the first character and "G" as the seventh character. The other characters in the first part of the CHAIN do not correspond to those in the

† Ivan Flores, *Computer Design*. Englewood Cliffs, N.J.: Prentice-Hall, Inc., 1967.

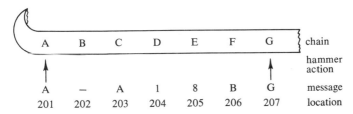

A	B	C	D	E	F	G	chain

| | | | | | | | hammer action |

| A | — | A | 1 | 8 | B | G | message |
| 201 | 202 | 203 | 204 | 205 | 206 | 207 | location |

Fig. 7.8.3 Correspondence between print chain and print message at one moment in time.

message. Hence, the message scan energizes HAMMERS at positions 1 and 7 corresponding to the A and G in the message.

At this point, we have examined each character of the message with respect to only *one* character in the alphabet. We wait until the CHAIN has positioned one character to the right, and then we perform another scan. This time "A" is sitting above the hyphen, "B" is above the 4, and so forth. We use as many scans of the entire message as there are characters in the vocabulary. Of course, the characters are put out on the CHAIN in a nonduplicating sequence.

The computer hardware coordinates with the PRINTER as illustrated in the flow chart in Fig. 7.8.4. The print message is located in a fixed area of MEMORY, positions 201 through 320. The *print* command synchronizes the operation of the PRINTER with the review of the message. A PRINTER signal tells when the CHAIN is aligned. Another PRINTER signal indicates the code for the character in the first position of the CHAIN.

Message review compares each character code in MEMORY with the print code for the character at the corresponding print position in the message. Since the positions along the CHAIN have different characters and, consequently, different codes, a new code is fabricated by CONTROL for each position. IBM examines every *third* character in the message, repeating this three times so that the entire message gets scanned. This detail should not confuse the issue. It is the complete scan which we refer to hereafter.

In the flow chart, after receiving the print character in the first position, we get a message character from MEMORY and compare the two codes. If the two are equal, we set up the HAMMER in *this* print position; otherwise, we check if this is the last character in the line. If not, we advance the MEMORY location. Scanning the line three times at every third character requires an incrementation of the message character address by 3 and a return to the beginning of the line when we reach the end. This consideration does not appear in the flow chart.

OPERATION

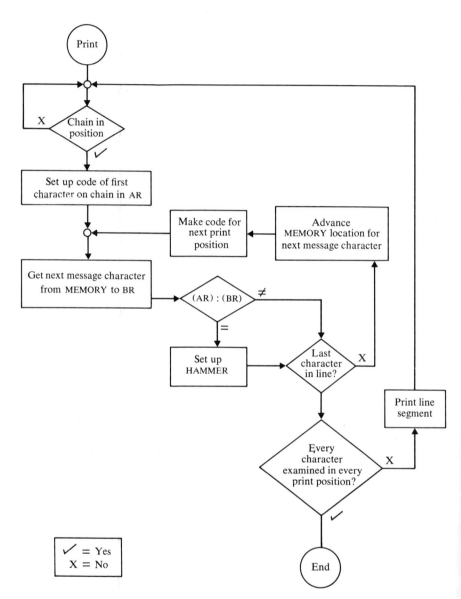

Fig. 7.8.4 Flowchart of print activity.

At the end of a scan, as we change the message character location, we also advance the print character code corresponding by augmenting the A REGISTER.

During comparison, the BR contains the message character and the AR contains the print position code. COMPARE determines if the two are equal and, if so, sends a message to energize the HAMMER position.

After a complete scan, we check to see if enough scans have been performed to print every character in every position. If not, we wait until the CHAIN has moved over one character position and then begin a new scan. There should be one complete scan for each character in the symbol alphabet of the PRINTER. However, a message scan can start with any character since the CHAIN position is transmitted to the computer at the beginning of the scan.

When all positions have been scanned through all characters, the print cycle is complete and the computer is released for other duties.

7.9   CHAINING

What is it?   The IBM 1401 programs frequently use two-address commands for *movement* and *arithmetic*. These commands require seven characters of storage for specification. More efficient use of MEMORY is made by chaining.

It is fortunate that the ADDRESS REGISTERS, AAR and BAR, hold the starting address of the *next* adjacent field *after* a command is executed. Three residual addresses are available to process fields which are adjacent in MEMORY. To do this, to **chain,** just the command mnemonic appears in the program. *Fetch* obtains only the command character—the next character has a WM. The new command in the OR uses the residual address in the AAR and BAR.

Example   In Fig. 7.9.1, we see a posting problem where activity information is to be entered onto a master record. For this payroll case, the gross weekly earnings, federal tax, and bond deductions are to be added to the year-to-date total in the master record for the employee for these same fields. Fields in the master record are larger than those in the activity record, for the totals they hold are similarly larger. This does not interfere with the chaining.

(a) Before

Location	901	902	903	904	905	906	907	908	909	910	911	912	913	914	915	916	917	918	919	920	921
Content	3	0̲	7	5	0	0	0̲	3	9	3	1	7	0̲	0	1	1	2	7	3	8	–
Function			YTD Bonds							YTD Tax							YTD Gross				

Location	566	567	568	569	570	571	572	573	574	575	576	577	578	579	580
Content	0̲	7	5	0	0̲	2	8	1	5	0̲	1	9	3	7	5
Function		Bond				Tax					Gross				

Location	350	351	352	353	354	355	356	357	358	359	360	361	362	363	364	365	366	367	368	369	370	371
Content	A̲	5	8	0	9	2	0	A̲	5	7	4	9	1	2	A̲	5	6	9	9	0	6	X̲
Function	Command							Command							Command							

(b) After

Location	902				906						912								920
Content	0̲	8	2	5	0̲	3	2	1	3	0̲	1	9	3	7	5	6	9	9	3

Location	569					574					580
Content	0̲	7	5	0	0̲	2	8	1	5	0̲	5

Location	350																					371
Content	A̲	5	8	0	9	2	0	A̲	5	7	4	9	1	2	A̲	5	6	9	9	0	6	X̲

Fig. 7.9.1 Three commands amenable to chaining with *before* and *after* for the computer MEMORY with respect to their execution.

COMMANDS

To do the posting without chaining, three commands are given as shown at the bottom of Fig. 7.9.1. Each command specifies an A field and a B field which, respectively, contain the active and the master record information location. After each command is performed, the B field contains the updated total; the A field still contains the activity quantity.

Chaining   Figure 7.9.2 shows the contents of various
requirements   REGISTERS after execution of the three posting
commands. It is apparent that the residual addresses from one command correspond to the actual addresses specified in the next command in the sequence of commands. The command sequence at the bottom of Fig.

Location	Command			Before			After		
				OR	A A R	B A R	OR	AAR	BAR
350	A	580	920	X	XXX	XXX	A	574	912
357	A	574	912	A	5 7 4	9 1 2	A	569	906
364	A	569	1919	A	5 6 7	9 0 6	A	565	899
371	X								

(a) without chaining

Location	Command		
350	A	580	920
357	A		
358	A		
359	X		

(b) with chaining

Location	350			357	358	359
Contents	A	580	920	A	A	X

(c) in MEMORY

Fig. 7.9.2 Chaining commands to do the job of Fig. 7.9.1.

7.9.2 chains these commands. When the A at location 350 is completed, the next *fetch* brings in A from location 357 to the OR. The next character obtained in the *fetch* comes from location 358 and is also A. When this character enters the BR, the word mark is detected, indicating it is part of the *next* command. (That new command consists of only the one character.) Therefore, at the end of this *fetch*, the IAR contains 359, the OR contains 357, and the residual addresses remain in the AAR and BAR.

Chaining occurs for the next *add* command at 358. The word mark in the fourth command, A, at 359 tells the fetch hardware that the residual information is properly oriented.

Although the foregoing sequence uses three add commands, any chainable commands may be chained.

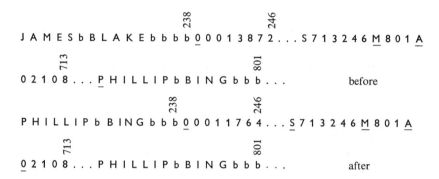

Fig. 7.9.3 An example of single-address chaining.

To process information *into* two adjacent fields from two nonadjacent fields, single-address chaining can be used, as illustrated in Fig. 7.9.3. As before, residual addresses are in the AAR and BAR. We want the residual destination address in the BAR but need a new source address for the AAR.

Using the example, after executing the subtract S713246, we find,

$$(\text{OR})=\text{S}; \qquad (\text{AAR})=708; \qquad (\text{BAR})=238 \qquad (7.9.1)$$

CONTROL reads in the next command, M801, and is halted by the WM in A. M is read into the OR and 801 is read into the AAR but *not into the* BAR. Hence we have,

$$(\text{OR})=\text{M}; \qquad (\text{AAR})=801; \qquad (\text{BAR})=238 \qquad (7.9.2)$$

which is equivalent to having given the command M801238.

PROBLEMS

7.1 What is the similarity between the 1401 and EAM equipment concerning (a) data; (b) commands?

7.2 Why is there no provision for indicating word marks on data entering the 1401 via punchcards?

7.3 How do WMs get into data?

7.4 When a program is brought in via punchcards, the segment in the *read* area contains no word marks. How can control be given to it?

7.5 Explain the scheme by which 16K of memory can be addressed with three characters.

7.6 What is a variable size command? Why is it used? Is this an advantage?

7.7 How does a *fetch* cycle distinguish variable length commands?

7.8 Why is a datum read from right to left?

7.9 Why is a command read from left to right? Is there any other alternative? Describe how you might design a CONTROL for a right-to-left command scan. How would this affect programming? What could the assembly do about it? Would other problems arise for the programmer (patching?) that you might foresee?

7.10 How is it possible for commands with the same opcode to have different lengths? Give examples. How are they used? How does CONTROL distinguish them?

7.11 Explain why there is only one conditioned *branch*.

7.12 How is the result of a COMPARE recorded? Used?

7.13 How is a *move* done? Why are there several kinds of *moves*?

7.14 How many memory accesses are required to move seven characters, including those for acquiring the command (without chaining)?

7.15 How does CONTROL affect the accessing of upper MEMORY?

7.16 How is arithmetic requested? Recorded? What about overflow? Sign?

7.17 How is *actual arithmetic* determined?

7.18 Why is recomplementation needed? Explain how its need is determined. How is it done (explain cycles)?

7.19 Why is the *edit* command so complicated? Explain the use of each control character. Why is & needed if a *blank* is called for?

7.20 Why are several *scans* required for *edit*? Explain each.

7.21 What is corner turning? How is it used?

7.22 Why can there be no simultaneity with the 1401 for the conventional devices?

7.23 Explain how a punchcard character gets into its MEMORY cell.

7.24 Why is IO limited to fixed areas of MEMORY?

7.25 Why do you think every *fourth* character on the print chain is scanned and a triple scan cycle is used? Examine the turning carefully.

7.26 Explain how a message gets printed.

7.27 What is chaining? What are its advantages? How does CONTROL *fetch* chained commands? Can *all* commands be chained? Why (not)?

8

HONEYWELL
200
SERIES

8.1 MEMORY AND ADDRESSING

Expansion   The Honeywell 200 Series is very similar to the IBM 1401, but the series includes computers which are much larger and more versatile. One way to increase the usefulness of a computer is to expand its MEMORY. This was done with the 200 Series so that the largest computers provide half a million *characters* of MEMORY. As with the IBM 1401, the word is one character. The problem is to make this much MEMORY addressable without using up many characters for calling out an address whenever MEMORY is accessed. To do this, Series 200 provides relative addressing which is automatically implemented but under the control of the program or software.

Indexing and indirection are two features which aid programming immeasurably. Although true hardware indexing is not provided in the 200 Series, this is unknown to the programmer. MEMORY indexing is effective but not as quick as with hardware REGISTERS.

Commands   The command for the H200 Series may contain up to four fields similar in use to those in the IBM 1401 command. This is a variable length command. The end of one command is distinguished by the field mark in the *next* command character.

In discussing the format, we refer to the four possible fields it might contain as F, A, B, and V. These fields must follow in the order they are named above, or

$$F \prec A \prec B \prec V \qquad (8.1.1)$$

where $\prec$ means "precedes."

Alternative formats for a command are presented by naming the fields and separating them by slashes. Thus the maximum format is F/A/B/V and the minimum is F.

The fields are

- F is a function code of one character.
- A is the A address field of two, three, or four characters.
- B is the B address field of two, three, or four characters.
- V is the variant character field; its nature is specified in the command description.

The lengths of A and B depend on the present addressing mode of the computer as described next. A and B are always the same length in a single command.

Addresses   To address half a million characters with the most efficient method—using straight binary addresses—requires nineteen bits. Using NBCD and four-bit numerics would require twenty-three bits. A mixed alphanumeric system as described for the IBM 1401 might require one or two more bits. Binary addressing is the best way to address MEMORY with the least number of bits, as in the 200 Series. The machine language programmer has to be familiar with binary and octal numbers. However, most coding is done at a higher level. **Easycode** is the assembly language for the 200. The responsibility to translate addresses from decimal to binary is on the assembler where it belongs.

In the largest 200 Series MEMORY, a nineteen-bit binary address is provided. If the user chooses a smaller MEMORY, the MEMORY ADDRESS REGISTER and all REGISTERS which handle addresses are trimmed to work for the chosen MEMORY size but no larger.

Addresses of operands are supplied in a command. As with the IBM 1401, an *A address* and a *B address* are specified in such commands as ADD or MOVE. Since commands address information in the same general area as the command itself, relative addressing is an expedient for shortening the operand address. This reduces the amount of space required for storing program information.

Addressing operates in three modes: four character, three character, and two character. Only in the four-character mode is total MEMORY addressable from the command; in the other modes, the base address provided by the most recent four-character mode command is retained and applied to the two- or three-character commands which follow.

Address recording   The relation of the address stored in the command to the address actually accessed in MEMORY is best explained by reference to Fig. 8.1.1.

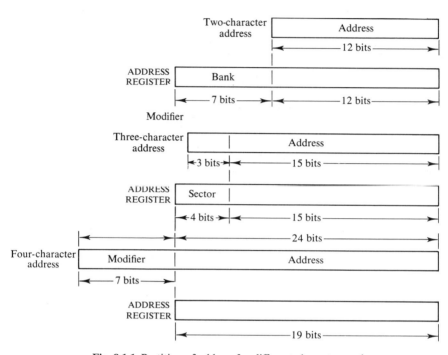

Fig. 8.1.1 Partition of address for different character modes.

TWO CHARACTER

A two-character address provides twelve bits of address information. For straight binary addressing, we can access 4K of MEMORY. If 500K of MEMORY is actually available, this leaves seven address bits unspecified. These **bank bits** have been set by a previous four-character command.

The effective address is composed by *concatenating*, stringing together, the two-character address in the command, as illustrated in Fig. 8.1.1.

THREE CHARACTER

Three six-bit characters provide eighteen bits; only fifteen of these are used to address one sector of 32K. Four bits, called the **sector bits,** are specified by the last four-character address. The effective address for direct addressing is composed by concatenating the four sector bits in a REGISTER with the fifteen address bits from the three characters in the command.

The three remaining bits from the command address are **modifier bits;** they indicate whether indirect addressing or indexing is requested.

The four address characters provide twenty-four bits—more than enough to address 500K. The least significant nineteen bits are the effective address for direct addressing. The remaining five modifier bits may request indexing or indirect addressing.

Changing mode A command with mnemonic CAM and opcode 42_8 changes the address mode from whatever it is to two-, three-, or four-character mode. The desired mode is indicated by the V character (Honeywell refers to this as a **variant character** and designates it as V instead of d). Thus, when we are in two-character mode and want to change to four-character mode, we give CAM with a variant character for four-character mode.

Indexing In the three- and four-character modes, the modifier portion of the address may carry index or indirection information. We restrict ourselves to three-character addresses. Modification of four-character addresses is similar and adequately described in the programmer's manual.

Of the eighteen bits in the three-character command, fifteen are the address portion; the most significant three bits indicate modification.

- 000 is for direct addressing.
- 111 is for indirect addressing.
- NNN is for index addressing where just one or two of the N's is 1 and NNN is the binary number for the INDEX REGISTER. For example, modifier bits 011 request indexing using REGISTER THREE.

Hardware INDEX REGISTERS are absent. The index tag is reinterpreted as a MEMORY location. If the same MEMORY CELLS were used as indexes regardless of the sector or bank being accessed, a complicated index access scheme would ensue. To simplify matters, INDEX REGISTERS are in a different location for each bank or sector in which the program might operate.

Thus, the first few CELLS of a bank are set aside for indexes. When indexing is specified and we are operating in bank three, one of the first few CELLS in bank three is accessed. If we change to bank two, one of the CELLS in the beginning of bank two is called for.

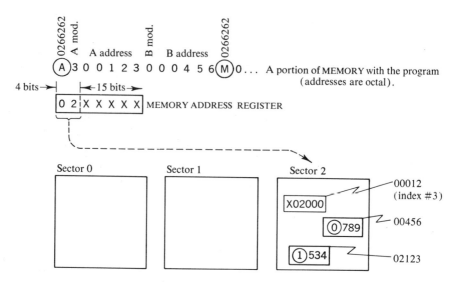

Fig. 8.1.2 An example of indexing.

Example   An example of indexing is presented in Fig.
8.1.2. Addresses that appear in the figure are (must be) octal; on the other
hand, data are alpha and/or decimal.

The MEMORY ADDRESS REGISTER holds seven octal digits. Actually, the
first digit can be only 0_8 or 1_8 since the REGISTER contains only nineteen bits.
For the three-character address command, sector information remains
constant. In the figure we are addressing the second sector.

The command *fetched* next is located (as shown in the figure) at address
0266262. Again the 02 designates the second sector. The opcode for *add*
is encircled thus: Ⓐ. A command begins with a word mark. Honeywell
indicates *their* word mark by encircling the character.

Twelve digits follow the opcode; these are *octal digits*—six per address.
We are now functioning in the three-character mode; each address
consists of three six-bit characters; each character is represented by two
octal digits.

The first octal digit (the leftmost) is the modifier digit. In the example,
the A modifier is 3, indicating a request for index 3.

Index 3 occupies the six octal digits in CELL locations which end at
000128 in MEMORY in the current sector. This is shown in the MEMORY map
at the bottom of Fig. 8.1.2. CELLS 00010_8 through 00012_8 in sector 2
contain X02000. X shows that the first three bits of the first character are
ignored. The remaining fifteen bits modify the A address portion of the
command being interpreted.

The five-character A address is 000123. To this we add the index
quantity, 02000, to form the effective address, 02123.

Although address fields are viewed as binary information, operand fields always contain alphanumeric information. Thus, the A field is *alpha information* which ends at location 02123. Its *beginning* is distinguished by word mark. If a field contains numeric information and is addressed by an arithmetic command, it is interpreted as a decimal number.

For instance, in the figure the effective A address is 02123: the datum lies between 02120 and 02123 inclusively; it is the decimal number 1534. Each decimal digit is coded into a six-bit character which, in turn, has a digit octal representation. For this example we have $1534_{\#} = 01050304_8$ since $4_{\#}$ is represented by 04_8, etc. Similarly, we find at locations 00453_8 through 00456 the field which is $0789_{\#}$ represented by 00071011_8.

Indirect addressing   In three-character address mode, the modifier character is 7_8 for indirect addressing. Multiple indirect addressing is permitted. Indirect addressing may terminate with an indexed address. Both direct and indexed addressing are terminal.

For indirect addressing, the address in the command is used to acquire the next address. The number of characters obtained during the chaining is determined by the mode. Indirect addresses are acquired starting with the designated address and proceeding from left to right (upward toward higher CORE).

Figure 8.1.3 shows an example of indirect addressing which terminates with index addressing.

The A field uses direct addressing as specified by the 0_8 of M, the first position of the *A address*.

The 7_8 in the *B address* indicates indirection. We are now operating in sector five and hence go to CORE location 0503456 to obtain the next three characters. These will be used for the *B address* of this command. Starting at that location, we obtain 200345.

The initial 2_8 indicates indexing using REGISTER 2. Its location is the three CELLS, the last of which is at 0500008. The six octal characters contained there are 010234. The first octal digit is ignored, and 10234 is added to 00345 to get 10601. This is prefixed by 05 (for operation in the fifth sector). Then 0510601 is the address of the B field operand.

8.2   CONTROL MEMORY

Need   The CONTROL MEMORY, CM, was chosen as a component to replace REGISTERS because it is less expensive than FLIPFLOP

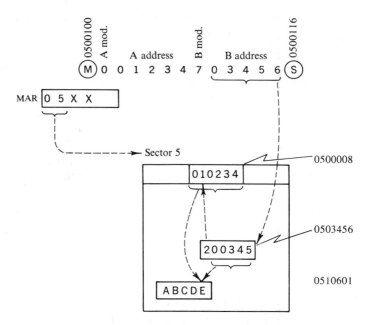

Fig. 8.1.3 An example of indirect and indexed addressing.

REGISTERS but faster than CORE MEMORY. It is really fast enough (half-microsecond access time) so that its use can be interspersed with cycles of MAIN MEMORY (two-microsecond access time) without losing any time between accesses. Further, as the versatility of the computer expands, more REGISTERS are required to hold intermediate results and/or addresses while processing is in progress. Adding new hardware REGISTERS increases the cost much more than if CONTROL MEMORY were simply expanded.

CONTROL MEMORY consists of somewhat more than sixteen CELLS of address size. Any CELL is available on demand from CONTROL for *recall* or *memorization*. Many REGISTERS previously incorporated in CONTROL for storing addresses are now in CM. Other REGISTERS associated with TRAFFIC CONTROL for PERIPHERAL DEVICES are also stored there. Finally, if the computer is to be expanded to new arithmetic functions which manipulate floating point numbers, these can also be stored in CONTROL MEMORY.

CONTROL MEMORY is a standard feature of all the Series 200 computers. However, more CM is provided in the larger models since additional functions are required there.

Content   The functions of some of the CELLS of CONTROL MEMORY are presented in Fig. 8.2.1. CM operates similarly to

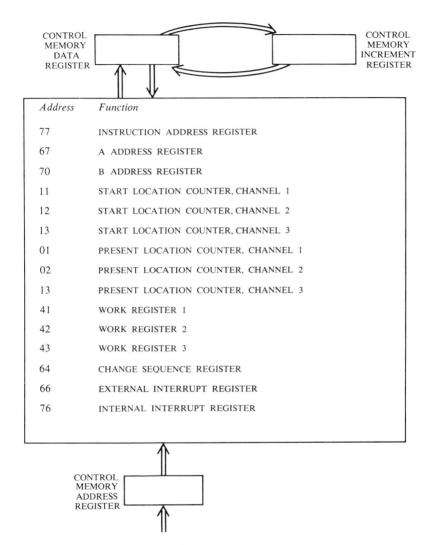

Address	Function
77	INSTRUCTION ADDRESS REGISTER
67	A ADDRESS REGISTER
70	B ADDRESS REGISTER
11	START LOCATION COUNTER, CHANNEL 1
12	START LOCATION COUNTER, CHANNEL 2
13	START LOCATION COUNTER, CHANNEL 3
01	PRESENT LOCATION COUNTER, CHANNEL 1
02	PRESENT LOCATION COUNTER, CHANNEL 2
13	PRESENT LOCATION COUNTER, CHANNEL 3
41	WORK REGISTER 1
42	WORK REGISTER 2
43	WORK REGISTER 3
64	CHANGE SEQUENCE REGISTER
66	EXTERNAL INTERRUPT REGISTER
76	INTERNAL INTERRUPT REGISTER

Fig. 8.2.1 The CONTROL MEMORY.

MAIN MEMORY. A CONTROL MEMORY ADDRESS REGISTER (CMAR) stores the address of a CM CELL. For *recall*, the content of this CELL is placed in the CONTROL MEMORY DATA REGISTER (CMDR). Often this datum is an address which is supplied to MAIN MEMORY, and thereafter, the address is altered (incremented or decremented) before it is returned to CONTROL MEMORY. Incrementation is performed in the CONTROL MEMORY

INCREMENTATION REGISTER (CMIR). An address may be sent there from CMDR; after incrementation, the address is returned to the CMDR and thence to CM.

Each CELL in the CONTROL MEMORY is of the same size—address size. Its length, in bits, is determined by the size of MM. For the largest MAIN MEMORY—half a million characters—the CM word is nineteen bits; smaller MM requires smaller words in CM.

Command fetch   The operation of the CONTROL MEMORY, during *fetch*, is presented in Fig. 8.2.2. *Fetch* obtains characters from MM and places them either in hardware or CONTROL MEMORY REGISTERS so that the command is ready for execution after *fetch* is completed. *Fetch* requires two cycles for *each* character in the command:
- Acquisition—the next character in the command is acquired and placed in the MDR.
- Distribution—the character in the MDR is transferred to a REGISTER position or in part of a CM word.

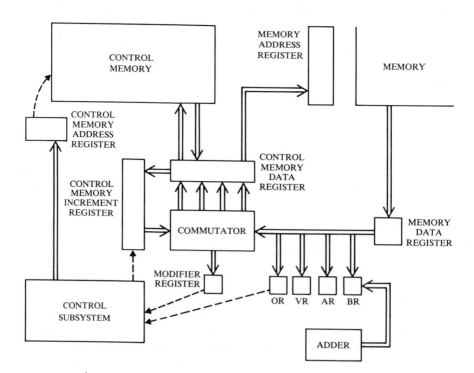

Fig. 8.2.2 Organization of the 200 system.

To acquire a character, furnish its address to the MAR as follows. CONTROL supplies [IAR] to CMAR. (IAR) goes to CMDR. From there it goes to the MAR and CMIR, and MM *recall* is initiated.

In the meantime, the CMIR adds 1 to the instruction address, since instruction character acquisition goes from lower numbered to higher numbered MAIN MEMORY locations. This incremented address is returned to the CMDR. The CMAR still contains the address of IAR. A CM *memorize* cycle is initiated.

In the meantime, the MM has acquired the next instruction character and has placed it in the MDR. It is distributed to a REGISTER or CM.

Table 8.2.1 ASSEMBLY OF A TWO-CHARACTER ADDRESS INSTRUCTION

Character	Type of Instruction			
Number	*A dup*	*B chain*	*F/A/V*	*F/V*
1	OR	OR	OR	OR
2	AR, BR, VR	AR, VR	AR, VR	VR
3	AR, BR	AR	AR	VR
4	BR	BR	VR	VR
5	BR	BR	VR	VR
6	VR	VR	VR	VR

Table 8.2.1 shows where each character goes for four possible instruction types for a two-address instruction with two characters per address. In all cases, the first character is passed over to the OPERATION REGISTER, OR, a FLIPFLOP REGISTER. The VARIANT CHARACTER REGISTER, VR, is also a hardware REGISTER.

Address assembly   Words in CM are large enough to address the MEMORY size option that the user has chosen—from twelve to nineteen bits. The number of bits changed in CM in two-character mode is less than the word size—not all the bits are changed. In general, the number of bits changed depends on the mode.

The technique of getting information into a CONTROL MEMORY word is presented in Fig. 8.2.2. The first character is inserted into the OR. Further characters from CM to the MDR by CONTROL are obtained as described before.

As the first *A address* character is entered into the MDR, the CONTROL MEMORY address of the AAR is passed over to the CMAR. CM brings the *A address* to the CMDR. The character now in the MDR is passed through the COMMUTATOR to the second character position from the right in the CMDR. A CM *memorize* cycle returns this to the AAR in CM.

If this character is also entered into the BAR, another complete CM CYCLE brings the *B address* into the CMDR, places the A character in the second position from the right, and returns it to the *B address* in CM.

The second A character is obtained and placed in the MDR by a *fetch* cycle. The *A address* is placed in the CMDR by a CM *recall* cycle as described just previously. Now the A character is passed from the MDR through the COMMUTATOR and is placed in the rightmost position. For a two-character address command, the *A address* is now complete. Twelve new bits have been furnished to the right-hand portion of the *A address*; the seven bank bits in the old *A address* are retained. The new *A address* refers to the same bank.

The same procedure is used to obtain the *B address*. The difference is that CONTROL places the [BAR] in the CMAR.

After the *A address* and *B address* are entered in CM, the remaining characters in the command are variant characters. As each one appears, it is passed over to the VARIANT REGISTER. The reader should note carefully that some commands *require* several variant characters, a difference from the IBM 1401.

Three-character address   For the three-character address, the first character contains three modifier bits and the three most significant bits of the fifteen-bit address. As this character appears in the MDR it is presented to the COMMUTATOR which separates these three bits, placing them in the MODIFIER REGISTER, MR. The other three bits go to bit positions fifteen, fourteen, and thirteen of the address word currently in the CMDR. The higher-order bits, the bank or sector bits, have been placed in the CMDR by a former CONTROL MEMORY cycle when the computer was in four-character mode.

The next two characters brought from MM are commutated in the second and first positions of the address word as described for the two-character address.

Four-character address   For the four-character address, the first character brought to the MDR contains a five-bit modifier and the most significant bit of the nineteen-bit address. This modifier information is siphoned off by the COMMUTATOR. The first five bits are placed in the MR. The remaining bit goes to the CMDR in the most significant bit position.

The next three characters that enter the MDR are passed through the

COMMUTATOR and are placed, respectively, in the third, second, and first positions of the address in the CMDR at the time.

8.3 INDEXING AND INDIRECTION

Preconditions   Indexing or indirection can occur only in three- or four-character mode. As an address is procured in the *fetch* cycle, modifier information is entered in the MODIFIER REGISTER.

Let us examine the case of the three-character address. The four-character address is handled using the same principles.

The discussion in the previous section made clear how the eighteen bits which make up an address are handled:

- The first three bits are the modifier. They are entered into the MODIFIER REGISTER, MR.
- The remaining fifteen bits are placed on the right-hand end of the ADDRESS REGISTER. Since the address can contain up to nineteen bits, the most significant bits remaining in the AR are designated as sector bits and are left over from the previous address.
- This applies to both *A addresses* and *B addresses*.

The descriptions which follow discuss how the *A address* is handled but apply equally to the *B address*.

Indirection   When the *A address* is acquired, a copy is placed into a WORKING REGISTER, WR1, in CM.

CONTROL uses the address in WR1 to make a new *A address*. Addresses are always obtained in the forward direction. Hence, we go through a sequence of obtaining characters designated by the contents of WR1. The number of characters we obtain is determined by the setting of the mode control and not by a word mark.

CONTROL sends [WR1] to CMAR. CM brings the latest *A address* from WR1 and places it in the CMDR. From there it goes to the MAR. MM gets a character which is placed in the MDR. Meanwhile, the contents of CMDR are passed over to the CMIR, where 1 is added to its contents. This is because we are looking *forward* in MEMORY to get *A address* characters. The contents of CMIR are returned to CMDR, and from there they are memorized in CM at [WR1].

The address character in the MDR is passed to the COMMUTATOR where it is separated into two parts. The first part goes to the MODIFIER REGISTER, MR; the second part is entered into the *A address* which was brought to the CMDR. To obtain the *A address*, [AAR] is entered into the CMAR; CONTROL MEMORY brings the *AA* to the CMDR for entry of the *new A address* character.

At the end of three MM accesses, a new *A address* should be secured in

INDIRECT ADDRESS CHARACTERS

the AAR contained in CONTROL MEMORY. The MR contains three bits which indicate if further indirection, indexing, or direct addressing is to be done.

Figure 8.3.1 contains an example of indirect address acquisition. Notice that this is *single* indirect addressing for the *A address* and simple direct addressing for the *B address*. The cycles which obtain the second *A address* are designated in the figure as AI1, AI2, and AI3.

Indexing   For indexing the *A address*, procure the *A address* and place it in the AAR in the CONTROL MEMORY as before. The modifier bits in the MR tell which INDEX REGISTER to use for modifying the *A address*. This set of bits, shifted two positions to the left, is inserted in a WORKING REGISTER, WR2. WR2 contains the sector bits presently applicable plus four times the binary number conveyed by the modifier bits. This is obtained by a shift left of two places in the index designation. It is the location of the terminal character of the INDEX REGISTER in MM.

We place the location of the *last* or right-hand *A address* in WORKING REGISTER WR1. This should be the same as the IAR setting when the last *A address* character was retrieved.

Indexing *adds* the contents of the designated REGISTER to the *A address*. To do addition, we obtain characters from right to left. An example is presented in Fig. 8.3.2.

In cycle ANA1, the right-hand *A address* character is obtained and placed in both the BR and AR. In the figure, these six-bit characters are represented in octal. In cycle ANB1, the index character is placed in the BR. In cycle ANC1, the contents of the AR and BR are added and the result placed in the BR. Also during this cycle, the contents of the AAR are placed in the CMDR. The COMMUTATOR is set so that the character in the B REGISTER is entered into the rightmost position of the CMDR. (We are going from right to left now.)

Cycles ANA2, ANB2, and ANC2, respectively, bring the next *A address* character and the next index character, add them, and place the result in the next position of the AAR in CONTROL MEMORY.

The same thing is done in cycles ANA3, ANB3, and ANC3. However, for this last character, the three least significant bits are the only ones of importance. These are entered into bits fifteen, fourteen, and thirteen of the AAR in CONTROL MEMORY. The remaining three bits would normally be the modifier bits, but indexing is terminal. Hence these bits are discarded, and we go on to pick up the *B address*.

Multiple indirect   It is possible to do multiple indirect addressing.
addressing;   Intermediate indirect addresses are tagged
indexing   111, indicating that further indirect addressing
is required. The technique for doing multiple indirect addressing is the

1100123

A 701234 034567

1101234

002345

Character	MDR	IAR	OR	AAR	BAR	WR1	MR	IFF
	XXXXXXX	1100123	X	11XXXXX	11XXXXX	XXXXXXX	X	0
Op	1100123	1100124	A	11XXXXX	11XXXXX	11XXXXX	X	0
A1	1100124	1100125	A	110XXXX	110XXXX	110XXXX	7	0
A2	1100125	1100126	A	11012XX	11012XX	11012XX	7	0
A3	1100126	1100127	A	1101234	1101234	1101234	7	0
AI1	1101234	1100127	A	1101234	1101234	1101235	0	1
AI2	1101235	1100127	A	1102334	1101234	1101236	0	1
AI3	1101236	1100127	A	1102345	1101234	1101237	0	1
B1	1100127	1100128	A	1102345	1131234	1101237	0	0
B2	1100128	1100129	A	1102345	1134534	1101237	0	0
B3	1100128	1100130	A	1102345	1134567	1101237	0	0

Fig. 8.3.1 Example of indirect address *fetch*.

Character	MAR	IAR	OR	AAR	WR1	WR2	MR	AR	BR
X	XXXXXXX	0500321	X	XXXXXXX	XXXXXXX	XXXXXXX	X	XX	XX
Op	0500321	0500322	A	05XXXXX	XXXXXXX	XXXXXXX	X	XX	XX
A1	0500322	0500323	A	050XXXX	XXXXXXX	XXXXXXX	3	XX	XX
A2	0500323	0500324	A	05040XX	XXXXXXX	XXXXXXX	3	XX	XX
A3	0500324	0500325	A	0504000	0500324	XXXXXXX	3	XX	XX
Set	0500324	0500325	A	0504000	0500323	0500012	3	XX	XX
ANA1	0500324	0500325	A	0504000	0500323	0500012	X	00	00
ANB1	0500012	0500325	A	0504000	0500323	0500011	X	00	23
ANC1	0500012	0500325	A	0504023	0500322	0500011	X	00	23
ANA2	0500323	0500325	A	0504023	0500322	0500010	X	40	40
ANB2	0500011	0500325	A	0505723	0500322	0500010	X	40	17
ANC2	0500011	0500325	A	0505723	0500321	0500010	X	40	57
ANA3	0500322	0500325	A	0505723	0500321	0500009	X	30	30
ANB3	0500010	0500325	A	0525723	0500321	0500009	X	30	62
ANC3	0500010	0500325	A	0525723	0500321	0500009	X	30	22
B1	0500325	0500326	A	0525723	0500321	0500009	X	30	22
etc.									

Annotations (memory contents):
0500321 ◁— A 304000 00 5000
221723
0500012
0500321

Fig. 8.3.2 Example of indexing.

same as that presented in Fig. 8.3.1. If the modifier bits picked up are 111, another set of cycles is initiated to obtain the next indirect address. A WORKING REGISTER is used to store the present *A address* while a new *A address* is entered into the AAR in CONTROL MEMORY.

The last address obtained by indirection may be direct or indexed as described in Fig. 8.2.2.

8.4 IO

The Honeywell Series 200 performs IO by cycle stealing, permitting simultaneity of IO and processing. At least three CHANNELS are normally provided. For the lower numbered models, a fourth (alternate) CHANNEL is available as an option. The fourth CHANNEL coordination is not described here to avoid needless complication.

In the higher numbered models, more CHANNELS may be provided when large MEMORY options are furnished. Then multiple sectors are available which are autonomous. Hence IO operation and information exchange can proceed in one sector independently of what is going on in another sector. Again, because of the complications which this adds to the explanation, these considerations are omitted.

Read write channel   For a system with three READ WRITE CHANNELS (RWCS), up to eight PERIPHERAL DEVICES may be provided. A READ WRITE CHANNEL is a crossbar-connected CHANNEL CONTROLLER. Each RWC can be connected to any one of the DEVICES, like the arrangement in Fig. 2.2.1.

Connected to the MAIN MEMORY is the TRAFFIC CONTROL, a MEMORY SCAN COMMUTATOR. In Fig. 8.4.1, each RWC is connected to the TRAFFIC CONTROL; also connected thereto is CONTROL and the PROCESSOR. Of course, the MEMORY is of major importance. TRAFFIC CONTROL determines who accesses the MEMORY and when.

The Honeywell 200 Series MEMORY operates with a two-microsecond-or-less cycle. Each RWC is entitled to one out of three MEMORY cycles. TRAFFIC CONTROL offers one MEMORY cycle, in turn, to each READ WRITE CHANNEL. Hence a MEMORY cycle is offered to each RWC every six microseconds. If an RWC does not require a cycle, the cycle is available to CONTROL or the PROCESSOR SUBSYSTEM—but the RWC has first priority.

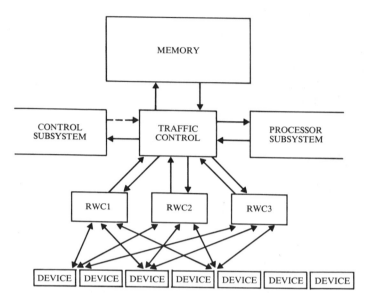

Fig. 8.4.1 TRAFFIC CONTROL can talk with any or all of the RW
CHANNELS.

If CONTROL is in the midst of a *fetch* (which may require several MM
cycles), *fetch* will be held up as long as RWCs request MM cycles. But it is
rare that there is activity on all cycles. Further, activity on RWC eventually
terminates so that its MEMORY cycles become available to CONTROL or the
PROCESSOR.

Similarly, when characters are being brought from MEMORY for
processing, their acquisition will be held up as long as there are RWCs
requesting cycles.

Peripheral data   Request for IO activity is made (by the
transfer   programmer) using a *peripheral data transfer*,
PDT. Its *A address* field contains the source (destination) starting MEMORY
location of the data for IO transmission. Information is read (written)
from (to) MEMORY starting at the left (lower numbered location) and proceeding to the right (higher numbered location).

The first variant character, V1, distinguishes the RWC activated. The
second variant character, V2, distinguishes the DEVICE and may also carry
information about the sector.

BUSY   If either RWC or DEVICE is busy, the transfer cannot begin. More
important, the computer is immobilized if the RWC and DEVICE cannot

accept the command. Therefore, tests should be incorporated in the program to verify that the RWC and DEVICE are free before a PDT is given, unless the programmer *really wants* the computer to be held up until they become free.

If both the DEVICE and RWC are available and no extraordinary conditions prevail, the DEVICE is activated. Data transmission begins after mechanical medium movement and positioning have occurred, and the DEVICE signals that it is ready to receive (or produce) information.

Data are transmitted to (or from) MEMORY, a character at a time or, occasionally, a fraction of a character at a time. Characters or fractions thereof can be transmitted between MEMORY and the DEVICE every six microseconds. If slower rates are appropriate to the DEVICE, then requests will be made at longer intervals (which is no problem).

The total number of characters transmitted between a DEVICE and MEMORY is generally determined by the DEVICE. Thus, in *reading* a card, eighty characters (columns) are transmitted from the card to MEMORY, and the programmer should allocate eighty free CELLS in MEMORY starting at the CELL designated in the command. For *reading* from an MTU, an *end of block* character noted by the MTU halts transmission. Here the programmer should leave sufficient space for the maximum size block.

The programmer can halt transmission on input by a record mark in MEMORY where the last character to be stored will be placed. Though characters may continue to emanate from the medium until an EoB is reached, they will not be stored.

Information is transferred serially by character. However, for corner turning, fractions of a character are transmitted, as typified by the IBM 1401, CARD READER, CARD PUNCH, and PRINTER. Their operations are similar in the Honeywell 200.

A complete character is transferred to (or from) MEMORY for the PAPER TAPE READER, PT PUNCH, MAGNETIC TAPE, MAGNETIC DISK, and MAGNETIC DRUM. For them, no corner turning is required.

Action of PDT command   During *fetch*, the first character obtained (conveying PDT) is placed in the OR.

Depending on the character mode, the next two, three, or four characters comprising the *A address* are inserted in the AAR in CONTROL MEMORY. Indexing or indirection, when requested, modifies the *A address* before variant characters are obtained.

(margin labels: TRANSMISSION DATA · TRANSMISSION TYPE)

The first variant character, when placed in the VARIANT REGISTER, VR, initiates two actions:

- The desired RWC is set to receive DEVICE information.
- The (AAR) is duplicated in CM at the RWC **starting location, RWCSL** (of data in MEMORY for transfer). One RWCSL is provided for each RWC.

The second variant character chooses an IO DEVICE. Activity is then initiated for that DEVICE by attaching it to the chosen RWC. Other variant characters which follow supply supplementary information about the DEVICE activity.

Single scan characters   We now describe IO activity for DEVICES such as the MAGNETIC TAPE UNIT, where only one MEMORY access per character is required.

For the MTU, the medium must be accelerated to speed before data transmission can begin. When up to speed in the case of reading, the DEVICE obtains the first legitimate character from the medium and notifies the RWC. The RWC reports to TRAFFIC CONTROL that it will need the next MEMORY cycle which becomes available to it within less than six microseconds.

For each RWC there are two CELLS in CONTROL MEMORY. Besides the RWCSL, there is also an RWC **present location cell,** RWCPL, which points to the *present* character.

Before the single character transfer operation begins, the *A address* which was stored in the RWCSL is duplicated in the RWCPL. The RWCPL is incremented whenever a character is transmitted.

We now look at IO somewhere in the middle of data transmission. The RWCPL is passed over to the CMAR. (RWCPL) is placed in the CMDR and is then passed to the MAR. Regardless of whether we are reading or writing, this character is brought from MEMORY to the MDR to check for a word or record mark (to determine whether the IO operation is to terminate). For writing, this character is passed over to the RWC; for reading, the character in the RWC is passed over to the MDR. Memorization is done, and the MM is free.

Meanwhile, the contents of CMDR are passed over to CMIR for incrementation. Thus 1 is added to the (RWCPL) so that the next time MAIN MEMORY is accessed, it gets a character in the CELL with the next higher address. The incremented address is returned to the CMDR and a CM *memorize* places it at [RWCPL]. RWCPL is now updated in CM.

If TRAFFIC CONTROL finds that the next RCW needs a MEMORY cycle, it is treated as above.

Multiscan CARD READER, CARD PUNCH, and PRINTER each
characters require *corner turning*. Information is transmitted only after a *ready* period. For *read*, the first scan not only enters
information but also clears the addressed MEMORY CELLS.

We examine CARD INPUT. Since its operation is the most complicated,
the operation of the other two DEVICES can be deduced from this explanation.

The 9 row is read first. First the CARD READER delivers the code for 9
via the RWC; it is entered into a WR in CM where it is available all during a
9 scan. Other rows report to CONTROL MEMORY similarly.

The CARD READER requires two cycles for *each* hole site in *each* row.
The first cycle gets the column read thus far from MEMORY and places it in
BR. The second cycle adds the code of the row scanned to that in the BR,
checks for legality, and returns the code to MEMORY.

At the beginning of each row scan, CM is cycled so that the RWCSL is
installed into the RWCPL. The row code is placed in a WORKING REGISTER,
WR3. Now character cycles begin. The [RWCPL] goes to the CMAR;
(RWCPL) is entered into the CMDR. From there it is passed over to the MAR.
The character is entered into the MDR. This character goes to a WORKING
REGISTER (say, WR4) in the CONTROL MEMORY to be available for the next
RWC cycle for this DEVICE.

On the next RWC cycle, the character from MEMORY is brought from
WR4 in CM and stored in the BR. If there is a punch in this card in the
column and row scanned, the code corresponding to that row is brought
from WR3 to the AR. If there is no punch, 0 is put in the AR. The contents
of the AR and BR are added in the ADDER and returned to the BR. The
result is checked for validity and, if invalid, reading hangs up.

Meanwhile, the (RWCPL) is withdrawn from CM and placed in the MAR.
The valid character code is transferred from the BR to the MDR. A MAIN
MEMORY cycle then places the character code in MEMORY. Before the
present location is returned to CONTROL MEMORY, it passes through the
INCREMENTOR so as to call for the next character when the next RWC cycle
comes around.

Inquiry For an RWC to accept a PDT command, both
the RWC and DEVICE must be available; otherwise, the computer hangs up
until the two are free. For the programmer to avoid this hang up, we give
him a check on DEVICES and RWC.

CARD READER

ACQUISITION

CHANGE

The *peripheral control and branch* command, PCB, has the format F/A/V. There is no *B address*. The first variant character distinguishes the RWC and DEVICE tested; the second variant character indicates a condition—generally we check for *busy*. If the condition being checked applies—if the DEVICE and CHANNEL are busy, for instance—then the next command is taken from the *A address*. If the condition is absent, we continue to the next command.

The PCB may contain additional variant characters to request other operations. These must be nondata operations, such as *seeks* for DISC and *rewinds* for TAPE. Also, they may precondition a DEVICE for errors. For instance, the CARD READER CONTROL can be conditioned to reject illegally punched cards, to generate a busy signal for illegally punched cards, or both, depending upon variant characters in PCB. Finally, variant characters may be used to condition interrupt operation.

The inquiry command PCB checks if an RWC and DEVICE are busy. If the system has received an interrupt, PCB determines whether a DEVICE and RWC have become free and whether a noted condition has arisen. The interrupt discussed in Section 8.5 initiates interrupt service for the RWC and DEVICE. After this service routine has taken effect, the programmer is sure that the RWC and DEVICE are no longer busy. He can then give a PDT command without fear that the computer will become immobilized. Hence a PCB command can be eliminated in this case.

IO without   Interrupt is an optional feature on some
interrupt   Honeywell 200 systems. Without it, how does
IO function smoothly? Recall that the RWC is connected by a crossbar so that any DEVICE may function on any RWC. In dispatching a DEVICE, then, any RWC can be called for as an intermediary between the DEVICE and MEMORY. But we don't wish to give a PDT to an RWC which is busy or for a DEVICE presently attached to another CHANNEL, for this will hold up the computer until the pair are free.
    To ascertain:
    • which RWC is free
    • if the DEVICE is free
a series of PCBs is incorporated by the programmer in his program. He may give a simple DEVICE check first so that, if the DEVICE is presently operating, he may skip the RWC check and just go on with the rest of his program (if he can). If he finds the DEVICE free, he may give PCBs which test RWCs and, when he finds a free one, he may then give the PDT appropriate to the task. If he finds no RWC free, he may pause or go to a different part of the program.

8.5 SEQUENCE CHANGE

Operation   A **sequence change** requests the CM to interchange the contents of the INSTRUCTION ADDRESS REGISTER, IAR, with another REGISTER. The other REGISTER can be:

- the CHANGE SEQUENCE REGISTER, CSR;
- the EXTERNAL INTERRUPT REGISTER, EIR;
- the INTERNAL INTERRUPT REGISTER, IIR.

Interchanges can be initiated by

- a request from the programmer;
- a trap by the hardware.

In all cases, the purpose of the sequence change is to stop the problem program and to go to routine elsewhere in MEMORY to

1. service the interrupt.
2. do some other job.

When we do this, we must save our place in the program because, when interrupt service is completed, we pick up the problem program where we left off. Some *saving* of other REGISTERS and INDICATORS may be necessary to provide properly for the sequence change.

PURPOSE

Change sequence   CSM causes the computer to operate in *change sequence* mode (another name for subroutine operation). It simply interchanges the IAR with the CSR. It is useful to subroutine linkage.

If the CSR contains the starting point of a subroutine, SRSTART, then CSM can link with the SR. CSM interchanges the contents of IAR and CSR. Sequencing of the computer continues from here using the *present contents* of the IAR. Therefore, steps performed after CSM are those of the SR.

At the end of the subroutine, another CSM command is given which interchanges the CSR and IAR. But the CSR contains the *old* IAR contents—the address of the next instruction in the main program. After the switch, the old program continues as though nothing had happened (except execution of the subroutine).

LINKAGE

How does SRSTART get into the CSR? Two commands make this possible:

- *Load Control Memory*, LCM, loads the location in CONTROL MEMORY specified by the variant character, with the contents of the *A address* field specified in the command.

LOADING

- *Store Control Memory*, SCM, places the contents of the location in CONTROL MEMORY specified by the variant character in the location in MAIN MEMORY specified by the *A address* field of the command.

To get the starting location of the subroutine SRSTART into the CHANGE SEQUENCE REGISTER, the programmer sets aside a location in MM which contains SRSTART. Then, before he issues CSM, he gives an LCM command specifying the CELL containing SRSTART in the *A address* as the source; the CSR is specified as the destination by a variant character.

NESTING

For one subroutine to call upon another, *save* is required. Suppose that, in an outer subroutine, I wish to switch to an inner subroutine. The CHANGE SEQUENCE REGISTER contains the place of the main program where I am to return. This must be stored in some CELL such as MBLOC by SCM before *another* CSM is given. Of course, CSM is also preceded by an LCM command installing the starting location of the *inner* SR in the CSR.

The inner SR, upon completion, gives CSM which takes us back to the outer subroutine. Immediately thereafter, we wish to do an LCM addressing MBLOC and restoring it to the CSR for our return jump.

Interrupt by sequence change   The 200 Series provides (in some models optionally) two levels of interrupt called **external interrupt** and **internal interrupt.** There is an INTERRUPT REGISTER provided for each type of interrupt. These are called, respectively, the EXTERNAL INTERRUPT REGISTER (EIR) and the INTERNAL INTERRUPT REGISTER (IIR).

When an interrupt occurs, its type is determined and an exchange is made between that INTERRUPT REGISTER and the INSTRUCTION ADDRESS REGISTER. This exchange is made only when permitting conditions prevail so that program information can be maintained. Sequencing continues; but now, commands from the interrupt service routine are executed rather than those in the problem program. However, our place in the main program is preserved in the INTERRUPT REGISTER and is available when we have finished our servicing.

Information about the type of interrupt and its cause is stored in FLIPFLOPS called INDICATORS and made available to the interrupt service routine by commands discussed in Section 8.6. During the course of the interrupt, information may be stored in INDICATORS normally used by the problem program. But what about the information previously held in these INDICATORS (before interrupt)? For the external interrupt, this information is placed in an AUXILIARY INDICATOR REGISTER (AIR) so as to be preserved during the interrupt.

Interrupt hierarchy   There are several statuses in which the
machine may operate:

- **Single cycle status** is under the control of the operator who
  presses a manual advance button to advance from *fetch* to
  execute for each command.
- In **normal status,** the machine has not been interrupted.
- In **internal interrupt status,** the machine has been interrupted by
  one of the causes classified as internal.
- For **external interrupt status,** the machine has been interrupted
  by a cause classified as external.

Let us now examine the hierarchy of interrupts. That is, we examine
which interrupts may occur in each status.

- In normal status, both classes of interrupts are permissible.
- In internal interrupt, the machine can be interrupted by an
  external interrupt; when the internal interrupt has been serviced,
  we return to the main program.
- In external interrupt, the machine is no longer interruptable.
  Return is made to the previous status. Hence, if the external
  interrupt occurred in run or in internal interrupt mode, return
  is made, respectively, to *run* or *internal interrupt* mode.
- In single cycle mode, the machine is not interruptable. Interrupt
  information is saved, however, and when the machine is returned
  to normal status, prevailing interrupt information causes a
  sequence change if this is in order.

External interrupt   An external interrupt can be caused by:

- a report on any one of the READ WRITE CHANNELS;
- a monitor call instruction, MC;
- the operator can indicate his desire for an interrupt on the
  CONSOLE CHANNEL.

The interrupt is registered on the EXTERNAL INTERRUPT FLIPFLOP, after
which the interrupt becomes effective when these conditions prevail:

1. The computer is not in single cycle operation.
2. The computer is not in external interrupt status.
3. Command execution is completed.
4. A MEMORY cycle is available to CONTROL.

When the foregoing conditions prevail, the EXTERNAL INTERRUPT
FLIPFLOP causes certain INDICATORS to be placed in the AUXILIARY
INDICATOR REGISTER, AIR: ARITHMETIC INDICATORS, COMPARISON INDICATORS,
ADDRESS MODE INDICATORS, etc. These INDICATORS are then cleared for use
by the interrupt routine. Automatically, we enter the three-character mode

and set the computer into external interrupt status. Finally, the contents of the EXTERNAL INTERRUPT REGISTER are exchanged with those of the INSTRUCTION ADDRESS REGISTER.

The interrupt condition is maintained until one of these situations arises:

1. A PDT command is given to an RWC.
2. A PCB command is given which contains a request to turn off the interrupt.
3. The computer is initialized.

COMPLETION

8.6   INTERRUPT ASSIST

Save and unsave   When an interrupt is established, the computer becomes dedicated to servicing it. All REGISTERS of importance to a user program must be stored in MEMORY. These REGISTERS occupy addresses in the CONTROL MEMORY. The interrupt routine can store REGISTERS using the SCM command. We must also store the contents of the ADDRESS REGISTERS, AAR and BAR, because the user program may be chaining commands at the time of interrupt. The next command might be an *add* referencing the updated *A* and *B addresses* stored in AAR and BAR.

But even when chaining is not done, the contents of the AAR and BAR contain the bank or sector bits required while operating in two- or three-character mode, respectively, to which we adjoin address characters contained in the command. If the AIR and BAR are not preserved and bank or sector bits are altered by the interrupt routine, then the main program will reference areas of MEMORY different from those intended by the programmer.

When interrupt service is completed, REGISTERS in CONTROL MEMORY must be restored. This is the obligation of the interrupt service routine; the problem program finds REGISTERS intact upon return. Hence, at the end of the service routine, we find a number of LCM commands.

Save INDICATORS   There are a number of INDICATORS associated with a running program. Some of these are stored automatically, but many are not. The command, *store variant and indicators*, SVI, is provided to store the character remaining in the VARIANT REGISTER and/or various INDICATORS. The format of the command is F/V.

CONTROL knows which INDICATORS are stored from the bits in the
variant character for SVI. Each of the six positions in V indicates a unique
set of INDICATORS to be stored.

Here is a list of the *set* of INDICATORS stored by SVI, going from least
to most significant bit in its variant:

1. The variant *now* in the VARIANT CHARACTER REGISTER.
2. PROGRAM INDICATORS including ARITHMETIC, COMPARISON, and ADDRESS MODE.
3. The contents of the AIR which are the same as in (2), but which are placed in the AIR on an external interrupt.
4. Information associated with the scientific (floating point) option.
5. INDICATORS associated with the protect, proceed, and relocation options (see Section 8.7).
6. INDICATORS associated with interrupt source and status.

$$(8.6.1)$$

For each set of INDICATORS, one character of storage is required—
as many characters of storage as there are 1's in the variant of the SVI. The
characters which now hold INDICATOR information are placed in locations
immediately following the variant for the SVI. It is up to the programmer
to leave space following this instruction.

To save three sets of INDICATORS, give the instruction:

SAVE   SVI   45 $$(8.6.2)$$

Octal 45 contains three 1's corresponding to (1), (3), and (6) of (8.6.1);
hence, three sets of INDICATORS are saved. They will be placed at the
character positions SAVE+2, SAVE+3, and SAVE+4. (What happened
to SAVE+1?)

RESTORE   We now need a means to get INDICATOR
INDICATORS   information from where it was stored, and
to reset the INDICATORS. *Restore variant and indicators* with the format
F/A/V; RVI does this. V indicates which *sets* of INDICATORS are restored.
The exception is that the interrupt source and status *cannot* be restored by
this command, or else we would be in trouble!

The command provides an *A address*, where the INDICATORS were
stored. The variant tells in which INDICATORS the information is installed
once retrieved from the A field. This is conveyed by the setting of the bits
in the variant character as presented in (8.6.1).

To restore the INDICATORS which were stored using (8.6.2), we give:

$$\text{UNSAVE} \quad \text{RVI} \quad \text{SAVE}+2, \quad 05 \qquad (8.6.3)$$

This command restores the two sets of INDICATORS (1) and (3), stored at SAVE+2 and SAVE+3, because octal 05 contains two 1's. Notice that the INDICATORS (6), stored at SAVE+4, are not restored; they were INTER-RUPT STATUS INDICATORS.

Monitor call   The single character command, MC, *monitor call*, causes an exchange of the contents of the IAR with those of EIR on program request (like the IBM System 360) SVC. The cause for this interrupt is recorded within MC and is available to the interrupt service routine.

Resume normal   The resume normal mode command, RNM, has the format F/A/V. What it does depends upon whether the computer is in external or internal interrupt status.

RNM in external status:

1. Turns off the EI FLIPFLOP.
2. Restores the INDICATORS whose contents were stored in the AUXILIARY INDICATOR REGISTER.
3. Sets the AAR from the *A address* in the command.
4. Sets the BAR from the *B address* in the command.
5. Swaps the EIR and the IAR.

RNM command if given in internal interrupt status:

1. Resets the II FLIPFLOP.
2. Restores the AAR and BAR from the *A* and *B addresses* in the command.
3. Swaps the IIR and the IAR.

RNM works properly when SMC, performed at the beginning of the interrupt routine, stores the AAR and BAR in the *A* and *B address* portions of the RNM *command itself*. How this is done is discussed briefly in Section 8.8.

8.7   PROTECT

The *protect and relocate* functions facilitate multiprogramming and protect the software resident in MEMORY. They divide MEMORY into two parts, one of which is protected while the other isn't. A running program is found in the unprotected area. It cannot reach into the protected area to harm either the software or other programs which may be there. Further, the (problem) program operating in the unprotected area cannot give any of a set of privileged commands. If this were not the case, it would be possible for the problem program to remove all protection from MEMORY and then clobber the previously protected software or programs.

Setup of protected areas and other important activities is restricted to the software residing in the protected areas since only privileged commands are available. This software in protected MEMORY can be entered only by an interrupt; the privileged commands can be given only while an interrupt is in effect. During interrupt, a program formerly running in the open area can be retired, and a new one may take its place at the discretion of the SYSTEM. SYSTEM changes protection boundaries to exclude the former problem program and include the new program.

Function   With the *protect* feature, the MEMORY is divided into one protected and one unprotected area. If the *relocation* feature is not incorporated, then only a single division line is provided. With it, the top area of MEMORY is protected, and the bottom is unprotected.

We confine our discussion to when the *relocation* feature is included. This provides an upper and lower dividing line. The unprotected area lies between, and the areas above and below the dividing lines are protected. Of course, the dividing lines can be placed anywhere. If placed at the top and bottom of MEMORY, then all MEMORY is unprotected.

When operating in normal status with protection and relocation features enabled by SVI, the problem program can address only the middle, unprotected area. If it tries to address a protected area, a protection violation occurs, causing an internal interrupt. Further, programs in the protected area may not address locations in the protected area in normal status. This does not cause a problem because, to get to the protected area, we have to enter interrupt status. Therefore, we never expect to be in normal status while operating in the protected area.

Boundaries   The lower boundary to the unprotected area is contained in the BASE RELOCATION REGISTER (BRR). Its setting indicates the *upper* bound of the *lower* protected area. This is just below the *lower* bound of the unprotected area. It also provides automatic relocation: A program which tries to access a lower area will have its operand relocated into the open or unprotected area.

The upper extremity of the unprotected area is contained in the INDEX-BARRICADE REGISTER (IBR) which is also the lower bound for the upper protected region. Commands in the unprotected program which try to access the upper protected area or, after relocation, which are found to address the upper protected area are declared to be in protection violation and cause an internal interrupt.

Boundary setup   To set up the boundaries, we require additional commands. These are described below in the case where both the protect and relocate features are supplied.

LIB

The *privileged* command, *Load Index-Barricade register*, LIB, has the format F/A/V. Its purpose is to load both of the REGISTERs which divide the MEMORY. It takes the contents of the *A address* and places them in the IBR; it takes the contents of the *B address* and places them in the BRR.

SIB

The privileged command, *Store Index-Barricade register*, SIB, reverses the steps taken by the LIB. The contents of the IBR are stored in the *A address* of the command; the contents of BRR are stored at the *B address* of the command.

Wraparound   The Honeywell 200 Series has a wraparound
MEMORY   MEMORY. If locations past the upper limit of MEMORY are addressed, these locations are accessed as though they still lie in MAIN MEMORY—this is a modulo *M* system, where *M* is the size of MEMORY. To find the location addressed, we subtract a multiple of the MAIN MEMORY size such that the number remaining is positive and smaller than *M*.

For instance, suppose we have 4K of MEMORY. The actual number of locations contained in MEMORY is 4096, and they are numbered from 0 to 4095. A request for CELL 4096 addresses CELL 0. A request for CELL 4097 addresses CELL 1. A request for CELL 8194 addresses CELL 2, and so forth.

Round binary   This wraparound scheme works only when *M*
number   is a power of 2 so that we get a well-behaved binary number. It works for 1K, 2K, . . . , 65K, etc. But suppose the user has a multiple of MEMORY which Honeywell furnishes but which is not a round binary number such as 48K. If I call for a location just a little bit higher than 65K, I will end up in a legal CELL in lower CORE. But if I call for locations between 48K and 65K where wraparound *does not exist* and CELLs have not been provided, I am making a request for CELLs which are nonexistent and hence not protected. This situation is handled as an

internal interrupt with addressing of the nonexistent core being noted as the reason for the interrupt.

Internal interrupt

There are three causes of an internal interrupt:

1. Addressing a protected area of MEMORY while in the normal mode.
2. Addressing nonexisting MEMORY (as explained earlier).
3. Giving a privileged opcode while in normal status.

The need for privileged opcodes was explicated at the beginning of the section. Other opcodes are classified as privileged because they cause an internal interrupt. An interrupt due to an opcode occurs because:

1. The opcode is a combination of bits for which no operation has been defined.
2. A proper opcode for a feature not in the user's system.
3. Opcodes for the following mnemonics:

H	SVI
LCR	RVI
PDT	RNM
PCB	LIB

8.8 SOFTWARE INTEGRATION

General scheme   The steps to be taken in servicing an interrupt are, in essence, those described in Chapter 4:

1. The interrupt sets the associated INDICATORS.
2. A jump is made to the interrupt routine by exchanging the contents of the INTERRUPT REGISTER with those in the INSTRUCTION ADDRESS REGISTER.
3. A *save* frees the CONTROL MEMORY and REGISTERS from the original program by placing pertinent information in storage location.
4. Tests find the cause of the interrupt.
5. The appropriate service routine is chosen and entered.
6. An *unsave* operation is performed to return the computer to its original condition.
7. Return is made to the original program.

We shall now examine how the hardware mediates between the program and the software.

Interrupt is During interrupt, all MEMORY is accessible to
privileged the interrupt routine and all commands are
available to it. Finally, note that an external interrupt cannot be interrupted. However, an internal interrupt may be interrupted by an external one.

Example A typical initial and final portion of an interrupt service routine is illustrated in Fig. 8.8.1. It starts in the middle of the page at START, the SVI instruction. The symbolic address which follows, INDS, is actually a variant character. This character is defined in line 3 above, by the pseudo CEQU. Its operand is #1C73. Here #1C conveys a literal consisting of exactly one character; 73 is the octal representation of the character: 111011. This variant character tells which INDICATORS to store.

A space of five characters is required to store all the INDICATORS since 73_8 contains five ones. This information is stored directly after the instruction SVI, which, with its variant, takes up two characters. At START+2, the pseudo DCW with operand #5 sets aside five characters of storage following SVI.

The next command, CAM, places the computer in four-character addressing mode.

The two commands which follow are SCR commands. Each has in its first operand field the symbolic address of a save area for the AAR and the BAR, namely, SAVEA and SAVEB. Space for these areas is provided by the DCWs on lines 5 and 6. This completes the *save*.

At the end of the interrupt routine, we *unsave* the information we have put away. Beginning on line 8 at location RESTOR (we jump there from the end of the interrupt routine, line 17), two LCRs restore the A and B ADDRESS REGISTERS. Next we restore the INDICATORS with the command RVI. It uses the *four* characters starting at location START+2. Although we placed *five* characters in this area, we only withdraw four. The fifth of these characters contains the old interrupt status.

Since we are only restoring four sets of INDICATORS, the variant character of RVI is different from that for SVI. It's symbolically called INDR and is defined on line 4 by the CEQU.

On line 11, RNM exits to the problem program by interchanging the present setting of the INSTRUCTION ADDRESS REGISTER with the contents of the INTERRUPT REGISTER. The INTERRUPT REGISTER to be used is determined by the *interrupt* state (internal or external).

Line	Location	Command	Operand	Comments	Type of Command
1	AAR	CEQU	#1C67	AAR variant code	Pseudo
2	BAR	CEQU	#1C70	BAR variant code	Pseudo
3	INDS	CEQU	#1C73	Variant to store INDICATORS	Pseudo
4	INDR	CEQU	#1C33	Variant to restore INDICATORS	Pseudo
5	SAVEA	DCW	#4C	Storage for AAR	Pseudo
6	SAVEB	DCW	#4C	Storage for BAR	Pseudo
7		ADMODE	4	Set maximum addressing mode	Macro
8	RESTOR	LCR	SAVEA, AAR	Unsave starts here; this restores the AAR	Mnemonic
9		LCR	SAVEB, BAR	Unsave the BAR	Mnemonic
10		RVI	START + 2, INDR	Restore requested INDICATORS	Mnemonic
11		RNM		Exit	Mnemonic
12	START	SVI	INDS	Save required INDICATORS	Mnemonic
13	START + 2	DCW	#5	Storage for the INDICATORS	Pseudo
14		CAM	MAX	Enter four-character addressing mode	Mnemonic
15		SCR	SAVEA, AAR	Save AAR	Mnemonic
16		SCR	SAVEB, BAR	Save BAR	Mnemonic
		.		Interrupt routine	
17		B	RESTOR	Jump to the unsave point	Mnemonic

Fig. 8.8.1 An example of coding for the internal interrupt routine prologue and epilogue in Easycoder.

Notice how RNM just precedes START. We have planned things this way so that we go a full circle. Upon completion of the interrupt routine, we find START, the location of the interrupt routine, in the IAR. Now, after RNM, the return to the normal mode, the proper starting place of the interrupt routine is in the INTERRUPT REGISTER.

PROBLEMS

8.1 Explain how, for a given Model of H200, a program can include two, three, or four character addresses?
   (a) What is the form in each mode?
   (b) What limitations are there in the amount of MEMORY addressable in each mode?
   (c) How does the three character address differ from that of the IBM 1401?
   (d) How does one change modes?

8.2 How is indexing done?
   (a) How is the index specified?
   (b) Where is the INDEX REGISTER located?
   (c) What happens in each mode?

8.3 How about indirect addressing?
   (a) Specification?
   (b) Method?
   (c) Can it be combined with indexing?

8.4 What is the CONTROL MEMORY?
   (a) What does it contain?
   (b) How is it used?
   (c) Explain a three character *fetch*.

8.5 How are the work registers in CM used?

8.6 What is the RWC? How is it like a CHANNEL? How does it differ?

8.7 What is TRAFFIC CONTROL? Describe how it works.

8.8 What is a *scan*?

8.9 What is PDT? What do the letters mean? What does it do?

8.10 PDT uses two variants, V1 and V2.
   (a) What does each convey?
   (b) How?
   (c) How can *two* variants be obtained in the *fetch*?

8.11 What happens for a PDT if RWC or DEVICE is busy?

8.12 How is data transmitted on a PDT?

8.13 What and where is the RWCSL, and what is its purpose?

8.14 How about the RWCPL?

8.15 Explain corner turning in the H200.

8.16 What is the PCB?
  (a) Explain F/A/B/V for PCB.
  (b) What does it do?
  (c) When should it occur in the program?

8.17 Since INTERRUPT is optional, how does the program request and schedule IO without it?

8.18 What is a sequence change? What happens? Explain CSR, EIR, and IIR.

8.19 Explain CSM. How is it used? What happens for CSM?

8.20 What is LCM and SCM?
  (a) How are they used for linkage?
  (b) What REGISTER(s) do they affect?
  (c) Where do they appear in the program?

8.21 How does the computer interrupt?
  (a) Explain the interrupt hierarchy.
  (b) What happens during the interrupt of a subroutine?
  (c) Is this a problem?

8.22 Explain MC thoroughly.

8.23 Explain the need for SVI. What does it do? How does it specify what is to be done?

8.24 Explain the complementary effect of RVI. How does it differ from SVI?

8.25 Explain the alternative operations done by RNM according to present mode.

8.26 What are the BRR and IBR?
  (a) How do they afford protection?
  (b) What do they have to do with relocation?
  (c) With indexing?
  (d) What happens when protection is violated? Explain.

8.27 What are LIB and SIB? How are they used? What do they do?

8.28 What is wraparound MEMORY? How is it helpful? Harmful?

8.29 What are privileged *opcodes*? Enumerate.

8.30 In Fig. 8.8.1, explain what each of these does and how: (a) CEQU; (b) DCW; (c) ADMODE; (d) SCR.

9

SYSTEM

360

9.1 INTRODUCTION

Aim IBM developed System 360 to suit all possible users. To expect a single computer system to satisfy everybody, from small users to large, would be imprudent. A number of models were developed, each for a different price field. Except for the IBM Model 20, the same machine language was kept throughout all the models. Further, each machine should, to at least some degree, suit both the business and scientific community. To be universally acceptable, a small data quantum was chosen and named the *byte*. As originally defined by IBM, a byte referred to a group of contiguous bits appropriate to a given application. IBM has chosen to redefine the **byte** as *exactly eight bits*.

A common machine language made possible product line compatibility in the basic programming sense. The software was also supposed to be compatible at all the levels.

Difficulties In trying to suit every user in all disciplines, many problems arise:
- One must have a plethora of commands.
- All data formats must be provided for.

228

For series compatibility, the small computer is straddled with a number of handicaps.

- It uses a large command format.
- The CHANNEL CONTROLLER approach is applied where it may be too sophisticated.
- Multiprogramming provisions are made, consuming time and space:
  * memory protect
  * interrupt
  * program status word
- For compatible software, much MEMORY (so valuable to the small computer) is consumed.
- A MEMORY hierarchy is expensive at the low end of the spectrum.

In the attempt to make the series compatible, the large computer models have disadvantages foisted upon them:

- Compatibility downward must be maintained.
- More commands than necessary appear in the repertoire.
- A universal software could work at higher efficiency in a larger machine.

Although the computers seem identical and compatible on a superficial level, they have quite different hardware. Further, it has been impossible to create universal software to work equally well in all models. A large array of different packages had to be constructed to meet the user needs at each level.

Design center   It is impossible to look at all the models of the series for lack of space. The Model 50 is the design center of the series. It has all the features of interest to the small- to medium-sized computer user. Time sharing for Model 67, interleaved instruction handling for Model 91, and large, fast buffer MEMORIES for Model 85 are indeed interesting topics, but they must be left for a different volume.

9.2 PROGRAMMER'S VIEW OF

SYSTEM 360

System   Figure 9.2.1 shows the bare essentials of System 360. Central to the system is MAIN MEMORY. The PROCESSOR communicates with it. CONTROL gets its directions from MEMORY. At our

(Margin notes, top to bottom: SMALL COMPUTER, LARGE COMPUTER, RESULT)

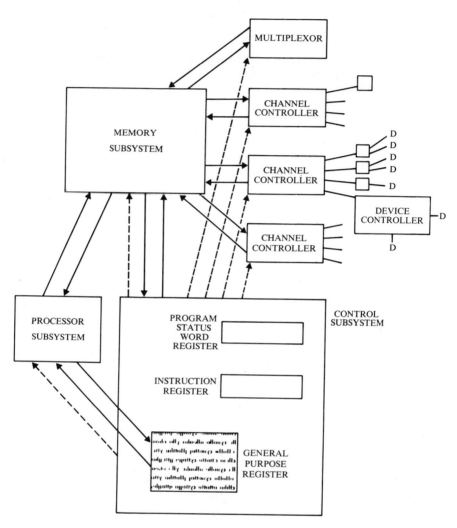

Fig. 9.2.1 Programmer's view of System 360.

initial examination of the computer system, information was *never* sent *from* the CONTROL SUBSYSTEM *to* the MEMORY. If we consider the GENERAL PURPOSE REGISTERS part of CONTROL, this would be an exception to that rule. Hence, to keep a consistent view of computers, we might regard the GPRs as part of MEMORY.

All IO functions are performed by CHANNEL CONTROLLERS as described in Chapter 2.

MAIN MEMORY is a single port system which operates as described in Chapter 1. CHANNEL CONTROLLERs have the highest priority for use of the MEMORY; CONTROL and the PROCESSOR have the least priority. A main (MULTIPLEXOR) CHANNEL is furnished with the system; additional regular CHANNELS (up to three) may be obtained as options.

The PSWR is supplied for the program status word (described in Chapter 4). The M REGISTER, MR, generally holds part or all of the instruction during *fetch* and *analysis*. The IAR stores the instruction address. All command decoding, function allocation and signal gating is done via the READ-ONLY MEMORY described in Section 9.4. There are no hard REGISTERS set aside specifically for indexing. Indexing is done using the GPRS as below. Some command arithmetic is required for CONTROL. This is done by sharing the PROCESSOR hardware; hence, it is indeed hard to see where CONTROL leaves off and the PROCESSOR begins. No indirect addressing is possible via the hardware.

GENERAL PURPOSE The programmer is aware of sixteen
REGISTERS *fixed point* GPRs. Each stores a four-byte (thirty-two bit) quantity. Also available to him, if he has the floating point option, are four *floating point* GPRs, each storing sixty-four bits.

All GPRs are addressable when they participate in a command. Fixed point GPRs are numbered consecutively from 0 to 15. Floating point GPRs are numbered 0, 2, 4, and 6 (they are eight-byte REGISTERS). Fixed point commands refer to fixed point GPRs; floating point commands refer to the floating point GPRs. Variable length decimal and character commands do not use GPRs. Hence, there is no ambiguity in labeling GPRs. When a GENERAL PURPOSE REGISTER is called for, the one named in the command is used.

The GPRs are implemented by a LOCAL MEMORY. This is high speed (half a microsecond access time) CORE MEMORY. It has sixty-four REGISTERS; the additional ones, other than the GPRs, are used for other purposes. These are not available to the programmer and are discussed in Section 9.4.

GPRs are used by most commands. They are the heart of the machine and serve the following needs:

1. They hold operands for fixed and floating point arithmetic and logical operations.
2. They hold index quantities and are referenced by commands which permit indexing.

3. They hold base or relocation quantities. It is important for both the programmer and the hardware man to distinguish between relocation and indexing. One of the main limitations of this particular system is the comparatively few GPRs available for these separate but equal functions.

Byte orientation   The various models of System 360 have different word sizes (as originally defined by me in Chapter 1)—the quantum of information obtained during the MEMORY cycle. The designers wished to give all models of the series functions which were independent of their word sizes. Hence, the byte was chosen as a quantum to fill this need and suit the spectrum of uses. It is defined as eight bits by IBM and other manufacturers of similar series.

The byte can be considered as:
  • a single eight-bit alphanumeric character code;
  • two four-bit NBCD digits;
  • a portion of a binary number.

As is usual, most commands (which process data) are data dependent: Decimal commands expect to find two decimal digits per byte; fixed point commands manipulate binary numbers; floating point commands expect fractions and exponents in a specific form; etc.

IBM, RCA, and others use particular names to apply to a collection of bits. In particular, they use "Word." **Word,** here, has a particular meaning: thirty-two bits or four bytes of information. To distinguish the manufacturer's use of *Word* from my use of *word*, I use an initial capital to set off the former (particular) one. Manufacturers also talk about **halfWords** (two bytes) and **doubleWords** (eight bytes). Their use is clear from the original definition of *Word*. Among the programmer's slang, **nibble** is applied to a halfbyte. I will *nibble* when needed.

By my definition, the word size of System 360 varies from one byte for the Model 20 to eight bytes (double Word) for the Model 65, and higher.

Bytes   A byte is simply eight bits. When speaking of the *value* of such a byte, it is inconvenient to use the straight binary notation consisting of only 0's and 1's. We might use three-digit octal notation, but the manufacturers did not favor this because:

1. Three digits are required;
2. It does not represent decimal numbers well;
3. It is not amenable to shift operations;
4. It is wasteful of punchcard columns or media space.

Instead, they have gone to a *base sixteen* system called **hexadecimal.**

To use a base of sixteen, we need zero and fifteen other digits. However, the decimal system provides us with only ten usable digit symbols. Hence, as auxiliary symbols, the first six capital letters of the alphabet are used. Each symbol has a four-bit code corresponding to it. These codes change in natural succession in the same way that the binary numbers do. Further, the order of the codes assigned is the same as the order of the letters. This code should be called natural binary coded hexadecimal or NBCH. Sometimes it is simply called NBCD. A table of NBCH codes appears as Table 9.2.1.

Table 9.2.1 THE DECIMAL AND HEXADECIMAL DIGITS AND THE FOUR-BIT NBCH
CODE FOR THEM

Decimal	Hexadecimal Digit	NBCH Code	Decimal	Hexadecimal Digit	NBCH Code
0	0	0000	8	8	1000
1	1	0001	9	9	1001
2	2	0010	+	A	1010
3	3	0011	−	B	1011
4	4	0100	+	C	1100
5	5	0101	−	D	1101
6	6	0110	+	E	1110
7	7	0111	−	F	1111

To illustrate how NBCH is used, two examples follow:

$$11001000 \quad 11110101 \equiv C8F5 \qquad (9.2.1)$$

$$00111010 \qquad\qquad \equiv 3A \qquad (9.2.2)$$

A byte can hold two decimal digits in NBCD form. The digits may be placed into a designated byte by the command, PACK, described later. Decimal arithmetic commands expect to find two decimal digits per byte. This format is called *packed decimal*. Each digit is coded in NBCD using the first ten codes in Table 9.2.1. Thus, each byte is considered as two nibbles, each of which is a four-bit code. Only ten combinations are admissible NBCD symbols. The other six are admissible as plus or minus signs, as noted from the table, only when they appear in the rightmost nibble of a decimal field. In any other position, a sign is recognized as invalid data.

When a byte carries alphanumeric information, all eight bits participate. This presents 2^8 or 256 combinations per byte. Two standard eight-bit codes are available. They are called ASCHII-8 and EBCDIC. The meanings of the initials and the codes themselves are found in System 360 manuals.

With so many combinations available, we find many unassigned combinations in each code. Even so, there are codes for the following:

1. Digits.
2. Uppercase alphabetic.
3. Lowercase alphabetic.
4. Special characters such as asterisk, question mark, etc.
5. Special symbols such as carriage return, line advances, and so forth.

Packing   Originally transcribed data are always transmitted to the computer from input in **unpacked** form with one digit, character, or symbol per byte. Numerals are a subset of the eight-bit input code. There is no reasonable way to have the INPUT DEVICE handle numerical and alphabetic information differently. Thus, information from punchcards, paper tape, consoles, and so forth is *unpacked* in alphanumeric form even if it is numeric. Numerals which will not be processed can be left *unpacked* and then transferred directly as any other *alpha* byte to an area for output without intermediate conversion.

Numeric data which are subjected to arithmetic must be *packed*. The command, PACK, takes numerals coded in eight-bit form, changes them to four-bit NBCD form by stripping the left four bits, and then *packs* them two digits per byte. This takes time and also requires MEMORY for storing both forms of the same number.

Unpacked decimal bytes contain 1111 in the left nibble and the NBCD equivalent of the digit in the right nibble. The exception is the least significant digit which may have another combination in the left nibble for sign. *Packed* data always contain the sign in the rightmost nibble. Then *packing* preserves the sign nibble, positioned as in Fig. 9.2.2.

Other decimal nibbles are prepared by *stripping* the left nibble from the *alpha* byte. These are assembled to produce the proper NBCD image as shown in Fig. 9.2.2.

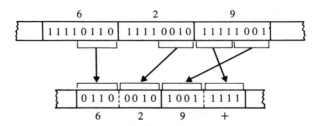

Fig. 9.2.2 Operation of the PACK command.

Consider that, if *alpha* rather than *numeric* data are used inadvertently for *packing*, *stripping* is performed automatically. If arithmetic is later performed on these *packed* data, an error may be detected since invalid codes may appear in nonsign positions—only nonsign combinations should appear there.

To *unpack* numeric data (N), using the unpack command, UNPK, the reverse operations are done (see Fig. 9.2.2) to produce an *unpacked* field (U):

1. The N rightmost (sign) nibble is placed in the left nibble of the U rightmost byte.
2. The next (going leftward) N nibble is placed in the right U nibble.
3. Succeeding N nibbles (going leftward) are placed in right nibbles of succeeding (going leftward) U bytes.
4. 1's are placed in the left nibbles of all U bytes.

Conversion   When fixed point binary arithmetic is used, *packed* (decimal) information must next be converted into binary form using the *ConVert to Binary* command, CVB, before binary arithmetic can be requested. We do binary arithmetic with thirty-two bit, fixed length Words.

When binary information is ready for output, it must go through both *reconversion* and *unpacking* procedures. Using the *ConVert to Decimal* command, CVD, we go from binary to packed decimal; we go from packed decimal to input alphanumeric using UNPK.

Only when information is for later computer consumption and is not to be used by the humans can we really take advantage of packed decimal or fixed word binary format. In this case, a CORE image can be dumped onto MAGNETIC TAPE, DISC, or DRUM without conversion and later returned to CORE MEMORY in its original state.

9.3   COMMANDS

Multiple length   The advantages of multiple length commands became apparent before the inception of the IBM 1401 and have been carried over to System 360. This philosophy provides:

- Two-address commands for requesting processing in a single command and providing reference to all three operands involved.
- One-address commands where direct addressing suffices: Although zero-address commands are useful for the IBM 1401,

implied addressing is not required in System 360 since GPRs are always named in the command.

- Effective use of MEMORY which is not wasted for fixed formats of extra length when smaller commands will suffice.

In the case of System 360, we find byte orientation instead of the field mark orientation. There must be some way to distinguish the size of commands. Actually, there are only three sizes: two-, four-, and six-byte commands. Command size is conveyed by the first two bits in the opcode.

We now examine the various fields which comprise the command.

REGISTERS   Of the sixteen GPRs, one to three of them may be called for in a command. When a REGISTER is referenced directly, as an OPERAND REGISTER, it is referred to symbolically as R. The number of the REGISTER is noted in binary; one nibble per REGISTER indicates REGISTER 0 through 15 (0 through F, hexadecimal). When GPRs are used as DESTINATION or SOURCE REGISTERS, they are designated by labels R1 or R2, respectively, depending on whether they are used for the first (both source and result destinations) or second (source only) operand.

When a GPR holds an index quantity (acts as an INDEX REGISTER) it is symbolically referenced as X. Again, a nibble suffices to label the REGISTER.

When a GPR is used as a BASE REGISTER for relative addressing, it is symbolically referred to as B, and a nibble suffices to call it out.

Addresses   When CORE MEMORY is referenced, a specific location is called for by a binary number. This number occupies twenty-four bits, enabling us to address about sixteen million bytes of MEMORY.

The effective address of an operand is formed by adding as many as three quantities together:

1. D is a displacement of twelve bits (one and a half bytes) contained in the command.
2. B is a BASE REGISTER. The GPRs contain thirty-two bits, but the address portion consists of only the rightmost twenty-four bits.
3. X is a GPR when used for indexing. Again, only the rightmost twenty-four bits are used for addresses.

M, the effective MEMORY location, is defined as:

$$M = D + (B)_M + (X)_M \qquad (9.3.1)$$

where $(B)_M$ and $(X)_M$ are the rightmost twenty-four bits of the GPR. (These subscripts are omitted later when no confusion will arise.) *All* MEMORY references include both a displacement and a BASE REGISTER specification; only certain specific commands permit indexing.

When a command contains an operand byte (immediate addressing), this byte is designated as I. Only one command byte can be immediately addressed.

Variable field length (VFL) commands operate upon fields, where the length of a field is specified in the command. When both source and destination fields are required to be the same length, the single byte specifier, L, indicates these lengths as 1 (L = 0) to 256 (L = 256$_\#$ = FF$_H$) bytes. When two fields of different lengths are used for decimal arithmetic, the nibble designators L1 and L2 are used to show fields of one (L = 0$_H$) to sixteen (L = F$_H$) bytes each.

Format   There are five formats for System 360 commands, and they are illustrated in Fig. 9.3.1. We discuss each.

The RR or REGISTER to REGISTER command references two GPRs. Each GPR specification requires one nibble; one byte specifies opcode. An example of such is LR or *Load Register*. It requests that the contents of R2 be duplicated into R1:

$$\text{LR:} \qquad (R2) \rightarrow R1 \qquad\qquad (9.3.2)$$

For RX commands, a REGISTER and an indexed MEMORY location are operands for the command. An example is *Load*, L, which requests that the contents of a MEMORY location be copied into a specified GPR thus:

$$\text{L:} \qquad (M2) \rightarrow R1 \qquad\qquad (9.3.3)$$

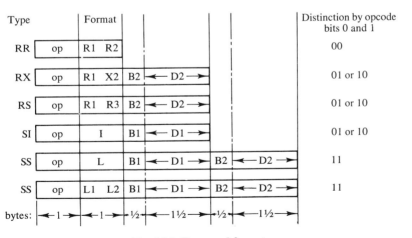

Fig. **9.3.1** Command formats.

Table 9.3.1 OPCODES AND MNEMONICS FOR IBM SYSTEM 360

TYPE RR

XXXX	Branching and Status Switching (0000XXXX)		Fixed Point, FullWord, and Logical (0001XXXX)		Floating Point Long (0010XXXX)		Floating Point Short (0011XXXX)	
0000			LPR	Load Positive	LPDR	Load Positive	LPER	Load Positive
0001			LNR	Load Negative	LNDR	Load Negative	LNER	Load Negative
0010			LTR	Load and Test	LTDR	Load and Test	LTER	Load and Test
0011			LCR	Load Complement	LCDR	Load Complement	LCER	Load Complement
0100	SPM	Set Program Mask	NR	*And*	HDR	Halve	HER	Halve
0101	BALR	Branch and Link	CLR	Compare Logical				
0110	BCTR	Branch on Count	OR	*Or*				
0111	BCR	Branch/Condition	XR	*Exclusive Or*				
1000	SSK	Set Key	LR	Load	LDR	Load	LER	Load
1001	ISK	Insert Key	CR	Compare	CDR	Compare	CER	Compare
1010	SVC	Supervisor Call	AR	Add	ADR	Add N	ALR	Add N
1011			SR	Subtract	SDR	Subtract N	SER	Subtract N
1100			MR	Multiply	MDR	Multiply	MER	Multiply
1101			DR	Divide	DDR	Divide	DER	Divide
1110			ALR	Add Logical	AWR	Add U	AUR	Add U
1111			SLR	Subtract Logical	SWR	Subtract U	SUR	Subtract U

TYPE RX

XXXX	Fixed Point, HalfWord, and Branching (0100XXXX)		Fixed Point, FullWord, and Logical (0101XXXX)		Floating Point Long (0110XXXX)		Floating Point Short (0111XXXX)	
0000	STH	Store	ST	Store	STD	Store	STE	Store
0001	LA	Load Address						
0010	STC	Store Character						
0011	IC	Insert Character						
0100	EX	Execute	N	*And*				
0101	BAL	Branch and Link	CL	Compare Logical				
0110	BCT	Branch on Count	O	*Or*				
0111	BC	Branch Condition	X	*Exclusive Or*				
1000	LH	Load	L	Load	LD	Load	LE	Load
1001	CH	Compare	C	Compare	CD	Compare	CE	Compare
1010	AH	Add	A	Add	AD	Add N	AE	Add N
1011	SH	Subtract	S	Subtract	SD	Subtract N	SE	Subtract N
1100	MH	Multiply	M	Multiply	MD	Multiply	ME	Multiply
1101			D	Divide	DD	Divide	DE	Divide
1110	CVD	Convert-Decimal	AL	Add Logical	AW	Add U	AU	Add U
1111	CVB	Convert-Binary	SL	Subtract Logical	SW	Subtract U	SU	Subtract U

Here, as in the remainder of the chapter, M2 is the effective address of the second operand and is defined by:

$$M2 = (X2) + (B2) + D2 \qquad (9.3.4)$$

where the subscript, M, has been elided.

In this command, two REGISTERS and an immediate operand are called for. An example of this is *Load Multiple*, LM:

$$\text{LM:} \quad (M2) \rightarrow R1, R1 + 1, R1 + 2, \ldots, R3 \qquad (9.3.5)$$

Here the contents of the MEMORY CELL, M2, given by

238

Table **9.3.1** (CONT.)

	Branching Status, Switching, and Shifting		Fixed Point, Logical, and Input/Output			
XXXX	1000XXXX		1001XXXX		1010XXXX	1011XXXX
0000	SSM	Set System Mask	STM	Store Multiple		
0001			TM	Test Under Mask		
0010	LPSW	Load PSW	MVI	Move		
0011		Diagnose	TS	Test and Set		
0100	WRD	Write Direct	NI	*And*		
0101	RDD	Read Direct	CLI	Compare Logical	None	None
0110	BXH	Branch/High	OI	*Or*		
0111	BXLE	Branch/Low-Equal	XI	*Exclusive Or*		
1000	SRL	Shift Right SL	LM	Load Multiple		
1001	SLL	Shift Left SL				
1010	SRA	Shift Right S				
1011	SLA	Shift Left S				
1100	SRDL	Shift Right DL	SIO	Start IO		
1101	SLDL	Shift Left DL	TIO	Test IO		
1110	SRDA	Shift Right D	HIO	Halt IO		
1111	SLDA	Shift Left D	TCH	Test Channel		

TYPES RS AND SI

			D Logical		F Decimal	
XXXX	1100XXXX		1101XXXX		1110XXXX	1111XXXX
0000						
0001			MVN	Move Numeric		MVO Move with Offset
0010			MVC	Move		PACK Pack
0011			MVZ	Move Zone		UNPK Unpack
0100			NC	*And*		
0101		None	CLC	Compare Logical	None	
0110			OC	*Or*		
0111			XC	*Exclusive Or*		
1000						ZAP Zero and Add
1001						CP Compare
1010						AP Add
1011						SP Subtract
1100			TR	Translate		MP Multiply
1101			TRT	Translate and Test		DP Divide
1110			ED	Edit		
1111			EDMK	Edit and Mark		

TYPE SS

Note: N = Normalized   DL = Double Logical   S = Single
SL = Single Logical   U = Unnormalized   D = Double

$$M2 = D2 + (B2) \qquad (9.3.6)$$

are copied into REGISTERS numbered from R1 through R3, inclusively.

The SI command conveys an immediate operand and a MEMORY address. The immediate operand in the command is a single byte labeled I. An example of this *MoVe Immediate*, MVI, places a character into a specified location in MEMORY:

$$\text{MVI}: \qquad I \rightarrow D1 + (B1) \qquad (9.3.7)$$

239

Table 9.3.2 ALPHABETIC LIST OF STANDARD SYSTEM 360 INSTRUCTIONS

Standard Instruction Set

Name	Mnemonic	Type		Code
Add	AR	RR	C	1A
Add	A	RX	C	5A
Add Halfword	AH	RX	C	4A
Add Logical	ALR	RR	C	1E
All Logical	AL	RX	C	5E
And	NR	RR	C	14
And	N	RX	C	54
And	NI	SI	C	94
And	NC	SS	C	D4
Branch and Link	BALR	RR		05
Branch and Link	BAL	RX		45
Branch on Condition	BCR	RR		07
Branch on Condition	BC	RX		47
Branch on Count	BCTR	RR		06
Branch on Count	BCT	RX		46
Branch on Index High	BXH	RS		86
Branch on Index Low or Equal	BXLE	RS		87
Compare	CR	RR	C	19
Compare	C	RX	C	59
Compare Halfword	CH	RX	C	49
Compare Logical	CLR	RR	C	15
Compare Logical	CL	RX	C	55
Compare Logical	CLC	SS	C	D5
Compare Logical	CLI	SI	C	95
Convert to Binary	CVB	RX		4F
Convert to Decimal	CVD	RX		4E
Load Positive	LPR	RR	C	10
Load PSW	LPSW	SI	L	82
Move	MVI	SI		92
Move	MVC	SS		D2
Move Numerics	MVN	SS		D1
Move with Offset	MVO	SS		F1
Move Zones	MVZ	SS		D3
Multiply	MR	RR		1C
Multiply	M	RX		5C
Multiply Halfword	MH	RX		4C
Or	OR	RR	C	16
Or	O	RX	C	56
Or	OI	SI	C	96
Or	OC	SS	C	D6
Pack	PACK	SS		F2
Set Program Mask	SPM	RR	L	04
Set System Mask	SSM	SI		80
Shift Left Double	SLDA	RS	C	8F
Shift Left Single	SLA	RS	C	8B
Shift Left Double Logical	SLDL	RS		8D
Shift Left Single Logical	SLL	RS		89
Shift Right Double	SRDA	RS	C	8E
Shift Right Single	SRA	RS	C	8A
Shift Right Double Logical	SRDL	RS		8C
Shift Right Single Logical	SRL	RS		88
Start IO	SIO	SI	C	9C

Name	Mnemonic	Type	C	Code
Diagnose		SI		83
Divide	DR	RR		1D
Divide	D	RX		5D
Exclusive Or	XR	RR	C	17
Exclusive Or	X	RX	C	57
Exclusive Or	XI	SI	C	97
Exclusive Or	XC	SS	C	D7
Halt IO	HIO	SI		9E
Insert Character	IC	RX	C	43
Load	LR	RR		18
Load	L	RX		58
Load Address	LA	RX		41
Load and Test	LTR	RR	C	12
Load Complement	LCR	RR	C	13
Load Halfword	LH	RX		48
Load Multiple	LM	RS		98
Load Negative	LNR	RR	C	11
Store	ST	RX		50
Store Character	STC	RX		42
Store Halfword	STH	RX		40
Store Multiple	STM	RS		90
Subtract	SR	RR	C	1B
Subtract	S	RX	C	5B
Subtract Halfword	SH	RX	C	4B
Subtract Logical	SLR	RR	C	1F
Subtract Logical	SL	RX	C	5F
Supervisor Call	SVC	RR		0A
Test and Set	TS	SI	C	93
Test Channel	TCH	SI	C	9F
Test IO	TIO	SI	C	9D
Test Under Mask	TM	SI	C	91
Translate	TR	SS		DC
Translate and Test	TRT	SS	C	DD
Unpack	UNPK	SS		F3

Decimal Feature Instructions

Name	Mnemonic	Type	Code
Add Decimal	AP	SS T, C	FA
Compare Decimal	CP	SS T, C	F9
Divide Decimal	DP	SS T	FD
Edit	ED	SS T, C	DE
Edit and Mark	EDMK	SS T, C	DF
Multiply Decimal	MP	SS T	FC
Subtract Decimal	SP	SS T, C	FB
Zero and Add	ZAP	SS T, C	F8

Protection Feature Instructions

Name	Mnemonic	Type	Code
Insert Storage Key	ISK	RR Z	09
Set Storage Key	SSK	RR Z	08

Direct Control Feature Instructions

Name	Mnemonic	Type	Code
Read Direct	RDD	SI Y	85
Write Direct	WRD	SI Y	84

SS   These commands involve two operands, each of which is drawn from a MEMORY location. In all cases, we deal with VFL data; hence, a length specifier is required. Where the strings are of different lengths, the specifiers, L1 and L2, are both nibbles. Where the fields are of the same size, a single-byte length specifier, L, suffices. An example of the latter is *MoVe Character*, MVC, described thus:

$$\text{MVC:} \quad (M2) \rightarrow M1$$
$$(M2 + 1) \rightarrow M1 + 1$$
$$\cdots$$
$$(M2 + L - 1) \rightarrow M1 + L - 1 \tag{9.3.8}$$

where

$$M2 = D2 + (B2); \quad M1 = D1 + (B1) \tag{9.3.9}$$

Repertoire   The entire repertoire of System 360 is tabulated according to machine language code in Table 9.3.1. The first opcode nibble in *hex* partitions the repertoire into sixteen groups of up to sixteen opcodes each. Actually, only twelve groups of commands are used, each group has distinctive properties, some of which are discussed later.

The standard set and some features of interest are presented by mnemonics alphabetically in Table 9.3.2.

9.4   HARDWARE-INCORPORATED

MEMORIES

Altered system   Figure 9.4.1 is a system block diagram showing
concept   a revised view of System 360. MAIN MEMORY is central. However, when we speak of MEMORY, there are two other possibilities for our referent. MAIN MEMORY (MM) contains data and programs. It operates at two microseconds per access (less for some higher numbered models) and contains hundreds of thousands of bytes. The program found here in the machine language program is usually produced by the assembler or compiler.

There are other larger MEMORIES with which the computer communicates such as DISC or DRUM and which I prefer to consider AUXILIARY STORAGE DEVICES.

Within the computer proper, System 360 provides two additional MEMORIES:

- The READ-ONLY MEMORY, RM, provides a sequence of operations for each command in the form of microprogramming.

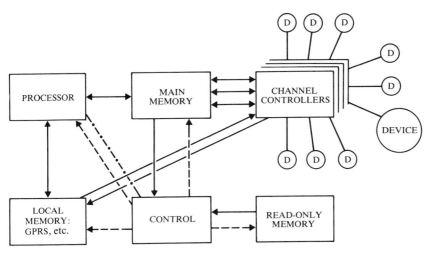

Fig. 9.4.1 System 360 block diagram.

- The LOCAL MEMORY, LM, holds the GPRs and other working
  REGISTERS.

CONTROL obtains instructions from the MAIN MEMORY and interprets
them. An instruction may refer to operands stored in MAIN MEMORY or
LOCAL MEMORY. In the latter case, only the GPRs are available to the
programmer, but they are available more quickly than from MM.

LOCAL MEMORY contains not only GPRs, but other CELLs which are
used as REGISTERS. To facilitate discussion, I will call these LM cells
"REGISTERS." Although LM REGISTERS are slower than electronic REGISTERS,
the saving in cost over the latter is considerable. To make effective use of
LM, increased complexity in timing provides overlap during reference to
other MEMORIES. Additional complexity is compensated for by lower total
cost.

The purpose of the READ-ONLY MEMORY is to reduce decoding and
analyzer hardware. The cost of this MEMORY is low because the computer
never writes into it.

Hence, these two additional MEMORIES reduce hardware cost without
reducing hardware function.

MEMORY function   The general MEMORY structure presented in
Chapter 1 prevails for MEMORIES encountered here. In Fig. 9.4.2, we see
this structure as it applies to the three MEMORIES of System 360.

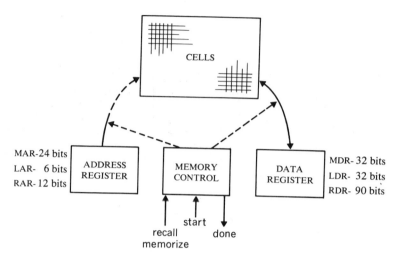

Fig. 9.4.2 General MEMORY structure.

There are three MEMORY functions:
- *store*—the MEMORY holds information without permitting it to evaporate.
- *recall*—a word whose address appears in the ADDRESS REGISTER is placed in the DATA REGISTER.
- *memorize*—the word in the DATA REGISTER is placed at the address contained in the ADDRESS REGISTER.

The four functional units of the MEMORY are shown in Fig. 9.4.2: CELLS; DATA REGISTER, DR; ADDRESS REGISTER, AR; CONTROL UNIT, CU. When one of these units is discussed, it is prefixed by a letter indicating the type of MEMORY to which it belongs.
- M for the MAIN MEMORY
- L for the LOCAL MEMORY
- R for the READ-ONLY MEMORY

Thus MAR is the MAIN MEMORY ADDRESS REGISTER, LR is the LOCAL MEMORY DATA REGISTER, and RCU is the READ-ONLY CONTROL UNIT. The complete MEMORIES are called MM, LM, and RM.

Figure 9.4.2 shows the size of REGISTERS associated with each MEMORY.

MAIN MEMORY   Model 50 MM may contain up to 256K bytes or more. Since these are accessed as Words, the MEMORY consists of up to 64K or more thirty-two bit Words.

Information in MAIN MEMORY is byte addressable: a byte or group of bytes may be addressed by an instruction. To make the MEMORY compatible with MEMORIES of the larger models of the series, 24 bits are reserved for this byte address. The size of the MAR in theory is 24 bits. In actuality, 16 bits suffice to address 64K Words for the Model 50.

A MM access cycle takes two microseconds or four subcycles of a half microsecond each. The first two subcycles are designated *R1* and *R2*; the second two are *W1* and *W2*. The first two cycles read a word for *recall* or clear a CELL for *memorize*.

R1 can only follow the *W2* cycle. A request to use the MDR causes a **read holdoff.** During *R2*, the MDR is available for use. This is the only subcycle during which the MDR is available: a MEMORY *recall* or *memorize* request is accepted then. If no request occurs, succeeding cycles are also designated as *W2*.

The MEMORY, the entire processing, and the control of the computer have been designed around these subcycles. A PROCESSOR *cycle* identically corresponds to the MAIN MEMORY *subcycle* and is so timed. It lasts for a half microsecond (500 nanoseconds).

Alignment   Fixed length fields, such as halfWords and doubleWords, must be located in MM on an **integral boundary** for that unit of information. A boundary is called integral when its address is a multiple of the length of the unit in bytes. Words must be located in MM so that their addresses are a multiple of 4. A halfWord must have an address that is a multiple of 2, and doubleWords must have an address that is a multiple of 8.

For MM addresses in binary, we find that integral boundaries for halfWords, Words, and doubleWords end with one, two, or three zeros, respectively. For example, the integral boundary for a Word is a binary number which ends in two zeros.

Variable fields are not limited to integral boundaries and so may start at any MM byte.

LOCAL MEMORY   The Model 50 LOCAL MEMORY contains sixty-four Word-size CELLs. To address them, the LAR is six bits long. To hold a Word, the LDR is thirty-two bits long.

The LM has a cycle time of half a microsecond. This is overlapped with MM cycles so as to increase the hardware efficiency.

The LOCAL MEMORY contains the following items:
- The fixed point GPRs labeled 0 through 15.
- The floating point GPRs labeled 0, 2, 4, and 6. Each double Word, floating point GPR requires two LM Words. The first Word is an even-numbered LM address; the second is at the next successive odd address.
- For each channel, there are four CHANNEL words (the MULTI-PLEXOR CHANNEL uses more):
  * the SUBCOMMAND LOCATION REGISTER
  * the CHANNEL CONTROLLER DATA ADDRESS REGISTER

* the CHANNEL CONTROLLER COUNT REGISTER
* the ASSEMBLY BUFFER REGISTER, AR
- Working storage—a number of REGISTERS hold intermediate results during a microprogrammed command sequence.
- Backup for some electronic REGISTERS including
  * the PSWR
  * the IR
- An INSTRUCTION BUFFER, IB.
- Spares.

LM is addressed during command execution by information in the word provided by the RM.

READ-ONLY
MEMORY
RM consists of over 2800 words of 90 bits each. RM is a 500-nanosecond MEMORY coordinated with the other two to increase hardware efficiency. RM replaces coding and analysis equipment in CONTROL.

It is possible but not customary to change RM mechanically before installation. A different MEMORY can provide a completely different command repertoire for the machine.

RM is often referred to as **microprogram** MEMORY because it controls all computer activities. Sequences stored in RM, besides controlling individual commands, also control *fetch*, CHANNEL CONTROL operations, and interrupts. There are microsequences for each command and/or for groups of commands in the System 360. The more complicated commands actually use loops set up in RM; SS commands, where a number of bytes of information are processed identically, exemplify this. Such a processing loop is performed once for each byte of data, as specified in the length field of the instruction.

Figure 9.4.3 shows how the RM is integrated with the rest of CONTROL. After an instruction is *fetched* completely, it generally resides in the MR where it is interpreted. The first byte contains the opcode. A portion of this code is entered into the RAR to access the RM. The word produced appears in the RDR. Here it is applied to the GATES in CONTROL and in the PROCESSOR to open or close appropriate GATES. This controls the flow of information for the next PROCESSOR cycle.

Part of the RDR contains all or part of the address of the next micro-command to be executed. This information is passed through the SWITCH to the RAR along with control signals from the IR. This SWITCH is controlled by another part of the RDR word so that the next word from RM for control of the forthcoming PROCESSOR cycle may be obtained and entered into the RDR.

When *execution* is complete, the next address to be entered in the RAR from the RDR is that of the *fetch* sequence so that the next command can be

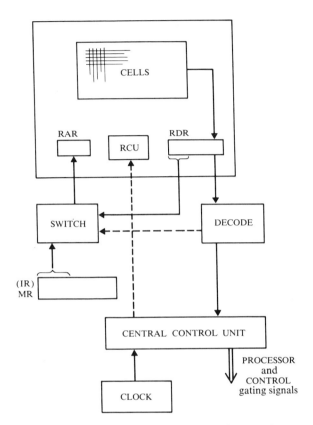

Fig. 9.4.3 READ-ONLY MEMORY—CONTROL subsystem interrelation.

procured. This may be overriden by interrupt or service request from a
CHANNEL which initiates an interrupt or a stolen cycle instead.

9.5 HARDWARE

Subsystems   The subsystem arrangement discussed in
Section 9.2 and presented in Fig. 9.2.1 is what the programmer sees. The
interrelation of the MEMORIES was just discussed. We look next at the
functional blocks contained in the PROCESSOR and CONTROL. These
subsystems are contained in a single main frame so that it is hard to
distinguish one from the other.

CHANNELS communicate directly with the MAIN MEMORY. However, as we shall see, they use CONTROL to facilitate this communication without much additional cost: they call forth their own microprogram sequences.

The interrelation of the three levels of MEMORY is important when examining the functional layout, Fig. 9.5.1:

- MAIN MEMORY contains programming information and data to be processed:
  * commands pass from MEMORY via the MDR, the ADDER output bus and the input SWITCHES, and thence they pass to the MR
  * data are routed according to the command in execution by the microprogram
- LOCAL MEMORY contains GPRS and other working REGISTERS
- READ-ONLY MEMORY is the source of all microprogram commands:
  * the RDR is the mechanism for controlling all the rest of the main frame
  * it also controls RM sequencing

REGISTERS and functions   Figure 9.5.1 shows the hardware REGISTERS of System 360 and their interrelation to the MEMORIES and SWITCHES. Although sketchy and imprecise, this is the "big picture"—it's not intended for the field service engineer. First examine main REGISTERS which, unless stated, are Word size; then find what each usually holds.

IAR

The INSTRUCTION ADDRESS REGISTER generally contains the address of the *first* byte of the *next* instruction to be executed; however, for long instructions, it may contain the address of bytes of the current instruction which has not yet been procured. The IAR is part of the PSWR and, when an interrupt occurs, the IAR is stored in MM with the rest of the contents of the PSWR in the old PSW location associated with the interrupt cause.

PSWR

The PROGRAM STATUS WORD REGISTER contains information about the running program which is not stored elsewhere in the hardware. For instance, it contains:

- instruction address (in IAR)
- activity masks
- condition code (in CCR)
- instruction length code (in ILCR)
- protect key (in PKR)

All these are HARD REGISTERS and are immediately available to guide the program together with the microprogrammed commands contained in the RDR. We sometimes refer to these SUBREGISTERS individually, such as the

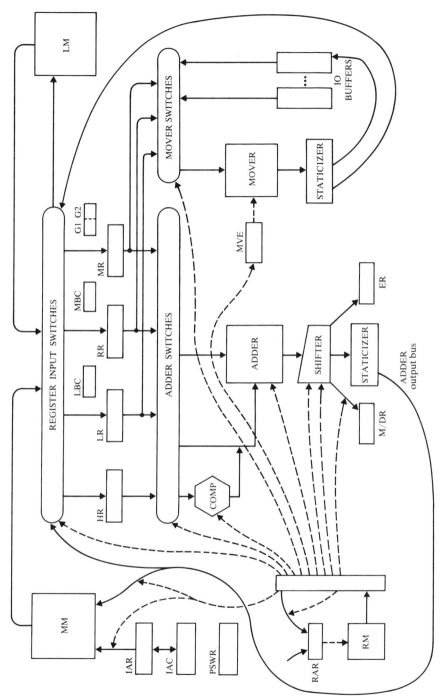

Fig. 9.5.1 System 360, Model 50 hardware.

249

IAR and the condition code register, CCR. This PSW information is also contained in a backup location in the LM.

IAC

During the *fetch* cycle, the INSTRUCTION ADDRESS COUNTER increments by two (or sometimes by four) the address contained in the IAR.

LR AND RR

The LEFT REGISTER and RIGHT REGISTER can communicate directly through SWITCHES with the LDR. They generally receive GPR or working storage information. They can hold operands of fixed length or bytes of VFL data during processing. These REGISTERS also hold operand addresses.

HR

Since the H REGISTER is not connected to the MOVER, it does not usually hold operands, but rather addresses. During interrupt, it receives the contents of the IAC to note our place in the program.

MR

The M REGISTER serves at least two functions. It is the INSTRUCTION REGISTER when the instruction is being *fetched*. But the instruction need not be maintained statically. After *fetch* and effective address calculation, it is no longer needed except to get the RM started on the proper microprogram sequence. This is discussed in Section 9.6. When the microprogram for a specific command is in control (replacing the *fetch* microprogram), there is no need for the MR to keep the instruction. Hence it is free for other tasks such as to hold VFL destination information during formation and assembly of words for storage with VFL commands.

BYTE COUNTERS

There are two byte COUNTERS to keep track of the most recent byte obtained or operated upon within a word in a REGISTER. The LEFT REGISTER COUNTER, LRC, generally keeps track of bytes in the LR, and the M REGISTER COUNTER, MRC, keeps track of bytes in the MR; but they may count bytes in other REGISTERS.

To keep track of bytes remaining during processing, the two length REGISTERS, G1 and G2, are the repository for the length descriptors L1 and L2. When there is only one length descriptor, L, these two REGISTERS operate together and are referred to as G1G2 or sometimes simply GR.

STATS

STATS are FLIPFLOPS which hold the transient states as they are observed in the main frame. They can be referenced by the microprogram, and decisions are made according to their settings. STATS are probably so called because they are single-bit static REGISTERS and store "states." For simplicity, no STATS are shown in the figure.

There are at least two 4-bit REGISTERs which store various quantities and counts during processing. Two of these are called the FR and the M/DR. They are used during arithmetic and function storage. They are also used to extend the SHIFTER as described later.

ADDER   The ADDER for the Model 50 is fullWord, thirty-two bit, parallel ADDER with carry lookahead. Each state provides two functions:

- What I call the carry *propagate* function is termed *transmit*.
- What I call carry *generate* is so named here.

The carry lookahead ADDER is described in detail in *The Logic of Computer Arithmetic*.† This ADDER has seven zero-level lookahead units and one first-level auxiliary lookahead.

Subtraction is performed by the ADDER using complementation and addition. A premature end-around carry is supplied by the microprogram. Multiplication and division require special microprograms which are supplied as an option for Model 50 users.

Decimal addition and subtraction are described in Section 9.10. Two or three cycles are required for each Word of decimal digits, depending upon the magnitude of the result. The parallel binary ADDER is used with an extra correction cycle.

SHIFTER   The output of the ADDER is entered into a SHIFTER which can be controlled for:

- direction of shift—right or left
- quantity of shift—zero, one, or four places

These functions are under the control of the microprogram.

Shifting may move information out of the direct line output of the ADDER or enter new information into the direct line of the ADDER. To hold appended and/or deleted information, EXTENDERs are required: FR and M/DR generally serve. Further, STATs may store the states of different areas within the ADDER after its function is performed, e.g., interdigit carries and overflows.

After ADDER information passes out of the SHIFTER, it is staticized onto FLIPFLOPS. The FLIPFLOPS present the sum of the ADDER onto the ADDER output bus which is routed to the entry GATES of most of the REGISTERs.

MOVER   The MOVER performs logic on a pair of bytes furnished at its inputs which are referred to as the U and V inputs. Most

† Ivan Flores, *The Logic of Computer Arithmetic.* Englewood Cliffs, N.J.: Prentice-Hall, Inc., 1963. See Chapter 5.

bytes of most REGISTERS are available to one or another input of the MOVER. In particular, LR, RR, and MR can be thus manipulated. To gate out the desired byte, the LBC and MBC are used.

The logical function to be performed upon the pair of bytes by the MOVER function is stored in the MVF, the MOVER FUNCTION REGISTER. Function information is placed there by the microprogram or from the auxiliary REGISTERS, FR or M/DR.

The result of the various functions which the MOVER can perform, described in Section 9.9, is always a single byte. This is staticized by the MOVER on its OUTPUT LATCHES and furnished to the MOVER output bus. From there it is entered into the required byte of the desired REGISTER by the microcommand. The MOVER is the only means for performing logical operations on information—no bit-picking facility is provided. All such operations are done by user-provided masks.

SWITCHES   SWITCHES are found at the input and output of most REGISTERS and the FUNCTIONAL UNITS. There are a large number of SWITCHES required; for clarity, they are indicated in Fig. 5.9.1 simply by an oval. All SWITCHES and FUNCTIONAL UNITS are controlled by the microprogram. They are driven by the information in the static data REGISTER of the READ-ONLY MEMORY, the RDR.

9.6 FETCH

Completed   Activity performed during *fetch* depends on
instruction   the *completeness* of the last command Word.
Information is accessed in MEMORY in terms of Words. If the last Word brought from MM for instructions is all used up, if all of its four bytes have been interpreted during the last execution, we say that the previous instruction was **completed.** If there remains command information (bytes) from the last instruction Word, then the command is said to be **uncompleted.**

Figure 9.6.1 illustrates three alternatives for *completed* instructions:
- The last instruction was RR, with the command occupying the right-hand halfWord.
- The last instruction was RX, RI, or SI, beginning on a Word boundary.
- The last instruction was SS, ending on a Word boundary.

Uncompleted instructions end on a halfWord boundary as shown in the figure.

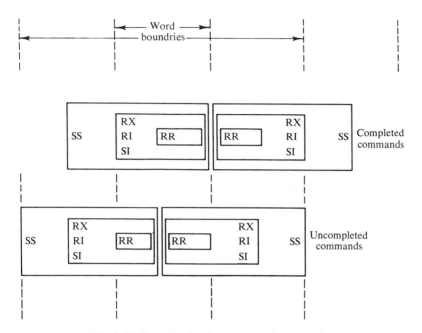

Fig. 9.6.1 Completed and uncompleted commands.

Action   The action for a *completed* instruction is
shown in Fig. 9.6.2. The IAR contains the address of the next instruction
(which begins on a Word boundary). This is sent to the MAR and *recall* is
initiated. The contents of the MDR are placed in the MR and entered into
LM in the INSTRUCTION BUFFER, IB.

The left-hand portion of MR determines the instruction type. For RR
instructions, the contents of the IAR are passed over to the IAC where they
are incremented by 2. In all other cases, including SS instructions, the
IAR is incremented by 4 using the IAC. For the SS instruction, another
MEMORY access is required to enter to obtain full operand information.

Uncompleted   The action for an uncompleted instruction
instruction   is shown in Fig. 9.6.3. An MM *recall* is
started; but what if CONTROL INDICATORS show that the last instruction
ended at a halfWord boundary? The last instruction may be obtained
from the IB in LM rather than using MM. Since LM *recall* requires only half a
microsecond, it is preferable.

Obtain the datum from the IB, shift it left, and enter it into the MR. Then
increment the IAR by 2 using the IAC, thereafter initiating an MM *recall*.

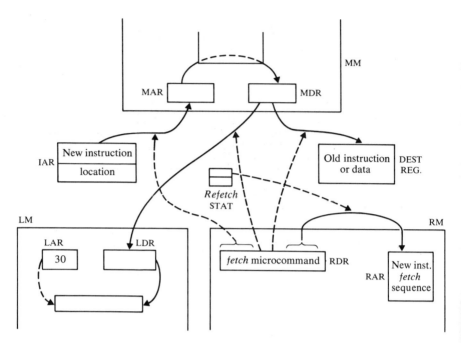

Fig. 9.6.2 *Fetch* for *completed* command.

Check the opcode in MR. For an RR instruction, *execute* it without further MM reference. Meanwhile, the next instruction is being obtained.

If the instruction in MR is not of type RR, then the rest of the instruction is placed by the MM *recall* in the MDR and then in the MR. From there, this word is passed over to the IB for future use. It may contain the last halfWord of an SS command or the first halfWord of a new command.

The left halfWord in the MDR is passed over to the right halfWord of the MR. We now have a fullWord in MR and can start *execution*. For an SS instruction, the remaining halfWord is in the IB.

Again we check the left side of the MR for instruction type. If this is a fullWord instruction, the first halfWord of the *next* instruction is in the IB. We set a STAT to indicate this and then increment the IAR by 2. For the SS instruction, we increment the IAR by 4, also indicating that the remainder of the instruction is in the IB.

Fetch; completed command   With the end of *execution*, the *fetch* microcommand sequence start address is placed in the RAR. The first *fetch* microcommand is brought to the RDR to commence *fetch*, Fig. 9.6.2. If the REFETCH STAT is set, a *completed* command is now in the MR. New command bytes are not in the LM and hence must be brought from MM.

The microcommand in the RDR causes the IAR contents to go to the MAR. The new command goes to the MR and also to LM at the IB (INSTRUCTION BUFFER) location.

Fetch; incomplete command   The *fetch* microcommand procures the IB contents from LM since the REFETCH STAT is *reset;* it generally is in this case, unless an *interrupt*, or something, has happened. This causes the contents of the IAR to be incremented by 2 in the IAC and sent over to the MAR. Thus the *recall* of the next four instruction bytes from MM is initiated regardless of the opcode of *this* instruction, which is now being brought from the IB. The *classification* cycle which follows will determine that.

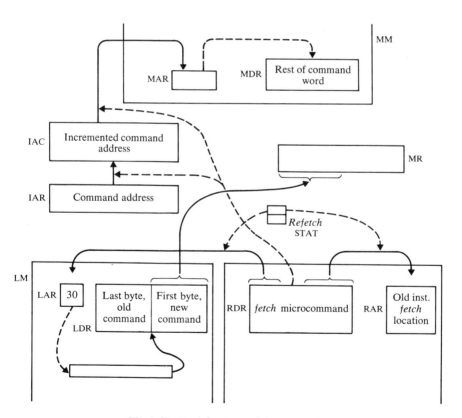

Fig. 9.6.3 *Fetch* for *incomplete* command.

Command Type	1L	1R	2L	2R	3L	3R	4L	4R
RR	opcode		R1	R2	X	X	X	X
RX	opcode		R1	X2	B2		D2	
RS	opcode		R1	R3	B2		D2	
SI	opcode		I2		B1		D1	
SS	opcode		L1	L2	B1		D1	
			L					

(heading above table: Byte, MR)

Fig. 9.6.4 The contents of the MR after the *fetch* activity for various types of commands.

Preclassification   After *fetch*, the command (or semicommand) is oriented in the MR as displayed in Fig. 9.6.4. It is evident that the MR serves as the INSTRUCTION REGISTER during *fetch, classification,* and part of the *execute* cycles of System 360.

The salient advantage of the asynchronous MEMORIES is that we get

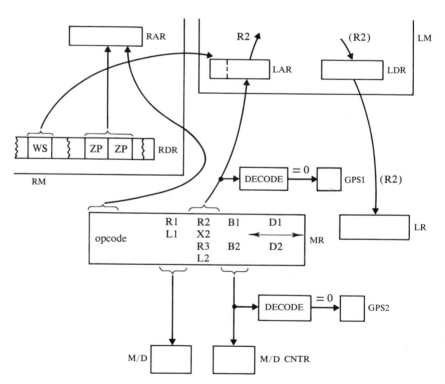

Fig. 9.6.5 GPR identification routing and acquisition during classification.

hardware command processing started before command acquisition is complete. From one to three GPR contents (Fig. 9.6.4) may be required for calculation of the effective address. GPR contents can be procured as soon as GPR identification is available in the MR. One way GPR identification is routed is shown in Fig. 9.6.5. The two half bytes of the second byte are stored in the REGISTERS called the M/DR and the JR. The JR is actually the least significant four bits of the LAR; the other two bits of the LAR are set by the field called WS (working storage) in the microcommand found in the RDR. This way we address the GPRs and not other LM CELLS. *Recall* is started; the destination of the datum (the GPR contents) after receipt by the LDR is the LR.

The left half of the third byte in MR is a GPR identifier. When the MR has been filled, this identifier is stored in the counter, MDC. Status REGISTERS, GPS1 and GPS2, are set if the last two half bytes are empty.

Classification   The first two bits of the opcode distinguish four classes of commands. A different microroutine is entered for each class. The RM address of the routine is formed from these two bits and the ZD and ZF fields of the current microcommand. A finer classification is done on the first few steps of each group microroutine.

9.7   REGISTER COMMANDS

Types   Table 9.3.1 classifies System 360 commands by opcode and type. Fixed Word REGISTER commands have opcodes for which the left nibble is between 0 and 7. Let us look at these on the chart:

> 0—Branch and status switching commands are discussed in Section 9.8.
>
> 1—Fixed point fullWord logical commands are discussed later.
>
> 2, 3—Load and arithmetic floating point commands are not discussed in this book.
>
> 4—Some are fixed point halfWord commands for which *execution* is very similar to fixed point Word commands. Wherever "Word" appears in the discussion, substitute "halfWord." Branch commands of this group are discussed in Section 9.8.
>
> 5—These fixed Word commands specify one operand from MEMORY rather than from a REGISTER.
>
> 6, 7—Indexed floating point commands are not discussed here.

Data   Data for all arithmetic commands in group 0 through 7 must be formatted according to the data group of the command.

Thus, when fixed point fullWord arithmetic is called for, a fullWord is operated upon, assuming that it is a thirty-two bit signed binary number. Similarly, floating point information should be Word or double Word of the form described in the manual. HalfWord commands manipulate sixteen bits of binary information using the right-hand two bytes of a REGISTER. The sign bit in the result is duplicated in the remaining sixteen bits to the left.

NOTATION

System 360 uses two's complement notation for fixed point arithmetic. This is thoroughly described in Chapter 2 of *The Logic of Computer Arithmetic*.† The first bit of such numbers is zero for positive numbers, and the remaining bits are a straight binary representation of the number. Negative numbers are the two's complement of the positive number to which this number corresponds; their left-hand bit is always 1.

Format   RR commands specify two GPRs, one in each of the two nibbles of the second command byte. During *fetch*, these nibbles locate the operands in the LOCAL MEMORY; microcommands bring them to the RR and LR where they may be operated on by the adder.

For RX commands, one field, R1, of one nibble specifies a GPR. The three other fields determine an operand address, M2, which is formed by the ADDER. The operand at M2 may then be obtained. We examine operand acquisition next.

RR operand   An RR command does the following task:
acquisition

$$(R1) \, \theta \, (R2) \rightarrow R1 \qquad\qquad (9.7.1)$$

The operands are contained in two of the GPRs, and the operation performed is indicated as θ. Before we acquire the operands and at the end of the classification cycle, the REGISTER situation is as shown in Fig. 9.6.5. The contents of R2 have been obtained by the following typical chain of events:

- The R2 field is extracted from the command in MR.
- It is sent to the JR portion of LAR.
- The remaining two bits of the LAR are supplied from the WS field in the RDR.
- The proper GPR contents are obtained from LM and entered into the LDR.
- These contents are sent from the LDR to the LR.

† Ivan Flores, *op. cit.*

It remains to obtain the other operand. This is in R1, and it is obtained by the following typical set of operations:
- The R1 field is extracted from the MR and sent to the LAR.
- The WS bits in RDR supplement the other four bits in the LAR.
- The contents of the indicated REGISTER are sent to the LDR.
- They are passed over to the RR.

Note that this is a *typical* sequence because of the crash manner in which the Model 50 was designed, where different microprograms were written by different engineering groups. Hence we find little consistency from one command to another as to how the addresses are prepared and REGISTER contents held.

RX command   A glance at Table 9.3.1 reveals that there are many commands in group 5 which have the same title as those in group 1 except that the suffix R is missing from the mnemonic. These truncated mnemonics apply to commands which are similar to commands with untruncated mnemonics except for the method of operand acquisition: group 5 commands get one operand from MEMORY; group 1 commands find both operands stored in a GPR.

For group 5 (RX), to obtain the operand, we first calculate its address, M2, given by

$$M2 = (X2) + (B2) + D2 \qquad (9.7.2)$$

The calculation requires the contents of INDEX REGISTER, X2, and BASE REGISTER, B2. Both of these are actually GPR designations but are in different fields in the command.

In Fig. 9.6.5, the same method used to obtain (R2) for RR commands has obtained (X2) for the RX commands.

Since the second operand is in MAIN MEMORY, whereas the first operand is in LOCAL MEMORY, it is expedient to calculate the second operand address, M2, before we obtain R1. Then this latter operation can be overlapped with a MAIN MEMORY acquisition cycle.

We might obtain the base modifier with this typical series of operations:
- Route B2 to the LAR from its field in the MR.
- Route the prefix bits from WS in the RDR to the LAR.
- Obtain (B2) from the LM and place it in the LDR.
- Route it over to the RR.

During this time, an addition *may* be taking place:
- Enter the displacement, D2, from the MR, into one input of the adder.
- Take the contents of the LR, (X2), and add it to the former.
- The result, (X2) + D2, is routed to the LR.

After these two operations are completed—getting (B2) and calculating (X2) + D—we add (B2) to the latter quantity in the LR, placing the result in RR. Meanwhile, we do another LM acquisition obtaining the first operand, (R1), from LOCAL MEMORY.

When the calculation of M2 is complete, it is sent over to the MAR to *recall* the operand, (M2), placing it in the LR via the MDR.

Microprogramming   All operations of the computer are controlled by the microprogram, a sequence of microcommands contained in the RM. Whenever an *execution* phase is completed, the *fetch* microprogram is initiated and its first microcommand brought to the RDR. It is interpreted there, and the *fetch* cycle proceeds.

After the first two or four bytes of the command have been established in the MR, the type of command is distinguished by the first two bits of the first byte. This causes a microprogram *branch* to the proper operand acquisition routine. Thus RR and RX commands are distinguished, and the computer can proceed to obtain (R2) or (M2). During these micro-routines, there is a close coordination between the computer LM and RM. The MM is called upon only to get the contents of M2.

The microprogram controls all the FUNCTIONAL UNITS in the PROCESSOR, including the ADDER, the MOVER, and all GATES involved. For instance, for the ADDER, the microprogram determines which two of all the REGISTERS are connected to the ADDER inputs and whether either of these inputs is complemented. Masks may be set up at the ADDER inputs so that selected bytes may be added instead of a complete Word. The microprogram also controls what is done with the ADDER overflow, how many places are shifted, etc.

Transfers; logic   We now examine four types of commands:
- load—a Word or portion thereof is entered into a REGISTER.
- store—the contents of the GPR are placed in MEMORY.
- logical—the logical function is performed on two operands and the result placed in a GPR.
- compare—two operands are compared and the condition code is stored in the CONDITION CODE REGISTER, CCR.

LOAD

Load enters a Word into a GPR. The operand is obtained from either LM or MM. For the former, an RR command, LR, suffices to specify that the contents of one GPR are copied into another GPR. For the RX command, the contents of the MEMORY CELL, M2, are copied into the GPR, R1, using L. The operand address, M2, is prepared as described, and the operand is procured and placed in the LR. From there, it is sent to the LDR. Meanwhile, R1, from its position in the MR, is sent over to the LAR. A *memorize* cycle is requested and the LM *loaded*.

Store enters a Word from a GPR into a MEMORY CELL, four bytes starting at M2; an RX command, ST, is required. While the address, M2, is being prepared, (R1) is obtained and placed in the LR. This is passed over to the MDR while M2 is passed over to the MAR and placed in MM with a *memorize* cycle.

STORE

The contents of the GPR, R1, are passed over to the LR. The second operand may come from R2 or M2. In any case, it is passed over to MR. The logical operation is performed on a byte basis. Respective bytes of the LR and MR are passed over to the MOVER. The MBC keeps track of the byte being worked on. The MVF contains a pair of bits which are set by the microprogram to the function performed by the MOVER during the logical command, *and*, *or*, or *exclusive or*. We keep track of what goes on in the MOVER and set the CCR accordingly. As the MOVER performs the function on its byte, the new byte is passed to the MOVER output bus. This is returned to the source position in the MR.

LOGICAL

When all four bytes are processed, the result in MR is passed over to the LM using the R1 address stored in one of the other REGISTERS.

Compare starts like a logical command. The operands are placed, respectively, in the MR and LR. They are then operated upon by the MOVER. However, the result of the MOVER operation is not returned to the MR, which is hence unaffected. The MOVER output is examined, and the CCR is set according to this output. No *memorize* cycle is required at the end of the *compare* since only the setting of the CCR is important in this command.

COMPARE

Arithmetic   Fixed word arithmetic is performed upon binary numbers in two's complement form. Both addition and subtraction are done using only *true* add or *complement* add. No recomplementation cycle is required because the numbers are in two's complement form.

ADD/SUBTRACT

An algebraic function is performed; the *actual arithmetic* done is determined by the signs of the two operands and whether addition or subtraction is requested.

Fixed word multiplication uses binary numbers in two's complement form. The operands are obtained as described, one going to the RR and another to the LR. The sign of the numbers determines the sign of the product which is then stored. The numbers are converted into *magnitude*

MULTIPLY

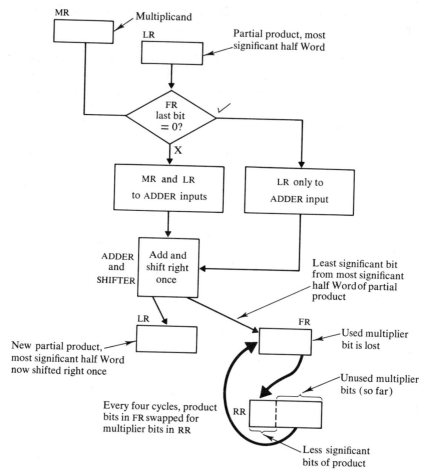

Fig. 9.7.1 Multiply flowchart.

form and switched, if necessary, so that, at the beginning of multiplication proper, the larger is *always* in the MR and the smaller in the RR.

Fixed positive multiplication takes place as shown in Fig. 9.7.1. Clear the LR which will contain the most significant partial product Word. The RR contains the multiplier; it will contain part of the multiplier and part of the partial product, the least significant part during intermediate cycles; on completion, the RR contains the less significant product Word.

Take a nibble from the RR and put it in the FR, a NIBBLE REGISTER. The least significant bit in the FR determines the next multiplier cycle: if it is 1, add the multiplicand to the partial product; if it is 0, add nothing (all 0's).

In both cases, the output of the ADDER is shifted right once as it is entered in the LR. The bit shifted *out* of the ADDER to the *right* is inserted at the *left* of the FR; the *right-hand* bit of the FR is shifted out and lost.

The foregoing operations continue for three more cycles to develop a less significant partial product nibble in the FR. On a separate cycle, this nibble is shifted from the FR into the RR upper end; then the least significant nibble from the RR is shifted into the FR. This new multiplier nibble is used for four more cycles. COUNTERS keep track of how many multiplication cycles are performed.

Upon the completion of thirty-two cycles, the product is contained in the concatenation of the LR and RR. It is then stored in LM at R1 and R1 + 1. Multiplication produces two Words; also, each of the operands is of Word size. Hence, to store the product, we require two GPRs. It is up to the programmer to set aside two GPRs starting at R1 in LM to store the product. System 360 requires that the R1 specification be an even number so that the microprogram for multiply can access LM most easily.

Fixed division of binary numbers in two's complement form is non-restoring. The process is reciprocal to multiplication described above:
- The sign of the quotient is determined from the signs of the operands.
- Numbers are placed in magnitude form:
  * the divisor goes to the LR
  * the more significant dividend Word goes to the RR
  * the less significant Word goes to the MR
  * the leftmost nibble of the MR goes to the FR

The situation is shown in Fig. 9.7.2. As long as the remainder is positive, we subtract the RR from the LR; otherwise, we add the RR and the LR. The FR may be considered a left extension of the RR for each set of four cycles. A subtraction (addition) is performed. A quotient bit is determined: 0 for a negative partial remainder; 1 for a positive remainder. The ADDER output most significant bit is placed into the right bit position of the FR. Simultaneously, we shift the RR and the FR one position to the left, entering the leftmost bit of the FR into the rightmost bit position of the RR. Since the FR was filled with the most significant bits of the low-order portion of the dividend, this process provides significant bits of the partial remainder to the RR.

Note that as dividend bits in the FR are used up, quotient bits are placed there. At the end of four cycles, the FR contains a quotient nibble and no more dividend bits. Place the quotient nibble into the right nibble position of the MR, and shift off a new dividend nibble from the left of the MR into the FR.

DIVIDE

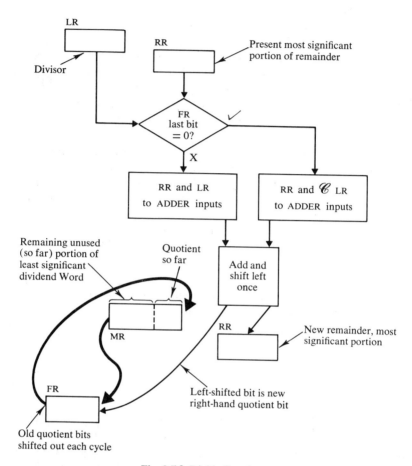

Fig. 9.7.2 Divide flowchart.

Sets of four cycles continue thus until the entire quotient is made. The quotient then sits in the MR, with the remainder in the RR. These two Words are entered into LM to complete division. As noted for multiplication, a double REGISTER is specified for the dividend both to call for a double Word dividend and to provide room for the quotient *and* remainder. Again, it starts on an even number to facilitate LM accessing.

Convert to decimal   There is a single command to convert a binary number to decimal, **CVD**. The computer does this with the **double-dabble** system, shown in Fig. 9.7.3, which we now explain.

Start with a sum of 0, and examine from left to right the number to be converted. Take what we have so far, double it, and add the next digit. The first time, we double 0 and add 1 to get 1. Next we double 1 and add 1 to it to get 3; and so on. As you can see, the eight-bit number in the figure converts to 229 in decimal. The name, double-dabble, arose since, in converting, we either *double* or *double* and *add* 1 (*dabble*).

We apply the same principle to NBCD numbers, except that, instead of storing decimal numbers in arabic numerals, we store them in their NBCD code. To double any small digit, we simply shift the code leftward one position. Thus, the code for number 3 is 0011; the code for 6 is 0110—the code for 3 shifted leftward one position.

This works well until we come to digits which number 5 or greater. When larger NBCD codes are shifted, we get a hexadecimal representation which means something, but which is an incorrect NBCD code for the doubled digit. The correction is to add the code for 6 (0110) whenever we encounter a *large* digit to be doubled.

To convert from binary to decimal we:

1. shift the new number leftward one place, adding corrections detected on a previous cycle;

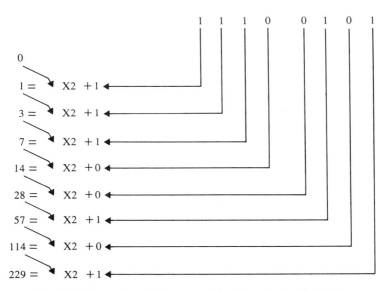

Fig. 9.7.3 Conversion of binary to decimal by the double-dabble method.

2. append the next left-hand bit to the right-hand position of the number we are forming;
3. check to see if any digits should be corrected;
4. set up the correction term for addition on the *next* cycle.

REGISTERS   The PROCESSOR REGISTERS which take part in conversion contain the following:

- The RR—initially set to 0. Eventually, it contains the result from conversion, the code for the corresponding decimal number.
- The LR—which temporarily stores correction factors.
- The FR—which holds four bits at a time of the binary number being converted.
- The MR—which initially contains the entire binary number being converted.

EXAMPLE

Figure 9.7.4 is a sample conversion as done by the computer. On line 1 the RR is cleared and the FR is filled with the first four bits of the number for conversion. The LR is also set to 0 since no correction is used on the first cycle. On line 2 we add the correction to form a sum, line 3. At the same time, a bit from the FR is spilled off and placed into the FR as the sum is shifted left and placed in the RR. The output of the ADDER is examined. If a digit position registers 8 or greater, a correction factor is inserted in the LR for that digit.

On lines 4, 5, and 6; and 7, 8, and 9; and 10, 11, and 12 the same three cycles are repeated:

- add in the correction factor
- shift left one position
- append the next digit

In all these cycles, the correction factor is 0.

On line 12, the output of the ADDER is E_H, which is a code combination greater than 8. It calls for a correction factor to be inserted into the LR, namely, 0110, line 13. This is added in line 14, and the sum produced is now 8 bits long, line 15.

Notice that, as we proceed, we make correction factors for two or more digits. Actually, the PROCESSOR always examines a fullWord to make up the correction factors; we have been examining only the significant portion of the word. Notice that, on line 22, both codes are greater than 8, and two correction factors are set into the LR.

Decimal to binary   To convert a decimal to binary using CVB, we do just the opposite operations:

1. Halve the decimal number.

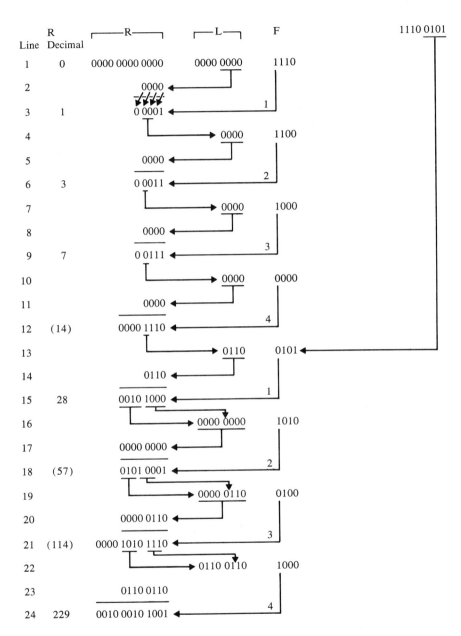

Fig. 9.7.4 Machine conversion from binary to decimal.

2. The remainder is the next bit developed, and it goes to the left of the previously developed bits.

3. A correction term is necessary because of XS6 (excess six) notation.

To halve a number coded in NBCD, each digit is shifted rightward. However, this will produce some digits incorrectly coded. We detect this when a 1 is about to pass from one digit rightward to the next. At this point, a correction is necessary.

The correction consists of subtracting 6 from the position to the right.

The necessity for correction is noted when we examine the output of the ADDER. Whenever a 1 appears in the second bit of a digit, the correction must be made upon the next digit to the right, after that digit has been shifted right one position.

The correction term is entered into the LR. An NBCD 6, 0110, is entered into that portion of the LR. On the next halving operation, this quantity is subtracted. Recall that, to subtract, we *add* the one's complement of the number in the LR. A precarry is necessary to give the two's complement; this is jammed into the carry-in position of the ADDER by the microcommand in the RDR.

The RR contains the decimal number to be converted, and the LR contains correction terms as they are generated during processing. The FR receives the bits as they are shifted out during addition. The MR receives the quantity placed in the FR every four cycles to expedite the conversion process.

Figure 9.7.5 is an example of conversion from decimal to binary. To make it simpler to follow, we convert decimal 229 into binary to observe that the process is just the reverse of that portrayed in Fig. 9.7.4.

Correction is done by sensing the output of the ADDER. A special initial cycle is required to shift the original quantity to the left and then again right. This forces a quantity out of the ADDER from which to derive the correction term for the first actual conversion cycle.

When 1 is sensed on the ADDER output in the second bit position of a digit, 0110 is entered in the next rightward digit position in the LR. In the figure, the double initial cycle is omitted since it is easy to see that correction terms are required in both positions of the LR, line 1. This correction applies to the halved output which is a halved number, line 2. The correction is performed by adding the one's complement of the LR and a precarry to get an end-around carry. The output of the ADDER generates the next correction term. The output of the ADDER is shifted to the right and entered into the RR. As the shift is performed, the right-hand bit from the ADDER is entered into the FR.

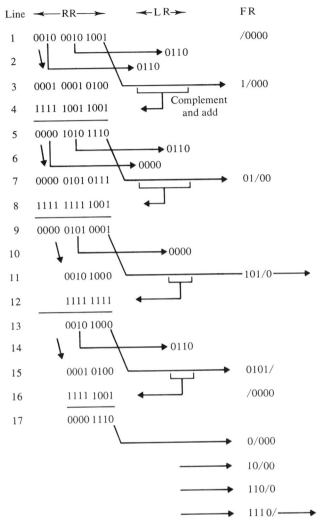

Fig. 9.7.5 Decimal to binary conversion

Cycles continue thus until four bits are accumulated in the FR. These are then sent off to the proper position in the MR.

Sets of four cycles continue until the entire thirty-two bit number is prepared.

At the beginning of a cycle, the present version of the number to be converted is in the RR. The correction term for it is in the LR. The correction is subtracted from the halved number by the ADDER by complement addition. The result coming out of the ADDER is stored, and the new correction factor is inserted in the LR. The right-hand bit from the ADDER is pushed into the FR, and the remaining bits are entered into the RR.

9.8 REFLEXIVE COMMANDS

Reflexive commands cause the computer to deviate from its normal sequence. We review normal sequencing first.

Normal operation   During *execution* proper, the INSTRUCTION ADDRESS REGISTER, IAR, contains the first byte address of the next instruction. When a command *execution* is complete, the *fetch* microprogram is called. If the assigned STAT shows that a *completed* instruction was just finished, bytes for the next instruction are obtained from MM using the IAR address. For an *uncompleted* instruction, the two bytes of the new command available in LM are obtained and placed in the MR for instruction interpretation.

As each pair of instruction bytes is obtained, either from LM or MM, the IAR is advanced by 2 to reflect the address of the next byte pair, regardless of whether *all* the bytes in the instruction have been procured.

The MR cannot hold an entire six-byte instruction. Hence, *fetch* is broken into two stages. The M1 address is calculated and stored before the third pair of bytes, when needed, is placed in the MR.

A common deviation from normal operation is a *jump* or, in IBM's terminology, a *branch*. The *branch* replaces the contents of the IAR by an address calculated from the *branch* command.

FORMAT

Branch on condition   This command can be either RR or RX and is formatted thus:

RR-BCR: 07 R1 R2   (9.8.1)

RX-BC: 47 R1 X2 B2 D2   (9.8.2)

where the fields have these meanings:
- R1 is a mask indicating the conditions for which a branch is taken.
- R2 *contains* the address of the branch—(R2) is the address of the branch.
- M2 *is* the branch address: $M2 = (X2) + (B2) + D2$.

Table 9.8.1 MASK BITS, BC AND BCR COMMANDS

	R1			*CC*	
B8	*B9*	*B10*	*B11*	*Octal*	*Binary*
1	X	X	X	0	00
X	1	X	X	1	01
X	X	1	X	2	10
X	X	X	1	3	11

The CCR, part of the PSWR, holds two bits. This permits four combinations, reflecting four conditions which may arise. R1 in BC or BCR conveys to CONTROL the branch requirement by stating a unique *set* of these four conditions. There are four condition codes which CCR might hold. There are sixteen combinations for which codes will or will not be tested. Hence, there are actually sixteen possibilities to be designated; when present, only a condition code belonging to the designated set will cause a branch.

Four bits can distinguish sixteen specific *combinations*, the sets of conditions, any *one* of which may cause a jump. These combinations of conditions are conveyed by R1 with bits designated B8, B9, B10, and B11. If one of these positions contains 1, a corresponding code in the CCR causes a branch. These mask codes are shown in Table 9.8.1.

When R1 is 6_H, condition codes 01 and 10 apply. Thus, a *branch* is taken for the *less* or *greater* conditions and no others. In other words, the branch occurs only for *unequal*.

The condition code in the CCR is set by many commands, including arithmetic. These are listed in the IBM System 360 manual. The most important use for the condition codes occurs after a *compare*.

Table 9.8.2 shows examples of masks used to cause jumps for various condition combinations.

Table 9.8.2 EXAMPLE OF MASKS AND THEIR CONDITIONS FOR BC AND BCR COMMANDS AFTER A *compare*

R1, hexadecimal	*R1, binary*				*CC*				*Meaning*
					=			None	
	B8	*B9*	*B10*	*B11*	0	1	2	3	
2	0	0	1	0	0	0	1	0	>
6	1	1	1	0	0	1	1	0	≠
C	1	1	0	0	1	1	0	0	≮
0	0	0	0	0	0	0	0	0	NOOP
F	1	1	1	1	1	1	1	1	UCJ

When R1 is 2_H in Table 9.8.2, when B10 only is set to 1, the jump occurs only when the condition code is 10: the last previous comparison must produce *greater* for the jump to occur.

When R1 = C_H, condition codes 00 and 02 are called for and a branch is taken on *less than* or *equal* conditions.

When R1 is 0_H, *no* condition code causes a branch; this is equivalent to a NOOP.

When R1 is F_H, *any* condition code will *cause* a branch. Since *one* of the four possible condition codes must be present, this mask causes an unconditional branch or UCJ.

When a branch is next taken, the address of the first byte of the next command is found in the IAR. If the branch *is* taken, (R2) is placed in the IAR for BCR; M2 is formed and placed in the IAR for BC. A *fetch* is then instituted.

Branch and link   These commands have the format:

RR-BALR: 05   R1   R2   (9.8.3)

RX-BAL: 45   R1   X2   B2   D2   (9.8.4)

Both provide links with subroutines. This *branch is unconditional*. The place where we left the main program is left in GPR R1. The contents of the IAR, the command length code, the condition code, and a program mask are all put in R1. In other words, the left Word of the doubleWord PSW is transferred into R1, and we jump to the operand address:

- the *contents* of R2 for BALR
- *M2* for BAL

To perform this command, the left PSW Word is prepared and placed in the LR. Its destination, R1, is obtained from MR and placed in the LAR. LM *memorize* places this information into LM. The branch address is obtained (BALR) or prepared (BAL) and placed in the IAR, and *fetch* is initiated.

Branch on count   These commands have the format:

RR-BCTR: 06   R1   R2   (9.8.5)

RX-BCT: 46   R1   X2   B2   D2   (9.8.6)

They decrement GPR R1 by one and then test it. The branch is taken when (R1) is nonzero. Otherwise, we continue in sequence. This command is especially useful for loops performed a number of times, determined by a count stored in R1. Remember, though, that sequencing through a list cannot be done with this command *alone*. When an INDEX REGISTER is used to monitor a list, the length of each datum must be kept in mind. For fixed data size, the INDEX REGISTER must be incremented or decremented by the *number of bytes* required for each datum. For instance, in sequencing through a list of items each of Word size, the increment or decrement is 4.

For both BCTR and BCT, (R1) is brought from LM and placed in the LR; then 1 is subtracted from it by passing it through the ADDER. On leaving the ADDER to go to the LDR, (R1) is tested against zero. If *unequal*, the branch address is prepared and entered into the IAR. If (R1) is zero, command execution is terminated; the IAR is unaffected. The decremented contents of R1 is always returned to R1.

Execute   The *execute* command format is:

$$\text{RX-EX:} \quad 44 \quad \text{R1} \quad \text{X2} \quad \text{B2} \quad \text{D2} \qquad (9.8.7)$$

It allows us to go outside the program stream and execute exactly one command, thereafter automatically returning to the program stream. We might call this indirect command addressing. The command to be executed is at M2.

This leaves the field R1 to be explained. IBM System 360 *execute* is distinctive because the last byte of the instruction at M2 is *or*'ed with the second byte of the contents of the specified GPR. This permits modification of the *executed* instruction in various ways not described here. The MEMORY image of the *executed* command (at M2) is unaffected by this.

The benefits of being able to *execute* one command outside the program string are not described here. However, it should be recognized that there is a limitation imposed by not permitting *execute* commands within the range of *execute* commands. This is similar to contrasting single in-direction with multiple indirection in addressing systems.

To fulfill an *execute* command, we first form M2. We then get the command situated at M2, simultaneously getting the contents of R1. The new command is installed in the MR, and the *or* procedure is performed by using the MOVER and reinstating the new byte into its proper position in the MR. The new command is executed as though it had been obtained originally from the address previously in the IAR.

When an SS command is the *executed* command, six bytes must be obtained somewhere along the line. The bytes used so far are kept track of in backup CELLS in LM. The new bytes are procured after the M2 address of the *executed* command has been formed and stored in the hardware REGISTERS of the PROCESSOR.

The command in the MR is treated as any other command. Upon its completion, the microprogram is switched to a *fetch* cycle. The IAR still contains the address of the next command (after the *execute*).

Supervisor call   With the format:

$$\text{RR-SVC:} \quad \text{0A} \quad \text{R1} \quad \text{R2} \qquad\qquad (9.8.8)$$

this command causes an interrupt, transmitting the pair R1R2 (not their contents) to the PSWR and therefrom to the old PSW location. The resulting interrupt is handled as described in Section 9.12.

Other   There are a few more reflexive commands. Their purpose is status switching or augmenting. They are:

- SPM—set program mask. This permits alteration of the interrupt code in the PSW.
- SSK—set storage key. This permits the software to assign a key to blocks of MEMORY. Actually, it sets a *lock* rather than a *key*.
- ISK—insert storage key. This command permits the same key to be set up in a REGISTER for eventual insertion into a PSW so *that* PSW will have a key to the blocks of MEMORY for which a similar lock has been assigned.

9.9   VARIABLE FIELD LENGTH

COMMANDS

Format   Variable field length (VFL) commands have an opcode DH, where H is a hexadecimal digit. Each contains a length specifier tag, L, and two addresses, M1 and M2. Each effective address is formed by adding the displacement, D, contained in the command to the contents of the GPR, B, designated in the command.

M2 is the address of the first (leftmost) byte of the source datum of length given by L. L is one less than the desired length in bytes: M1 is the address of the leftmost byte of the destination field whose length, again, is given by L. Then M1 and M2 specify two fields; the opcode describes an operation to be performed on the operands. The result is placed in the destination field starting at M1.

A VFL field can begin at any byte in MEMORY—there are no boundary limitations.

MOVE   There are three commands which *move* VFL operands. As would be expected, M2 is the starting address of the source, and M1 is the starting address of the destination.

MVC, with opcode D2, moves characters without alteration.

MVN, with opcode D1, moves the right (numeric) nibble of each source
byte into the right nibble of its corresponding destination byte.
The destination field is altered only in the right nibble positions.
MVZ, with opcode D3, moves the *zone* or *left nibble* similarly to the
numeric for MVN described before.

The three commands, NC, OC, and XC, with opcodes D4, D6, and
D7, respectively, perform the logical functions *and*, *or*, and *exclusive or*,
respectively. These are performed on a bit basis: Corresponding bits of
each field have the logical function performed on them, and the resulting
bit is placed in that position in the destination field.

LOGICAL

CLC, with opcode D5, compares the two fields logically on a bit-for-
bit basis, viewing the fields as binary numbers of length 8L and determining the larger number of the two. The result of the comparison is
recorded in the condition code:

COMPARE

$$0 \quad \text{for} \quad (M1) = (M2)$$

$$1 \quad \text{for} \quad (M1) < (M2)$$

$$2 \quad \text{for} \quad (M1) > (M2)$$

$$3 \quad \text{for} \quad \text{none}$$

There are four other commands in this group which are used to
translate and *edit* information. *Translate* commands perform a table
lookup function which is quite valuable; *edit* commands check sign and
append and delete information similarly to those of the IBM 1401. These
are not described here.

OTHERS

Address
preparation
During the first phase of the *fetch* operation,
the M REGISTER receives the first four bytes of
this six-byte command. The opcode distinguishes it as a VFL command.
L is obtained from the second byte and entered into the concatenated
counter called G1G2. The next nibble contains a GPR indication, B1; the
next three nibbles are the displacement, D1.
To prepare M1, we get the contents of B1. B1 is sent to JR, the four
least significant bits of the LAR. The microprogram sets the two leading
bits to point to the GPRs. The quantity from LM is placed in the LDR and
then routed to the LR. Now the contents of the L REGISTER, (B1), are added
to the displacement field, D1. The result is returned to the H REGISTER as
M1 and also recorded in LM at the working STORAGE CELL, ws1: The
microprogram sets the LM address of ws1 into the LAR; the ADDER output
bus is connected to the LDR and the LM *memorizes*.

During this period, we start acquisition of the last two bytes of the SS command. If the previous command was *uncompleted*, these two bytes are in LOCAL MEMORY. We initiate a LM *recall* cycle with the microprogram furnishing the address of the INSTRUCTION BUFFER to the LAR. If the previous command was *completed*, the MM has the remaining two bytes.

The last two bytes are found either in the LDR or the MDR. For the LDR, the two right bytes are set to the right-hand position of the MR. For the MDR, the left-hand halfWord is routed to the right-hand halfWord of the MR. Also, it is advantageous to store this new instruction datum; hence, the Word in the MDR is also routed to the LDR. The microprogram starts the storing of this word in the IB in LM.

Now, in Fig. 9.9.1:
- HR contains M1;
- MR contains the opcode, L, B2, and D2;
- LR contains the contents of B1 left over from the last cycle;
- the contents of RR are unspecified.

The microprogram sets up the LAR for the GPR, and the B2 nibble is sent over to the JR. LM *recall* brings (B2) to the LR.

Fig. 9.9.1 The REGISTERS after preparing first operand address.

Next, (LR) and the D2 nibbles pass from the MR, through the ADDER, to form the address, M2, placed in the RR.

The ADDER output is also passed over to the LDR to keep a record of this address. The microprogram inserts the address of the ws2 into the LAR, and we *memorize* M2 at ws2, Fig. 9.9.2.

The new state of affairs is reflected in Fig. 9.9.3:
- The FR and the M/DR hold the function information which operates the MOVER—this was obtained from the first byte of the MR.
- L is in G1G2.
- The HR contains the first operand address, M1.
- The two least significant bits of M1 are stored in the MB COUNTER, MBC.
- The second operand address, M2, is stored in RR.
- Its least two significant bits are stored in the L-BYTE COUNTER, LBC.

HR controls the acquisition of M1 words into the MR; RR controls the acquisition of M2 words into LR.

(SECOND ADDRESS)

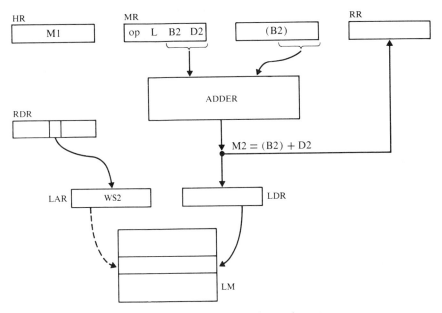

Fig. 9.9.2 Second address preparation and LM storage.

Overlap   System 360 DH-type commands permit overlap of fields M1 and M2. Operations are described to the programmer in
terms of bytes. Thus, if the M2 field is one byte to the left of the M1 field,
the first character of the M2 field will be moved into the first character of
the M1 field. This is also the second character position in the M2 field.
Subsequent moves will put this byte into the rest of the M1 field. When
fields overlap, the microprogram logic performs operations as though done
on a byte basis. Actually, they are done on a Word basis as shown below.
It would serve little purpose to describe the interlocks necessary for proper

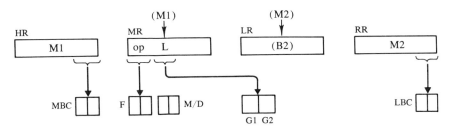

Fig. 9.9.3 After M2 is made, MR will store the first operand, LR will
store the second operand.

overlap of byte operation. Consequently, we simply describe nonover-lapping VFL operations as represented by the equation

$$M2 \ \theta \ M1 \to M1 \tag{9.9.1}$$

Here, θ indicates an operation to be performed as specified by one of the opcodes above.

Types of cycles   VFL data need not be aligned on boundaries. But, since Model 50 is Word oriented, it is advantageous to arrange to have at least the *destination* field aligned on a Word boundary as soon as possible during *execution*. Then we need only one M cycle to get a Word and one MM cycle to return a Word. We then distinguish three types of cycles:

- The initial cycle handles enough bytes to get the M1 field onto a Word boundary.
- Intermediate cycles handle fullWords of information from each field as long as they are still available.
- A final cycle, when necessary, handles the remaining fraction of the Word.

Intermediate cycle   The intermediate cycle finds M1 aligned on a Word boundary. If M2 is also aligned on a boundary as shown in Fig. 9.9.4, both MBC and LBC contain 00. MM *recall* cycles alternate as follows for the *both-on-boundary* case:

1. (HR) is entered into the MAR.
2. *recall* is instituted.
3. The datum is passed to the MDR and then to the MR.
4. (RR) is sent to the MAR.
5. A *recall* is instituted.
6. The datum passes to the MDR and then to LR.
7. The two operands are operated upon.

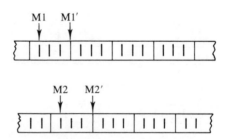

Fig. 9.9.4 M2 Word boundary aligned for intermediate cycles.

8. The result is returned to the MR.
9. The contents of the HR are sent to the MAR.
10. The contents of the MR are sent to the MDR.
11. A *memorize* cycle is performed.
12. Both the HR and RR are incremented by 4.

When the M2 operand is not aligned on a Word boundary, as shown in Fig. 9.9.5, (MBC) = 0 but (LBC) ≠ 0. We go through phases which prepare one source Word in a REGISTER by taking parts of it from two successive MEMORY Words. We save time in this operation since the last M2 MEMORY word received is in LM.

To see this more clearly and also to clarify the terminology, notice in Fig. 9.9.5 that we have typically,

MEMORY Words: FFF0F1F2;   C3C4C6C8;   etc.

source Words: F1F2C3C4;   C6C8F3F4;   etc.

Figure 9.9.5 shows an unaligned M2 field after an initial cycle. The old source Word (which crosses a Word boundary) is the one that we have just finished working upon. The new source Word is the one which we shall prepare next.

Figure 9.9.6 shows how we prepare the new source Word. In the figure, LM at [ws3] stores the most recent MEMORY Word. Its right portion, C6C8, will be placed in the left portion of the LR. This is the first part of the source Word. We also need another portion which is from MAIN MEMORY. The next MEMORY Word is F3F4F5F8. We initiate MM *recall* as well as LM *recall*.

To get the left data part, the microprogram places the location of ws3 in the LAR and requests a *recall*. The LDR receives this word. The desired portion, C6C8, is determined by the LBC and is routed to the left portion of the LR. Meanwhile, the contents of RR are sent over to the MR.

M2 OFF BOUNDARY

EXAMPLE

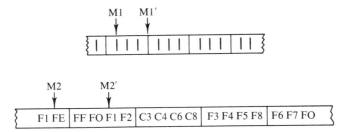

Fig. 9.9.5 M2 NonWord boundary aligned for intermediate cycles.

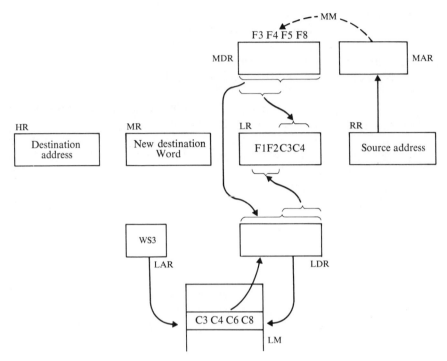

Fig. 9.9.6 Acquisition and assembly of a Word in an intermediate cycle in the M2 off boundary case.

A *recall* is requested. The left portion of the MEMORY Word, F3F4, goes to the right part of LR. The entire MEMORY Word, F3F4F5F8, is also routed to the LDR. The LAR still contains the address of WS3. A *memorize* puts the new Word away. The contents of RR are incremented by 4 to point to the next data byte.

VFL functions are performed entirely by the MOVER. After situating both a source and destination Word as in Fig. 9.9.7, the MOVER function is set up in the MVF, and one of the *move* operations shown in Table 9.9.1 is called for.

Initial cycle   Figure 9.9.8 shows two fields, neither of which is aligned on a Word boundary. The number of bytes handled by the initial cycle is determined only by the number of bytes in the first (*incomplete*) MEMORY Word of the destination field. In the figure, the first MEMORY Word destination bytes in hexadecimal are A1B2C3. The source bytes corresponding to these three bytes are 112233 in hexadecimal.

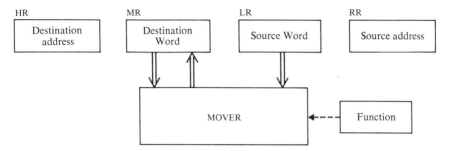

Fig. 9.9.7 The MOVER performs a function (θ) on (MR) and (LR), placing the result in MR.

Notice that they overlap two source Words. After the initial cycle, the destination operand is aligned on a Word boundary, namely M1'. Yet the source MEMORY Word is not aligned on a Word boundary; it starts at M2' in the figure.

In the first phase, Fig. 9.9.9, we bring in the *incomplete* destination Word; it is known to be incomplete since MBC contains a nonzero quantity. M1 is sent from HR to the MAR. Since the final bits are truncated in addressing MAIN MEMORY, the entire Word, including the initial byte, FF, is brought into the MDR. From there, it is transferred to the MR.

In Fig. 9.9.10, we acquire the first MEMORY source Word containing the first portion of the source field. We send the address, M2, from RR to MAR and bring that Word to the MDR. In passing the Word over to the LR, the LBC determines the skew to which it is subjected: Only one byte of the source is used, determined by counting up LBC until it hits zero. The MBC is also counted this number of times (once), as is the RR and the HR. The other bytes of the LR are filled with 0's.

Table 9.9.1 FUNCTIONS OF VFL COMMANDS

Mnemonic	Code	Description	REGISTER Function	None
MVC	D2	(M2) → M1	(LR) → MR	move character
MVN	D1	(M2)$_N$ → M1†	(LR)$_N$ → MR	move numeric
MVZ	D3	(M2)$_Z$ → M1†	(LR)$_Z$ → MR	move zone
NC	D4	(M1) ∧ (M2) → M1	(LR) ∧ (MR) → MR	*and* character
OC	D6	(M1) ∨ (M2) → M1	(LR) ∨ (MR) → MR	*or* character
XC	D7	(M1) ⊻ (M2) → M1	(LR) ⊻ (MR) → M	*exclusive or* character

† Subscript N is used for right halfbytes and Z is for left halfbytes.

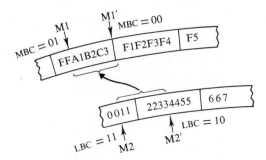

Fig. 9.9.8 Initial cycle of an MVC where intermediate cycles find M2′ off boundary.

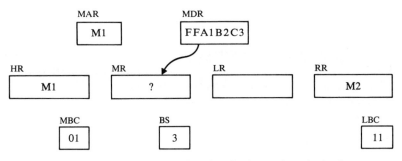

Fig. 9.9.9 First, in the initial cycle, the incomplete destination Word is brought to the MR.

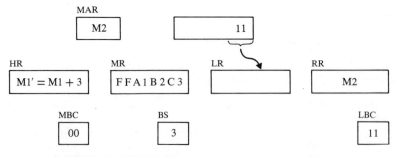

Fig. 9.9.10 Next, for the initial cycle, the first part of the source Word goes to the LR.

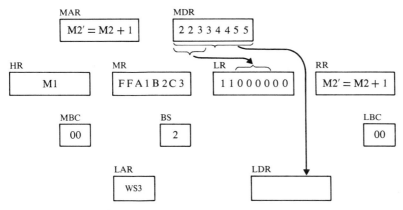

Fig. 9.9.11 Then, for the initial cycle, the second part of the source Word is obtained for the LR. It is duplicated in WS3.

Now the REGISTERS appear as in Fig. 9.9.11. For next source Word, (RR) is sent over to the MAR. The datum appearing in the MDR is sent to the LDR for the next intermediate cycle. The address of WS2 is placed in the LAR, and a *memorize* cycle also places this Word in LM.

To form the remaining portion of the Word in the LR, count up the MBC to 00 to find the number of bytes needed. The number of places to shift right depends on the number of significant bytes in the LR, as recorded in the byte by STATS. In the example, we enter two bytes, shifting them right one position as shown in the figure. So doing, we count up the two REGISTERS RR and LBC. The count in LBC is the number of bytes out of step between the two fields. After this, the REGISTERS are as in Fig. 9.9.12. The

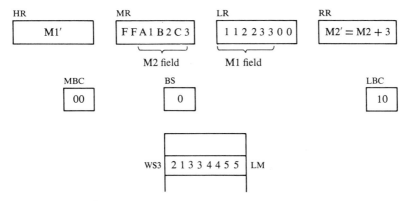

Fig. 9.9.12 The initial cycle and the operation are ready to be done.

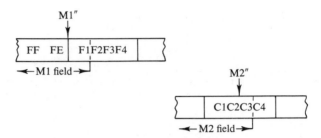

Fig. 9.9.13 Addressing on a final cycle.

MOVER then operates on the indicated fields according to the opcode in the FR. The size and position of the fields used are noted on STATS, not shown. The next cycle is an intermediate cycle (except when L gets very small).

Final cycle   We determine that this is a final cycle by examining the content of G1G2 and finding it less than 04_H. An example of this is shown in Fig. 9.9.13. As expected, the M1 address, M1″, points to a Word boundary. The M2 address, M2″, need not point to a Word boundary.

The operations performed in procuring the operands are portrayed in Fig. 9.9.14. All of the source Word is resident in LM. No MEMORY word is needed. The microprogram sends the location of ws2 over to the LAR to procure the last MEMORY Word. In being passed to the LR, this last Word is

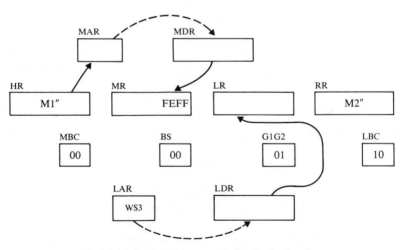

Fig. 9.9.14 Getting the operands for the final cycle.

shifted as many positions as indicated in the STATS. Meantime, we obtain the destination operand by sending the contents of HR, $M1''$, over to the MAR. The datum is returned to the MDR and thence placed in the MR. No further information is required to compile the source operand since G1G2 tells us (in the example) we need only one byte of information.

The operands are properly positioned in the MR and LR as shown in Fig. 9.9.15. But only one byte of each is needed. Hence the MOVER imput is so gated. The function performed has been recorded and affects only those bytes of the receiving field in the MR which are to be altered. G1G2 is reduced to zero (showing *execution* is complete), and the quantity in MR is stored at the address found in the HR.

Compare   *Compare*, CLC, is similar to other commands examined except that we may *stop* at some point before all L bytes have been examined. As long as comparable bytes are equal, the comparands appear to be equal, and the condition code in the CCR remains zero. As soon as an unequality is found, the condition code is changed and operation terminates. Bytes are examined from *most* to *least* significant position. Once an inequality is found, this inequality *is* the *result* for CLC.

Two fields of equal length are to be compared in Fig. 9.9.16: the source field starts at M2; the destination field starts at M1. Corresponding bytes of each are compared, bit for bit, only until an inequality is found.

Figure 9.9.17 shows in tabular form what happens during *compare*. Again, three kinds of cycles are used: initial, intermediate and final. Since the details of operand acquisition were discussed, we look only at the processing required.

EXAMPLE PROCESSING

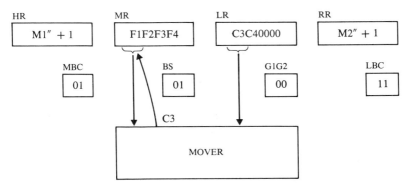

Fig. 9.9.15 Last operation on the final cycle for an MVC using the fields shown in Fig. 9.9.13.

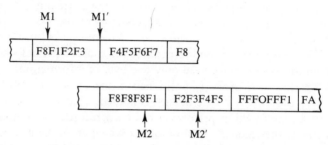

Fig. 9.9.16 Two fields to help us examine CLC operation.

Comparison is done by complementing one of the comparands and adding it to the other through the ADDER:

- If the result is zero, the comparands are equal.
- If the result is nonzero, the comparands are unequal.
- A carryout from the ADDER indicates which comparand is greater.

The operations required are numbered in Fig. 9.9.17 to correspond to the sequence of their occurrence.

1. Bring the source comparand to the L REGISTER and set all the bits of the MR to 1 (hexadecimal F's). The M/DR is set to the complement of LBC—the number of bytes in the initial Word.
2. There is only one byte of significance in the example as determined by LBC. It goes to the second position in the M REGISTER as determined by the MBC. If there were two bytes of significance in the LR, their destination in the MR would still be determined by the MBC. Then the second byte in the MR becomes 0E, the complement of the last byte in the LR; other bytes in MR are unaffected. Complementation is done by the MOVER by an *exclusive or* of:
   (a) the LR bytes;
   (b) a set of all-zero bytes.
3. Obtain the second portion of the M2 Word, placing it in the LR.
4. This Word is placed in location ws3 of LOCAL MEMORY because all of it is not used for this comparison cycle. The M/DR indicates that two bytes in the LR are of importance. These two bytes are positioned at the right end of the Word in MR. They are complemented as they are passed over. The left byte in the MR is not touched. The source comparand is now completely assembled.
5. Obtain the destination comparand, placing it in the LR without alteration.
6. The comparison operation is performed by the ADDER. However, we gate into the ADDER only those bytes which are to be compared, namely, the three right-hand bytes. Since the total of the two

No.	Operation	L	LBL	M	MBC	ADDER	WS3	G1G2	M/D	CC
1	First M2 Recall	F8F8F8F1	01	FFFFFFFF	11	?	?	3F	11	00
2	First M2 Position			FF0EFFFF	00				10	
3	Second M2 Recall	F2F3F4F5								
4	Second M2 Position			FF0ED0C	10		F2F3F4F5		00	
5	First M1 Recall	F8F1F2F3	00							
6	Add and Set					XX000000				
7	Third M2 Recall	F2F3F4F5		FFFFFFFF					00	
8	Third M2 Position			0B0AFFFF	00				10	
9	Fourth M2 Recall	F1F0FFF1								
10	Fourth M2 Position			0B0A000E	10		F1F0FFF1		00	
11	Second M1 Recall	F4F5F6F7								
12	Add and Set					FFFFF705				10

Note: The table only indicates when a REGISTER changes.

Fig. 9.9.17 Operation of *compare* for the fields shown in Fig. 9.9.16.

comparands is zero, without a carry, this portion of the comparands is equal; continue the comparison. The condition code remains unchanged.

7. Retrieve the source comparand from LOCAL MEMORY; gate the next two bytes for comparison.

8. These are complemented as they are entered into position in the MR.

9. Without enough bytes, go to MAIN MEMORY and gate the next Word, placing it in the LR.

10. The two left bytes in the LR remain to be entered in the MR. They are complemented as they are put in the right side of the MR.

11. The source comparand is obtained from MAIN MEMORY and placed in the LR.

12. Addition is performed as shown in Fig. 9.9.18. Since a nonzero result is produced without a carry, the condition code is set to 10.

(MR):	0000	1011	0000	1010	0000	0000	0000	1110
(LR):	1111	0100	1111	0101	1333	0110	1111	0111
	1111	1111	1111	1111	1111	0111	0000	0101
ADDER output:	F	F	F	F	F	7	0	5

Fig. **9.9.18** Addition for comparison, Fig. 9.9.17.

We need no longer make comparisons since a complete result is available. This is the end of the command.

9.10   DECIMAL COMMANDS

Nature   All decimal commands are SS format and have the opcode F*H*—all begin with hexadecimal F and have another hexadecimal digit in the second halfbyte.

Decimal commands handle information from right to left—contrary to field specification: a decimal field is specified by the address of its left-hand byte and the number of bytes it contains. However, for arithmetic, we examine the sign first; furthermore, as the digits of each number are operated upon, carries may be propagated leftward. Examination should therefore proceed leftward.

• Arithmetic commands require two operands.
• There are three single operand commands:
  * MVC move with offset
  * PACK
  * UNPK

Address formation   All commands, even those using a single operand, require two operand addresses. In the case of single operand commands, we specify a source and a destination address: a field is *moved*, *packed*, or *unpacked* from a source field into a destination field.

An operand address, designated M1 or M2, is formed using the base and displacement specified in the command. But M1 and M2 are left-hand byte addresses, while decimal commands require the right-hand operand addresses; call them M1″ and M2″. They are given by

$$M1'' = M1 + L1; \qquad M2'' = M2 + L2 \qquad (9.10.1)$$

LENGTH

Although the length specifiers, L1 and L2, run from 0 to 15, they specify fields of length 1 through 16. This works out very well: If a specifier is 0, the right-hand address is also the left-hand address. This choice of L's turns out properly for all values of M1 and M2.

PROCEDURE

To determine the right-hand operand addresses, M1″ and M2″, first form M1 and M2 as described for the variable field length commands and store them in LOCAL MEMORY. To each of these add, respectively, L1 and L2 to form M1″ and M2″, and store them in different CELLs in LM. All this is part of *fetch*, *classification*, and *initiation*.

fetch COMPLETION

Figure 9.10.1 shows the main frame REGISTERs when the individual decimal command microsequence takes over.

MVO   Examine the operation of the single operand command, MVO, *move with offset*. Suppose the computer is left in the state shown in Fig. 9.10.2 which also portrays the objective of MVO. The M2 field is to be moved to the M1 field so that the right-hand digit of the M2 field is placed in the right-hand digit position of the M1 field. Notice that the M2 field is unsigned, whereas the M1 field *is* signed, and that sign is preserved.

REGISTERS

Here's how REGISTERs are used during this command:
- MR is for assembly of the destination Word.
- HR holds the address of the Word assembled in the MR.
- LR is for disassembly—it holds the source Word from which pieces are being transferred to the MR.
- RR holds addresses for the source Word being disassembled.
- BS (BYTE STATS) keep track of bytes being worked upon.

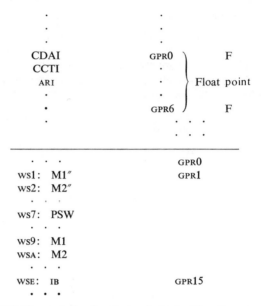

Fig. 9.10.1 The contents of LM during decimal arithmetic commands.

OPERATION

Figure 9.10.3 shows how the information manipulated in the fields presented in Fig. 9.10.2 are operated upon. The MR actually holds portions of two Words. It is simpler to fill it up completely before doing any storage operations. Numbered as in the figure, the operations are:

1. The destination Word is brought to the MR because we need its sign. We also have a source Word sitting in the LR.
2. 6 from the LR is placed in the left-hand position of the MR, completing the first destination byte. The MBC is hence stepped down to 11.

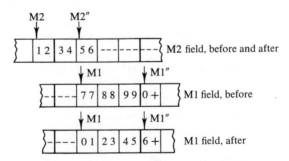

Fig. 9.10.2 Example of the job done by MVO command.

Line	HR	MBC	MR	LR	LBC	BS	RR
1	M1″	00	0 + X X X X X X	3 4 5 6 X X X X		0000	M2″
2			6 + X X X X X X			1000	
3		11	6 + X X X X X 5			0000	
4			6 + X X X X 4 5			0001	
5		10	6 + X X X 3 4 5		00		
6				X X X X X X 1 2	11		M2″ − 4
7			6 + X X 2 3 4 5			0011	
8		01	6 + X 1 2 3 4 5				
9			6 + 0 1 2 3 4 5			0111	

Fig. 9.10.3 REGISTER changes for MVO for fields shown in Fig. 9.10.2.

3, 4. Two more halfbytes are assembled. They go into the right-hand byte of the MR.

5. We use up the last digit from the LR.

6. To continue, we procure another word from MEMORY.

7, 8. The two remaining useful digits are taken from the LR, aligned, and placed in the MR.

9. The one digit of the MR which is undetermined is set to 0.

This occurs because the L2 count sitting in G2 has been reduced to 0. We now have all the information for the M1 field, and we place it in MM using two *memorize* cycles.

Pack and unpack   We have discussed PACK, presented in Fig. 9.2.2. UNPK is just the reverse of this. Both of them are done from right to left and similarly to MVO as far as assembly and disassembly are concerned.

For PACK, the source field, (M2), is brought, a word at a time, to the LR. The first byte has its two halfbytes reversed as it is entered into the MR. For the remaining nibbles, the numeric nibble from each source byte is obtained from the LR and packed into the MR. The zone fields are stripped at this time.

For UNPK, again nibbles of the right-hand byte are reversed. Thereafter we take a nibble at a time, from right to left, from the LR. We place it in the right half of a byte in the MR and place a hexadecimal F to the left of it. Thus each nibble in the LR becomes a byte in the MR.

Decimal add and   First, let us examine the principles of XS6
subtract   arithmetic discussed in detail in connection with the design of an NBCD ADDER in *Computer Design.*†

† Ivan Flores, *Computer Design.* Englewood Cliffs, N.J.: Prentice-Hall, Inc., 1967. See Section 12.6.

```
X:  00765400
6:  66666666
H:  66DCBA66
Y:  00765401
T:  67530E67
E:  99FFF999
             1
    ─────────
S:  01540801
```

Fig. 9.10.4 An example of decimal addition.

ADDITION

Addition is performed as in Fig. 9.10.4 by first converting one of the operands, call it *X*, into XS6 form, calling the result *H*. This is done by adding 6 to each digit. The computer adds the *code* for 6 to the *code* for the digit. No overflow occurs since no decimal digit is larger than 9.

To the result, *H*, we add the other operand, *Y*. Call this sum *T*. *T* is in XS6 form for some digits, but not for others. Those for which a carry has occurred are not in XS6 form—they are in their proper form; those for which no carry has occurred are still in XS6 form.

To correct *T*, subtract 6 from all digits where no carry occurred. However, instead of subtracting, the computer adds and complements. We add 9 (complement of 6 with respect to *F* in hexadecimal) wherever *no* carry has occurred in forming *T*; we add an *F* (complement of 0 with respect to *F*) where a carry *has* occurred (to make things uniform). Positions where a carry occurs in forming *T* are underlined in the figure. The correction factor in the figure is called *E*. When *E* is added to *Y*, an end-around carry may be produced; it is added in to produce the final sum, *S*.

SUBTRACTION

Figure 9.10.5 shows a decimal subtraction of *X* from *Y* to find a difference, *D*. Find the complement of each digit of *X*, with respect to F_H. Call this *W*. Add *W* to *Y* with a precarry to get *G*. Some of the digits of *G* are in true form; others are in XS6 form. They are in true form whenever an interdigit carry has occurred; they are in XS6 form where *no* carry has occurred. The latter need to be corrected.

```
Y:      00321000        Y:  00321000
X:      00297600        W:  FFD689FF
──────────────                     1
Y − X:  00023400        ──────────────
                        G:  00089A00
                        K:  FFF999FF
                                   1
                        ──────────────
                        D:  00023400
```

Fig. 9.10.5 An example of decimal subtraction.

A correction is subtracted where necessary by complement addition. Hence the correction factor, K, has F's where a digit is in true form and 9's where it's in XS6 form. We correct G by adding K and an end-around carry to get the difference, D.

Operation   Operation of the hardware during addition is divided into several phases:

(a) Determine the *actual arithmetic* performed; algebraic addition (or subtraction) can call for either addition or subtraction. The desired process is stored in STATS along with the sign of both operands.
(b) Acquire and properly align the operands.
(c) Add, using XS6 arithmetic, and store the intermediate result. If a carryout is present, it is noted.
(d) The intermediate result is stored in the M1 field.
(e) Steps (b), (c), and (d) may be repeated up to four times more; for L, up to 16 times.
(f) Recomplementation may be required.

The right-hand byte addresses, M1″ and M2″, lead us immediately to Words containing sign bytes for each field. These are stored separately in STATS. *Actual arithmetic* is determined from the sign bytes stored in the STATS and from the command opcode and requests the proper microprogram, *add* or *subtract*.

Actual arithmetic   *Actual arithmetic* determination is made first because, as M2 digits are obtained, we should know if they should be stored in true or complement form.

The number of digits operated upon in the first cycle is determined by the boundary position of the M1 field (if L1 is large enough). This may be 2, 4, 6, or 8 digits. That many M2 digits are obtained and aligned with the M1 Word. During acquisition, we may find that:
- one or two Words from the M2 field are required;
- digits may or may not be left over from the M2 fields.

The first instance is determined by watching the condition of the BYTE COUNTER for the M2 field during assembly and alignment of that field. If we run out of digits, the BYTE COUNTER will so indicate, and we will have to acquire a new M2 Word. If digits are left over during assembly and alignment, these are stored in LM so that another MM reference is not required during the next phase.

SIGN AND OPERATION

Example   An example of how addition is performed is
shown in Fig. 9.10.6. The M1 contains 0765331C; here, C_H represents a
plus sign. M2 contains 44222C. To add these fields, first find the address
of the last byte of the M1 and M2 fields: M1″ and M2″, respectively.
Neither M1″ nor M2″ lie on a Word boundary in the example; so fractions
of a Word are added in the first cycle. There is only one byte addressed in
the first M1 MEMORY Word. Therefore, we take only one byte from the M2
MEMORY Word although the M2 field addresses two bytes in that Word.

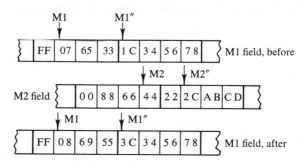

Fig. 9.10.6 Example of the job done by decimal add command AP.

FIRST CYCLE   The first cycle is shown in Fig. 9.10.7. On line 1 we obtain the M2
MEMORY Word. From it we take one byte to match up with the first and
only byte addressed in the M1 MEMORY Word. This source byte, 2C, is
taken from the LR and placed in the MR in the left-hand position. The C_H
is replaced by a 0, as are all the other nibbles to the right of this one. Since
there is at least one more useful (left-hand) byte left in the Word in the MR,
it is placed in LM for later.

The quantity in the MR is coded in NBCD; we want it in XS6. A series
of 6's are placed in the LR. The contents of the MR and LR are added
together and the result placed in the MR on line 4.

One more correction constant enters the sign into this M2 quantity.
This adjustment figure is placed in the LR, line 5, and the contents of the LR
and MR are added together to produce the sign-adjusted, XS6, M2 field
quantity in the LR.

Next we get the M1 Word and place it in the MR. Zeroes are entered
in the right-hand four nibbles of the Word since they do not belong to the
M1 field being added. The next two nibbles to the left are set to FF for sign
adjustment, line 8. Finally, the addition is performed, using the quantities
in the MR and LR; the result is placed in the MR, line 9. As this is done,
the ADDER notes those digits for which overflow occurs and F's are

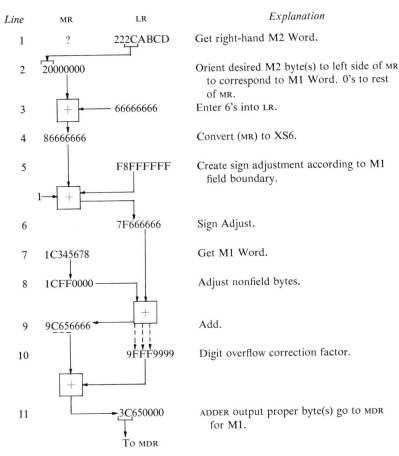

Line	MR	LR	Explanation
1	?	222CABCD	Get right-hand M2 Word.
2	20000000		Orient desired M2 byte(s) to left side of MR to correspond to M1 Word. 0's to rest of MR.
3	+	66666666	Enter 6's into LR.
4	86666666		Convert (MR) to XS6.
5		F8FFFFFF	Create sign adjustment according to M1 field boundary.
6		7F666666	Sign Adjust.
7	1C345678		Get M1 Word.
8	1CFF0000		Adjust nonfield bytes.
9	9C656666		Add.
10		9FFF9999	Digit overflow correction factor.
11		3C650000	ADDER output proper byte(s) go to MDR for M1.

To MDR

Fig. 9.10.7 First phase of decimal addition example.

entered into the LR in these positions. 9's are placed in the other positions to obtain the overflow correction quantity. Another addition is performed. The output of the ADDER is now correct, at least for the two digits with which we were working. These are sent to the MDR, where they may be entered into MAIN MEMORY for storage.

For larger fields, intermediate cycles of addition would add full Words, eight digits each. We now look at a final cycle of addition where again a partial word is being added in Fig. 9.10.8. First we assemble an M2 Word. Generally, there is a part of a Word left over in LM. On line 1 we obtain this word and place it in the LR. The left byte is usable. It is placed to the right of the MR, which is cleared, line 2.

FINAL CYCLE

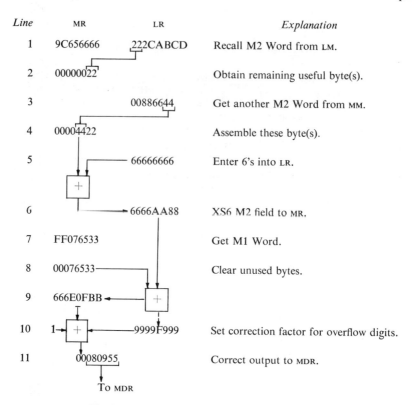

Line	MR	LR	*Explanation*
1	9C656666	222CABCD	Recall M2 Word from LM.
2	00000022		Obtain remaining useful byte(s).
3		00886644	Get another M2 Word from MM.
4	00004422		Assemble these byte(s).
5		66666666	Enter 6's into LR.
6		6666AA88	XS6 M2 field to MR.
7	FF076533		Get M1 Word.
8	00076533		Clear unused bytes.
9	666E0FBB		
10	1	9999F999	Set correction factor for overflow digits.
11	00080955		Correct output to MDR.

To MDR

Fig. 9.10.8 Last phase of decimal addition example.

More bytes are required; so we go to MM and get a new Word, line 3. Only the right-hand byte is needed because the length specified is now used up. This byte is placed to the left of the last byte that was put in the MR, line 4. To convert the number in the MR to XS6 form, the LR is loaded with 6's, line 5. After adding (LR) to (MR), the LR gets the M2 number in XS6 form, line 6.

We get the next M1 field from MEMORY. The last *three* bytes will be used for addition; the first byte is cleared to zero, line 8. Notice that the M1 field is larger than the M2 field. We add, placing the result in the MR, line 9. Digits for which an overflow occurs are detected by the ADDER, and the correction factor is set into the LR, line 10. A correction addition cycle is performed, and the result appears on the ADDER output bus, line 11. This is gated to the proper positions of the MDR to complete addition.

Multiplication   The *decimal multiply* command, MP, for *multiply packed*, uses the M2 field as the multiplicand and the M1 field as the multiplier, placing the product in the M1 field. In multiplication, the product is generally larger than either the multiplicand or the multiplier, and sufficient space must be provided for it. We restrict the multiplicand to eight or less bytes (fifteen digits plus sign, or less). The multiplier is then assumed to consist of a field whose length is the difference, L1 — L2. This assures there will be sufficient room in M1 for the product.

Decimal numbers are stored in sign and magnitude form. For multiplication, the absolute value of the product is the same regardless of the signs of the operands. Hence, the product sign is determined only by the signs of the multiplicand and multiplier on an initial cycle, and it is stored in the M1 field in LM.

Consider multiplication of a single Word of four bytes or less. The reader may extrapolate to a multiplicand which is larger, but the complications do not justify the explanation.

(M2) is obtained and aligned at the right with 0's entered on the left. The sign digit is removed so that the rightmost digit is numerical. From the multiplicand, call it X1, we calculate its double, X2. X1 and X2 are stored in LM CELLS WSA and WS8. To start multiplication proper, obtain a digit at a time of the multiplier. From a Word of multiplier digits, extract the rightmost digit and store the rest in LOCAL MEMORY. As new multiplier digits are needed, they are obtained from LM. When LM multiplier digits are exhausted, get the next M1 multiplier Word and disassemble it similarly.

MULTIPLE ADDITIONS

The partial product is in one REGISTER. Obtain a multiplicand multiple, X1 or X2, and place it in another REGISTER. Perform addition, reducing the multiplier digit in M/DR by one or two accordingly. This continues until the M/DR reaches zero. The partial product now contains the correct rightmost digit. This is entered into a PRODUCT REGISTER in LOCAL MEMORY and the partial product is shifted within its REGISTER.

Now obtain the next multiplier digit, place it in the M/DR, and perform another set of multiple additions of the multiplicand (multiple) to the shifted partial product.

TERMINATION

G1 initially contains L1. It is decremented each time a new multiplier digit is used. When it reaches zero, it indicates when multiplication is complete. The product Words now in LM should be returned to the M1 field. To do this, we must reinstate M1″ as well as L1. These have also been kept in LM and are now made available. With as many cycles of MM as required, the product now in LM is transferred to the M1 field in MM.

Division   The decimal division command references the M1 field as the dividend and the M2 field as the divisor. Division is reciprocal to multiplication; hence, the length of the quantities involved are similar. Using a divisor of length L2 and a dividend of length L1, we develop a quotient of length L1 − L2. The rest of the M1 field, L2 bytes (the same as the divisor length), is free to hold the remainder. The quotient and the remainder occupy the left and right portions, respectively, of the M1 field at the end of division.

Each quotient digit is developed in the PROCESSOR REGISTERS using *restoring* division. This is explained in *Computer Design*, Sections 14.4–14.6. Repeated subtractions of the quotient from the partial remainder are performed, each one being recorded by incrementing the M/DR. When the partial remainder becomes negative, it is restored by a cycle addition. The M/DR is decremented, and this is the next quotient digit to be recorded in the QUOTIENT REGISTER in MAIN MEMORY.

Sign preparation is similar to that for multiplication.

9.11 IO

Commands   There are four IO commands with the following mnemonics:

- SIO—start input/output
- TIO—test input/output
- HIO—halt input/output
- TCH—test channel

$$\left.\right\} \quad (9.11.1)$$

These commands may be given *only* in supervisory state and have the same format:

$$\text{IO:} \quad 9H \ X \ B1 \ D1 \qquad (9.11.2)$$

where H is one of four hexadecimal digits, X is undefined and one byte long, and B1 and D1 are base and displacement, respectively. The address M1 is the sum of the contents of the GPR designated by B1 and the displacement D1. But for an IO command, we address a DEVICE on a CHANNEL rather than MAIN MEMORY. Hence, the Word, M1, is viewed as three components:

$$\text{M1:} \quad Y \ C \ D \qquad (9.11.3)$$

where:

Y is the left twenty-one bits which are ignored;
C is a three-bit CHANNEL designator;
D is an eight-bit DEVICE designator.

To reiterate, from the base and displacement in the command, the PROCESSOR forms M1 which, in turn, designates a CHANNEL and DEVICE.

You may wonder why eight bits are required to designate a DEVICE. Both the multiplexor channel (which we do not discuss here) and the SELECTOR CHANNEL consist of SUBCHANNELS. One use of the SUBCHANNEL is to accommodate the DEVICE CONTROLLER which, in turn, communicates with several DEVICES. The four bits of D designate a SUBCHANNEL designator; the other four bits designate a DEVICE on this SUBCHANNEL.

TIO and TCH test to determine the status of the DEVICE and CHANNEL; HIO may *halt* an IO operation before it would otherwise terminate. However, TIO, HIO, and TCH have so many ramifications regarding conditions and alternatives that it does not pay to examine them in detail.

SIO is the most useful and most used command. It initiates IO activity in most situations:

- during traps under JOCS
  * for errors
  * normal completions
  * exception
- starting from scratch

Most of our attention in what follows goes to SIO.

IO operations   We review SIO activities on *data transfer*.

1. SIO is encountered in program in supervisor mode.
2. B1D1 is converted into M1.
3. M1 is broadcast to CCS as C D.
4. The status of the CHANNEL, SUBCHANNEL, and DEVICE is examined.
5. The SIO is accepted or rejected; the condition code records this:

   0—SIO accepted.
   1—CSW notes disposition.
   2—CHANNEL or SUBCHANNEL is busy.
   3—CHANNEL, SUBCHANNEL, or DEVICE is not operational.

6. Assuming acceptance, the channel address word CAW is obtained from MM for the CC and placed in the CR (actually stored in LM). The CAW contains the protect key and the subcommand (CCW) starting location.
7. The first channel control word (CCW) is brought to the SUBCOMMAND REGISTER, SCR (actually in LM). Each CCW contains:
   (a) a subcommand code describing the desired DEVICE activity;
   (b) an MM address to or from which data are moved;
   (c) a count of bytes to be moved;
   (d) flags for chaining, skipping, interrupting, etc.

8. The IO task is delegated to the DEVICE and the program allowed to proceed simultaneously.

Information may flow either way: we examine inbound data.

9. Character codes are:
   (a) read from the input medium;
   (b) transmitted from the DEVICE to the CC;
   (c) sent to the commutator;
   (d) positioned in the ASSEMBLY REGISTER, AR.
10. When the AR is full, a cycle is stolen:
   (a) For the IBM 360, an MM cycle can be stolen at specified steps in a microprogram during either *fetch* or *execution*.
   (b) CC to MM uses the PROCESSOR for cycle stealing.
   (c) The microprogram is reinstated thereafter.
   (d) The SCR is updated.
11. When a subcommand is completed, the activities which follow depend on which is specified:
   (a) data chaining;
   (b) subcommand chaining;
   (c) neither.

12. A command is completed when:
   (a) the DEVICE reports an exception or error;
   (b) the DEVICE reports normal completion and there is no subcommand chaining.
13. Completion causes an interrupt.

Fetch operations   *Fetch* for IO commands is the same as for other four-byte commands. A command is obtained and placed in the MR. B1 is extracted from its position in the MR and sent over to the LAR. The BASE REGISTER contents are brought from LM and placed in the LR. The displacement field is added to the contents of the LR to form the M1 address which is returned to the LR. Then the IO microprogram is called for.

Setup   The IO microprogram gets the **channel address word (CAW)** from its fixed location (byte 72 in MM) and places it in the RR. The CAW contains three fields:

1. The protect key indicates which banks in MEMORY are available to the IO command.
2. An intermediate field contains four zeros.

3. The last field of three bytes, the address at which commands to the CHANNEL begin, is called the channel control address and abbreviated **CCA.**

Subcommands via the CHANNEL to the DEVICE are contained in a doubleWord called the channel control word and abbreviated **CCW.** The first Word of the pair is **CCW1**; the second is **CCW2.** The next microprogram task obtains CCW1. The CAW is obtained from the RR and sent over to the MDR. *Recall* is initiated and the Word which is recovered is sent to the MR. Notice now that the MR no longer contains useful information:

- The M1 address fabricated from (B1) and D1 now resides in the LR.
- The opcode contained in the MR has caused a transfer to the microprogram specific to this command.

The CCW1 contained in the MR has two main fields:

1. The first field, f, indicates function.
2. The second field, *loc*, is the source or destination address in MEMORY for IO data.

The microprogram has momentarily completed its tasks. To transmit information to the desired CHANNEL requires the attention of logic called the COMMON CHANNEL. The COMMON CHANNEL communicates between the CHANNEL CONTROLLERS and the CPU. During this period, the CPU enters what is called the **countdown state:** it remains inactive until the disposition of the CHANNEL in question is known.

COMMON   In communicating between the CHANNELs and
CHANNEL   the CPU, the COMMON CHANNEL responds to
the command at the CPU by determining the present states of the CHANNEL and DEVICE addressed. There are four states which the CHANNEL may occupy:

A—it is available for use.
I—it has terminated its activity and has an interrupt pending.
W—it has an assignment and is working.
N—it is not operational; it is either disconnected or there is no DEVICE attached to this DEVICE CONTROLLER.

$$(9.11.4)$$

The first thing the COMMON CHANNEL does in handling an SIO is to determine if the command presented is legal. If not, it sets up a **FOUL.** This is an unlikely event and requires special handling for recovery.

For no FOUL, the COMMON CHANNEL checks the CHANNEL addressed. This CHANNEL may be in any of the four states just noted, or it may have a terminating activity or lower priority activity, in which case the COMMON CHANNEL waits or pushes aside the lower priority activity.

If the CHANNEL addressed is idle, the COMMON CHANNEL causes the CHANNEL addressed to pick up the Words from LR, MR, and RR by initiating the SIO transfer microprogram. While this is in progress, the COMMON CHANNEL requests another microprogram to procure CCW2 as soon as the first microprogram is done. The address for CCW2 is CAW+4.

The CHANNEL CONTROLLER checks CCW1, when received, for subcommand validity. The process is aborted and an interrupted state entered for an invalid subcommand.

DEVICE select   If the subcommand is accepted, then the CHANNEL determines the state of the DEVICE addressed. A DEVICE may occupy one of four states described in (9.11.4): A, I, W or N. The DEVICE may accept a subcommand only in the available state, A. The CHANNEL broadcasts the DEVICE address. If the DEVICE address is illegal, a "not operational" signal is returned to the CHANNEL and relayed to the microprogram, thus aborting the subcommand.

If available, the DEVICE so indicates. The CHANNEL then sends the subcommand to the DEVICE which prepares to execute it and transmits a status signal when it has determined whether the subcommand is acceptable.

The DEVICE and CHANNEL talk back and forth, and eventually a status signal is sent from the DEVICE to the CHANNEL CONTROLLER. Similarly, the CHANNEL CONTROLLER transmits a status report to the COMMON CHANNEL. Finally, the COMMON CHANNEL transmits a status signal to CONTROL which is then recorded and takes CONTROL out of *countdown* state.

When CONTROL pops out of *countdown*, it is free to enter a *fetch* state for the next command. Meanwhile, the CHANNEL CONTROLLER and DEVICE are busy executing the first subcommand in the sequence indicated in the CAW for the SIO.

CHANNEL   Some of the hardware of the CHANNEL
REGISTER   CONTROLLER is shown in Fig. 9.11.1. The main REGISTER used for communication between CONTROL and CHANNEL is designated by me as the CHANNEL REGISTER, CHR. IBM calls this the "GENERAL PURPOSE REGISTER." However, if we call it this, it can be easily confused with the GPRs in LM.

The CHR receives information from the CPU which it promptly staticizes to other REGISTERS. To send information to the CPU, information from these other REGISTERS is placed into the CHR and dispatched from there.

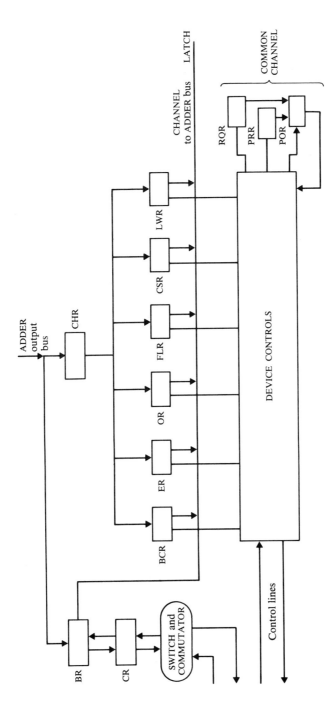

Fig. 9.11.1 REGISTERS in each CHANNEL CONTROLLER.

303

Let us see the use of some of the REGISTERS in the CHANNEL CONTROLLER:

- The BYTE COUNTER, BCR, points to the byte being assembled or disassembled.
- The END REGISTER, ER, notes termination conditions.
- The OPERATION REGISTER, OR, holds information about the function the DEVICE is to perform.
- The FLAG REGISTER, FLR, describes the data flow during the subcommand and how we continue to the next subcommand.
- The CHANNEL STATUS REGISTER, CSR, tells the present status of the CHANNEL; it tells whether errors or exceptions have arisen and their cause.
- The LAST WORD REGISTER, LWR, gives information about the three DATA REGISTERS. Data for transmittal between the CHANNEL CONTROLLER and MAIN MEMORY may be found in one or more of the following:
    * the C REGISTER, CR, used for assembly and disassembly;
    * the BUFFER REGISTER, BR, for local hardware buffering of the C REGISTER;
    * the LOCAL MEMORY BUFFER REGISTER, AR, which stores a datum just before it is placed into MM.

CONTROL   Initiation of activity within CONTROL (starting a new microprogram) by the CHANNEL CONTROLLER uses three registers contained in the CHANNEL and falling to the COMMON CHANNEL:

- The REQUEST REGISTER, RQR, holds indication of the type of microprogram which the CHANNEL would like the CPU to perform next.
- The PRIORITY REGISTER, PRR, indicates the priority of the request in the RQR.
- The POSITION REGISTER, POR, indicates the microprogram now in execution.

Requests for activities are made automatically by examination of the states of REGISTERS in the CHANNEL and in the DEVICE. If the request sent to the RQR has a priority higher than that noted in the PRR, it is placed in the RQR, evicting the previous occupant and setting up the higher priority in the PRR. When the POSITION REGISTER indicates that no microprogram is presently being requested, the information, RQR and PRR, is entered into the POR.

The POR talks to CONTROL via the COMMON CHANNEL. The COMMON CHANNEL monitors the CPU activity, and before a new *fetch* is initiated, CHANNEL requests are made for microprograms to service the CHANNEL. Such CHANNEL requests permit cycle stealing and enable the microprogram to service the CHANNEL without substantially slowing down CPU activity.

Assembly and The CR is the assembly (or disassembly)
disassembly REGISTER for the CHANNEL. Information exchanged between a DEVICE and the CHANNEL uses only the CR.

All DEVICES transmit information a byte at a time. However, MM and the CHANNEL handle information on a Word basis. The CR assembles bytes into Words or disassembles Words into bytes.

Reading information from a DEVICE requires the *assembly* of a Word in the CR. After a Word is assembled, we clear out the CR as soon as possible so that the next byte from the DEVICE can be placed into the CR without clobbering information before it gets into MM.

The BR is a buffer for the CR; it enables us to free the CR immediately. When the BR is full, we empty it as soon as possible so that when the CR becomes full, we will have a place for its datum. This requires the intervention of a microprogram.

A microprogram can store the Word from the BR directly into MM provided it can break into CONTROL operations presently under way without harming them. To save time, another REGISTER in LM, called the AR, is used for backup for the BR. There is one such REGISTER for each CHANNEL. This permits us to service a CHANNEL immediately and put away the Word in AR at our leisure.

Let us now reverse the process and see what happens on writing from MEMORY to a DEVICE:

- A MEMORY Word is stored in the AR.
- Words from the AR are sent to the BR if the CR is full, or to the CR directly if it is empty.
- The CR is loaded from the BR by the CONTROLLER when it is ready to disassemble a new Word.
- Bytes are sent from the CR to the DEVICE as they are needed by the DEVICE.

Read and write Figure 9.11.2 shows the microprograms called
operations during a *read*. Each microprogram is in a "rectangle" whose left side is a semicircle. Boxes are numbered to correspond to the text. The SIO operation immediately initiates the STARTIO microprogram (1). It also calls for the CCW2 (2). After the CCW is checked (3), the UNIT SELECT microprogram is called in (4). If all is well (5, 6), the IO UNIT transmits information to the CR for assembly (7). When information is to be stored in MM, a storage chain is entered (8–10). If more is done for this CCW, CONTROL returns to the DEVICE (11–13, 7).

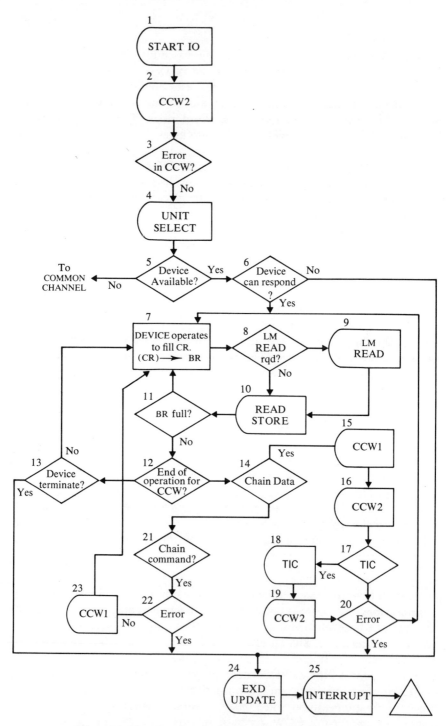

Fig. 9.11.2 Flowchart for microprograms and decisions for *read*.

306

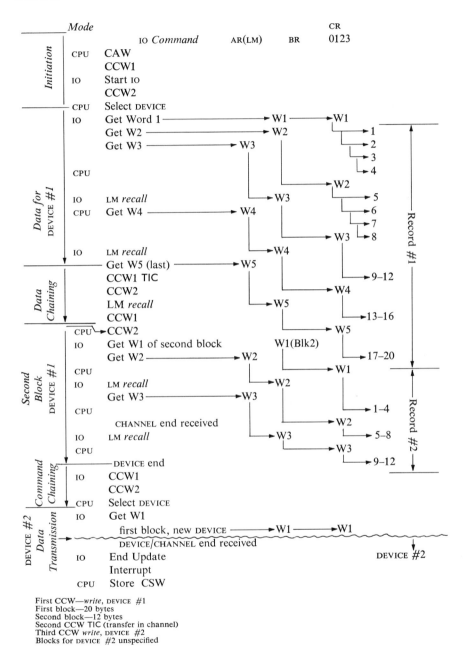

Fig. 9.11.3 *Write* operation.

For the end of a CCW operation (12), we check for data chaining (14) and command chaining (21). When chaining occurs, we get new CCWs (15, 16) and make checks on them (17–20). There are several ways to terminate the operation (6, 13, 20, 22). Upon termination, the microprograms for *end* and *interrupt* are called upon (24, 25). The interrupt takes us from the microprogram into the software.

WRITE

Operations which take place for write commands are presented in Fig. 9.11.3. This is shown in a different format. It indicates at which point the microprogram is operating in CPU mode or IO mode. It also indicates what is going on at each moment. The next two columns to the right show what is contained in each of the BUFFER REGISTERS. Finally, on the extreme right, the information being presented for output is detailed.

Breakin and **breakout** constitute the initiation and termination of stealing, as discussed in Chapter 2. How these are done for System 360 is described next.

9.12   CYCLE STEALING

AND BREAKIN

Breakin and breakout   System 360 is organized around the CENTRAL PROCESSOR cycle. Recall that there are four half-microsecond CPU cycles in one MAIN MEMORY reference cycle of two microseconds. Each CPU cycle is under the control of a single microprogram step. This relieves the limitations upon cycle stealing which were present in second generation computer systems:

- There, we could break in only after the completion of instruction.
- In the third generation system, we can break in at the end of almost any CPU cycle.

The only precautions which must be observed after the breakin occurs within an instruction are the following:

- Mark the place within the broken-into microprogram.
- Preserve REGISTERS used by the breakin microprogram.
- Provide a means to return to the broken-into microprogram.
- Prohibit breakin during breakin.

All servicing of CHANNEL traps is done by CPU cycle stealing as described below.

Traps require return to the software and therefore are subject to more limitations than simple CHANNEL servicing regarding when they may occur.

Example   An example of cycle stealing is presented in
Fig. 9.12.1. We see there the normal sequence of events occurring in CPU
mode. The first microactivity is the *fetch* operation. This is followed by a
classify operation. Then come activities in the operation of the command,
labeled here CM1, CM2, etc.

During the *i*th microactivity of the command, CM(*i*), the COMMON
CHANNEL receives a request from the CHANNEL CONTROLLER communicating
that cycle stealing is necessary. The COMMON CHANNEL sets up so that, at
the end of CM(*i*), the breakin occurs. Of course, this happens only if the
proper priority and availability prevail.

The *control* goes over to the breakin hardware. This is hardwired logic.
It places the computer in IO mode and then begins the microprogram
requested by the COMMON CHANNEL. During each of these microoperations
in IO mode, further breakin is impossible—it is suspended.

After the last CHANNEL service microoperation, a breakout is entered.
This causes the computer to re-enter CPU mode and to return to the next
microoperation required to fulfill the main program command being
executed, CM(*i*+1).

Breakin initiation   Figure 9.12.2 is a block diagram of hardware
which participates in cycle stealing. The COMMON CHANNEL has several
inputs: one from each SELECTOR CHANNEL, and one from the MULTIPLEXOR.
Each of these inputs may or may not have a *request* for an IO microprogram.
When a *request* is present, a priority indication appears also. When a
request appears on one or more of these lines, the COMMON CHANNEL
raises the *request* line. This signal is routed through the RM ADDRESS
DETERMINATION LOGIC (RMADL). The purpose of this LOGIC is to take
information from the RDR and other signals from the CPU to determine
what the next read address will be. Normally this address would be sent
over to the RAR to *request* the next microoperation Word to be placed in
the RDR.

Since a request is present, we do not wish the next normal microoperation to be obtained. Instead, its address is entered into the READ ADDRESS
BUFFER REGISTER, RABR—this will be kept to return us to the main microsequence after breakout is completed.

The address of the CHANNEL service routine is supplied by the COMMON
CHANNEL. It is routed by the determination of the RMADL to the RAR. One
more thing that the RMADL does: it places the computer in IO mode by
setting the MODE FLIPFLOP. All this is done only after the RMADL receives a
signal indicating the end of a CPU cycle.

As long as the CPU is in IO mode, further breakins are prevented by
suppressing COMMON CHANNEL signals.

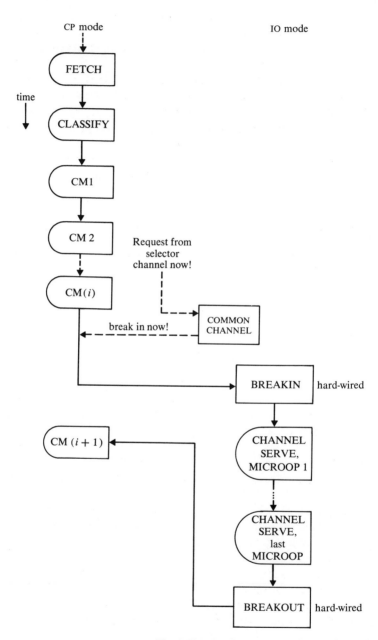

Fig. 9.12.1 Breakin.

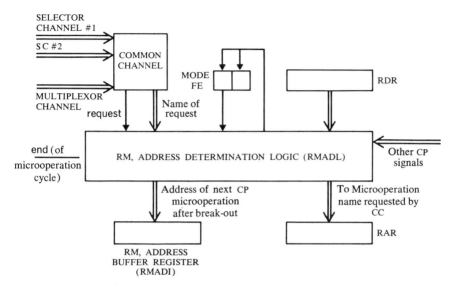

Fig. 9.12.2 Hardware used in breakin and breakout.

Breakout   A breakout occurs after the last micro-operation of the IO service routine has been done and provided that no request is pending on the COMMON CHANNEL.

The tasks of breakout are opposite to those of breakin:

1. The next micro address for the broken-into microprogram is obtained from the RABR and is placed in the RAR.
2. Further addresses from the RMADL are routed directly to the RAR.
3. We now enter the CPU mode.

Chaining   If, during IO servicing, another CHANNEL comes up with *requests* for a microroutine, then we do not wish to enter breakout; it would only be followed by breakin. A service mechanism is provided so that, if a breakin is to occur—if any CHANNEL request is pending—we can suppress breakout. Then, instead of returning to the broken-into microprogram, we permit the *request* pending on the COMMON CHANNEL to pass through the RMADL and into the RAR. When the last IO microroutine is completed and there are no COMMON CHANNEL requests pending, a breakout is performed.

IO microroutine   An IO microroutine is always entered on the initiation of the COMMON CHANNEL. It, in turn, receives a signal from one of the CHANNEL CONTROLLERS. Only the request with the highest priority is applicable to the next cycle steal. Since only one request can occur from a given CHANNEL, it is clear that the CHANNEL with the highest priority *request* will dominate.

This CHANNEL transmits its number. The IO microroutine needs this number to service properly the CHANNEL by communicating with the area assigned to that CHANNEL in LOCAL MEMORY. For each SC, we find in LM an area of four Words allocated for these functions:

1. the subcommand address;
2. the data address;
3. the data count;
4. the AR.

Four areas times four Words each takes up sixteen words of LOCAL MEMORY. Knowing the number of the *requesting* CHANNEL permits the microroutine to address the four Words allocated to the requesting CHANNEL. Besides IO microroutine initiation by CHANNEL requests, other IO microroutines are initiated by commands in the program sequence. Thus, the command SIO should start an IO microroutine. Actually, the computer remains in CP mode during the *fetch* and *classify* phase of the SIO command. Normally, a microroutine checks the SELECTOR CHANNEL and the reply comes back through the COMMON CHANNEL. It is this reply which acts like any other CHANNEL request and causes the CP to enter IO mode in the manner described above.

Interrupt   The interrupt microroutine, INT, is initiated through a CHANNEL request as are all other IO microroutines. It is routed through the COMMON CHANNEL; however, it has the lowest priority because it requires the use of all the hard REGISTERS of the CP. For that reason, INT can take control only after all the micros for a command have been completed and just before *fetch* for the new command takes place.

The properties of INT are:
- It has the lowest priority.
- It can take place only after *execution*.
- It uses the CP REGISTERS.

The REGISTERS are filled with information required to build the channel status word, CSW, and with data for the interrupt software. CP REGISTERS contain:

MR: UNIT status
RR: key, command address
LR: UNIT address, CHANNEL address

The microroutine INT may be chained with other microroutines; but it may not be chained with another INT microroutine. Obviously, if this were permitted, the contents of the REGISTERS would be destroyed before the CSW Word could be prepared and put away.

Trap   The events preceding, during, and following interrupt are presented in Fig. 9.12.3. After the interrupt has occurred,

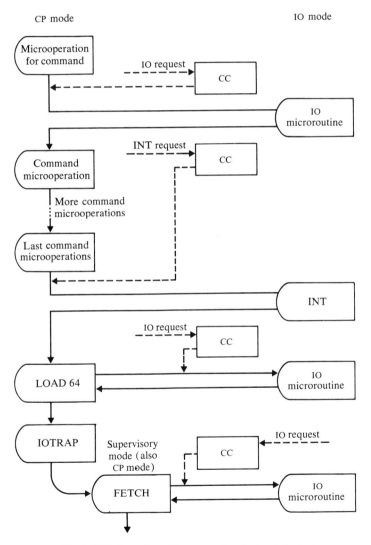

Fig. **9.12.3** Operation of microroutine during interrupt.

we do not wish the computer to continue with commands in the problem program. Instead, we wish it to enter an *interrupted* state and begin *trap* processing routine. But even before this is done, we must put away the channel status word with the microroutine called LOAD64 (so named because byte 64 is loaded with the CSW). LOAD64 is done in CPU mode because we want it to be interruptable for IO servicing by breakin. This ensures proper storage for continuing operation of the PERIPHERAL DEVICES. Figure 9.12.3 shows a cycle steal operation during LOAD64.

The CSW, whose loading is the objective of LOAD64, contains the following fields:

- CCW + 8
- UNIT status
- count

When LOAD64 is completed, it automatically goes to the next microroutine, IOTRAP. It gets us into supervisory mode and lets the software take over. To do that:

- IOTRAP puts the old PSW, formed from data now existing, into REGISTERS;
- this is stored in the old PSW location for the IO trap;
- the new PSW is brought from its location and installed in the PSWR;
- finally, control is turned over to SFETCH, the *fetch* microroutine in supervisory mode.

During IOTRAP, IO microroutines may interrupt for servicing. Of course, this is also true for all microroutines operating in supervisory mode.

PROBLEMS

9.1 Explain hexadecimal for number, bytes, signs.

9.2 Explain byte, Word, halfWord, nibble, doubleWord.

9.3 What do PACK and UNPK do?

9.4 Explain the various command formats and their uses.

9.5 How is an effective address calculated?

9.6 For the three MEMORY subsystems, explain
   (a) the need for three;
   (b) the names of the components of each;
   (c) each.

9.7 Describe one use for each of the following:

- IAR
- IR
- IAC
- PSWR
- PKR
- CCR
- ILCR
- LR
- RR
- HR
- MR
- BYTE CNTRS
- STATS
- MOVER
- SHIFTER

9.8 For *three* command lengths it may not be possible to acquire the entire command in one MEMORY *recall*.
(a) Explain.
(b) Examine *fetch* for three sizes, two kinds of completion.
(c) How is LM used?
(d) What is the REFETCH STAT for?

9.9 How are command types distinguished? How does *classification* use this information?

9.10 Describe what the typical RR command does. What is done by the corresponding RX command?

9.11 Describe a typical calculation for M2 in terms of REGISTER and LM transfers. Use arrow notation, completely detailed.

9.12 What uniformity is there about all RR and RX commands except *store*, ST?

9.13 How are A and S done?

9.14 Describe what happens to the operands and GPRs for M and D.

9.15 Work out another CVD example as shown in Fig. 9.7.4.
(a) Convert (by yourself) 185 to binary.
(b) Show the setup of RR, LR and FR as CVD begins.
(c) Go through all the conversion steps from binary to decimal.

9.16 Now do 9.15 in reverse, as would be done by CVB, again using decimal 185.

9.17 In assembly language, the mask for BC and BCR is decimal. Make a table of decimal numbers versus MEMORY for all sixteen masks.

9.18 Describe BAL, BALR, BCT, BCTR in arrow notation. Then explain how each is done, assuming M2 already available.

9.19 When R2 = 0 for BALR, it acts as a NOOP as far as the branch is concerned, but R1 still keeps the present program position.
(a) Put in arrow notation.
(b) How might Model 50 do this?

9.20 From the *Principles of Operation* manual find the description of BXLE and BXH.
(a) Put in arrow notation.
(b) Explain how Model 50 might do them.

9.21 Describe address preparation for VFL commands.

9.22 (a) Describe the three kinds of VFL cycles.

(b) Why *are* there three kinds of cycles?

(c) Why are there several intermediate cycles?

9.23 *Compare* uses the ADDER.

(a) How?

(b) When does it terminate?

(c) Create another example such as that in Fig. 9.9.17 to show *compare* activity.

9.24 (a) Why is the final character required for *decimal* commands?

(b) Why are two length fields, L1 and L2, used?

(c) Why might L1 and L2 be different?

(d) What is L1 for a four digit packed number?

9.25 Describe PACK and UNPK in arrow notation.

(a) For either, can M1 = M2?

(b) Can L1 = L2 for either? With what constraints?

9.26 Create two new examples similar to Figs. 9.10.4 and 9.10.5.

9.27 How do the cycles of addition differ? What happens on overflow? How can the program test for overflow? With what command?

9.28 (a) Draw a flowchart of decimal multiplication, MP.

(b) Give an example.

9.29 Repeat 9.28 for DP.

9.30 In SIO, how are DEVICE and CHANNEL specified? Explain. What do you think the programmer usually uses for B1?

9.31 How does the address of the CHANNEL program get into the CAW?

9.32 Where do the CCWs come from?

9.33 Where is the COMMON CHANNEL? What does it do? How many are needed?

9.34 For Model 50, cycle stealing requires that processing be held up for a few CPU cycles.

(a) Why?

(b) What happens?

(c) Is processing really interfered with?

(d) Is this like interrupt? How (not)?

9.35 Describe multiple breakin and breakout.

9.36 When and how does interrupt occur?

9.37 Explain the microprogram of Fig. 9.12.3.

10

SPECTRA

70

10.1 INTRODUCTION

Contrast with   Spectra 70 and System 360 are comparable
System 360   on a machine language basis:
- The two systems use the same set of opcodes.
- They are both byte-oriented computers.

Both are a series of computers which cover a very large range of size, speed, and MEMORY capacity. This book is not meant to cover either series completely but rather to direct attention to a single model within each series.

For good contrast and comparison, I have chosen the Spectra 70, Model 45, because it is comparable in speed for sample problems to the Model 50, though it is somewhat lower in cost. It is *the* Spectra 70 model most similar to the Model 50, even though the word size of the former is half that of the latter. Some of the other differences are discussed below.

Word size   Sticking to our definition of word size, the System 360 model is a Word computer, whereas Spectra 70, Model 45, is a half Word computer—two bytes. Smaller word size means lower MEMORY cost. Smaller words require more references and more processing transfers for the same program. Apparently speed is picked up elsewhere, for the speed cost-contrast between the two systems is favorable to the Spectra 70.

LOCAL MEMORY   Model 45 provides 128 Words of high speed MEMORY. This enables many important control words to be stored in a more accessible place, saving MAIN MEMORY cycles. It also permits GPRS for all the states to be stored in LM so that software *saving* and *unsaving* operations are reduced.

Four states   Four different operating states are provided in the Model 45. This may help software transition and modularization.

Processing by byte   Another way to reduce cost is to reduce the amount of hardware. Model 45 has a small ADDER LOGIC UNIT. This ALU, as RCA calls it, does both arithmetic and logic by the byte. Cost is lower, but so is the speed; however some speed difference may be masked.

10.2 OPERATIONAL STATES

AND TRANSITION

The states   Recall that System 360 has exactly two states: the program state and the supervisor state. In the supervisor state the full command repertoire prevails, whereas the program state had a restricted repertoire. There is a separate set of GPRs for each of the four CPU states.

For the Spectra 70, there are four machine states, described in Table 10.2.1.

WHY FOUR STATES?

In examining the Spectra 70 and observing four states, the question immediately arises: Why are four states necessary when IBM gets away with two? Here are just a few reasons why four states might be preferable if the implementation cost is comparable:

- There is isolation of function.
- Software modules may be constructed to be fairly independent.
- If LOCAL MEMORY REGISTERS are provided separately for each state, as they are in the Spectra 70, the interrupt procedure in the software program may be considerably reduced.
- Four states provide for easier fault isolation within and between the hardware and the software.
- An interrupt priority system can be provided without using the program status word concept.
- The interrupt class concept is no longer required.
- Interrupt transition can use LM instead of MM and, hence, may initiate traps with greater speed.

Table 10.2.1 SPECTRA 70 MACHINE STATES.

State	RCA Description	Description, State
W	P1	Worker—User programs operate only in P1. None are permitted elsewhere.
X	P2	Executive—Most software runs in this state.
I	P3	Interrupt—All interrupts except machine errors are taken to the state.
M	P4	Machine—All machine errors are interrupted to this state where they are resolved.

Transition   An interesting way to present states and the
transitions among them is found in Fig. 10.2.1, the state transition diagram.
- . Heavy arrows indicate transitions which take place because of
  interrupt.
- Light arrows indicate program-initiated transitions.

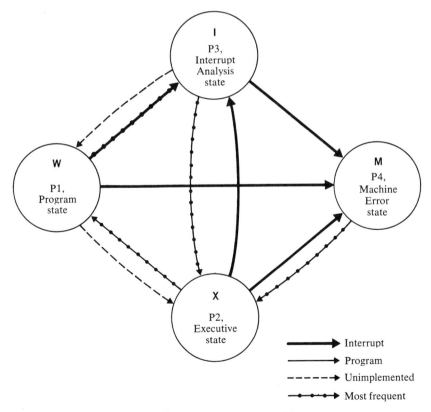

Fig. 10.2.1 PROCESSOR state transitions.

- Dotted arrows show most frequently used transitions.
- Dashed arrows indicate transitions which might have been incorporated into the equipment but which are absent and are no loss to smooth operation.

Before examining the states carefully, let us make a few observations.

- The only way to get out of state **W** is by interrupt.
- The only way to get into state **M** is through an interrupt.
- The only way to get into state **I** is through the interrupt.
- The only way to get back to state **W** is by a program controlled jump from state **X**.

All user programs operate in state **W**, where they have a limited repertoire as contrasted to the full repertoire available in the other three states. A program cannot get to another state except by an interrupt. But, as in System 360, we have the artifact **SVC**, the *supervisor call*, which is a program-initiated interrupt to state **I**. This was discussed in detail in Chapter 9.

Interrupts may arise from various sources. System 360 classifies them into five different classes. Here there is no class structure. Most interrupts take us to state **I**, with the exception of machine-error interrupts. These take us to state **M**.

Most interrupts take us to state **I**. It would be more correct to call this an *analysis* (inalysis?) state rather than an *interrupt* state, since here interrupts are analyzed to find:

- their sources;
- the cause specific to that source.

The analysis routine then determines the proper routine in state **X** and turns control over to it.

Most software routines run in state **X**. We get into one of these routines from state **I**. When this service required of the software is performed in state **X**, we return, under program control, to state **W**.

When machine errors are discovered, an interrupt takes us to state **M** where the error is analyzed and remedied if possible. Otherwise, we make use of software routines which operate in state **X** to which we turn over control.

If the error is catastrophic, a routine in state **X** prints out a message to the operator and then causes the machine to idle while the operator performs a corrective action, if he can. Upon completion, he presses the *restart* button. This gives control to a routine in state **X** and, if the machine is fully operative, thence to the worker program in state **W**.

(margin labels) WORKER STATE / INTERRUPT STATE / EXEC STATE / MACHINE ERRORS

10.3   MEMORIES

As in System 360, Spectra 70 has three entirely different MEMORIES. The characteristics of the MAIN MEMORY differ among the models.

Characteristics
- word size—two bytes
- MEMORY size—16K to 131K
- cycle—1.44 microseconds

- word size—four bytes
- MEMORY size—16K to 545K
- cycle—840 nanoseconds

(side labels, top to bottom: MODEL 45 MM · MODEL 55 MM · READ-ONLY MEMORY · LOCAL MEMORY)

Hereafter, we look at Model 45 only.

Each word in a READ-ONLY MEMORY is 53-bits wide. 2K of MEMORY is provided to hold the main microprograms without the emulation feature. RM operates at 960 nanoseconds per cycle. This is slow compared to the desired speed. To make RM seem faster, it is split into two banks. The operation of the banks are overlapped with each other. The words are separated into banks by the least significant bit. This enables them to overlap operations and generally to achieve an effective speed of 480 nanoseconds per cycle.

RCA calls their LOCAL MEMORY a *scratch pad* MEMORY, but we maintain the title LM as before. Each word in LM contains four bytes, a Word. There are 128 Words in the MEMORY which operates at a speed of 300 nanoseconds per Word. Thus, LM, for the Model 45, is larger and faster than that of the System 360, Model 50.

LM has many functions which we discuss later but pause to summarize here. It contains:
- one set of GPRs for each of the four program states;
- INTERRUPT REGISTERS for all states;
- CHANNEL CONTROL REGISTERS for all CHANNELS;
- UTILITY REGISTERS for the PROCESSOR, regardless of the states.

LOCAL MEMORY map   In succeeding sections we discuss the role of LM in the computer as a whole. It is wise to examine the LM map presented in Fig. 10.3.1, which shows the function of each Word in LM.

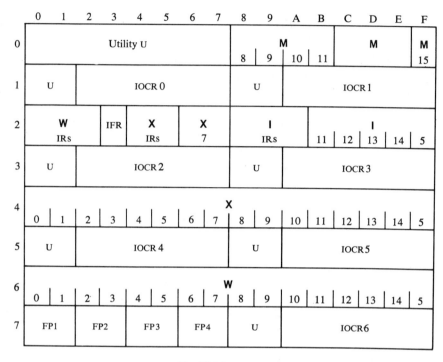

Fig. 10.3.1 LM map.

In areas where the letter U appears, the Words in LM act as UTILITY REGISTERS. Their areas are reserved for different modes and contain a mode designator as follows:

- **W** for worker or program worker;
- **X** for executive or supervisor mode;
- **I** for interrupt or analysis mode;
- **M** for machine-error mode.

We now examine the contents of LM, but not necessarily in a particular order.

The sixteen GPRs for state **W** are found in row 6. The four FLOATING POINT GPRs are in row 7.

WORKER GPRS

Row 4 contains all the state **X** GPRs, a full complement of sixteen. Notice that LM contains only one set of FLOATING POINT REGISTERS (4) for state **W**, since they are generally only used in the program state.

Row 2 contains five GPRs used for interrupt analysis. We also find in this row three sets of INTERRUPT REGISTER groups which are discussed in Section 10.4. They post interrupt activity for three modes. Since software in state **I** analyzes interrupt source and cause, it can most easily use this information in a form where it can be addressed by GPR notation. Row 2 also contains the INTERRUPT FLAG REGISTER, IFR.

Row 0 contains five GPRs available in state **M**. It also contains the IR group for state **M**. This is all that is needed in state **M** for error analysis.

Each CHANNEL has associated with it six REGISTERS which facilitate its activities. These six REGISTERS comprise a CHANNEL REGISTER group. Seven such groups are scattered through LM. Although Model 45 can have only five CHANNELs attached to it, the other groups are provided for compatibility. The CR group is discussed in more detail in Section 10.6.

SUPERVISOR GPRS

INTERRUPT GPRS

MERS

CHANNEL REGISTERS

10.4 INTERRUPTS

Sources   Thirty-two sources of interrupts are shown in Table 10.4.1.

1. The first column gives interrupt source by name.
2. The second column gives state initiated upon the interrupt.
3. The third column shows the hexadecimal weight assigned to this source. This weight is entered into GPR15 for the interrupted state, where it can be picked up by the interrupt routine to determine what the interrupt source was.
4. The last column shows the priority number of the interrupt, the lowest being the most important. This is also the bit position of the flag and mask bits.

The first two entries in the table are the only ones which take us into a state **M**. They are due respectively to power failure or parity error in one

Table 10.4.1 INTERRUPT CONDITIONS

Source	State Initiated	Hexa-decimal Weight	Mask Bit and Priority
Power failure (1 millisecond warning)	**M**	00	0
Machine check (MAIN MEMORY or SCRATCH PAD error)	**M**	04	1
External signal No. 1	**I**	08	2
External signal No. 2 (Used with optional	**I**	0C	3
External signal No. 3 "direct control" feature	**I**	10	4
External signal No. 4 for MULTIPROCESSOR	**I**	14	5
External signal No. 5 complex.)	**I**	18	6
External signal No. 6	**I**	1C	7
Not specified (Used in special purpose PROCESSORS.)	**I**	20	8
SELECTOR CHANNEL NO. 1	**I**	24	9
SELECTOR CHANNEL NO. 2 (IO termination	**I**	28	10
SELECTOR CHANNEL NO. 3 interrupt or program-	**I**	2C	11
SELECTOR CHANNEL NO. 4 controlled IO interrupt.)	**I**	30	12
SELECTOR CHANNEL NO. 5 (SELECTOR CHANNELS on	**I**	34	13
SELECTOR CHANNEL NO. 6 optional features.)	**I**	38	14
MULTIPLEXOR CHANNEL	**I**	3C	15
ELAPSED-TIME CLOCK (Time-out) (Optional feature)	**I**	40	16
Console interrupt request (COIN button)	**I**	44	17
Not specified (Used in special purpose PROCESSORS.)	**I**	48	18
Not specified	**I**	4C	19
Supervisor call instruction	**I**	50	20
Privileged operation (in nonprivileged state)	**I**	54	21
Opcode trap (Unassigned operation codes)	**I**	58	22
Addressing error (Improper MEMORY or REGISTER address)	**I**	5C	23
Data error (Packed decimal format check)	**I**	60	24
Exponent overflow (Floating point exponent 127)	**I**	64	25
Divide error (Result too large)	**I**	68	26
Significance error (Floating point result fraction = 0)	**I**	6C	27
Exponent underflow (Floating point exponent 0)	**I**	70	28
Decimal overflow (Result too large)	**I**	74	29
Fixed point overflow (Result too large)	**I**	78	30
Test mode (Automatic interrupt after each instruction)	**I**	7C	31

of the MEMORIES. The next higher priorities go to external signals. These are available only as a special option for users. They permit communication lines to get immediate attention.

The next set of priorities go to SELECTOR CHANNELS. The lowest number CHANNELS have highest priority and should get the fastest DEVICES. The MULTIPLEXOR CHANNEL, being the last, has the lowest CHANNEL priority.

The next two interrupts are for an ELAPSED-TIME CLOCK and CONSOLE, discussed in Chapter 3. SVC (program-initiated interrupt) is next and gets service before program-originating errors, the remaining interrupt sources.

REGISTERS   Several REGISTERS are associated with interrupt. The INTERRUPT FLAG REGISTER, IFR, and a group of registers called the IF group, one for each mode, serve the needs of interrupt.

There is only one IFR. Providing several would require that each be updated during an interrupt. But only one is necessary. It contains one bit for each possible interrupt source, as indicated in Table 10.4.1. There is a zero in this bit position if no interrupt has occurred for that source or if an interrupt has occurred and has been detected and acknowledged by the software. There is a one in a bit position if the source has signaled an interrupt, but that interrupt has not yet been acknowledged by the software.

IFR

There is one IR group for each of the four program states. Each group contains three REGISTERS, Fig. 10.4.1:
- PCR is the PROGRAM COUNTER REGISTER:
- IMR is the INTERRUPT MASK REGISTER; it determines which interrupts to respond to;
- ISR is the INTERRUPT STATUS REGISTER which records other information important to the activity.

IR GROUP

The IMR contains thirty-two bits which are identically labeled for sources, as is the IFR. A zero in a bit position suspends interrupts for this source which are recorded but not otherwise responded to; 1 permits a trap to occur when sensed for that source.

IMR

The PCR records information about a state when we leave it. For instance, when an interrupt occurs in state **W**, the next **W** instruction is recorded in PCR. The four items recorded in PCR are:
- next instruction location
- condition code
- instruction length
- program mask

PCR

We have not discussed the program mask, a set of four bits in the PCR which permits or inhibits certain PROCESSOR interrupts. The four bits correspond to the following four processing difficulties:
- significance error
- exponent underflow
- decimal overflow
- fixed point overflow

The program mask is settable in any mode. Thus, the program has control in state **W** as to whether any of the foregoing errors will cause an interrupt.

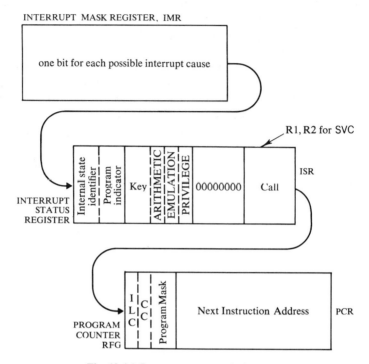

Fig. 10.4.1 Interrupt REGISTER (IR) group.

The INTERRUPT STATUS REGISTER stores another set of data important to the program just interrupted:

- the protect key;
- whether we are using EBCDIC or ASCII characters;
- if emulation is in progress;
- if privileged mode prevails;
- R1, R2 for the first SVC.

Interrupt microroutine   An interrupt can occur when the computer is in any one of the four states **W, I, X, M** (generally all interrupts are suspended in state **M**). The interrupt microroutine responds in the same way regardless of the state of the computer at the time. It performs these tasks in order:

1. Receives the interrupt.
2. Identifies the source of the interrupt, giving it a number between 0 and 31, corresponding to its position in Table 10.4.1.
3. Obtains the contents of IFR.

4. Places 1 in the position corresponding to the interrupt source.
5. Returns this word to the IFR.
6. Gets the contents of the IMR for this state.
7. Compares the contents of the IMR with those of the IFR. The criterion used is the presence of 1 in the same bit position of both words. Should this condition arise, initiate an interrupt procedure. Otherwise, continue with the program.

For Interrupt Completion Only

8. Assuming that an interrupt is under way, its weight is placed in GPR15 for the state to be entered.
9. The PC word for the state that we leave is prepared and placed in that PCR.
10. The IS word is also made up and placed in its proper ISR location.
11. The PCR for the state being entered is obtained from LM and entered in the hardware REGISTERS.
12. Now *fetch* the new command in the new state.

Interrupt state jobs   When we enter I state, the IMR will probably be set so that only machine errors can interrupt during this activity. If not, it is up to the interrupt state of the machine to so set IMR. Next, the interrupt routine goes to GPR15 and takes out the weight constant. The systems programmer determines how much analysis is done in state I and how much in state **X**. The weight in GPR15 distinguishes the source of the interrupt. We may now go to a source table and find the location in state **X** where the service routine for that source is found.

Suppose, however, that not only source but also the cause of interrupt is desired. Then the aforementioned table will lead us to a specific source/cause analysis routine. For instance, for a CHANNEL, this routine finds which DEVICE has caused the interrupt and for what reason. This can be determined by *inquiry* commands.

To reiterate, cause determination routines may be found in either state I or state **X**; the next routine called in is a cause-specific service routine.

Again, suppose that source and cause have been determined in state I. To enter state **X**, the PC command automatically does two things. It:

- resets the PCR for this state to a quantity incorporated in the command. This enables a new interrupt to take over, not from the last instruction, but at the beginning of the analysis routine.
- goes into state **X** using the PC of the PCR for state **X** as the beginning of the executive routine.

PC has the format:

$$PC: \quad 82 \quad I2 \quad B1 \quad D1 \qquad (10.4.1)$$

where $M1 = (B1) + D1$, and $M1$ is the address to be stored in the PCR of this state. Furthermore, $I2$ has the form:

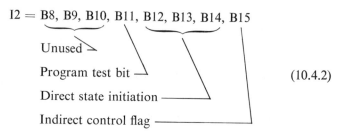

$$I2 = B8, B9, B10, B11, B12, B13, B14, B15$$

Unused

Program test bit

Direct state initiation

Indirect control flag

(10.4.2)

If we disregard the test bit which has esoteric uses, the direct state bits specify states as follows:

B12	B13	B14	
0	0	0	$= \mathbf{M}$
0	0	1	$= \mathbf{I}$
0	1	0	$= \mathbf{X}$
0	1	1	$= \mathbf{W}$

(10.4.3)

If $B15 = 1$, we use the state bits in the ISR to determine the next state entered, disregarding the direct state bits.

Executive state   All servicing is done in the executive state. The amount of analysis conducted in this state, as mentioned earlier, depends on system design. IO required by JOCS is also done here. Further, job and task sequencing go on in this state.

When the executive routine is complete we return to the main program by the PC command. This time the beginning of the executive program is set into the **X** PCR and the place to return to the main program is taken from the **W** state PCR.

Program errors in   Should a program fault or arithmetic error
state X   arise in state **X**, return is made to state **I**. Such errors should not occur with properly debugged software. Emergency routines must be called in to handle them.

State M errors   We go to state **M** because of power failure or MEMORY error. When power is failing, we have about one millisecond to rescue the computer. Any information which is hurt by power failure can be placed in CORE MEMORY where it is safe. It is set up so that it can be reinstated when the *restart* button is pressed. After this, the machine goes to state **X** where, if there is time, a message is printed to inform the operator.

When power resumes, the operator can press the *restart* button. The computer goes to state **X** to reinitialize the problem. It then returns to the place the program left off and returns to state **W**.

For MEMORY parity errors we can only retry to interrogate MEMORY. If this fails, the equipment must be shut down and the service engineer called.

Multiple interrupts   Again, the problem arises: What do we do if an interrupt develops while an earlier interrupt is being serviced? The interrupt mask will suspend some interrupts. Servicing proceeds to completion in state **X**. Then we return to state **W**, but before doing anything there, we check the interrupt state flag against the IMR in the **W** state. If there are one or more interrupts pending, a microprogram selects the one with the lowest number and places its weight in GPR15, state **I**. Then it takes off to service that new interrupt.

10.5 HARDWARE

A basic hardware block diagram is presented in Fig. 10.5.1.

Bus system   A large data bus, DB, is divided into three lines labeled DBO, DB1, and DBA. DBO is a byte line which carries the less significant of two bytes when information is being transferred; DB1 carries the more significant byte. DBA is a two-bit bus which supplements the other sixteen bits when the MAR is addressed. This is required because addresses can be eighteen bits long for the largest MEMORY option for Model 45.

The data bus is simply a set of lines which connect to and from most of the REGISTERS in the computer. The SOURCE REGISTER for the DB is determined by the S field in the RDR; the destination is set by the RDR D field. If the data bus is not used by an EO (elementary operation—microop), the S and D fields are free for other uses. This is the case for EO's whose purpose is a test operation.

The diagram would become much more complicated if we tried to show how the S and D fields affect the data bus; this is left to the reader's imagination.

LOCAL MEMORY   The LOCAL MEMORY ADDRESS REGISTER, LAR, receives addresses for any word to be memorized in LM. Addresses for the

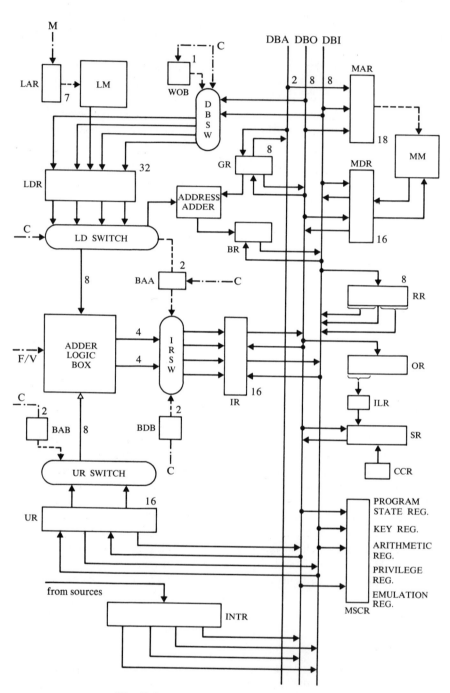

Fig. 10.5.1 Spectra 70, Model 45 hardware.

LAR may be produced in several ways:

1. During both the *fetch* and *execute* phases of a command, locations in LM are addressed by the EO by transferring all or part of the M field in the RDR to the LAR.
2. During RR and RX instructions, GPR designators are stored in the R REGISTER, abbreviated RR (for REGISTER REGISTER). To form the GPR address, the EO provides: part of the RR; the PROGRAM STATE REGISTER, PSR; one or two bits on its own. The PSR is a two-bit REGISTER indicating in which of the four program states the CPU now resides.
3. For RR, RS, and SS commands, a GPR is specified as a base. This designation is generally kept in the BASE REGISTER, BR. Its location in LM is formed using PSR, the PROGRAM STATE REGISTER, and part of the M field.

The LOCAL MEMORY DATA REGISTER, LDR (called the DR by RCA), receives the thirty-two bit data word from the LM. To be distributed, this word passes through the LD SWITCH. Only one byte at a time may be absorbed by the ADDER LOGIC BOX, discussed below. This byte is chosen by the C field of the EO. It also may be controlled by the FLIPFLOP, BAA.

The LDR is loaded from the data buses. To position the two-byte information into the four-byte REGISTER, SWITCH DBSW is used. This is controlled by the WDB REGISTER or from the EO itself.

ADDER LOGIC BOX   The ADDER LOGIC BOX, ALB, has two inputs, each providing a single byte. The first input comes from the LD SWITCH which is controlled by EO field C and BA. The other input comes from the UTILITY REGISTER, UR, a two-byte REGISTER. The byte used is selected by the UR SWITCH, set by REGISTER BAB, which, in turn, is controlled by the C field of a previous EO.

The ALB does all processing for the computer, a byte at a time. What it does during any EO is determined by the F and V fields of that EO.

The output of the ALB is always routed to the two-byte INTERMEDIATE REGISTER, IR. The ADDER LOGIC BOX produces a single output byte, divisible into two nibbles, each of which may be routed to any nibble position in the IR through the SWITCH, IRSW. IRSW is controlled by two small REGISTERS, BAA and BAD, set previously by the C field of an EO.

COMMAND REGISTERS   Command information from MAIN MEMORY appears in the MDR; from there it is placed on the data buses. The first pair of command bytes is routed to the OPERATION REGISTER, OR, and the REGISTER REGISTER, RR. The OR stores the opcode throughout *execution*.

When the next two command bytes appear, they are routed to the BR and UR, UTILITY REGISTER. The BR gets the first nibble; the UR gets the next three nibbles. The top nibble position of the UR is set to 0_H so that the displacement is a proper halfWord. For SS commands, the BR and UR are used in the same fashion. For MEMORY operand instructions, two operand addresses are prepared in operations described in Section 10.7. They are stored in LM in two positions, designated AAD for M1 and BAD for M2. Figure 10.5.2 is a summary of REGISTER contents for command information.

REGISTER	Holds
OR	OP
RR	R1R2, L1L2, R1X2, or L
BR	B1 or B2
UR	D1 or D2
AAD	M1
BAD	M2

Fig. 10.5.2 REGISTER contents relative to commands.

Other REGISTERS   The two high-order bits of the OR store the length code duplicated in the ILR. The CCR holds the two-bit condition code at the end of an instruction. The S REGISTER is used for various purposes, one being the assembly of part of the PC word. Hence it has inputs from the ILR, CCR, and DBO.

A single-byte register, GR, occasionally takes part in address calculation. There is a group of miscellaneous REGISTERs which I have called MSCR. Their uses are labeled in the diagram.

The fullWord INTERRUPT REGISTER, INTR, receives interrupt information from IO CHANNELS, the CPU, and EXTERNAL DEVICES. There is one bit for each source. When this source wishes to interrupt, it sets this bit to 1. This REGISTER is used for posting to the IFR and for comparing with the IMR.

10.6 MICROPROGRAMMING

AND COMMAND EXECUTION

This section examines Spectra 70 microprogramming.

The microprogram   The data word from the READ-ONLY MEMORY
word   is placed in the RDR where it controls the
computer just as in System 360. A microcommand is called by RCA an

elementary operation and is abbreviated as EO. An EO word in Fig. 10.6.1 contains these fields:

F—the function to be performed by the ADDER LOGIC BOX, ALB.

V—variations upon the function F.

C—a COUNTER and address constant.

M—control bits to tell LM what to do.

S, D—source and destination for data buses, Fig. 10.5.1.

T—test conditions.

N, A—normal and alternate RM address for *true* and *false* tests.

E—exception check.

I—IO breakin inhibit.

How these fields are specified and used would be an irksome task to describe. It would make service engineers out of all of us.

Address for RAR   Of special interest is how the next RM address is prepared and controlled by an EO. This is demonstrated in Fig. 10.6.1. The T field of the EO in the RDR contains bits which specify REGISTERS in the CPU and states which should prevail on them. If these states *do* prevail, the EO chooses the normal address specified by N for the RAR; otherwise the alternate address A goes to the RAR.

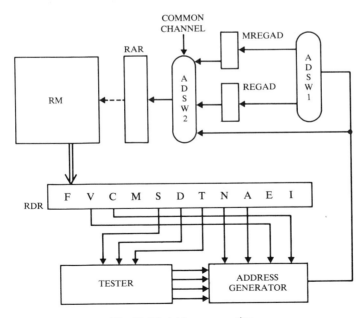

Fig. 10.6.1 Address generation.

This provides a binary choice. To make an address dependent on multiple conditions, the D and S fields supply further REGISTER conditions to be checked. The D and S fields can be used for this purpose only when the data bus is not called for. The C and V fields of the EO then furnish additional addresses for these branches. The TESTER is furnished with the T, D, and S fields and decides, by examining CPU REGISTERS, which of the four addresses goes to the RAR. These addresses are forwarded to the ADDRESS GENERATOR which produces an address routed to the ADDRESS SWITCHES.

Normally, an address, when fabricated, is sent to the RAR to procure the next EO. Further, as we recall from the System 360, a breakin from a SELECTOR CHANNEL may be in progress. This is communicated through the COMMON CHANNEL which causes an alternate address to be placed in the RAR. To keep our place in the RAR, the address of the next command for normal execution is put in a BACKUP REGISTER. For Spectra 70 there are *two* BACKUP REGISTERS: MREGAD is the MULTIPLEXOR REGENERATING ADDRESS REGISTER used only for MULTIPLEXOR breakin; RAGAD is the other REGENERATING REGISTER used for all other breakins.

Then the address for the RAR is controlled by the two switches, ADSW1 and ADSW2, which provide an address:

- Normally, the RAR is furnished an address from the ADDRESS GENERATOR.
- In breakin, the address from the ADDRESS GENERATOR goes to the BACKUP REGISTER: the address for the RAR is obtained from the COMMON CHANNEL.
- For breakout, the address comes from a BACKUP REGISTER.

RR commands We now examine the *fetch*, *classify*, and *execute* for a typical RR command. Each command does several functions; each function has an EO associated with it. Each EO may provide a number of data paths and transfers outlined in arrow notation below.

FETCH

Several EO's are required to perform an RR *fetch*. The first gets the PROGRAM COUNTER from LM. The PROGRAM COUNTER accessed depends upon the state of operation. The first EO procures the PC address.

$$[\text{PC}] \rightarrow \text{LAR} \qquad (10.6.1)$$

The PC is then sent to the MEMORY ADDRESS REGISTER:

$$(\text{LDR}) \rightarrow \text{MAR} \qquad (10.6.2)$$

In the meantime, after incrementing the LOCAL MEMORY DATA REGISTER which contains the PCR, we return its contents to that PROGRAM COUNTER location:

$$(\text{LDR}) + 2 \to \text{PCR} \qquad (10.6.3)$$

Before the next EO, we wait for MEMORY to complete a *recall*, bringing the next datum, the first two bytes of this command, into the MDR. The next EO places the command in CPU REGISTERS:

$$(\text{MDR}) \to \text{OR, RR} \qquad (10.6.4)$$

The next EO classifies the command in the OR by checking the first two bits. They are 00 for the RR command. The last *classify* EO brings the less significant halfWord of the contents of R2 to the UTILITY REGISTER.

$$(\text{RR2}) \to \text{LAR} \qquad (10.6.5)$$

$$(\text{LDR2}) \to \text{UR} \qquad (10.6.6)$$

Here, "RR2" means the right half of RR; etc.

The reader should bear in mind the important differences in the size of the REGISTERs between the Model 45 and the System 360, Model 50:

- MM words are halfWords for Model 45.
- Most of the CPU REGISTERs are consequently two bytes long.
- Addition and logic done in the ADDER LOGIC BOX, ALB, are performed upon only one byte.
- All LM words are four bytes long for both models.

As a typical RR instruction we examine the logical *and*, NR with hexadecimal code 14. It *and*s the two Words contained in the GPRs designated by R1 and R2.

After the *fetch* and *classify*, the opcode causes a branch to the first EO for NR. It sets the ALB for *and*.

The second EO gets the lesser halfWord of R1. *And* is then done upon the (LDR) and the (UR), which contains the lesser halfWord of R2. The result is put in the intermediate register, IR.

$$\text{R1} \to \text{LAR} \qquad (10.6.7)$$

$$(\text{LDR2}) \ \& \ (\text{UR}) \to \text{IR} \qquad (10.6.8)$$

We have only half of the result. We must now get the more significant halfWord of R2.

$$\text{R2} \to \text{LAR} \qquad (10.6.9)$$

$$(\text{LDR1}) \to \text{UR} \qquad (10.6.10)$$

Next we set the address of R1 into the LAR.

$$[\text{R1}] \to \text{LAR} \qquad (10.6.11)$$

Now we do two things at once. We put away the result halfWord that is in the IR, placing it in the second half of the LDR.

$$(\text{IR}) \rightarrow \text{LDR2} \qquad (10.6.12)$$

We also perform *and* on the contents of the UR and the first half of the Word in the LDR, placing the results in the IR.

$$(\text{LDR1}) \;\&\; (\text{UR}) \rightarrow \text{IR} \qquad (10.6.13)$$

The last EO places this half of the result in the first half of the LDR,

$$(\text{IR}) \rightarrow \text{LDR1} \qquad (10.6.14)$$

and then returns the complete result to LM.

$$(\text{LDR}) \rightarrow [\text{R1}] \qquad (10.6.15)$$

RX fetch   The RX command has the format:

$$\text{OP} \quad \text{R1} \quad \text{X2} \quad \text{B2} \quad \text{D2} \qquad (10.6.16)$$

Fetch for RX commands is the same as for RR commands, so that at its end, we have OP in the OR and R1 in RR.

CLASSIFY

The first EO gets the second command halfWord. First put the address of the PROGRAM COUNTER into the LAR:

$$[\text{PCR}] \rightarrow \text{LAR} \qquad (10.6.17)$$

The LM quantity is sent to the MAR:

$$(\text{LDR}) \rightarrow \text{MAR} \qquad (10.6.18)$$

Before returning the PCR quantity, we add 2 to it so that it points to the next pair of instruction bytes.

$$(\text{LDR}) + 2 \rightarrow \text{PC} \qquad (10.6.19)$$

The two bytes obtained from MM are placed in REGISTERS so that they may be operated on as the base and displacement. The first nibble, the base specifier, is put into the BR; the remaining three nibbles are placed in the UR. Since the UR is a halfWord REGISTER, the first four bits are set to 0. We have:

$$(\text{MDR}) \rightarrow \text{BR}, \text{UR}; \quad (\text{BR}) = \text{B2}; \quad (\text{UR}) = \text{D2} \qquad (10.6.20)$$

The next task is to make the MEMORY operand address, M2. We access the GPR in LM. This EO takes the four bits in the BR and constructs the LM address of B2, placing it in the LAR.

$$\text{B2} \rightarrow \text{LAR} \qquad (10.6.21)$$

As the base quantity is brought from LM, it is added to the displacement and placed in the IR.

$$(\text{LDR}) + (\text{UR}) \rightarrow \text{IR}; \qquad (\text{IR}) = (\text{B2}) + \text{D2} \qquad (10.6.22)$$

The next EO distributes the partial MEMORY address to the UTILITY REGISTER.

$$(\text{IR}) \rightarrow \text{UR} \qquad (10.6.23)$$

To make M2, we need the index quantity, (X2). Its address is in the second half of the RR, and this is sent to the LAR.

$$(\text{RR2}) \rightarrow \text{LAR} \qquad (10.6.24)$$

The partial address in UR is added to the quantity obtained from LM and the result returned to the IR.

$$(\text{LDR}) + (\text{UR}) \rightarrow \text{IR} \qquad (10.6.25)$$

We now have the operand address. A CELL in the LM, called the BAD for B address, is set aside for this address. Recall that MM is organized by halfWord. To obtain the operand requires two MM accesses. This EO puts away the operand address.

$$[\text{BAD}] \rightarrow \text{LAR} \qquad (10.6.26)$$

$$(\text{IR}) \rightarrow \text{LDR} \qquad (10.6.27)$$

$$(\text{LDR}) + 2 \rightarrow \text{LM} \qquad (10.6.28)$$

Notice that 2 is added to the operand address as it is stored in LM. Instead of pointing to the *true* operand address, it points two bytes ahead. There is a good reason for this. In doing fullWord arithmetic, we wish the less significant two bytes of an operand to be obtained first. By moving the operand address ahead two bytes, MEMORY reference, which is done in halfWords, now procures this less significant pair of bytes first.

RX execute   We examine the fullWord RX subtract command with mnemonic, S, and hexadecimal opcode 5B. It does this job:

$$\text{S:} \quad (\text{R1}) - (\text{M2}) \rightarrow \text{R1} \qquad (10.6.29)$$

The first EO sets the ALB to perform subtraction and also to obtain the operand address:

$$[\text{BAD}] \rightarrow \text{LAR}; \qquad (\text{LDR}) \rightarrow \text{MAR} \qquad (10.6.30)$$

Notice that the address was sent over to the MAR to start a MEMORY *recall* cycle.

As the operand address is put away, it is decremented by 2 so that it will point next to the *more* significant pair of bytes in the operand.

$$(\text{LDR}) - 2 \to \text{BAD} \qquad (10.6.31)$$

When the operand arrives at the MDR, it is sent over to the UTILITY REGISTER.

$$(\text{MDR}) \to \text{UR} \qquad (10.6.32)$$

To save time we start the MEMORY retrieving the *first* pair of bytes while we operate with the second.

$$[\text{BAD}] \to \text{LAR}; \qquad (\text{LDR}) \to \text{MAR} \qquad (10.6.33)$$

Now we get the other operand for subtraction. The minuend is contained in the GPR named R1. The less significant halfWord is obtained from LM and the contents of UR are subtracted from it. The result goes to the IR:

$$[\text{R2}] \to \text{LAR} \qquad (10.6.34)$$

$$(\text{LDR2}) - (\text{UR}) \to \text{IR} \qquad (10.6.35)$$

We wait for the first pair of bytes to arrive from MEMORY and then send them to the UTILITY REGISTER.

$$(\text{MDR}) \to \text{UR} \qquad (10.6.36)$$

The result halfWord is withdrawn from the IR and placed in the right halfWord of the LDR. Meanwhile the rest of the subtraction takes place.

$$(\text{IR}) \to \text{LDR2} \qquad (10.6.37)$$

$$(\text{LDR1}) - (\text{UR}) \to \text{IR} \qquad (10.6.38)$$

The difference word is assembled in the LDR and the result is now returned to LOCAL MEMORY.

$$(\text{IR}) \to \text{LDR1} \qquad (10.6.39)$$

$$(\text{LDR}) \to \text{LM}; \qquad (\text{R1}) = (\text{R1}) - (\text{M1}) \qquad (10.6.40)$$

10.7   SS COMMANDS

Fetch   The *fetch* and the first part of *classify* look like those used for the RX command. At the end of this we have:

$$(\text{AAD}) = \text{M1}; \qquad (\text{RR}) = \text{L} \ \text{or} \ \text{L1L2}; \qquad (\text{OR}) = \text{OP} \quad (10.7.1)$$

The PROGRAM COUNTER stored in the PCR in LM points to the third byte pair in the instruction. To get this halfWord, we send the PROGRAM COUNTER to the MAR.

$$[\text{PCR}] \to \text{LAR} \qquad (10.7.2)$$

$$(\text{LDR}) \to \text{MAR} \qquad (10.7.3)$$

The PROGRAM COUNTER is incremented as it is returned to LM.

$$(\text{LDR}) + 2 \to \text{PCR} \qquad (10.7.4)$$

The last command halfWord is now in the MDR. It is distributed to BR and UR.

$$(\text{MDR}) \to \text{BR, UR}; \quad (\text{BR}) = \text{B2}; \quad (\text{UR}) = \text{D2} \qquad (10.7.5)$$

We obtain the contents of the BASE REGISTER.

$$[\text{B2}] \to \text{LAR} \qquad (10.7.6)$$

When the contents appear at the LDR, the ADDER is activated and they are added to (UR). The result is passed over to the IR.

$$(\text{LDR}) + (\text{UR}) \to \text{IR}; \quad (\text{IR}) = \text{M2} \qquad (10.7.7)$$

This is the second operand address, and it is placed at BAD in LM.

$$[\text{BAD}] \to \text{LAR}; \quad (\text{IR}) \to \text{LDR} \qquad (10.7.8)$$

VFL commands   As described, AAD and BAD contain the first and second operand starting addresses. This is proper for transfer and logical commands such as MVC.

For decimal arithmetic we operate on data fields from right to left instead of from left to right. We need the address of the last data byte pair for each operand: AAD and BAD should point to this last byte pair. It is prepared by adding the length specifier to the operand address so that we have:

$$(\text{AAD}) = \text{M1}' = \text{M1} + \text{L1} \qquad (10.7.9)$$

$$(\text{BAD}) = \text{M2}' = \text{M2} + \text{L2} \qquad (10.7.10)$$

During *fetch*, RR contains L1L2. Each nibble is a length specifier for one of the operands. After M1 is prepared, it is simple for M1′ to be prepared in a few EO's. M2′ is similarly prepared.

Types of cycles   We look at *MoVe* Character, MVC, and distinguish the kinds of cycles which are required. For Model 45 with halfWord access, instead of being concerned with Word boundaries, it is a halfWord boundary which is important.

As in Section 9.9, we distinguish three kinds of cycles:
- An initial cycle gets M1 to a halfWord boundary.
- Intermediate cycles fill halfWords in the M1 field.
- A final cycle is necessary if there is one byte left over in completing the operation.

Actually, the only four cases in dealing with transfers are presented in Fig. 10.7.1.

1. Both source and destination fields are on halfWord boundaries.
2. Both fields are off a halfWord boundary.
3. Only the M1 field is on a halfWord boundary.
4. Only the M2 field is on a halfWord boundary.

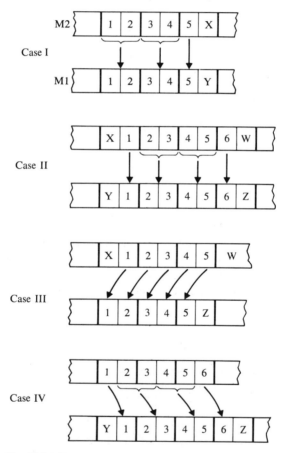

Fig. 10.7.1 Four cases in decimal character commands.

Case I   For this case we immediately start intermediate cycles. Everything is properly aligned. We first get the M2 field.

$$[\text{BAD}] \rightarrow \text{LAR}; \quad (\text{LDR}) \rightarrow \text{MAR} \quad\quad (10.7.11)$$

$$(\text{MDR}) \rightarrow \text{IR}; \quad (\text{LDR}) + 2 \rightarrow \text{LDR} \quad\quad (10.7.12)$$

The source halfWord is now in the IR. It is now put away in the destination field.

$$[\text{AAD}] \rightarrow \text{LAR}; \quad (\text{LDR}) \rightarrow \text{MAR} \quad\quad (10.7.13)$$

$$(\text{IR}) \rightarrow \text{MDR}; \quad (\text{LDR}) + 2 \rightarrow \text{LDR} \quad\quad (10.7.14)$$

We decrement the length and return it to its REGISTER.

$$(\text{RR}) - 2 \rightarrow \text{RR} \quad\quad (10.7.15)$$

We check the length remaining:

$(\text{RR}) \geqslant 1:$ continue; $\quad (\text{RR}) < 0:$ stop;

$$(\text{RR}) = 0: \quad \text{final cycle} \quad (10.7.16)$$

For the first condition, we continue intermediate cycles as described by (10.7.11) through (10.7.16). If a final cycle is required, instead of replacing the entire MDR, only the more significant byte from IR is inserted in the MDR before *memorization*.

Case II   Here we require an initial cycle to transfer one byte from source to destination. We simplify the arrow notation, indicating in one equation that we get the first source halfWord and place it in the IR.

$$((\text{BAR})) \rightarrow \text{IR} \quad\quad (10.7.17)$$

We then bring the destination halfWord to the MDR.

$$((\text{AAR})) \rightarrow \text{MDR} \quad\quad (10.7.18)$$

Now only the second byte from IR is placed in the second byte position of the MDR; the first byte in the MDR is unchanged.

$$(\text{IR2}) \rightarrow \text{MDR2} \quad\quad (10.7.19)$$

The remaining source and destination fields are now aligned on halfWord boundaries, and we revert to case I described above.

Case III   Here the source field is not aligned with the destination field. Only the second byte of the source halfWord is to be transferred to the destination field. We get this halfWord:

$$[\text{BAB}] \rightarrow \text{LAR}; \qquad (\text{LDR}) \rightarrow \text{MAR} \qquad\qquad (10.7.20)$$

We take the second byte and place it in the first byte position of the IR:

$$(\text{MDR2}) \rightarrow \text{IR1} \qquad\qquad (10.7.21)$$

We increment the byte address.

$$(\text{LDR}) + 2 \rightarrow \text{LDR} \qquad\qquad (10.7.22)$$

Now we get the next source halfWord. The first byte of this halfWord goes into the destination halfWord we are forming; the remaining byte is for the next destination halfWord. We have:

$$[\text{BAB}] \rightarrow \text{LAR}; \qquad (\text{LDR}) \rightarrow \text{MAR} \qquad\qquad (10.7.23)$$

The source halfWord is placed in the UTILITY REGISTER and the source address is incremented.

$$(\text{MDR}) \rightarrow \text{UR}; \qquad (\text{LDR}) + 2 \rightarrow \text{LDR} \qquad\qquad (10.7.24)$$

The first byte in UR is passed over to the second byte of the IR through the ADDER, so that we now have assembled the destination word in IR.

$$(\text{UR1}) \rightarrow \text{IR2} \qquad\qquad (10.7.25)$$

It is placed in the MDR.

$$(\text{IR}) \rightarrow \text{MDR} \qquad\qquad (10.7.26)$$

Now the second half byte in UR is passed over to the first byte position in IR to get ready for the next destination word.

$$(\text{UR2}) \rightarrow \text{IR1} \qquad\qquad (10.7.27)$$

We get the destination address,

$$[\text{AAD}] \rightarrow \text{LAR}; \qquad (\text{LDR}) \rightarrow \text{MAR} \qquad\qquad (10.7.28)$$

and store the destination word. After this, we increment the destination address.

$$(\text{LDR}) + 2 \rightarrow \text{LDR} \qquad\qquad (10.7.29)$$

The length specifier is now decremented.

$$(\text{RR}) - 2 \rightarrow \text{RR} \qquad\qquad (10.7.30)$$

Tests are performed as in (10.7.16) to determine if more halfWords are to be processed.

Case IV   For this case, the first destination halfWord will receive a source byte only in its second position. The first byte of the destination halfWord remains unchanged. An initial cycle is required to take care of this first halfWord; thereafter, processing of future halfWords proceeds as described for Case III.

Other commands   The *move* command that we have examined here does not use information in the destination field. Other decimal commands such as AP and SP *add* and *subtract*, respectively. Using the information in the source field for the arithmetic requested, it is simple to see how these operations are done using the REGISTERS as described above and using the procedures examined while pursuing the logic of System 360.

10.8 IO

IO control   To expedite IO activity, all IO control is in LM. We do have to reference MM to obtain subcommands (CCW's) and for data transfer.

The IO CONTROLLER is delegated a task with the *start device command*, SDV. This is equivalent in all respects with the System 360 command, SIO. Other commands which are parallel to those of System 360 are HDV, IDV, and CKC.

SDV has this format:

$$\text{SDV:} \qquad \text{OP} \quad I = 0 \quad \text{B1} \quad \text{D1} \qquad\qquad (10.8.1)$$

Here M1 distinguishes the CHANNEL and DEVICE desired. The CHANNEL address word, CAW, is stored at the decimal address 72. It contains a key and an address. The key is the protect key to be used by the CHANNEL in addressing MEMORY. The address is that of the first subcommand.

LM for each   One CR group in LM is set aside for each
CHANNEL   CHANNEL. Its contents are displayed in Fig. 10.8.1. Notice the CAW REGISTER, CAR, the two CCW REGISTERS, CCR1 and CCR2, and a new designation, the CHANNEL assembly and status word, CASW. Only one REGISTER is used for assembly and status posting, the CASR. This is because MM word size is two bytes. Of the remaining two LM bytes of the CASR, one is wasted and the other is used to hold status

	CAR	CCR2	CCR1	CASR	CUR1	CUR2	

Fig. 10.8.1 The CHANNEL REGISTER (CR) group.

information. Finally, two CHANNEL UTILITY REGISTERS, CUR1 and CUR2, are provided which are unique to a given CHANNEL. These enable the CHANNEL microprogram to leave messages for itself.

CHANNEL service input   Whenever a word—two bytes—is assembled in a CONTROL BUFFER REGISTER, the CONTROLLER issues a *request for service*. Since several *requests* may appear at once from different sources, some CENTRAL LOGIC is required to determine which request is serviced first. RCA calls this the CONTROL ELECTRONICS, but we maintain our previous term, COMMON CHANNEL.

When one or more *requests for service* arrive at the COMMON CHANNEL, it selects the one with the highest priority. It then sets a FLIPFLOP in the CPU which is checked by certain EO's. If the I field in an EO is set to 1, COMMON CHANNEL requests are ignored; if it is set to 0, a breakin may be initiated. Breakin is similar to that described for System 360. RAGAD is the BACKUP REGISTER for the next RM microroutine address for the command being executed. The address provided by the COMMON CHANNEL is loaded into the RAR to start the IO microroutine.

Data transfer   A data transfer microroutine transfers half-Words between MAIN MEMORY and a SELECTOR CHANNEL or other source in a manner similar to that described for System 360.

Interrupt   Interrupt procedure for the Spectra 70 is different from that for System 360 and hence is described here.

Whenever a source has an interrupt pending, it immediately transfers this information to the interrupt register, INTR. This REGISTER is ignored until the end of either a *fetch* or *execute* cycle. Generally both cycles must be completed; but there are some exceptions.

The *interrupt* microprogram takes over and inserts the address of the IFR into the LAR, obtains the interrupt flag, and posts the INTERRUPT REGISTER's contents onto it.

Now we wish to see if the pending interrupt is permitted. To do this we must get the contents of the IMR. We have:

$$[IMR] \rightarrow LAR; \quad (IMR) \rightarrow LDR \quad (10.8.2)$$

The mask in the LDR is compared with the pending requests in the INTR, and if we cannot find corresponding 1 bits, we go on with the main program.

$$(LDR) \,\&\, (INTR) = 0 \quad fetch$$
$$\neq 0 \quad CHST \quad (10.8.3)$$

When an interrupt is required, we enter the microprogram which I have labeled CHST (for *change state*) and which does the following:

1. determines the next state from the bit setting in INTR;
2. assembles PCR information from CPU REGISTERS;
3. sets the PC in the PCR for this state;
4. creates a weight from information in the INTR;
5. places this weight in GPR15 for the new state;
6. forms the address of the PCR for the new state;
7. gets the *new state* PCR;
8. installs PCR information in the CPU REGISTERS;
9. goes on to the *fetch* microprogram.

PROBLEMS

10.1 (a) Explain the advantages of four modes.
(b) How is each mode used?

10.2 Explain Fig. 10.2.1.

10.3 What difference have you observed in command mnemonics? Comment.

10.4 Explain how machine interrupt on power failure can work.

10.5 What and why is the CHANNEL REGISTER group?

10.6 Explain
- IFR • IRG • PCR
- IMR • ISR

10.7 Describe how the interrupt is handled.

10.8 How are interrupts enabled or disabled?

10.9 How are multiple interrupts to different states handled?

10.10 Why is the two bit bus DBA required? Why isn't it larger?

10.11 How does the ALB work? Explain its size.

10.12 Design one bit of the ALB.

10.13 Explain the general use of
- OR • RR • BR
- AAD • BAD • UR

10.14 What is an EO? Explain the fields.

10.15 How is the *next* RM address required calculated?

10.16 Explain conditional EOs.

10.17 Explain RR and RX *fetch*. How is M2 calculated? Stored?

10.18 Explain completely the *execute* phase of A in arrow notation.

10.19 Describe how VFL *fetch* works.

10.20 Why another *four* cases for Model 45 VFL character commands? Explain what's done with each.

10.21 Explain AP in arrow notation. Discuss L1 and L2.

10.22 How does SIO differ from SDV?

10.23 What is RAGAD, and how is it used?

11

UNIVAC

9000

SERIES

11.1 INTRODUCTION

The small
byte-oriented
computer

The smaller business user wants a small computer which is inexpensive and for which he is willing to accept a small MEMORY and make a sacrifice in speed. At the low end of the small computer spectrum, we find the UNIVAC 9200 and 9300 systems. Other similar computers are the IBM System 360, Model 20, and the Spectra 70, Models 15 and 25. The other 9000 Series member is the UNIVAC 9400; passing mention is given to it, when pertinent, and Section 11.7 covers other features.

In designing a series of computers, the aim is to make as much compatibility from one model in the series to the next. Then, when the user finds his application has become too big for his present model, it is easy for him to replace it with a larger model in the same series and have his old programs run identically on the new model, except at a higher speed. This has been the policy for all these systems, at least on the high end. Making very small computers places constraints which don't lend to compatibility.

Small MEMORY The user of a small machine does not require much in the way of MEMORY. If he had to pay for more MEMORY, it would be advisable for him to go to a larger machine and get all the other advantages which would accrue to him.

Then, expecting the small computer user to have modest MEMORY requirements, we can make it easier for him to access all of his MEMORY

347

directly, without the use of BASE REGISTERS, although the machines in use have GPRs for other uses. In so doing, we consequently alter the command structure. The advantage of making all MEMORY accessible directly to the command becomes a disadvantage when upward compatibility becomes important.

Hardware   To keep the cost of the computer low, it is important to reduce the number of hardware REGISTERS to a bare minimum and to keep their lengths small. Further, the functional units, such as the ADDER, are restricted to byte length, if not smaller.

Microprogram   Microprogramming has the advantage of reducing the amount of instruction decoding but the cost disadvantage of adding another complete MEMORY UNIT. At the low price level, the disadvantage outweighs the advantage. This is especially true when we pare the instruction repertoire to a minimum, thereby reducing significantly the decoding requirements.

At the low end of the price scale, microprogramming is absent and control is hardwired into the computer.

LOCAL MEMORY   Again, austerity requires that we trim off the fat—this time, by eliminating LOCAL MEMORY and without adding hard REGISTERS. Since the REGISTERS in LM are required in one form or another, they are replaced by fixed locations in MAIN MEMORY. "Registers" in MM are not truly REGISTERS. But to maintain our shorthand form, we symbolize MM REGISTERS in small capitals hereafter anyway.

IO   Again, to keep the cost down, the number and types of IO DEVICES are kept to a minimum. The interface between the DEVICE and the PROCESSOR is necessarily simple:
- It does provide for cycle stealing or a simultaneity.
- It does provide for an interrupt for software monitoring of user programs.

Salient features   The points to keep in mind when examining the small byte-oriented computers are:
- microprogramming and RM have been eliminated;
- hardware CONTROL takes its place;
- LOCAL MEMORY is eliminated and replaced by restricted areas in MM;
- MAIN MEMORY is kept small—there is only one MEMORY;

- the command repertoire has been trimmed;
- the command structure is altered to make MAIN MEMORY totally addressable;
- peripheral equipment, while having interrupt and cycle stealing capabilities, does not use our previous concept of the CHANNEL CONTROLLER in its entirety.

Except for the first and last, these statements are also true at the bottom of competitive series: IBM System 360, Model 20; RCA Spectra 70, Model 15.

11.2   9300 COMMANDS AND DATA

The UNIVAC 9200 and 9300 are the same except for speed characteristics. Hereafter, we refer only to the UNIVAC 9300.

Word size   All MM references procure or store a single byte. Therefore, word size for this computer is one byte—eight bits. An interesting feature is the great speed of MAIN MEMORY (or simply MEMORY), which performs a complete cycle in 600 nanoseconds.

GPRs   There are only eight GPRs in this small machine. There are several reasons for reducing the number of GPRs; among them are:
- The command structure cannot provide reference for more than eight REGISTERS.
- Neither relative addressing nor relocation is required, so that fewer REGISTERS suffice.

GPR size is smaller. They are only two bytes or one halfWord long. GPRs are used for most of the same reasons as in larger machines: indexing, storing data, other programmer needs.

Data   There are several kinds of data, even for the smaller byte machines.
- Unpacked alphabetic information is coded in one of the two standard forms.
- Packed decimal format uses two digits per byte.
- It is the binary information that is different: it is a halfWord, with the sign in the left-hand position.
- Hardware floating point is not supplied even as an option.

Commands   The command repertoire for the 9300 provides no RR commands. None are really required, since substitution of
other commands, namely RX type, can be made. Since such RX commands did not exist in the System 360 repertoire, new ones were created.
System 360, Model 20, *does* provide RR commands, but only three of them.

The three types of 9300 commands are RX, SI, and SS, presented in
Fig. 11.2.1. They are similar to those discussed earlier, except for the
following conditions:
- The operand address is formed by referencing no more than one
  GPR.
- The combined B and D field in the command is interpreted
  differently than in the other machines.

The use of the base and displacement fields is presented at the top of
Fig. 11.2.1 and is radically different. The left bit of these combined fields
determines whether absolute direct addressing or indexing is done. When
it is 0, the remaining fifteen bits are an absolute address in MEMORY. This
permits addressing of 32K of MEMORY. This machine does not permit a
larger MEMORY option; so this suffices.

When the left bit is 1, indexing is requested. The REGISTER to be used,
called B, is designated by the next three bits. The remaining twelve bits are
the "displacement" to be added to the contents of B.

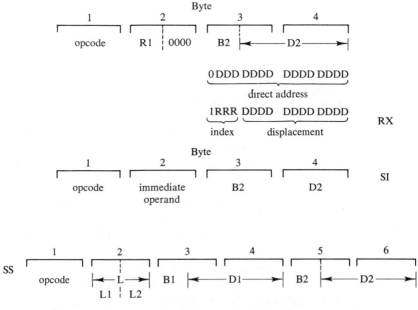

Fig. 11.2.1 Commands for the Univac 9300 (and Univac 9200 and
IBM System 360, Model 20).

Other than this, the format of the commands are similar to those of System 360 with one further exception: RX commands require all 0's in the X field to provide upward consistency to the UNIVAC 9400.

Repertoire   Table 11.2.1 is the command repertoire for the 9300. The three commands with opcode A6, AA, and AB are

Table 11.2.1 SUMMARY OF 9300 SYSTEM INSTRUCTION REPERTOIRE

Operation	Op code	Instruction	Mnemonic	Format
Binary	4 0	Store halfWord	STH	
	4 8	Load halfWord	LH	RX
	4 9	Compare halfWord	CH	
	A 6	Add immediate	AI	SI
	A A	Add halfWord	AH	
	A B	Subtract halfWord	SH	RX
Logical	9 1	Test under mask	TM	
	9 2	Move immediate	MVI	SI
	9 4	*And*	NI	
	9 5	Compare immediate	CLI	
	9 6	*Or*	OI	
	A 9	Halt and proceed	HPR	
Decimal	D 1	Move numeric	MVN	
	D 2	Move character	MVC	
	D 4	*And*	NC	
	D 5	Compare logical	CLC	SS
	D 6	*Or*	OC	
	D C	Translate	TR	
	D E	Edit	ED	
	F 1	Move with offset	MVO	
	F 2	Pack	PACK	
	F 3	Unpack	UNPK	
	F 8	Zero and add	ZAP	
	F 9	Compare decimal	CP	SS
	F A	Add decimal	AP	
	F B	Subtract decimal	SP	
	F C	Multiply decimal	MP	
	F D	Divide decimal	DP	
Branch	4 5	Branch and link	BAL	
	4 7	Branch on condition	BC	RX
State	A 0	Store state	SPSC	
Control	A 8	Load state	LPSC	SI
Special	A 1	Supervisor call	SRC	SI
IO	A 4	Execute IO	XIOF	SI
	A 5	Test IO	TIO	

necessarily different from those in System 360 (since these opcodes are illegal in System 360). The distinction is that arithmetic overflow for these commands does not cause the machine to stop (as in the Model 20); instead, it sets an OVERFLOW FLIPFLOP which can be tested by the programmer or ignored, if he so chooses.

11.3   MEMORY MAP, CONTROL

STATES

Map   MEMORY serves the purposes of both LM and MM for the larger machines. Since there are so few hard REGISTERS in the computer, MEMORY is used to hold just about everything while a command is in progress. However, INDEX REGISTER designations for the programmer use all four bits. Thus the lowest-numbered available REGISTER is 8_H for 1000_2; C_H designates GPR 1100_2, the fifth GPR, for instance.

Figure 11.3.1 demonstrates just how much is stored in MEMORY. The first four bytes of MEMORY store the PSC described below, which is similar to the PSW discussed earlier for System 360—it contains the IC. The next

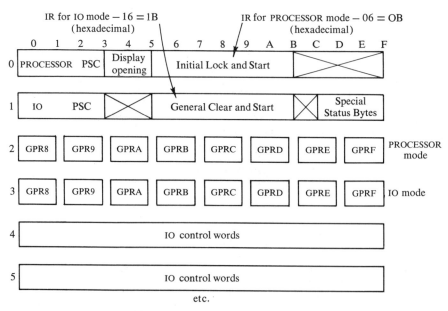

Fig. 11.3.1 MEMORY map, Univac 9300.

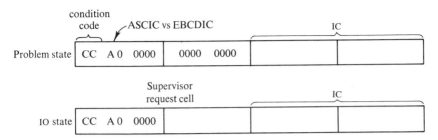

Fig. 11.3.2 The program state control to word (PSC) containing the
INSTRUCTION COUNTER.

two bytes are console control bytes. Next we have six bytes which hold the
complete *instruction register*. This includes the opcode and the effective
operand addresses calculated during *fetch*.

The next sixteen bytes of MM serve a duplicate function to the first
sixteen, except that they apply to IO mode. UNIVAC distinguishes modes
of operation as *problem* and IO. The two console control bytes are missing
for IO mode, but the final set of status bytes is present. The next set of
thirty-two bytes is provided for the GPRs, a separate set for each mode.
This duplicate set of GPRs is a convenience which RCA provided with
their Spectra System.

The first sixteen bytes of MEMORY are restricted and protected. Another
big chunk of low MEMORY is reserved for use by IO but is also available to
the program.

Figure 11.3.2 displays PSCs for the two states. At the left of the PSC
is the two-bit condition code, the same as for the other machines. The A
bit distinguishes the kind of codes we are using for symbols ASCIC,
EBCDIC. Only sixteen bits are required for the INSTRUCTION COUNTER
(at the right) because of the MEMORY size restrictions. Notice the SRC
position in the IO PSC. When the command SRC is given, the I field of that
command is placed in this position of the IO PSC. The SRC command is:

$$\text{SRC} \quad \text{I} \quad \text{B1} \quad \text{D1} \qquad\qquad (11.3.1)$$

Since SRC "should" be an RR command, and there are none in the 9300,
the address portion of this command is ignored.

11.4 HARDWARE

MEMORY   MEMORY is somewhat unconventional. It is
made of wire plated with thin magnetizable film. It is very fast: 600

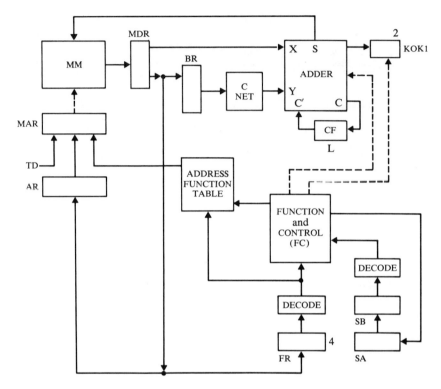

Fig. 11.4.1 Functional block diagram of Univac 9300.

nanoseconds per cycle. A further speed advantage is optional non-destructive readout which permits a read cycle without write back when the computer designer chooses to use it thus.

As shown in Fig. 11.4.1, the MEMORY ADDRESS REGISTER points to the location to be referenced in MEMORY. Information is placed in the MAR from the AR or from the ADDRESS FUNCTION TABLE. Address entry is controlled by the FUNCTION and CONTROL UNIT (FC).

Readout from MAIN MEMORY is always into the MDR; but unlike other MEMORIES, writing is not done from this REGISTER, but rather from the output of the ADDER. Hence, any REGISTER output to be written must pass through the ADDER. The ADDER may be doing a function upon different source bytes, and then the result word is placed in MEMORY.

REGISTERS   The MDR is not only the MEMORY DESTINATION REGISTER for MM, but it also stores operands used by the ADDER. Any word destined for another REGISTER must be temporarily stored in the MDR.

The BR holds a second operand during arithmetic. This byte originally came from the MDR. Its byte may be blocked, complemented, or otherwise operated on by the C NET.

The FUNCTION REGISTER, FR, holds the operation being performed after extraction from the command word. RR holds a GPR designation.

Functional units   The C NET operates on a second operand before it is entered into the ADDER.

The ADDER is a single-byte device with inputs from the MDR and the C NET. Its output is *always* returned to MEMORY at the CELL designated by the MAR. When a carry is produced, it is stored in the CARRY FLIPFLOP, CF. The function which the ADDER performs is determined by the FUNCTION and CONTROL UNIT, FCU.

The timing of all operations is done by CLOCK which produces four pulses: TP1, TP2, TP3, and TP4. These activate two COUNTERS, SAC and SBC. Signals are gated to these and the address table by FCU. Other hardware included in the computer is discussed in Section 11.7.

11.5   FETCH

For the 9300, *fetch* means placing the next command with one or two effective operand addresses into a low-order MEMORY position assigned to act as the INSTRUCTION REGISTER. Thus, although the INSTRUCTION REGISTER is a set of MEMORY CELLS, for ease of reference, we talk about it as though it were a hard REGISTER in the computer and call it IR.

Example   An example of *fetch* is shown in Fig. 11.5.1. The IC points to 0770, the starting byte of a command. The command is AA, the *add halfWord* command. The second pair of bytes in the instruction word is D0, calling for REGISTER 13 as the destination GPR. The operand address is C454, indicating indexing by GPR12 and a displacement of 454. The opcode is transferred during *fetch* to the OR (a position of the IR in MEMORY). Also the address portion of the IR is filled with the effective operand address. Then 454 is indexed by REGISTER 12 which contains 1666. After *fetch*, the command sits in MEMORY in IR as shown at the bottom of the figure.

Opcode   The entire *fetch* is outlined in Fig. 11.5.2 in arrow notation. We examine, first, how the opcode is obtained. Remember everything is done by manipulating single bytes. The numbers in

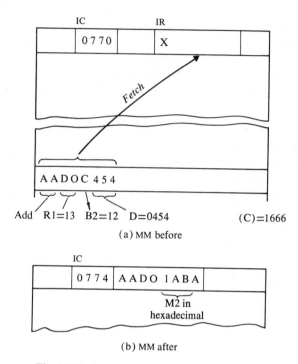

Add R1=13 B2=12 D=0454   (C)=1666

(a) MM before

M2 in
hexadecimal

(b) MM after

Fig. 11.5.1 An example of a *fetch* for the 9300.

the text refer to the lines of arrow notation in the figure. The address of the second byte of the INSTRUCTION COMPUTER is passed to MAR (1). That byte is obtained (2) and passed to the second half of AR (3). We add 2 to the COUNTER in the MDR so that it points to the next pair of instruction bytes. However, this is the *less* significant byte of the IC byte pair. If a carry is created, it is stored in CF (4).

We get the next byte of the INSTRUCTION COUNTER (5, 6, 7). If there is a carry from the previous addition, it is added to the contents of the MDR and this is put away as the new IC, first byte (8).

Now the AR contains the INSTRUCTION COUNTER. It is passed over to the MAR (9) and the first byte of the instruction is put in the MDR (10). The address of the first IR byte is placed in the MAR and the first opcode byte is put away (12).

To get the next instruction byte, we advance the AR address and place it in the MAR (14); the next instruction byte is brought out from MEMORY (15) and then returned in its IR position (16, 17).

Other instruction   After obtaining the first two bytes of the
bytes   instruction and putting them in the IR we get
the next two bytes. The *address* of the first of these two bytes (the *third*

1.	{IC2} → MAR	⎫
2.	(IC2) → MDR	⎬ get (IC), byte 2
3.	→ AR2	⎭
4.	(MDR) + 2 → {IC2}; cy → CF	increment IC
5.	{IC1} → MAR	⎫
6.	IC1 → MDR	⎬ get (IC) byte 1
7.	→ AR1	⎭
8.	(MDR) + (CF) → {IC1}	restore IC recognizing the carry
9.	(AR) → MAR	⎫
10.	CM1 → MDR	⎬ get opcode
11.	→ FR	⎭
12.	{IR1} → MAR	⎫ place in IR
13.	(MDR) → MM	⎭
14.	(AR) + 1 → MAR	⎫ get R1 for RX or L for SS
15.	CM2 → MDR	⎭
16.	{IR2} → MAR	⎫ place in IP
17.	(MDR) → MM	⎭
18.	Repeat 1–8 so that (AR) = (IC) again	
19.	(AR) → MAR	⎫
20.	CM3* → MDR	⎬ establish R2 or B1 and part of D2 or D1
21.	→ RR	⎪
22.	→ BR	⎭
23.	{IR3}* → MAR	⎫ and place in IR
24.	(MDR) → MM	⎭
25.	(AR) + 1 → MAR	⎫
26.	CM4* → MDR	⎬ get rest of D2 or D1
27.	→ BR	⎭
28.	{IR4}* → MAR	⎫ and put in IR
29.	{MDR} → MM	⎭
30.	Continue if relativizing or indexing requested	
31.	(RR) + 1 → MAR	⎫ get index quantity, least bit
32.	(R2 − 2)* → MDR	⎭
33.	{IR4}* → MAR	⎫ place effective address in IR
34.	(MDR) + (BR) → MAR; cy → CF	⎭
35.	(RR) → MAR	⎫
36.	(R2 − 1)* → MDR	⎬ get rest of index quantity
37.	→ BR	⎭
38.	{IR3} → MAR	⎫ and rest of displacement
39.	D − 1 → MDR	⎭
40.	(MDR) + (BR) + (CF) → MM	place rest of effective address in IR
41.	Repeat 18–40 for SS only so that M2 → IR5 ⌣ IR6	

* For the SS instruction for (41), these operations are relabeled appropriately.

Fig. 11.5.2 *Fetch* in arrow notation for the Univac 9300.

instruction byte) is pointed to by the IC; it is obtained and installed in the AR (18). We then go to MEMORY and procure the instruction byte itself. The left nibble of this byte is a REGISTER designation; the second nibble is part of the displacement. We place this byte into the RR and the BR (19–20) and return it to the IR (23–24).

The fourth instruction byte is obtained from MEMORY (25–27) and put into the IR and the BR (28–29).

When relativizing or indexing is requested, as determined by RR, we calculate the effective address. If the first bit of RR is 0, no address calculation is made. Obtain the least significant byte of the indicated GPR from MEMORY (31–32). The address of the fourth IR byte is given to MEMORY (33), and an addition is performed to fabricate the last byte of the effective address carry from the addition; it is recorded by CF (34). The next byte of the effective address is calculated and put away by a similar sequence of operations (35–40).

When an SS instruction has been determined by the contents of the FR, we go through the same sequence (9–40) to determine the fifth and sixth bytes of the instruction and to place the effective address therein.

HalfWord acquisition The word size of the UNIVAC 9300 is one byte. *Fetch*, described above, is oriented toward a command which consists of two or three halfWords. Frequently, a byte address is increased or decreased by 1. This is not done by the ADDER. It is a simple hardware feature stemming from a convention imposed on the programmer: *instructions and binary data are always found on halfWord boundaries*. Hence, the first byte in every instruction is at an address which ends in 0; the second byte address ends in 1. The addition indicated in Fig. 11.5.2 consists of jamming 1 into the least significant of the addresses.

Whether we want the first or the second byte of halfWord depends on the action at the moment: for instruction procurement, we generally go from left to right; operations for arithmetic are examined from right to left, as we might suppose.

11.6   EXECUTION

Analysis *Fetch* has left us with an opcode in the FR which the attached DECODE can classify. Further, the opcode and its effective address are now situated in a CELL of MM referred to as the IR.

There is only one MEMORY in the 9300—there is no microprogramming to sequence hardware operations. Sequencing is hardwired into the computer. Let us examine examples for two types of commands.

RX As with the System 360, RX commands reference one GPR and one MEMORY location. For the 9300, both are

actually in MM. One effective address and one GPR designator are now in
the IR. It is a simple matter to place one operand in the MDR and the other
in the BR. Let us see what happens in the case of halfWord addition.

We get the MEMORY operand address first. We procure its address from
the third and fourth bytes of the IR. Then we get the least significant byte
of the MEMORY operand, placing it into the BR. GPR identification is in the
RR. This actuates the MAR and therewith obtains the GPR contents which
are brought to the MDR. The ADDER operates on (MDR) and (BR) to produce
a result which is returned to the GPR using the address now in the MAR.
A carry may be recorded in CF. This completes one byte of addition.

The second half of addition is the same as the first, with the simple
exception that the carry in CF is now entered into the ADDER as addition is
performed.

SS commands   For SS commands, the IR contains a length
and two addresses. Since MEMORY has a word length of one byte, the word
boundary problem encountered in the two previous chapters no longer
exists here.

Four operations are necessary for each byte.
- Get the address of the first operand from the IR.
- Place the byte in the BR.
- Get the address of the second operand byte from the IR.
- Place that byte in the MDR.

Of course, the destination byte is obtained last because *memorizing* and
processing occur simultaneously. The ADDER is activated to process the
two bytes according to the opcode in FR: a source byte is in the BR; a
destination byte is in the MDR. The result from the ADDER is returned to
the destination position in MEMORY. As these operations go on, we have
to do some accounting.
- Carries are kept track of.
- Byte addresses have to be incremented or decremented (depending on whether we are moving or doing arithmetic).
- Length has to be decremented.

A complication occurs with subtraction when recomplementation is
necessary. A working storage location is needed to keep track of the
actual length of the result for recomplementation.

11.7   UNIVAC 9400

HalfWord   The UNIVAC 9400 is most like the IBM
MEMORY   Spectra 70, Model 45, or System 360, Model
30: MEMORY has a word size of a halfWord of two bytes. This, together

with additional hardware, made this computer much more like the other byte-oriented computers. The command repertoire is much the same. RX commands permit modification by two GPRs. RR commands are present. There are one or two different SUPERVISER mode commands.

Characters   An enumeration of the characteristics of the UNIVAC 9400 follows; emphasized are the similarities and differences among it, the other UNIVAC 9000 series, and its competitors.

1. There is only one MEMORY; the MAIN MEMORY, consisting of 24K to 131K bytes of MEMORY.
2. Since there is only one MEMORY, no microprogramming is provided.
3. LOCAL MEMORY functions are furnished by the MAIN MEMORY; hence, GPRs and such are found in restricted areas of MM.
4. The IO subsystem is more similar to System 360 and less similar to the other 9000 series members (which we have not really discussed).
5. There is a larger instruction repertoire:
   * All RR instructions are present.
   * No floating point instructions are included.
   * Only a few new opcodes were added.
6. The MEMORY protect feature, the key and lock system described in the IBM 360, is absent. We have in its place the LIMIT REGISTER system described below.
7. The GPRs are full size.
8. A PSW instead of PSC is used for interrupt. Further, each SELECTOR CHANNEL has its own PSW location in MM.
9. There is a separate set of GPRs for user and supervisory mode.
10. The user GPRs are available to the supervisor.

LIMIT REGISTERS   A LIMIT REGISTER is provided in the 9400; it determines the upper and lower bounds to the area which may be accessed by the command now in control. This REGISTER can be set only by a special privileged instruction. Thus, once the user's program has been set up and the LIMIT REGISTER established, the user's program cannot harm other programs residing in MEMORY. If it tries to do this, MEMORY protect violation occurs which takes us into supervisor mode.

The LIMIT REGISTER is sufficient with the other paraphernalia to make multiprogramming possible. When a program is finished or gets into trouble, it reports to the supervisor. The supervisor resets the LIMIT REGISTER and the PSW and starts another program presently residing in MEMORY.

A program must occupy contiguous storage locations. The LIMIT REGISTER establishes bounds using the most significant bits in the MEMORY address in units of 516 bytes. This allows us to ignore the last nine bits in an address, checking only the upper, more significant bits.

Implementation   The 9400 MEMORY has a half Word word and is fast—600 nanoseconds per cycle. To service a wider MEMORY requires wider REGISTERS. The 9400 has more and larger REGISTERS than its smaller brothers. More REGISTERS are required because of the expanded functions such as the LIMIT REGISTER and the expanded command repertoire.

To make half Word REGISTERS operate faster, a half Word ADDER is supplied.

Control functions are more complicated because of the increased repertoire and the larger number of REGISTERS to be contended with.

PROBLEMS

11.1 Describe LM and RM for UNIVAC 9000.

11.2 (a) Explain the GPRS in both states.
(b) Explain the states.

11.3 (a) Explain the RX format.
(b) How is indexing requested?
(c) What does this have to do with the number of GPRS?
(d) How is the base register specified in RX?
(e) How does this effect relocation?

11.4 (a) What about RR commands?
(b) What provisions are made for RR commands?
(c) Explain SRC.

11.5 Describe "9300" registers. What are their names, and how are they used?

11.6 How is a *fetch* done? Explain Fig. 11.5.2.

11.7 Describe A in arrow notation.

11.8 Describe MVC in arrow notation.

INDEX

363

LIST OF ABBREVIATIONS

Abbrev.	Meaning	First Used Topic	Page
IR	Intermediate Register (2-byte)	SPECTRA 70	331
IR	Instruction Register	UNIVAC 9000	355
IRSW	IR Switch	SPECTRA 70	331
ISR	Interrupt Status Register	SPECTRA 70	325
JR	Least significant four bits of LAR	S/360	257
LAR	Local Memory Address Register	S/360	244
LCU	Local Memory Control Unit	S/360	244
LDR	Local Memory Data Register	S/360	244
LD switch	Local Memory Data Switch	SPECTRA 70	331
LM	Local Memory	S/360	243
LR	Left Register	S/360	250
LWR	Last Word Register in channel controller	S/360	304
M	Location in Memory (referred to in a command or subcommand)	Chan Cont	58
M	Effective Memory Address	IBM 1130	147
M	Machine State—machine errors (same as P4)	SPECTRA 70	319
MAL	Macro Assembly Language	Intro	29
MAR	Memory Address Register	Intro	14
MAR	Main Memory Address Register	S/360	244
MARP	Page portion (left 5 bits) of MAR	PDP-8	117
MARW	Word portion (right 7 bits) of MAR	PDP-8	117
MBC	M-register Byte Counter	S/360	250
MC	Monitor Call Instruction (causes external interrupt)	Hon 200	217
MCU	Memory Control Unit	Intro	14
MCU	Main Memory Control Unit	S/360	244
MDR	Memory Data Register	Intro	14
MDR	Main Memory Data Register	S/360	244
M/DR	Auxiliary Register (used as an extender when shifting)	S/360	251
ML	Code Indicating source of interrupt	Interrupts	85
MM	Main Memory	Chan Cont	49
MR	Modifier Register	Hon 200	205
MR	M Register (functions as IR, Instruction Register, during fetch and analysis; used to start RM on proper microprogram sequence; then available to hold VFL data)	S/360	231
MREGAD	Multiplexor Regenerating Address Register	SPECTRA 70	334
MSCR	Miscellaneous Registers	SPECTRA 70	332
MTU	Magnetic Tape Unit		
MVF	Mover Function Register	S/360	252
NBCD	Natural Binary Coded Decimal Code	Intro	5
NBCH	Natural Binary Coded Hexadecimal	S/360	233
nibble	Half a byte—4 bits (slang)	S/360	232
OP	Operation code field of command (5 bits)	IBM 1130	146

LIST OF ABBREVIATIONS

Abbrev.	Meaning	First Used Topic	Page
OPR	Operation Register (hold opcode)	IBM 1130	147
OR	Operation Register (upper half of instruction word)	SDS-92	140
OR	Operation Register (one character)	IBM 1401	162
OR	Operation Register	Hon 200	203
OR	Operation Register in channel controller	S/360	304
OR	Operation Register	SPECTRA 70	331
P	Program (present)	Interrupts	71
P'	Program (new)	Interrupts	71
P1	Worker state—user programs operate only in this state (same as W)	SPECTRA 70	319
P2	Executive State (same as X)	SPECTRA 70	319
P3	Interrupt State—all interrupts except machine errors (same as I)	SPECTRA 70	319
P4	Machine State—machine errors (same as M)	SPECTRA 70	319
PB	Page Bit (in command format)	PDP-8	116
PCR	Program Counter Register	SPECTRA 70	325
PCU	Processor Control Unit	Intro	15
PKR	Protect Key Register	S/360	248
POL	Problem Oriented Language	Intro	30
POR	Position Register in common channel	S/360	304
PRR	Priority Register in common channel	S/360	304
PSC	Program State similar to PSW	UNIVAC 9000	352
PSR	Program State Register	SPECTRA 70	331
PSW	Program Status Word	S/360 Int	89
PSWR	Program Status Word Register	S/360 Int	89
PT	Paper Tape		
QR	Quotient Register	Intro	16
RABR	Read-only Memory Address Buffer Register	S/360	309
RAR	Read-only Memory Address Register	S/360	244
RCU	Read-only Memory Control Unit	S/360	244
RDR	Read-only Memory Data Register	S/360	244
REGAD	Regenerating Address Register	SPECTRA 70	334
RI	Command format—referencing two GPR's and an immediate operand	S/360	238
RM	Read-only Memory	S/360	242
RMADL	Read-only Memory Address Determination Logic	S/360	309
RQR	Request Register in common channel	S/360	304
RR	Command format—referencing two GPR's	S/360	237
RR	Right Register	S/360	250
RR	Register Register	SPECTRA 70	331
RS	Command format—referencing two GPR's and one memory location	S/360	237
RWC	Read Write Channel	Hon 200	209
RWCPL	Read Write Channel Present Location (of character presently being transferred) (one for each RWC)	Hon 200	212

LIST OF ABBREVIATIONS

Abbrev.	Meaning	First Used Topic	Page
CCR	Condition Code Register	S/360	248
CCR	Condition Code Register (2 bits)	SPECTRA 70	332
CCW	Channel Control Word (subcommands for chan)	S/360 Ints	104
CCW1	First word of CCW double word pair	S/360	301
CCW2	Second word of CCW double word pair	S/360	301
CF	Carry Flipflop	UNIVAC 9000	355
CHR	Channel Register in channel controller (called "General Purpose Register" by IBM)	S/360	302
CI	Compare Indicator	IBM 1401	171
CM	Control Memory	Hon 200	199
CM1, CMi	ith microactivity of the command	S/360	309
CMAR	Control Memory Address Register	Hon 200	201
CMDR	Control Memory Data Register	Hon 200	201
CP	Central Processor	S/360	312
CR	Command Register (in Fig. 2.5.1 this is the IR, Instruction Register)	Chan Cont	65
CR	Control Register (same as IR—a full word)	SDS-92	140
CR	C Register in channel controller (for assembly and disassembly)	S/360	304
CR	Channel Registers (six in each channel)	SPECTRA 70	323
CSR	Change Sequence Register	Hon 200	215
CSR	Channel Status Register in channel control	S/360	304
CSW	Channel Status Word (info about an IO task)	S/360 Ints	104
CU	Control Unit (for a memory—MM, LM, or RM)	S/360	244
CUR1, 2	Channel Utility Register 1, 2	SPECTRA 70	343
D	Displacement Field (8 bits) of a command	IBM 1130	146
DB	Data Bus (consists of DB0, DB1, & DBA)	SPECTRA 70	329
DB0	Data Bus—byte line carrying least significant two byte	SPECTRA 70	329
DB1	Data Bus—carrying more significant byte	SPECTRA 70	329
DBA	Data Bus—two-bit line	SPECTRA 70	329
DBF	Data Break Facility ("a stripped down channel controller")	PDP-8	131
DBSW	Data Bus Switch	SPECTRA 70	330
DC	Device Information	Interrupts	85
DR	Divisor Register	Intro	16
DR	Data Register	Chan Cont	65
DR	Data Register (RCA name for LDR)	SPECTRA 70	331
EBCDIC	Extended Binary Coded Decimal Interchange Code	S/360	233
EIR	External Interrupt Register	Hon 200	215
EO	Elementary Operation (microop)	SPECTRA 70	329
EOJ	End of Job (macro instruction)	S/360	97
ER	End Register in channel controller (notes termination conditions)	S/360	304
EXT	Accumulator Extension Register	IBM 1130	149

LIST OF ABBREVIATIONS

Abbrev.	Meaning	First Used Topic	Page
F	Form bit of command (distinguishes long from short)	IBM 1130	146
FC	Function and Control Unit	UNIVAC 9000	354
FF	Flipflop (general)		
FI	Interrupt pending or in progress (signal from a flipflop)	Interrupts	84
FLR	Flag Register in channel controller	S/360	304
FR	Auxiliary Register (function)	S/360	251
FR	Function Register	UNIVAC 9000	355
G1, G2	Length Registers	S/360	250
GPR	General Purpose Registers (16 each fixed point, 32 bit, 4 byte; and possibly 4 each floating point, 64 bits)	S/360	231
GPS1, 2	Status Registers	S/360	257
GR	Length Register (G1 & G2 operating together)	S/360	250
GR	A processor register	SPECTRA 70	330
HIO	Halt IO (instruction)	S/360 Ints	102
HR	H Register (holds contents of IAC during interrupts)	S/360	250
I	Indirect address bit (long command form only)	IBM 1130	146
I	Interrupt state—all interrupts except machine errors (same as P3)	SPECTRA 70	319
IAC	Instruction Address Counter	S/360	250
IAR	Instruction Address Register (address of next instruction)	IBM 1130	149
IB	Indirect (addressing) Bit (In command)	PDP-8	116
IB	Instruction Buffer	S/360	246
IBR	Index Barricade Register (upper bound of unprotected area—lower bound of upper protected area)	Hon 200	222
IC	Instruction Counter	Intro	25
ICP	Instruction Counter—page part (left 5 bits)	PDP-8	116
ICW	Instruction Counter—word part (right 7 bits)	PDP-8	116
IFF	Interrupt Flipflop (in device)	PDP-8	129
IFR	Interrupt Flag Register	SPECTRA 70	323
IIR	Internal Interrupt Register	Hon 200	215
ILCR	Instruction Length Code Register	S/360	248
ILR	Instruction Length Register	SPECTRA 70	332
IMR	Interrupt Mask Register	SPECTRA 70	325
INC	Address Incrementor	IBM 1401	171
INTR	Interrupt Register	SPECTRA 70	332
IO	Input-Output (device or operation)	Chan Cont	49
IOCC	Input-Output Control Command	IBM 1130	153
IP	Interrupt Pending Signal		
IPFF	Interrupt Pending Flipflop (in PCU)	PDP-8	130
IR	Instruction Register	Intro	19